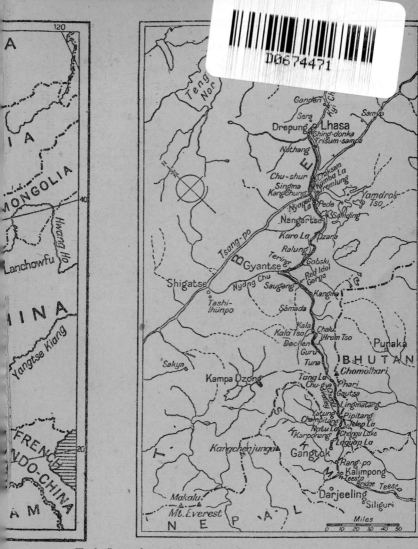

*Trade Route from Gangtok to Lhasa, followed by Lhasa Mission 1936/37*

492    693
       753

# MEMOIRS OF A MOUNTAINEER

Photograph by Mrs. Fullalove

THE AUTHOR

# MEMOIRS
## OF A
# MOUNTAINEER

### ' HELVELLYN TO HIMALAYA '
### AND ' LHASA : THE HOLY CITY '

### F. SPENCER CHAPMAN

*With 31 pages of illustrations*

### THE REPRINT SOCIETY
### LONDON

*Helvellyn to Himalaya*  FIRST PUBLISHED 1940
*Lhasa: The Holy City* FIRST PUBLISHED 1938
JOINT EDITION PUBLISHED BY THE REPRINT SOCIETY LTD.
BY ARRANGEMENT WITH CHATTO AND WINDUS LTD.
1945

PRINTED IN GREAT BRITAIN BY RICHARD CLAY AND COMPANY LTD.
BUNGAY SUFFOLK.

# ILLUSTRATIONS

The Author . . . . . . . *Frontispiece*
Climbing the Flake Crack, Scafell . . . *Facing page* 16
North-West Iceland : View near Cap Nord . . . 17
Alps : From the Requin Hut . . . . . . 17
Sledging Loads up a Frozen Stream . . . . 48
Himalayas : Two Episodes on Simvu . . . . 49
Siniolchu from the Langpo-La . . . . . 96
Climbing the Sphinx Arête . . . . . . 97
Reconnoitring the Fluted Peak . . . . . 97
Northern Face of Chomolhari . . . . . 160
Approaching the Ridge of the Langpo-La . . . 161
The Author after Chomolhari . . . . . 161
Crossing the Yamdrok Lake in February . . . 192
Tibet : Lhasa Personalities . . . . . 193
Gyantse Town and Monastery . . . . . 208
The Prime Minister with his Wife and Daughter . . 209
The late Dalai Lama . . . . . . 209
An Outcast's Tent . . . . . . . 224
Four Tibetan Portraits . . . . . . 225
Ceremonial Trumpets, Gundeling Monastery . . . 256
Pagoda covering the late Dalai-Lama's Tomb : Images . 257
Kampa Dancers . . . . . . . 288
A Tiny Incarnation-Lama in the Regent's Procession . . 288
Dance by Soldiers Wearing Ancient Armour . . . 289
Lhasa : An Official's House : A Street Scene . . 304
The Regent's Baggage passing Shing-donka . . . 305
The Potala from the South-West . . . . . 320
The Potala from the East. Nomads performing Holy Walk . 321
Norbhu Lingka Stables . . . . . . 336
Cloisonné, Lioness with her Cub . . . . . 337
Fresco, Mongolian Leading Tiger . . . . 337
Drepung Monastery, Largest in the World . . . 352
Monastery to the North of Lhasa . . . . 353
A Tibetan Lewis-gun Section . . . . . 384
Lhasa United Football Team . . . . . 385
Rugbeians All : Möndö, Kyipup, Ringang . . . 385
New Year Lama Dance at the Potala . . . . 416
Tsarong's Household . . . . . . 417

# HELVELLYN TO HIMALAYA

## CONTENTS

| CHAP. | | PAGE |
|---|---|---|
| I. | EARLY YEARS | 7 |
| II. | FURTHER AFIELD | 18 |
| III. | FROM LIVERPOOL TO THE HIMALAYA | 32 |
| IV. | FROM THE TROPICAL FOREST TO THE SNOWS | 45 |
| V. | SIMVU | 62 |
| VI. | PLANS AND COMPLICATIONS | 81 |
| VII. | THE PYRAMID AND THE SPHINX | 98 |
| VIII. | THE ASCENT OF THE FLUTED PEAK | 108 |
| IX. | CHOMOLHARI: PREPARATIONS | 121 |
| X. | CHOMOLHARI: THE ASCENT | 138 |
| XI. | CHOMOLHARI: THE DESCENT | 158 |
| | GLOSSARY OF MOUNTAINEERING TERMS | 171 |

# CHAPTER ONE

## EARLY YEARS

I HAVE not always been fond of mountains. The enthusiasms of one's childhood are settled by circumstance rather than by an inherent urge in any definite direction: one boy is brought up beside the sea and becomes an ardent yachtsman; another is much in contact with a man who has a passion for collecting fossils and is influenced accordingly. In other cases the environment of a boy's own home and the interests of his parents, curiously enough, have a contrary effect upon him, and he feels antagonism for the very things which his father hopes he is learning to love. I know a man whose heart has always been in the mountains; from earliest youth his children were taken up hills and made to bathe before breakfast in icy lakes, with the sad result that they have developed a violent distaste for the country, especially mountainous country, and are now happily living in cities. My own parents died when I was very young and I was brought up by an elderly parson and his wife in a village on the edge of the Lake District. As my guardian had little time to spare from his parish duties, my elder brother and I were left very much to ourselves. We used to go for long walks in the country; there were fells near at hand, but as far as I can remember we preferred the winding lanes and streams of the lower valleys. Our chief interest at that time, derived from the memory and books of our father, was in butterflies and wild flowers. Mountains hardly entered into our scheme of things, and rock-climbing we had not even heard of. Only once do I remember making a more ambitious expedition into the hills, and that was when my tutor took me up to the top of Dunmail Raise on the back of his motorcycle and we climbed Helvellyn by way of Grisedale Tarn and Dollywaggon Pike. This was a tremendous walk for a small boy and the apparent vastness of the Lake District fells stirred my imagination. It gave me an impression of beauty, immensity, and physical exhaustion which I shall never forget. But for some reason, this expedition, being so unlike any previous adventure, remained for many years an isolated experience, as if it were impossible to hope to repeat it.

After a disastrous term in the kindergarten of a girls' school in Kendal, I was sent, at the age of 8, to a private school at Ben Rhydding, on the edge of the Yorkshire moors. The head-master—a man of infinite kindness and understanding—was an enthusiastic entomologist; and here again the moors served as a happy hunting-ground for oak egger or emperor moth cater-pillars, and were not climbed for their own sake, with the excep-tion of the Cow and Calf rocks at Ilkley, whose attraction was that they were out of bounds. I also served a valuable apprentice-ship as a tree-climber, but here again the incentive was birds' eggs or chestnuts for " conkers ", and the fact that tree-climbing was forbidden.

I left my Private School with a good knowledge of gardening and a vast enthusiasm for all forms of natural history. Lessons, I considered, were things to be avoided by all possible means, fair or foul, and organized games were a waste of a fine afternoon. My love of adventure had led me into more scrapes than any other boy in the school, and as I did not excel at work or games I began to feel I was rather a failure. To vindicate myself to others I posed as one who had no regard either for authority or for his own safety, and to justify myself to myself I concentrated all my energies on my particular interests.

At the age of 14 I went to Sedbergh, a school which is set in the midst of wild moorland country; it was possible to run for twenty miles there without meeting another human being. I was not much good at class work, I loathed the monotonous bell-regulated routine of school life, and I still could not see any point in spending every afternoon hitting or kicking a leather-covered ball when I might have been fishing the Lune or trying to photograph the peregrine falcon's eyrie on Coombe Scaur. In my first summer term I was beaten by the Head of the House four days running for refusing to play cricket, then the matter was reported to my House-master, who was luckily a wise and sympathetic man. He said that if I really felt so strongly about it, I need not play cricket so long as I did not waste my time. And I did not waste my time. We had three half-holidays per week. That meant if I took lunch and supper with me—or did without—I was free from soon after one o'clock, when the morning's work ended, until seven o'clock, when preparation began. As I could travel at an average speed of six miles per hour over the fells, those six hours gave me a magnifi-

cent range of country to explore. I did no roped climbing at
that time, but some of the descents to ravens' or peregrines' nests
at Black Force, Cautley Spout and Coombe Scaur reduced the
margin of safety to its slenderest limit. Often my life depended
on a root of mountain ash or bunch of heather, and the screes I
ran—in gym shoes too—were steeper than I would choose to run
nowadays even in boots.

But it was good practice; it gave me self-reliance and I could
forget myself in the rhythm of tired muscles, in the fascination of
following a compass course over the hills in thick mist, in the
determination to go just one mile further before turning.

In the holidays I was much alone. My guardian had retired to
a village in Somerset, and I lived with another parson in the same
part of the Lake District; my debt to him is more than I can ever
repay, but he too was a busy parish priest, and my brother was
away from home. I spent nearly all my time wild-fowling and
bird-watching on the shores of Morecambe Bay. I suppose the
naturalist's and the hunter's instincts are equally strong; in those
days it did not seem odd that I could spend hour after hour in a
hide watching birds, learning their secret ways, more thrilled by
the sight of a new or rare species than by anything else in the
world, and then, in the winter months, plot to shoot those same
birds.

I used to go down to the shore before it was light to take up my
position in the hideout in the mud-flats. All the bird notes were
familiar : the soft purring of dunlin, the thin querulous whistle of
widgeon, the distant swelling chorus of thousands of curlew,
oyster-catcher, lapwing, ringed plover and redshank at the tide's
edge, and sometimes, if I was lucky, the loud distinctive whistle
of a greenshank or the plaintive note of grey plover. Then the
spell would be broken by the sudden whirring of wings overhead,
as yet indiscernible in the dim light. I could recognize them by the
sound : the sibilant whistle of golden-eye, as if their joints needed
oiling; the muffled throb of teal hurtling through the air; the
regular beat of mallard, at first faint, then strong, then fading
again into the distance, and from far off the thrilling sound of
geese launching themselves into the air, and calling to each other
with clear clarion cries. Will they come over the hide? Frozen
fingers close on the half-forgotten gun, the body becomes tense
as the air is filled with the beat of wings and the muttering under-

A 2

tone of grey geese as they keep in touch with each other. The gun's flash startles the quiet dawn. There is a thudding splash as a heavy body hits the sodden mud-flats. Nothing can be greater than the thrill of one's first goose.

When I was 15 I went to stay with a friend at Talyllyn Lake in North Wales. There I climbed Çader Idris, my first real mountain since the ascent of Helvellyn, in record-breaking time, and developed a great enthusiasm for trout-fishing.

About this time I learnt the art of poaching, which gave more scope for skill and excitement than anything I had known before, and I learnt to " guddle " trout, to set horse-hair snares for grouse, and to observe the tracks of game while leaving none myself. Sometimes it was too exciting. I remember well the pain that two of us suffered, extracting pellets from each other's backs with the point of a rusty penknife after a successful long-range right and left from an irate gamekeeper. And how one night netting salmon we were surprised by the beck-watcher, and had to spend a frozen hour hiding beneath the bank with only our heads above water while he and his dog systematically searched the waterside. But as one grew up these exciting pastimes had to be left behind and one was forced to accept an adult sense of the sanctity of possessions.

I learned to ride at about this time. It happened that a famous breeder of thoroughbreds lived in our village, and he was always glad of somebody who would help to exercise his horses. This suited me very well, and though it was rather anxious work with valuable animals which danced all over the road whenever a car passed, I became a tolerable rider. I also became a keen follower of the Kendal Otter Hounds and whenever possible went out with one of the Lake District packs of foxhounds, where all the field follow for miles and miles over the fells on foot.

Although the mountains of the Lake District were in sight of my home and of the shore where most of my day was spent, I had no great desire to visit them. We used to go there occasionally for picnics, but I was more interested in the birds or wild flowers that we found than in the hills themselves. I knew no mountaineers or rock-climbers among my contemporaries, and I had read nothing about their activities.

But when I went up to Cambridge in 1926, at informal Sunday evenings in the house of that great mountaineer, Geoffrey Winthrop

Young, I found myself suddenly in the midst of a set where the talk was all of belays, pitches and cornices. I had known Winthrop some years before, when he took a house in the Lake District, but as he had then only recently lost his leg in the war, and had not yet evolved the marvellous technique by which he subsequently climbed many of the major Alpine peaks with the aid of an artificial limb, he had not been disposed to talk of mountaineering in those days. I soon joined the Cambridge Mountaineering Club and started roof-climbing, as there were no rocks within a reasonable distance of Cambridge. We took this very seriously, using a rope, and working out the climbs with the greatest care. We did it partly to keep in climbing trim, and also because it provided some excitement in the routine of academic life in the fens. The climbing had to be undertaken in the small hours of the morning, and its dangers were enhanced by the need to avoid the vigilance of college porters and others. For the authorities took every possible step to prevent roof-climbing, which not only provided a means of getting out of one's college after the gates had been officially locked, but also did considerable damage to the roofs.

We were very strongly opposed to the people who advertised their activities by tying umbrellas or other articles to the summits of conspicuous buildings : such advertisement we considered unnecessary and in very bad taste.

My first real rock-climbing was done in North Wales in 1927. I bought an ancient motor-bicycle and sidecar for £8, and on this three of us travelled, with many strange adventures, from Cambridge to Capel Curig. We camped at the foot of Tryvfan and climbed the Milestone Buttress and spent some happy hours on the easier routes up the Idwal Slabs. I did not see the eclipse of the sun—which was one of our objects in going to North Wales —but I developed a strong liking for rock-climbing. It was an excuse to go camping in wild country, and provided an outlet for an unlimited amount of physical energy. It was also as dangerous and exciting as one cared to make it; I felt a strong satisfaction in having succeeded in getting up some climb, during which I had probably been more terrified than I would have admitted even to myself, for I have never been able to overcome an inherent fear of precipitous places. Finally, it introduced a new form of companionship and interdependence with the other men on the rope.

My chief training as a rock-climber was gained during the years I climbed with T. E. Hicks in the Lake District. Our first climb was the Little Gully on Pavey Ark in Great Langdale. We did this in walking shoes and without a rope. I remember it for the extraordinary profusion of wild flowers in the gully and for the fact that in the middle of the climb we surprised a fox. Later we must have done at least a hundred climbs together. He was a brilliant climber and, moreover, a very careful one. I was harder to tire than he was, but I was sometimes unable to follow him up a particularly difficult section. Together we did most of the better-known climbs in the Lake District. I enjoyed this climbing tremendously, but was usually very frightened on the really difficult pitches. A handhold might break away at the critical moment, and a bootnail could so easily slip from the tiny ledge on which one's whole weight was poised. The New West climb on Pillar, or Kern Knotts Crack on Great Gable seemed to me about the limit of reasonable enjoyment. Being normally muscular and stout-hearted but having no genius for acrobatics, I found such climbs as the North West on Pillar—especially the Oppenheimer's chimney pitch—most unpleasant. I was absolutely terrified, and though I was elated afterwards, I was miserable at the time, and used to swear I would give up climbing if I ever lived to reach the top.

I also climbed in the Snowdon District, on Ben Nevis, and in Skye. I did most of the climbs that were then classed as " severe ", but the "very severes" I usually avoided. Though I often climbed alone I did very little actual leading, as I was usually fortunate enough to be with more experienced men, better able than myself to take the responsibility for other people's lives.

For those who do not understand the art, I will explain the normal procedure of rock-climbing in this country so that they will understand the inevitable technicalities which—though I have reduced them to a minimum—are bound to occur in a book on mountaineering. Let us take a party of three people, all of whom have done some roped climbing, but the leader, we will suppose, has been in the same district before and knows many of the climbs. Guide-books are published by the various clubs and these give detailed descriptions of the climbs, pitch by pitch (a pitch is the name given to a section of a rock-climb), and a classification of the various climbs as to difficulty, such as very severe,

severe, difficult, moderate, etc. The older school of climbers almost invariably wore heavy boots nailed with soft iron nails called *clinkers* into which the rock can bite, or sharper hard nails called *tricounis* which give a grip on the minutest hold. These boots were equally useful for scree-running or fell-walking. The modern climber has invented many varieties of nails but prefers rubbers or rope soles. These make climbs possible which would be out of the question in boots, but on the other hand they become unsafe on wet rock.

The leader then, considering his own prowess, the weather, and the experience and equipment of his party, decides what climb he will take them up. It may necessitate a walk of several hours from the camp or inn to the foot of the climb. Personally, I like this just as much as the actual climbing, but nowadays many people seem to consider it merely a necessary nuisance. The leader then finds the foot of the climb, either from his previous experience or from the guide-book. Usually there is a small cairn there, and the scratches on the rock from the boots of previous climbers indicate the route. The party then ties on the rope, being careful to use the recognized knots, and the leader starts up the first pitch. The length of his lead depends on the amount of rope available, the frequency of suitable anchorages, and the confidence he has in himself and in his second man. Suppose the climb is not particularly difficult, and he leads out forty feet : he then finds a suitable stance and proceeds to make a belay. The object of this is to prevent his being pulled off the rocks if the second falls, and to enable him to anchor the second in such an eventuality. The form of belay depends upon the nature of the rocks. If possible, he knots a loop in the rope and puts it over some protuberance, then, standing as firmly as possible, he passes the rope over his shoulders in such a way that he can bear the greatest possible strain should the second fall off. Then, as the second climbs up to him, he takes in the slack so that the rope does not get in the way of the climber. Thus, if the second falls off, the weight comes on to the rope at once and is lessened by its elasticity, and the leader can easily hold him and either pull him up to the next hold or lower him to the last. The rope is only there in case of emergency, but it gives great confidence to the climbers and can also be used to make a hurried descent of the rocks if the party is overtaken by darkness or storm.

As soon as the second man reaches the leader's stance, the latter transfers his belay to him and the third man is brought up in the same way. If there is not much room, the leader starts on the next pitch before the third man comes up; if the climbing is easy, the first and last men move at once, the middle man acting as an anchor. It should therefore always be possible to hold the second and third men should they fall off, while the leader can only fall a limited distance. When traversing—that is, moving sideways across the rocks—the leader can probably hitch the rope over any protuberances as he passes, so that he will not fall far, and in any case he would probably swing pendulum-wise instead of falling vertically downwards. But it might happen that if the leader fell the second could not hold him. If he falls when he is thirty feet directly above the second, even if he does not knock him off his stance, a tremendous pull will come upon the unfortunate second from the resulting fall of sixty feet; if he does manage to hold him, his hands and shoulders will probably be skinned, and even then, with the leader's inert body dangling thirty feet below him, he may be unable to pull or lower him to a place of safety.

From all this it follows that the leader simply must not fall. If he is climbing on recognized routes, he must not tackle anything that might be beyond his powers, and in any case he must not climb a pitch unless he is certain he can get back again. It is only by adhering strictly to these rules that accidents are avoided. Often, watching inexperienced parties juggling with the rope on climbs which are obviously beyond their capabilities, I am amazed that accidents are not even more frequent. In the old days a climber served a long apprenticeship before leading, but nowadays this is not considered necessary, and the resulting increase in accidents—though admittedly the number of climbers has also increased—has brought great discredit on the mountaineering fraternity.

When men of equal ability are on the rocks together they will probably take it in turn to lead. In mountaineering, as in anything else, a man has his off-days, and moments when he feels that even the Central Buttress on Scafell would present no insuperable difficulties. Sometimes a party is composed of climbers each of whom specializes in one particular type of rock: one leads on exposed buttresses, another up chimneys and a third on bare slabs. Personally, I have been involved in very few rock-climbing accidents and I have never fallen when leading, or known my leader to fall. I remember once, at Cambridge, several of us decided that we could no longer bear the misty flat horizon of the fen country. We left Cambridge by car very early one Sunday morning bound for some rock slabs near Matlock. Gino Watkins was in the party, also Jack Longland, Lawrence Wager and Charles Warren, all of whom have since distinguished themselves on Everest. We were scrambling about, unroped, on the rocks. I was at the foot of the slabs watching the others. Suddenly Warren was seen to be in difficulties; his foothold had broken away and he was left hanging by his hands from a narrow ledge. He could not get down and he had not the strength left to pull himself up. Longland, who was climbing just above, rapidly came down to his aid and was able to grasp his wrists just as he was forced to let go of the rock. But, none too securely placed himself, Longland could hold him only for a few agonizing seconds before he had to let him drop. He fell for about twenty feet, landed on a grassy ledge, telescoped, then shot outwards again, to fetch up in a sycamore tree another twenty feet lower down. He was unhurt.

Occasionally when climbing with Hicks I had to accept the assistance of a gentle pull from the rope above me. Only once did I really fall, and there was some excuse for that. One very wet afternoon in October we were climbing Walker's Gully on Pillar Rock. We had already done several climbs and were rather tired. The climb is classified in the *Fell and Rock Climbing Club Guide* as "severe—last pitch very severe". We were almost at the top and were climbing a vertical wall from the temporary security of a small level platform in a gully which was just too wide to "chimney up", that is, to jam oneself between two rock walls and to wriggle up by extreme muscular exertion. Further out, the gully narrowed over a formidable overhand to the foot of the climb. The only hold to assist in leaving the platform was a tiny ledge, an inch and a half wide and sloping downwards. Hicks found that his nails would not grip the wet rock, so he removed his boots and clambered up in stocking-feet. Soon afterwards he found a stance out of my sight and shouted to me to come on. He had a very stout belay and advised me not to bother to remove my boots. Just as I had all my weight on the sloping hold, and before I had found the larger handhold above, my nails slipped off and I shot outwards, to jam in the narrower part of the chimney. Hicks, listening from above, heard my warning shout, felt a sudden pull, and then the rope became slack in his hands. Thinking that the rope had severed in some way, he strained his ears for a dull thud coming up from below. But instead of that he heard a cheerful voice saying that I had discovered an easier variation, for it was quite a simple matter to chimney up where the walls of the gully were nearer together.

Another time Hicks and I were standing on the level platform at the top of Easter Gully on Dow Crags and were just roping up preparatory to climbing Broderick's Crack. Suddenly there was a startling noise up above and we were just in time to dodge the body of a sheep which fell sheer for three hundred feet, to land with a thud where we had been standing. As we moved forward to examine it, several boulders, disturbed by the sheep when it lost its footing, crashed and broke into a thousand fragments in the very place from which we had just moved. The danger from falling stones, especially now that so many people climb, is one of the greatest perils on the rocks.

I did a certain amount of solitary climbing at this time. Though this practice is deprecated by many mountaineers, it certainly gives one confidence and helps one to attain that rhythmic speed of movement which is so necessary in the Alps or Himalaya when the whole party has to move together over difficult ground. I remember once in Skye I was climbing alone up the steep side of the so-called Inaccessible Pinnacle on Sgurr nan Gillean. As I reached the summit I met Bobby Woodhouse, a well-known climber of the old school, leading a party up the other side. He had taught me physics at Sedbergh, but in spite of that we were great friends. In answer to my cordial salutation he gave me a vigorous lecture on the iniquities and dangers of solitary climbing : I immediately descended by the way I had come up.

One of the most satisfactory climbs I have ever done was a solitary ascent of the Tower Ridge on Ben Nevis, the longest rock-climb in the British Isles. I had walked with a non-climbing friend to the summit in the afternoon ; we were due to leave Fort William the next day after breakfast. At three o'clock in the morning I slipped out of the hotel and ran to the foot of the rocks ; I forget how long it took to do the climb, including the more difficult Douglas Boulder, but I was at the summit of Ben

CLIMBING THE FLAKE CRACK, CENTRAL BUTTRESS, SCAFELL

NORTH-WEST ICELAND : VIEW NEAR CAP NORD

ALPS : FROM THE REQUIN HUT LOOKING OVER THE GEANT SERRACS TO
THE COL DU GEANT, COL D'ENTREVES AND THE TOUR RONDES

Nevis again soon after dawn and back in the hotel for breakfast at nine.

I have only once got into serious difficulties when climbing alone. That was in Wales, when we were camping at the foot of Tryvfan. Feeling energetic—and also because a stream had overflowed in the night and my sleeping-bag was more or less floating—I got up very early, and putting on shorts, a rugger jersey and gym shoes, I decided to run to the top of Tryvfan by following the Heather Traverse, a path that slants gently up the foot of the rocks until it doubles back along the easy summit ridge. The mist was down over the top of the mountain, and meeting what I realized later was only a dip in the track, I thought I had reached the place where the way led up over steep but not difficult rocks. I started to climb, and soon came on to a tiny grassy ledge where I suddenly saw, looming through the mist, a sheep and a lamb. I thought that if I advanced towards them they would show me the way up, but apparently I was guarding the only exit from the grassy ledge, and the sheep, fearing for her lamb, immediately charged. I threw myself flat on my face, and the mother, followed by her lamb, actually touched me as they fled past my inert body to safety. This was disturbing, but imagining that the summit ridge was only just above me, I decided to carry on upwards, still not realizing that I had left the Heather Traverse far too soon and was on the steep rock-face. I soon found the marks of climbers' nails on the rocks and worked my way up what I afterwards identified as the Gashed Crag route, one of the hardest climbs on the mountain, and certainly not one to be tackled alone in gym shoes, on wet rocks.

Rock-climbing in the British Isles, because of the variety, both in nature and severity, of the climbs, is a most valuable apprentice-ship for a mountaineer, and on no recognized climb in the Alps or Himalaya have I found any pitches more difficult than some of those on Snowdon or the Cuillins. But it is unfortunate that some of those who have not been lucky enough to graduate to mountains beyond our islands should concern themselves solely with technical problems and follow routes which strain the limit of safety to breaking-point. Surely they fail to appreciate the real spirit of mountaineering.

## CHAPTER TWO

### FURTHER AFIELD

IN the summer of 1928 I had my first taste of mountaineering as opposed to rock-climbing, as a member of a party which traversed the Meije in the Dauphiné Alps. F. R. G. Chew and I were staying at Grenoble, trying to learn French. It was very hot and muggy down there in August, though we had kept ourselves as fit as possible by working out some new routes up Les Trois Pucelles. Then we had a letter from Jack Longland and Lawrence Wager, who had been doing some serious climbing in the Dauphiné, asking us to join them on an unguided traverse of the Meije (13,500 feet). This is one of the longest and more difficult of the better-known climbs in the Alps; we were neither of us in very good training and I had never even handled an ice-axe— except on the winter cornices of Ben Nevis. It is a safe principle that in guideless parties every member should be capable of lead-ing; but if the two experts were prepared to take the risk we were certainly ready to join them.

The journey up to La Grave, where we were to start the climb, was memorable. We went up on my old motor-cycle, a machine more noted for its speed than its reliability. I remember we were held up behind a travelling circus on one of the steep winding Alpine passes; the truck containing the elephant was far too large for us to pass, and after roaring along in bottom gear for some time the engine seized up. However, at last we reached La Grave and I saw the full glory of Alpine flowers for the first time. I had found the rare *lloydia* and purple saxifrage among the rocks of North Wales, and the exquisite *Primula scottica* on the Sutherland hills, but here all the varieties whose single blooms one had sought in remote corners of the British Isles, or admired in the rockery of some skilful gardener, were growing in marvellous profusion: dense, flower-covered cushions of silene and androsace, masses of scarlet and white cyclamen, wild roses and almost luminous blue gentians.

That afternoon our companions appeared, looking grim and weather-beaten after a fortnight's serious climbing. We sought out the tiny inn where we were to stay. In the evening some men in curious helmets entered; we never discovered if they were the local fire brigade or some strange frontier militia, but a dance was given in their honour and we had no sleep that night. Music was provided by an ancient musical box in the room just beneath our bedroom: three tunes followed each other with maddening monotony. At 2 o'clock we got up. An hour later we left the hut and set off up the steep track towards the Brèche de la Meije, on the other side of which lay the Promontoire Hut where we were to spend the night. Soon we heard the shouts of what appeared to be a cragfast tourist on a grassy ledge of a steep precipice. But when we set about rescue operations he walked away with a bunch of flowers in his hand, still shouting. Apparently he was the village idiot. Then I met my first crevasses, great cracks and fissures formed in the glacier by irregularities in the bed over which the ice flowed, or by the sheer weight of the ice as it moved over a convex surface. The vast scale of these tangled ice serracs and cavernous gashes suddenly appearing in the rounded curves and hollows of the glacier was something I had been quite unprepared for.

Having reached the top of the Brèche we glissaded down to the hut, practising the use of the ice-axe on the way. This was frightening but exhilarating. The slope was so steep and the snow so hard that if we had once got out of control we should have slid downwards with ever-increasing velocity. But the rope and ice-axe were there to prevent this. By grasping the ice-axe firmly and leaning back on the shaft which drags in the snow it can be used as a brake. If one does lose control it is necessary to roll over on to one's front and to dig the longer spike of the axe into the snow so that, with all one's weight on the top of it, it acts as an anchor and gradually brings one to a standstill. How many times since then have I saved my own and others' lives by this means!

At the Promontoire Hut Chew and I had pemmican and porridge for the first time in our lives, and were both violently sick. Pemmican, the roast beef of explorers, is a very concentrated meat food containing a high percentage of fat and albumen which makes it an especially suitable diet in cold climates. It has the consistency and appearance of coffee fudge and tastes salty, gritty and not unlike the dregs of strong beef-tea. The Danish variety contains nuts and fruit. It can be eaten raw, but is usually made into soup, with or without the addition of oatmeal, which is very filling and extremely sustaining. It is thought that the Red Indians were the first to make it by pounding down dried buffalo meat and mixing it with fat. But whatever the truth of its history, it is an invaluable commodity which the traveller should not be without.

I also had my first experience of mountain sickness here, though how much of this was due to the pemmican I cannot say. I had a terrible headache, especially at the back of the eyes, violent diarrhœa and vomiting, and an overpowering desire to go to sleep and not to wake up again. Chew was in much the same state, so we went to sleep while the other two roped up and prospected the first part of the route we were to follow next day. However, we were soon disturbed by a noisy French party whose guides sang songs and drank red wine far into the night.

We left before dawn, carrying a lantern to light us up the first part of the climb. As it was still dark when we reached the rock the leader had to climb with the lantern held in his teeth. And the climbing was not at all easy. The chief difficulty was the speed at which we had to go. Frequently all four of us would be moving together over ground which we would have negotiated singly and with the utmost respect had it been on Scafell or Snowdon. I was terrified, but at the same time I found it strangely exhilarating to be climbing in the half-light over such difficult rock. I had never before realized how important rhythm is in climbing; I found I could overcome weariness and even fear by moving in a definite rhythm; my own momentum seemed to carry me on, or perhaps it was the momentum of the rest of the party. At last we reached the glacier Carré and stopped for a few minutes' rest and some breakfast. The French party passed us here and held us up later at the Cheval Rouge, a rock pitch as difficult as anything I had climbed at home. Soon after this we reached the summit of the Grand Pic. The view was superb. I never had much of a case against scoffers who asked why I did not go up by the ordinary route when I had sweated up some sodden gully on Pavey Ark, descended by another route and then followed a more exciting way to the top of the rocks again. But here it was different; there was no other way: only by undergoing all that hard work and terror could we be here at all, and it was also undeniable that our senses were somehow purged and quickened by the muscular and nervous effort. And there was another element in our triumph : the four of us had got here without guides, by our own efforts—though Chew and I could claim little credit for that—and we were dependent on one another to get safely back to the rest of the world, which seemed at that moment so remote.

The dawn had been gradual and unobtrusive; one moment it was night and then, before one was conscious of any great change, it was day. The frosty stars had been clear, but now it was overcast, and tiny crystals of snow were forming—so small that they dissolved the moment they landed on rocks or garments. A sudden gust of wind flurried the snow which lay in pockets of the rock. The experts feared that there was a blizzard brewing and told us we must make haste to get off the mountain. Chew and I had been climbing as fast as we thought humanly possible; now we must go faster still. A mile of knife-edge ridge lay between us and the next summit and then there was a perilous descent to the other hut. The French party descended into the Brèche Zsigmondy on a double rope, and we overtook them here and held our lead, although it was very difficult to get off the lower glacier out of the Brèche. The scramble along the knife-edge ridge to the next peak, the Doigt de Dieu, was a nightmare, but we reached it at last, and an hour's perilous descent, still at full speed, took us off the rock. We had been climbing for twelve hours. Longland and Wager, experienced climbers in perfect training, had been going as fast as they possibly could, and Chew and I, inexperienced and straight from the relaxing heat of Grenoble, had had to keep up with them. Our reaction on stopping was to be violently sick, but after a meal and a rest we were ready to descend the 5000 feet of easy rock and scree to La Grave.

This was not without excitement. Fine scree is easy to run. The small stones slide down with one, and if they start going too fast, it is easy to jump aside and let the moving staircase go on. With larger stones it is more difficult; not only does the scree run unevenly, but sometimes the large stones which are disturbed come rushing after one with terrific speed. It is therefore best, if a large party is descending a scree slope, for its members either to go singly or to follow different routes. On this occasion Chew and I took one scree shoot while Longland and Wager chose another well to the side. We agreed to meet at the bridge over the river which could be seen at the foot of the valley. Suddenly, as we were enjoying the change of exercise and the exhilarating descent, there was a noise like the whining of a shell over our heads, followed by a crash down below. Then several more missiles went whizzing just above us and we hastily took cover until the fusillade was over. Soon afterwards the other two appeared; apparently our screes had joined not far above and Chew and I, being some way ahead, were in the direct passage of the stones; as some of them were as big as footballs there would not have been much of us left had we been hit.

Next day I went up alone on my motor-bicycle to the top of the Col de Galibier. I was very lucky to reach the top at all, for on the way up, just as I was negotiating one of the many S bends, I suddenly caught sight of a large black-and-white shrike, of a species I had never seen before, and I was so thrilled by this new bird that I took my eyes off the road for a second and all but drove over the edge into the gorge below. When I reached the summit I walked up to the top of the hill, from which there was an excellent view of the Meije, and I tried to analyse the feelings which my triumph of yesterday had roused in me. I have tried to do the same thing many times since then: to formulate a philosophy of mountaineering; to try to justify to myself and others this overpowering desire to reach the top of a mountain. The attraction certainly cannot lie in the view to be obtained from the summit; for as a rule the view is better when you are looking *at* mountains, not *from* them. It is not solely for the physical satisfaction of making the ascent, though there is no better exercise in the world than climbing. I hope it is not simply in order to have the gratification of telling other people about one's achievement; nor for the self-justification of carrying out a difficult climb in spite of contrary odds. No, there is a greater satisfaction than that in it: the beauty and aloofness of high mountains and the hard physical effort which is required to visit them combine to produce an emotion which has an inexpressible charm for those who have experienced it. Mountains have always been acclaimed as the dwelling-place of the gods, and the mountain spirit reveals himself at such moments to his worshippers.

On the way home from Grenoble I had an adventure which very nearly ended my life. Suddenly, as I was speeding along a road, I felt a sharp and excruciating pain over my heart. I discovered that a hornet had become entangled in my woolly scarf and crawling inside my clothes had stung me. I felt very sick, but decided to make for Avallon, the next town, and see a doctor. The road was perfectly straight and I was going along it at about fifty miles per hour when I suddenly fainted and crashed into the rough ground beside the road. The motor-cycle was completely flattened but I was unhurt, except for a few bruises. A garage was able to do a very complicated operation on the machine, grafting in various parts of other wreckage they had in stock and I managed to catch the boat at Havre that night, none the worse.

In the summer of 1929, as soon as I had taken my degree at Cambridge, I organized an expedition to Iceland with two medical-student friends. Our alleged object was to collect plants and make bird observations for the British Museum, but actually I wanted to experience again the thrill of setting out on some difficult or dangerous enterprise with friends of similar tastes—in other words, to go on an expedition. Also, I had not decided what I was going to do for the rest of my life, and I felt that it would be easier to achieve the detachment necessary to make such a momentous decision in the clearer atmosphere of Iceland.

After calling at the Faroes and the Westmann Islands the three of us reached Reykjavik, travelling steerage on an ancient ship called the *Botnia*; then, having assimilated as much local knowledge as was available, we set off to walk right across the north of the country, carrying all the necessary equipment on our backs. That was the trouble; in our state of inexperience, everything seemed necessary, and we found ourselves starting off with ungainly loads of 70 or 80 lb. each. Here is an example of our extraordinary ignorance and lack of common sense: we had decided, to save expense, to have sleeping-bags made up in Reykjavik, where eiderdown is collected locally; when it came to designing the bags, I thought that as one normally slept with three or four blankets above and only one blanket and a sheet below, I would follow the same proportions and have eiderdown above and only one thickness of blanket below. But of course when one is camping most of the cold comes up from the ground, so we did not have much sleep our first few nights.

Although we saw many birds which were new to us, the scientific results of the expedition were not important. We slept in a tent, and though we took a basic ration of oatmeal, biscuit, chocolate, sugar and butter, we relied on the country for food in the form of ducks and ptarmigan which we shot with a ·410 gun, fish we caught in the lakes and rivers, and sea-birds' eggs which we collected along the shore. This Robinson Crusoe way of living has always fascinated me, and I am sure that our appreciation of the beauty of Iceland, as well as our great enjoyment of ordinary life when we again returned to it, was sharpened by the fact that our bodies were worn out by the weights we were carrying and the distances we walked.

After returning from Iceland I decided that I would teach, but I wanted to see a little more of life before settling down as a school-master.

In November 1929 I went out to Davos to ski. I had been to Maloja the year before and had found it a wonderful experience. I think ski-ing is the only sport I could ever have been really good at. I have all the necessary qualifications—a good eye, an excellent sense of balance, great staying power and enough foolhardiness to take almost any slope straight. After a few months' ski-ing I was able to take part in some of the great international ski races : the Parsenn Derby and the Arlberg Kandahar. I also did a certain amount of ski-ing up on the glaciers as an antidote to the gaiety and excitement of Davos. We used to go up to the high huts with food for a week or two and spend all the daylight hours on skis. On places where there was danger of crevasses we had to ski roped together, and carry ice-axes instead of sticks. This is the most exacting of all kinds of ski-ing. The rope must not be allowed to sag down on to the snow, and each ski-er must be careful not to tug the rope, or his companion will lose his balance. Sometimes a frail snow-bridge would collapse as soon as the first ski-er had passed over it; at other times it would be necessary to leap an open crevasse without checking speed.

Among many glacier tours, one, though it was not particularly successful, stays most clearly in my mind. In January 1930, R. H. L. Holdsworth (late Headmaster of Islamia College, Peshawar), M. J. Ingram (one of the Iceland expedition), and I, did a winter ascent of Pitz Kesch from the Porchobello Glacier. This was my first experience of crampons—a framework of metal spikes, generally about two inches in length, which are strapped beneath climbing boots to give a grip on hard ice. It was also my first lead on an important climb. The ascent was difficult, we had to move one at a time, clearing new snow from every hold, and the sun had set behind the distant triple peak of Monte Rosa by the time we reached the summit. We stood on the isolated peak, a head and shoulders higher than any other in the neighbourhood, torn between a desire to stop and stare at the lovely scene and a haunting fear that we were already too late to reach the Kesch Hut in safety. When we returned to our skis the sealskins had frozen on—we had foolishly omitted to remove them while they were still soft, and it took us some time to get them off. By the time we had started ski-ing it was moonlight. In spite of wind-swept snow the run down to the Porchobello Hut was a wonderful experience : we felt as though we were floating and had no contact with the earth. When we took our boots off, Holdsworth found that his toes were frost-bitten, probably from the tightness of his crampon-strap or ski-binding, and no amount of rubbing would restore the circulation to one big toe. Next day the weather had broken, and though we were able to make our way through the Vallorgia Pass to the Grialetch Hut, we had to abandon our plan of climbing the Pitz Grialetch and the Sarsura. We were forced by bad weather to spend two days in the hut. I remember Ingram smoked *brissagos* (rank cigars wound round a straw which has to be pulled out before they will draw) until the whites of his eyes went yellow, and I read *The Prelude* aloud and was very much hurt when Holdsworth went to sleep in the middle. When the weather cleared, a search-party of Davos guides arrived at the hut, and to our great surprise we discovered they were searching for us, having been sent by Ingram's family, who had become anxious for our safety. We were furious, because we had arranged beforehand that we would stay in the hut if it snowed. To cause people the trouble of sending a search-party is the greatest shame a mountaineer can suffer.

A climbing misadventure which I had at Davos must be told, though it is much to my discredit. In the middle of the big park at Davos Platz there is a large copper statue of a naked man with outstretched arms. One morning the inhabitants awoke to find the statue had been painted scarlet from head to toe. Actually I had done this only because somebody had dared a friend of mine to do it and he did not possess the necessary climbing skill—it was a very large statue on a high pedestal—but the officials took a very serious view, suspecting either an anti-nudist demonstration or some deep political plot, and the son of the man who was depicted in the statue came at full speed from Berlin to challenge the artist to a duel. I knew nothing of all this, and when a friend criticized the colour-scheme of my handiwork I went out again the next night and painted the statue white. Just as I was putting the finishing touches to the legs I heard the rattle of a police-dog's chain and saw several dark figures stealthily closing in on the statue. I made a run for it, was captured, escaped again, and after being hit on the head with a truncheon recovered consciousness in the municipal prison. It was a gloomy prospect : I think I was in the condemned cell, for there was a crude charcoal drawing on the wall of a man hanging from a gibbet, and beneath it, in German, which I was just able to translate, the words, " Only God can help you now ". The officials took an even more gloomy view of the incident than they had on the first day, and I think I should be in prison still had not somebody murmured the words " Student's Rag " at the trial. From that moment all went well from my point of view ; here was an explanation which they understood, and I was let off with a fine of £30 and costs— which could have been a very large sum, for the statue might have had to be sent to Berlin to be cleaned and re-processed. Doctor H., an English resident at Davos, came to my rescue with a cheque, the result of a collection among sympathetic friends, which was more luck than I deserved.

One day at the end of March, I was ski-ing home to my " hotel " (I stayed at the Station Inn, a house much frequented by the sledge-drivers, as the best food in Davos was obtainable there), when I met Gino Watkins. I had known him at Cambridge after he had returned from his Spitsbergen expedition, which he had led and organized at the age of 19. Since then he had wintered in Labrador with J. M. Scott.

" Hullo, Gino," I said. " How's Labrador? "

" Hullo, Freddy," he answered. " How's Iceland? What are you doing here? Come to Greenland? "

" Right you are," said I. " Why? "

" Well, I must get back to dinner now. Meet me tomorrow and I'll tell you all about it."

And so I found myself suddenly attached as ski expert and naturalist to the British Arctic Air-Route Expedition 1930–31.

The story of that, and of the Pan-American Arctic Air-Route Expedition 1932–33, I have told elsewhere.[1]

Life in Greenland was remarkably satisfactory. Our actual job was to investigate the possibilities of an air-route from Europe to America, utilizing the natural land-bridges across the Arctic, from London over the north of Scotland and the Faroe Islands to Iceland, across the grim ice-cap of Greenland to Baffin Land, and thence down the far side of Hudson Bay to Winnipeg, thus avoiding any sea-crossing of more than three hundred miles. The only unexplored part of this route was the district around Angmagssalik on the ice-bound east coast of Greenland, and here fourteen of us—pilots and a mechanic for the two Gipsy Moth aeroplanes, surveyors, a geologist, a meteorologist, a wireless expert and a doctor—were spending rather more than a year. In 1932, four of the original party went out to spend another year at a more suitable air base some miles further north.

I do not think that any part of my life has been or could be happier than those years in Greenland. We were a group of young men with more or less kindred interests and all intent on the same object. The work of mapping and flying over unknown country was inspiring, and the mere struggle to keep alive in the Arctic absorbed all one's spare energy, enthusiasm and inventive powers. Instincts inherent in man but dormant through long years of " civilization " were called into play. I experienced cold so intense that at one time or another I lost all my finger- and toe-nails from frostbite, and my breath froze into solid ice on my face. During the long winter journeys on the ice-cap I was sometimes so exhausted that I fell asleep as I walked along, and once, owing to the rough sea making landing impossible, I spent twenty hours in my kayak. I have been so hungry that I have eaten seal-skin boots and raw blubber. Sometimes we would be confined to our tents for four successive days by a raging blizzard. More than once I fell through a deep crevasse and only saved myself by catching hold of the handle-bars of the sledge, and once, far from land, the sea-ice broke beneath my dogs and sledge-runners, and only by driving on at full speed did I prevent the whole outfit from going through the ice. On another occasion two of us were camping out on the sea-ice when a violent storm arose and the ice started to break up and float out to sea. A crack, through which

[1] *Northern Lights, Watkins' Last Expedition,* etc.

we could see the surging water, appeared right across the tent, and next morning when the storm had abated we found that the ice had broken up on three sides of us and we were connected to the shore by only a narrow strip.

We learnt much from the Eskimos, a most delightful race. A family of twenty or thirty could live together for a whole winter in a single room without an angry word being said, and in time of famine or misfortune they showed a degree of fortitude and unselfishness which astonished us.

There was little actual climbing on these expeditions, but I learnt a great deal of expedition craft and was able to experiment with polar equipment and technique. I also learnt much about ice and snow. And I made another discovery, which is this: almost all difficulties can be overcome. Mere cold is a friend, not an enemy; the weather always gets better if you wait long enough; distance is merely relative; man can exist for a long time on very little food; the human body is capable of bearing immense privation; miracles still happen: it is the state of mind that is important. To Gino Watkins the word "impossible" simply did not exist. Lesser or greater risks might have to be taken, infinite patience might be necessary, but if the will was sufficient, success would come at last. Even the versatile and resourceful Nansen had said that it was impossible for Europeans to learn to roll the kayak and to harpoon seals from it; Watkins said, "Well, if the Eskimos can do it, we can too". So we had kayaks built, and most of us learnt how to roll them. In August 1932, Gino Watkins, at the age of 25, was drowned at Lake Fjord while hunting in his kayak. With him went not only a very great friend and leader, but many exciting plans for the future both in the Arctic and Antarctic.

In the year between the two Greenland Expeditions I was very busy lecturing and writing to help to pay off the expedition debt, but I found time to go in for the Fell Record, a thing I had long wanted to do. It is held by the man who walks or runs up the greatest number of Lake District peaks in 24 hours. Dr. Arthur Wakefield, of Everest fame, originated it in 1911; he set out from Keswick at midnight, climbed Skiddaw, Helvellyn and Scafell, and returned to his starting place within the 24 hours. Dr. Wakefield was a Sedbergian, and had been paced over part of his route by Bobby Woodhouse, a Sedbergh master. They were both very anxious that a Sedbergian should recapture the record, which was then in the hands of Mr. Eustace Thomas, who had added many peaks to the original three, but Woodhouse had made me promise not to attempt it until I was over 25. I stayed for some time in Borrowdale, as a long period of training is necessary before making such a sustained effort. Then I went to stay with Dr. Wakefield at Keswick, where I spent the mornings working on a book about Greenland and the afternoons and week-ends on the fells. On May 17th I was ready to try. It would have been better to have waited for the longer days and more settled weather, but I had to get back to London and had already left it as late as possible.

As is customary, I had arranged for pacers, who would have provisions ready and would at the same time act as witnesses, to meet me at certain places. May 17th was a dull day with mist on the hill-tops. I left Keswick market-place at midnight. The course I had worked out led along the road to Portinscale and then along the far side of Derwentwater to Newlands, then up Robinson, across to Hindscarth and over Dale Head to the top of Honister Pass. There was thick mist on the tops, but I knew the ground well. However, on the way down Dale Head I was running beside the remains of the fence when I was suddenly aware of a darker shadow in the swirling mist at my feet. I was just in time to stop on the edge of a gaping chasm where the slate quarry had encroached upon the fell.

My route then led over Brandreth and Green Gable to the top of Great Gable, where I found my next pace-maker awaiting me. As I was running down the far side of Gable to Kirk Fell my compass fell out of my pocket and broke among the rocks. Crossing the top of Black Sail pass I reached Looking Stead, then passed the summits of Pillar, Steeple, Red Pike and so down to Yewbarrow, whence a pleasant run down the screes brought me at 8 o'clock to Wastdale Head for breakfast. At 8.30 I left Wastdale and made my way to the top of Scafell. Then Broad Stand—the only piece of real rock-climbing on the route—had to be negotiated on the way to Scafell Pike. Between Scafell Pike and Great End I lost my way in the mist and having broken my compass was forced to descend below the mist to discover my whereabouts. I found I was in the head of Eskdale, so I climbed back to the summit of Great End and thence by Esk Hause to the top of Bow

Fell, where I found Bob Graham, the present holder of the record, awaiting me with hot cocoa. From here we cut across by Hanging Knott to the Langdale Pikes, each of which was climbed in turn, then High White Stones and Sergeant Man. Our route now lay along the top of Steel Fell to Dunmail Raise. Unfortunately, we again lost our way in the mist and wasted a good half-hour.

After a half-hour rest for lunch at the top of Dunmail Raise I went up Seat Sandal to Fairfield, then back over Grisedale and along the top of Dollywaggon to Helvellyn, where I found Dr. Wakefield with hot coffee, and over Stybarrow Dod, Great Dod, Clough Head and down to Threlkeld for tea. After half an hour there my pacer and I climbed up the long ridge of Saddleback and across to Great Calva. It was dark by now and raining hard. I was almost an hour behind time, and the man who should have been on the top of Great Calva with hot coffee had given me up and gone home; this was very disheartening, as it was then only just possible to get back to Keswick by midnight.

The long climb up Skiddaw seemed interminable. On the way down we tried to take a short cut to Keswick and became involved in some sort of a quarry which was so steep that we had to let ourselves down by holding on to heather and bracken. It was 1 o'clock by the time we reached Keswick market-place. I had taken 25 hours, so it was a failure so far as the record was concerned, but I mean to try it again one day. George Abraham, the famous mountaineer who lives at Keswick, estimates the route as 130 miles of walking and 30,000 feet of climbing—that is even if you don't get lost in the mist. I was not in the least tired until I reached Threlkeld, but the toil up Saddleback was exhausting and the final climb up Skiddaw almost a nightmare.

In 1934 I went up to the West Coast of Greenland to buy seventy huskies for John Rymill to take to the Antarctic on the British Graham Land Expedition. I longed to go with him, but I felt it was time to settle down and do some work. If I was going to be a schoolmaster and not an explorer-adventurer it was high time I began.

I could have made a living for a time, and a fairly good one too, by writing and lecturing in between expeditions, but an explorer's is an unsettled, unsatisfactory existence as a permanent prospect. To keep up my earnings I should have had to depend on publicity and stunts of one sort or another, for as the great explorer Stefansson once said, the story of a successful expedition makes dull reading, for there should be no adventures. I had followed carefully the careers of men who had been with Scott and Shackleton and on other expeditions, and I found that most of those who had kept it up too long had come to grief in one way or another. The only people who made a success of it were those whose jobs forced them to return to normal life as soon as the expedition was over—the scientists and men from the Services. Expedition life, if you are suited to it, takes such a hold of you that it makes all other occupations seem flat and dull in comparison and it is difficult to break away. Yet the break had to be made, so I became a schoolmaster at Aysgarth, a large, old-established private school in the North of England. The routine was irksome at first, but I enjoyed the work very much and made good use of my holidays.

One summer I went to Chamonix with two friends, but we had vile weather and were unable to do any of the major peaks. However, we climbed the Requin, the Tour Noir and the Aiguille d'Argentière, though we were turned back from the Grepon and Mont Blanc. Here I learnt more ice-work, and realized what I had missed by never having had the opportunity of climbing with good Alpine guides. The modern guideless climber is self-reliant and enterprising, but I am sure that on ice he lacks the flawless technique and easy speed of the older school.

In the Easter holidays, 1935, two of us went to Lapland. I wanted to see how travel with reindeer compared with dog-sledging, and to try out various details of polar equipment. We bought a reindeer, which we called Isaac, at Karesuando and drove him on a compass course to Karasjok, a distance of about 150 miles. As we did not take a Lapp guide with us and as reindeer are notoriously intractable, we chose one without horns in case it came to a hand-to-hand struggle. Unfortunately, we did not realize that reindeer rely to a certain extent on their horns [1] for digging through the snow to uncover the lichenous moss on which they are able—by some remarkable digestive process—to derive sufficient strength to travel prodigious distances in a single day. The

---

[1] Later observation has reluctantly convinced me that the reindeer relies solely on its hooves for digging through the snow. But I cannot spoil a good story.

consequence was that we had to spend precious hours digging moss for Isaac's supper when we should have been cooking our pemmican or sleeping. Isaac had large black and exceedingly sharp hooves which were valuable in supporting his weight in deep snow, but with which he could deliver phenomenally hard and vicious kicks in almost every direction at once. He also refused to pull our sledge, unless one of us went in front and pulled not only the sledge but Isaac too. Consequently, when we reached Karasjok we were very glad to sell Isaac to a butcher, in spite of considerable financial loss, and to complete the journey on skis, carrying our gear on our backs. Eventually, after turning back just in time from what proved to be a five-day blizzard on Lake Enari, we came out at Vadsö and returned by boat round the North Cape. This journey showed that it was possible to carry out quite exciting expeditions even during the normal school holidays, and I planned to take some of the boys another time, to give them a glimpse of the joy of an expedition before they settled down to modern life in cities.

After I had been at Aysgarth for two years, I accepted an invitation from Marco Pallis to take a term off and to join an expedition he was planning to the Himalaya. The object of the expedition was to visit the Zemu Glacier in the Kangchenjunga district of Northern Sikkim, and from there to attempt Simvu (22,360 feet) or Siniolchu (22,620 feet), and possibly other peaks if time and weather permitted.

## CHAPTER THREE

### FROM LIVERPOOL TO THE HIMALAYA

MARCO PALLIS is a very remarkable man. His father was a Greek who translated the Odyssey and the Bible into modern Greek. Later he became a British subject and settled at Liverpool. Pallis is a lover of all forms of art; for some years he has been working on an opera, composing the music, writing the words and designing the costumes; he is particularly interested in the viol and harpsichord and has studied under Dr. Dolmetsch at Hazelmere, where both he and Richard Nicholson, another member of the expedition, frequently play. Another of his interests is Tibetan art and philosophy; he finds himself closely in sympathy with the mysticism of the East, and has a very considerable knowledge of the Tibetan language. He did not take up mountaineering until he was over 30, and then, after several seasons in the Alps, he led an expedition to explore the Gangotri district of the Himalaya. T. E. Hicks and Charles Warren, who have deen mentioned before in this book, were members of that expedition, so also was R. C. Nicholson, who came again this time.

Nicholson, a son of C. E. Nicholson, the famous yacht-designer, had deserted office life in order to devote himself to music, and he and Pallis, having so many tastes in common, were inseparable. R. C. Roaf, the doctor of the expedition, was a son of the eminent professor of physiology at Liverpool. His experience of mountaineering was small, but he was extremely interested in Tibetan art and had already a fair knowledge of the language. J. K. Cooke, the fifth member of the expedition, worked in an insurance office in Liverpool. He used to escape to Snowdon during week-ends, and having had a season or two in the Alps, he had made a name for himself as a very skilful and daring rock-climber. The plans were that after we had all climbed for a month on the Zemu Glacier, Pallis, Nicholson and Roaf would, if permission could de secured, enter Tibet, while Cooke and I continued to climb in Sikkim.

The expedition was fortunate in being allowed to travel for a nominal sum in the Harrison Line cargo boat *Recorder*, which sailed from Brunswick Dock, Liverpool, on February 22nd, 1936. As we left the foggy Mersey behind us after the usual crowded last week of preparation I found it difficult to believe that I was really setting out for the Himalaya, the highest peaks in the world, the ultimate but rarely-found goal of all mountaineers. I was not on my way to attempt Everest, but this, I hoped, might be a preparation for such an expedition in the future.

The voyage was uneventful, but as it was my first journey to the East, it was full of interest for me. The Captain did not like passengers and did not disguise the fact. He was a keen golfer and used to practise his drive on the lower deck with a captive golf ball. Unfortunately its captivity was uncertain and balls whistling about the ship added to the excitement of an otherwise

B

uneventful trip. We used to keep fit by playing with a heavy medicine ball until it and all available substitutes had been hurled overboard by over-enthusiastic players. Entering the Mediterranean we saw to the south the snow-capped peaks of the Atlas Mountains and to the north the sunset glow on the Sierra Nevada. At Port Said, when we had to remove all brass fittings from the boat to prevent their being stolen, a wonderful collection of leering pock-marked rogues came on board to try and sell us things we did not want. The best turn was a man who described himself as an " A1 Barber"; his game was to come up behind someone with a pair of scissors and pretend to trim off a projecting tuft of hair and then quickly snip a furrow right up the back of the victim's hair, so that he was forced to have it cut. The redeeming features of Port Said were a row of exquisitely graceful fishing-boats lying at anchor, and the wonderful magenta-coloured blooms of the Bougainvillæa growing on the houses.

The Canal is cut straight through the desert with banks of sand up to 15 feet high on either side and is edged by concrete walls with frequent mooring-blocks in case ships have to pass. The best position is behind mail-boats or oil-tankers, as these—the latter being explosive—are hurried through as quickly as possible. We were unlucky though, and once had to tie up while eight ships passed us—two empty Italian troop-ships returning from Abyssinia, a Swedish timber boat from Göteborg, a French tramp, a large Japanese cargo-boat from Kobe, a wheat-boat from Latvia, a Dutchman from Rotterdam and a Brocklebank Line boat from Liverpool. Soon we passed the war memorial near where the Turks attacked in the last war, and by the time we had crossed the Great Bitter Lake and seen the remains of the ancient canal of the Pharaohs it was time to turn on the enormous searchlight which had been fitted to our bows at Port Said. After passing the Land of Goschen, where Jacob was sent by Joseph, we saw the line of lights which marked Suez, having traversed the 870 miles of the canal in just over twelve hours.

Going down the Red Sea we admired the magnificent rows of jagged mountains in the distance on each side; bleak and barren they looked, except when they were softened by the misty early morning sunlight. We saw no sign of Mount Sinai. There was never a patch of grass visible, not a leaf, not even a lichen, moss or cactus. Nevertheless there was plenty of colour;

bands of pale sulphur, ochre and chocolate zigzagged across the arid ridges. A dove with exquisite lilac-blue wings settled on the ship; then a kestrel and a short-eared owl. A flight of several hundred kites passed overhead, flying northwards. It was here that I saw flying fish for the first time and thought them most beautiful. The water was an oily blue colour, except where it reflected the terra-cotta tints of the mountains. Suddenly there emerged what appeared to be a dragon-fly, but with black and oval body, though sometimes the scales appeared to be of silver and the wings shone with rainbow lights. It flew fast with its gossamer wings vibrating, a thin double line of disturbance following it in the water until it rose clear. It did not fly more than a few feet above the water and every now and then it came low enough to touch the surface with its body, setting off again after each contact with renewed vigour, like an electric toy which has to stop and recharge itself. The end of the flight was disappointing: it fell back with a heavy splash, leaving only a few ripple-rings. Nearly every evening Pallis and Nicholson played their viols. I shall always connect the tune *Greensleeves* with the diaphanous wings of flying fish, and the unreal stage-scenery-like mountains of the Red Sea.

On March 16th we were off Minacoy, a small coral island between the Maldive and Laccadive Islands and the only land we saw between Perim and Ceylon. We were south of the north-east monsoon by then and it grew unpleasantly hot. Two days later we passed the south coast of Ceylon and saw the graceful catamarans (outrigger canoes) coming in from fishing. They are so light and stream-lined they seem to leap from crest to crest of the waves, a strong contrast to a large turtle which we saw swimming cumbrously alongside. Ceylon looked enchanting with its strip of golden sand and low palm-covered shore-line, and in the distance all varieties and shapes of deep blue hills, some ending in rock monoliths like buildings, others with their heads lost in heavy cumulus cloud.

On March 21st, after a voyage of four weeks, we landed at Vizagapatam, the new port two hundred miles south of Madras. The shore-line was not unlike Brighton beach and almost as crowded. Beyond the sand, where fishing-boats were hauled up, was a line of modern concrete villas and the low hills clothed with palm-trees and a few mosques and temples on the hill-tops.

We anchored at sunset and a pilot took us into the harbour up an attractive creek where I saw several grey kingfishers, many bee-eaters, a flock of white parrots, some cinnamon-coloured Brahminy kites and other new birds.

In the cool of the evening we set out for a walk, following a windy road lined with tamarisk, mimosa and acacia trees. First we passed some primitive native dwellings, mere booths of thatched palm with fairy lights inside. Outside them were goats and queer oxen with humps on their shoulders, hanging dewlaps and tucked-back ears. The shops were curious cupboard-like contrivances; they sold brass-ware, spices, sweets, curries and cereals and bottles of brightly coloured fizzy drinks. Huge trees hung over the road and the heavy air was loaded with their strong perfume. Crowds of dark-skinned people passed to and fro clad in gay loosely-hanging garments; there were many bicycles and occasionally a motor-car hooted its way through the press. Then a line of slow bullock-waggons would emerge from a side-street with a naked boy-driver standing importantly between two of the animals. A few mangy little ponies pulled dog-carts and " cabs," evil-looking boxes on wheels, into which their drivers tried to tempt us.

Standing back from the line of shops was a shrine of some sort, exquisitely coloured, and further along an opening into a cool garden, shaded by clumps of coconut palms and banyan trees. The wall was plastered with dung cakes drying for fuel. Cows and goats lay in the streets on the raised steps of the houses and men were sleeping beside them with pieces of brightly coloured cloth draped over their inert brown bodies. Women with straight supple figures went past carrying loads on their heads : an earthen-ware jar, a bundle of wood, or a round basket of mangoes. Another group with brass pitchers collected, gossiping, round a well. What an overpowering smell there was—of heat in the first place, and human bodies, warm dung, and a sudden heavy breath of flower scent that was like incense, then a nauseating reek of dirt and sour milk, and all the time the noise of cicadas and grasshoppers, holding its own against the soft voices of the crowd.

A wizened old man squatted in the dust and harangued a circle of attentive boys; a leper washed his mutilated limbs in the gutter; a thin voice at my elbow set up a wail of " Babu, Babu," and a wrinkled cringing beggar slapped his hollow stomach and followed us, clamouring, for some distance along the road. Hearing strange music, we turned up a side-street which was hung with paper decorations, and watched a group of hooded women in white robes come out of a house and cross the road; then a man appeared and asked us not to come any further, so we had to leave it as an unsolved mystery, the culmination of our dream-like walk. We checked our direction by the Pole Star—low on the horizon in these latitudes—and followed Canopus, winding our way through narrow mud-walled streets, and at last reached the shore, where the fresh salt air broke the spell and we realized that it was late and time to go to bed.

Next day we heard that owing to a bore that was expected in the Hooghli river our ship would have to wait for several days at Vizagapatam. Pallis and Roaf went on by train to Calcutta and thence to Kalimpong to make preparations for our transport, leaving the rest of us to follow with the *Recorder*. That night Cooke and I joined a party in the mate's cabin. We drank whisky and the mate strummed his banjo, with sweat pouring off his round red face, and sang nautical—some of them very nautical—songs. What a strange race merchant-seamen are! They seem to have no interest in the places they visit. Very often they don't even bother to go ashore, and when they do it is usually only for a debauch. "Oh! do you know Bahia Blanca?" says one. "Yes," answers another, "I was there in '32. Do you know the —— Bar?"

As we had a couple of days to fill in, we decided to go up by train to Salur at the foot of the Eastern Ghats. The train left at dawn and took us through some interesting country with paddy-birds and white egrets feeding beside sluggish streams. As we went inland coconut palms gave way to thatching and date palms. Cultivation increased; there were groves of huge-leaved banana trees, plantations of tobacco and betel-nut and fields of oil-seed and millet. All the square paddy-fields were surrounded by mud walls a foot high to hold the monsoon rains of July and August for the rice crop. Water is brought up from the river by means of a pole attached to a bucket and laid across a forked tree; one native walks up and down the pole so that the bucket alternately dips into the river and is lifted into the air; when it is in the latter position a second native empties it into a cut at a higher level. The fields are worked with primitive hoes and the ploughs

pulled by oxen. In clusters of trees are lovely mud-walled
native houses thatched with palm leaves. When we stopped to
change at a station, we heard the coppersmith bird calling in the
pepill trees, and saw sacred monkeys come down and walk among
the passengers. Iridescent king crows and blue jays sat on the
telegraph wires and vultures and kites circled overhead.

At Salur we watched them treading out the millet with oxen.
One man walked two bullocks round and round a small patch
of ground about ten feet square, while another swept the grain
in towards the centre. In the river they were washing clothes,
standing knee-deep in the water and continually beating the wet
garments on flat stones propped up at an angle of 45 degrees in the
water, hissing all the time like grooms and ejaculating " tsay "
at each smack.

In the market-place, the flies were a tribulation, beggars whined
on all sides and the heat was almost unbearable. At last our car
arrived, a rickety old Ford bus with no windows, and we set off
for the top of the Ghats, some twenty miles distant. We sped
along the dustiest road I have ever seen, with our horn blowing
all the time to stir the slow-moving bullock-carts and lines of
women carrying loads on their heads. We passed a leper colony
and the road started to wind upwards with frequent hairpin bends
and embankments. On each side were huge pyramidical peaks
of volcanic rock; the largest had a lovely temple on the summit.
In some places the slope was so steep that it was difficult to understand how the earth and trees clung on. This was the real jungle.
As far as eye could reach, on either side of the road the forest
stretched away into the distance. Down below, an impenetrable
undergrowth of prickly shrubs, many with exquisite flowers,
prevented all progress and surely hid all manner of wild beasts.
Here and there taller trees reared their heads above the general
level. The most spectacular, called Flame of the Forest, had no
leaves on the smooth grey branches, but at the top it broke into
a mass of crimson heads like sunflowers. On the way back we
encountered a dust-storm and had to stop for a few minutes as it
was impossible to see across the road. Then it rained as it can
rain only in the tropics, and from the train on the return journey
we saw that all the paddy-fields were squares of silver in the
moonlight.

The next day we sailed for Calcutta, which is very like an English city except for its cosmopolitan Eastern crowds and certain peculiarities which strike a stranger, such as pavements red with betel-nut spat out by addicts, and the sacred bulls which wander through the streets holding up the traffic, eating from the vegetable stalls, or sleeping on the pavements. The temperature was 104° in the shade and we felt as if we had been left all night in a Turkish bath.

On March 27th we left by train for Siliguri. The train travelled all night across the plain of Bengal, through paddy-fields, mud-walled villages and groves of palms, bamboos and bananas. At first sight Siliguri seemed to be a typical village of the Plains, but among the crowd in the squalid fly-infested bazaar there were a few hill-men, recognizable by their oblique eyes and high cheek-bones and their cheerful, independent manners. And already in the background could be seen the steep tree-covered foothills of the Himalaya.

We hired two open cars and set off for Kalimpong, a small town at 8000 feet, forty miles further north, on the border of Bengal, Sikkim, Tibet and Bhutan. For the first seven or eight miles the road led straight through a level stretch of tropical forest known as the Terai; then, accompanied by the narrow-gauge railway which runs from Siliguri to Darjeeling, it entered the Teesta gorge, where it followed the river between beetling cliffs which rose extremely steeply on either side. Once again I found myself marvelling how the trees and undergrowth could cling to rock at such a precipitous angle. About thirty miles from Siliguri we crossed the Teesta river by a modern concrete bridge hung with prayer flags by pious Buddhists. From Teesta Bridge the road soon took to the hills and after nine miles of twisting and turning through the forest we were at Kalimpong. In one place the road actually doubled over itself as railways do in Switzerland.

Kalimpong is a fair-sized village straggling along a saddle between two thickly-wooded hills. As the climate is good there are many Europeans here, the most eminent being the Very Reverend Doctor Graham, who came to Kalimpong some fifty years ago. He and his wife built up the excellent Kalimpong Homes for unwanted or poverty-stricken half-caste children. Dr. Graham's son-in-law, Norman Odling, is another well-known figure. He is in charge of the wool trade with Tibet, and with the help of his charming wife he runs the Kalimpong Arts and Crafts to encourage local industry. The Himalayan Hotel where we stayed at Kalimpong is managed by David Macdonald, who has lived longer in Tibet than any other English-speaking man. The son of a Scottish father and a Sikkimese mother, and married to a Nepali, he was for twenty years British Trade Agent at Gyantse, on the main trade route to Lhasa, which also he had frequently visited. He is an old man now, and has unfortunately become rather deaf. The hotel is looked after by one of his many daughters, who is married to an Englishman called Perry who was once attached to the escort at Gyantse.

It is difficult for me to describe Kalimpong, a place where I later spent many happy days as a guest of the Odlings. In my mind it is a confusion of disconnected but vivid pictures. The clearest, perhaps, is of the Odlings' bungalow, which is furnished like an English country-house, with the addition of rare Tibetan curios. The walls are hung with rich *thankas*—paintings of Buddhist deities framed in scrolls of rich brocade and hung from rollers. These are usually found in Tibetan monasteries and some of them are very valuable. They have also a very fine collection of Tibetan metalwork, twelve-foot-long monastery trumpets, silver prayer-wheels inlaid with turquoise, exquisite copper and brass teapots of curious design, and a number of jewelled charm-boxes. In their garden, all the ordinary English summer flowers were in bloom as well as plants which will not grow out of doors at home. On a clear day there was a wonderful view from it. The red and grey roofs of Kalimpong village showed through the tree-tops on its saddle-back ridge, and beyond that the land fell sharply, one wooded ridge after another, to the malaria-infested Teesta gorge. In some places the forest had been cleared and wrinkled paddy-fields had been laboriously carved from the steep hillsides. On the other side of the valley, clearings in the forest showed the site of the Darjeeling tea-gardens with trim lines of bushes surrounding the factory buildings. Ridge behind ridge paled into the distance, and beyond, poised high in the air as though in another world, were the eternal snows of the Himalaya. The first sight of these mountains was an unforgettable experience to one who had dreamed of them and read of them for years. Dominating the range was the solid mass of Kangchenjunga, a complete range of mountains in itself, shining with dazzling whiteness above the hazy valleys, and grouped around it were the more delicate peaks of many other mountains, including Simvu and the fearful pinnacle of Siniolchu with a great ridge running to the south.

The cosmopolitan market of Kalimpong is another vivid memory. The usual dark-skinned Hindus sat cross-legged in their shops; but up here they looked out of place; they were attenuated by malaria and the whites of their eyes were a sickly yellow. There were also sallow Chinamen dressed in long quilted robes, perhaps the remnants of the routed Chinese army which fled this way from Lhasa in 1911; lithe hustling Nepalis with small black embroidered fezes; timid-looking, pale-skinned Lepchas, the original inhabitants of the forest; independent and villainous-looking Tibetan muleteers with huge turquoise and gold ear-rings, pigtails tied round their heads, and whip-handles stuck into their girdles; short-haired Bhutanese, with striped home-spun robes and bare knees; and always crowds of silent Nepali and Lepcha women hurrying past with huge baskets for carrying stones attached to their foreheads.

Pallis and Roaf had been over to Gangtok, the capital of Sikkim, to see the Political Officer at the Residency, and now, owing to the infected dust of the highway, they were both suffering from inflamed throats. Their report was none too promising. Mr. Gould, the Political Officer, who is responsible for our dealings with the native states of Sikkim, Tibet and Bhutan, seemed to think there was little chance of any of the party being allowed into Tibet and he even discouraged the climbing part of our programme. Apparently the Kangchenjunga district is extremely holy to Buddhists, and the Maharajah of Sikkim did not want us to go; it was possible that we should be allowed to attempt some minor peaks, but neither Simvu nor Siniolchu comes under this category. Pallis was very depressed and retired to bed with a high temperature.

Ishwar Singh and Jun Singh, two Garwalis who had been with Pallis and Nicholson in 1936, joined us here. Ishwar Singh was to be the sirdah in charge of the porters, while Jun was to do the cooking.

On March 30th, Nicholson, Ishwar Singh and I went over to Darjeeling to choose the twenty porters whom we needed to carry our gear up the Zemu Glacier. Among these would be some of

the famous Sherpas who come down to Darjeeling in the early
summer to look for expedition work. They are men of Tibetan
stock who inhabit Sola Khombu, a high valley of Nepal. In the
winter time they are industrious farmers and in the summer they
attach themselves to climbing expeditions, partly for the wages
they earn, but chiefly for love of the job. In the last thirty
years they have built up a splendid tradition of trustworthiness
and fortitude and many of them are very skilful mountaineers.
The Himalayan Club, with a local secretary at Darjeeling, has all
the information about them carefully filed and docketed. Each
porter carries a passport with a photograph of himself, his signature
in the form of an impression of his thumb, and all particulars of
his career as a porter, the expeditions on which he has served,
the height which he reached, and signed comments on his
character and ability from the leader of each expedition. All
have pink cards with a medical report from a Darjeeling or
expedition doctor. They are a cheerful, improvident crowd,
many of whom drink or gamble away all their wages as soon as
they draw them.

Darjeeling, the centre of the tea-planting district and the
summer residence of the Governor of Bengal, is larger and more
prosperous-looking than Kalimpong, though it is built on similar
steep mountain slopes and has the same squalid bazaar and as great
a proportion of corrugated-iron and ramshackle, jerry-built
native dwellings.

Outside the house of Mr. Kidd, the local secretary of the
Himalayan Club, was a straggling crowd of fifty or sixty of the
wildest-looking men I had ever seen. Not many of them were
genuine Sherpas; most of them were Tibetans or Bhutias, and
one or two were rickshaw wallas from the Darjeeling bazaar.
Some had pronounced Mongolian features, others seemed almost
negroid, with thick lips and curly black hair. Many of them were
bare-foot, others wore scarlet and green muleteers' boots, while a
few had properly nailed climbing-boots, khaki puttees and
Balaclava helmets, perquisites from former expeditions. Some
wore their tangled hair hanging unkempt over their shoulders,
others had their long pigtails wrapped round their foreheads
and some had tied them round their battered felt-hats. One,
who appeared to be a lama of some sort, had short hair and wore
a long purple robe. One or two had been on Everest expeditions,

or had served with Paul Bauer and the Bavarians on Kangchenjunga; some had no experience at all.

It was a difficult and invidious job to choose the number we
wanted from among them; they all seemed so desperately keen
to come. We took a few who had obviously had some experience
of real climbing; we took the lama; we took the ugliest one,
a man with a single enormous tooth in the middle of his mouth;
we took the handsomest one, a rickshaw walla, who wore an
ear-ring set with a large turquoise in his left ear. Then we made
the remainder run up the hill and took those who seemed to be
in the best condition. At last we had chosen our twenty. We
wrote down their names, the names of their wives and to whom
their wages should be paid, their age, nationality and occupations,
and finally they had to sign the agreement with a thumb-print.
Their wages were to be one rupee per day (1s. 6d.) and a small
allowance for food; those who were taken on to the snow would
be paid slightly more.

While we were at Darjeeling, Wood Johnson, the Transport
Officer of the 1933 Everest Expedition, rang up and asked us to
stop and dine at Geille Tea Garden, where he was assistant-
manager. To reach his bungalow we followed a narrow road
through the forest down a remarkable number of S bends, some
of them so acute that we had to reverse to get round them, and,
below, the hillside dropped away almost vertically. Only the
smallest cars could negotiate the road at all. Soon the rhododendron forest gave way to lines of trim tea-bushes and thickets
of graceful olive-coloured bamboos. As soon as it grew dark
the air was full of fireflies, a strange owl hooted, and tiny lights
twinkled in the coolie lines. A tea-garden seemed a most romantic
place.

That night we talked Everest till the small hours. Was it
essential to go before the monsoon? What was the ideal number
for a climbing party? What was the ideal age? Should oxygen
be taken? What were the factors which controlled acclimatiza-
tion? Wood Johnson told us that some people's characters
changed completely at an altitude of above 20,000 feet and that
a certain climber had tried to murder another member of the
party. He himself had developed duodenal ulcers on the mountain and had almost died before they got him down. This year
(1936) they were attempting it again: would the monsoon be

kind to them—and to us, who were equally dependent on good weather?

When we returned to Kalimpong we found that Pallis was still laid up, so it was arranged that the rest of us should go over to Gangtok by car, as heavy rainstorms had now settled the dust on the road and conditions were ideal. The road took us down almost to Teesta Bridge and then we turned northwards and followed the river to Rangpo, being stopped at the frontier by native police who examined our passes. Then the road led through dense forest where the trees were festooned with huge ferns, mosses and all manner of creepers. Magenta orchids bloomed in the forks of trees; strange, gaily-coloured birds darted into sight, and clouds of enormous brilliant butterflies rose from wet patches on the road as the car approached. In one place we ran through rubber plantations, in another there were trim orange groves, and down by the river were occasional oases of terraced cultivation where natives could be seen ploughing the dark soil with clumsy water buffaloes. Troops of monkeys squatted beside the road or shook the tree-tops in anger or alarm. Now and then we passed a group of wild, long-haired, Red-Indian-like men with trains of mules and donkeys: these were Tibetan muleteers bringing wool down from the highlands of Tibet.

At last, after climbing steeply for several miles, we reached Gangtok, a small town with a busy street of market stalls and a few European-looking houses. At the top of the village was the Dak bungalow, or rest-house, which was in charge of a dirty-looking old man. There was a note for us, inviting Nicholson and myself to go up to the Residency. So we drove on past the bungalow up a trim tarmac drive lit by electric light. Soon we reached a beautiful stone house surrounded by green lawns, gay flower-beds and ornamental ponds. Here I met Mr. B. J. Gould, whom I was destined to see much of in the following years. He was a very tall, soldierly man of about 50, who had been in nearly all the danger spots of the Frontier from Quetta to Bhutan; in 1912 he was British Trade Agent at Gyantse and was a keen student of the Tibetan language; he had been at Gangtok for only a few months, having succeeded Mr. Williamson, who had died suddenly in Lhasa.

We found that the six bullock-carts which were to bring the expedition gear from Siliguri had not yet arrived but the twenty mules that were going to carry it on up to Lachen, fifty miles nearer the Zemu Glacier, were already waiting. The porters, meanwhile, had walked over from Darjeeling and were impatient to start. Some of them had started a riot in the bazaar the previous night.

The expedition plans were not much advanced; apparently Kingdon Ward and Ronald Kaulback had upset the Tibetan authorities, and, as British relations with the Lhasa Government were at that time very ill-defined, it was important that nothing should happen to complicate them further. We were to be allowed to visit the Zemu Glacier, but it seemed improbable that any of us would be allowed to enter Tibet.

On April 7th Pallis came over from Kalimpong. He still looked very ill but was fit enough to start for Lachen on the following day.

## CHAPTER FOUR

### FROM THE TROPICAL FOREST TO THE SNOWS

On April 8th—a lovely day—we were up at 6.30 and sorted loads and packed our personal possessions to the sound of strange music, as of bagpipes and trombones, which came up from the monastery. My hold-all contained the following :

> Grenfell-cloth wind-proof suit, with fur-edged hood,
> Balaclava wool helmet and a thinner wool hat, scarf, putties,
> Three pairs ordinary socks,
> Three pairs thick wool socks,
> One pair stockings,
> One pair felt-lined climbing-boots,
> Two pairs wool mitts,
> One pair wind-proof outer gloves,
> Two light wool jerseys,
> One heavier sweater,
> Two flannel shirts, one cotton shirt,
> Two pairs grey flannels,
> Two pairs cotton pants,
> Six handkerchiefs,
> Pyjamas, towel, sleeping-bag cover.

We carried our immediate necessities in our rucksacks; mine contained mostly cameras, also a sleeping-bag, washing-gear and a change of clothes, and weighed 25 lb. The fourteen mules came at 8.15, a motley collection of weary saddle-sore jades. Each should carry 150 lb., but as our boxes weighed 50 lb. each and the loads have to be evenly balanced they carried only 100 lb. The porters had light loads, so they were happy; they had only about 50 lb. each, which is half what they really can manage. Each man tied a scarf or other kind of primitive harness under the bottom of the load on his back and then over his forehead and this took all the weight. It is an interesting fact that nearly all the tribes in the world which are noted as weight-carriers support the load on their heads and necks.

We got away at 10. The mules bucked a bit to begin with, but soon settled down; indeed, they were remarkably quiet animals; the men walked all round as they loaded up and none of them tried to bite or kick. It was marvellous to be off at last. The lovely road wound round the hillside, continually crossing streams which poured from the steep forest above. There were quantities of tree ferns and masses of white, yellow and purple orchids. The undergrowth, mostly bamboo, was very thick. On the left were barley fields and meadows, and on the other side of the gorge, a great mountain slope so thickly covered with trees that not a rock was visible. I saw a white-capped redstart; cuckoos were very noisy and also a tiresome bird which called continually but missed four beats with maddening persistence.

Suddenly the road dived through a cutting and we were at the top of the Penlong La (" La " means a pass) unexpectedly soon. On the way down the other side we passed the porters drinking tea at a wayside bazaar. They seemed to be as glad as we were to be on the move at last. Soon afterwards, although we had only gone nine miles, we camped because we wanted to go right past Dikchu, a notoriously malarial spot, in a single march. There are bungalows every ten to fifteen miles but we avoided them, partly to save expense and also to get used to camping routine. We camped among some terraced paddy-fields, the only clearing we had seen in the dense forest. At the edge of the clearing there were too many leeches, so we put up the tents lower down. The porters cut beds of bracken and stretched tarpaulins above. We had tea and biscuits and jam. Every drop of water had to be boiled. The site of Phodang Monastery was revealed by a line of white prayer flags on the other side of the valleys. I could not persuade any of the others to walk across to it, so I went up into the jungle alone and had a bad time with the leeches; whenever I stopped to pull them off my shoes or clothes, new ones rushed in on me; it is an awful sight to see them standing on end blindly feeling for one's blood. I found a queer tin-roofed monastery with wonderful carving on the door, but I did not like to go inside. The Buddhism here is of a very primitive type, retaining much of the ancient Pön religion of pure animism; the native Lepchas are very close to the spirits of the forest.

A great deal of barley is grown here. One woman was threshing it with a hand-flail while another sifted the grain in a round tray. There was a fine view of pinnacled ridges, all forested, and the high snow-scattered hills of Tibet beyond. Rain threatened, so we dug dykes round the tent. Nicholson found a leech in his sleeping-bag and we cremated it horribly in the candle.

The next morning we were away by 7. We wandered down-hill to Dikchu. Soon the " motor road " stopped and gave place to a steep, winding, cobbled track. In one place a gang of Nepalis were building a fine stone bridge and many men and women were working on the road. They stared at us and the children said " salaam " and asked for money. It was terribly hot here and the forest had an overburdening and oppressive effect. Some of the tree-trunks were completely hidden by creepers with huge shiny kidney-shaped leaves; clumps of hound's-tongue fern clung to the sides of trees and grew in their own decaying vegetation, often completely obscuring the trunk. There were long serrated ferns, delicate feathery ones, innumerable kinds of mosses, and all sorts of flowering shrubs which we had not seen before. Brilliantly coloured butterflies hovered over the trees : black velvety swallow-tails as big as small birds, with curiously shaped underwings spotted with blue, pink or white; lemon-coloured swallow-tails with a network of iridescent green, and others that flashed deep purple as they flew, and orange, peacock-blue and scarlet—every colour imaginable—in hundreds at every wet place on the road, where they settle to suck the moisture.

At Dikchu, where three roads meet and there was actually a signpost, there are only a few dirty wooden huts, roofed with corrugated iron; the people looked very sallow and malarial. There is a fine suspension bridge across the Dik Chu (" Chu " is Tibetan for a river), just above its junction with the Teesta; the porters all picked a flower and dropped it into the water with a prayer as they crossed. All day we met natives carrying prodigious weights of grass for pony fodder and bundles of split bamboos for thatching. After the bridge there was a long pull uphill, and the path became very narrow and was paved with rough cobble-stones. In one place we crossed a precarious bamboo causeway built along a vertical rock wall over the foaming Teesta. It swayed with each step. Later we crossed the gorge of a tributary by a suspension bridge, 300 feet long and 300 feet above the river. Most of the people here were sallow-faced Lepchas; they seemed subdued and overpowered by the spirit of the jungle of which they are supposed to know every tree and every plant. They live by growing cardamom seed and a little maize and rice in clearings of the forest, but they are being driven further and further into the jungle by the more enterprising Nepalis, who are excellent business men. At 4 o'clock we reached Mangan, a few squalid tin-roofed huts on a hillside, and as it started to rain we put up our tents. Near by there was a considerable encampment of Tibetan muleteers with canvas tents. I wished I could talk to them. We found several leeches in the tent. Most of the natives we met had bleeding bites all over their bare feet and legs, but it did not seem to worry them; the cattle suffer terribly.

The view when we rose at 6 the next morning was magnificent. The whole valley was a hazy blue; pale, transparent bamboo thickets were grouped just below our camp and, away in the distance, framed by the steep sides of a tributary valley, were the high snows, dominated by Simvu and Siniolchu. Bulbuls and babblers were singing and vivid blue fly-catchers were flying to and fro. I took a photograph before we set off and stupidly left my ice-axe behind, so had to return several miles for it. The road was very busy and we saw many Tibetans with trains of mules and donkeys. The women are handsome; they wear silver charm-boxes studded with turquoise hanging round their necks, but some of them have red pigment plastered on their faces to protect their complexions. One family was taking dye-twigs back to Tibet; a tiny child carried a chicken in a bamboo cage; they had still a

SLEDGING LOADS UP A FROZEN STREAM

OUR HIGHEST CAMP ON SIMVU

"HI ! TAKE IN THE SLACK ON MY ROPE"
THE STEEP PITCH ON THE SIMVU RIDGE

month's journey before them. The leeches were very bad and began to get on our nerves. The bite passes unnoticed at the time, but it bleeds and bleeds and then tickles for days. Salt or dry tobacco leaf removes them at once.

We passed Singhik and then Tong, where we descended to cross the Teesta. Here the track is a lovely cobbled winding way with dense ferns and moss and sometimes wild strawberries on the banks. At the head of the valley there was usually a superb view of the snows. In some places the natives were burning the jungle to make clearings for barley and bananas. After a year or two they leave it to return to jungle and burn another clearing elsewhere. The Nepalis are very destructive and set fire to more than they need.

We stopped and made tea after waiting half an hour for the porters to come up. The sun left us about midday and the forest then became gloomy and sinister. A mile beyond the bridge we found a good camp site. We had done only ten miles, but they were long miles on this steep, stony track and we seemed to have been marching all day. Pallis' idea was that we should take it easy and build up our strength rather than use it up. Our three green trek-tents were on a level ledge—probably an old raised beach—30 yards wide and 30 feet above a bend of the Teesta. On the other side of our ledge was the track and then an almost vertical wall a thousand feet high. In spite of its steepness, trees covered most of it, and creepers, covered with strange flowers, hung straight down. At the foot was an enormous old tree whose trunk was almost completely hidden by orchids. Below, the Teesta disappeared at once round a bend, and the valley seemed to be completely shut in by the steep forested walls, but high up in this V appeared a rounded tree-clad mountain and above that a solitary, snow-capped peak; up-river, after several wooded spurs, was a brown hillside, apparently above the tree line, and beyond that again a great serrated wall of snow-spangled rock right across the valley.

We did not get away the next day until 10.30. Pallis thought it wicked to hurry in such country, but I was impatient to get on to the snow. We climbed and zigzagged along a carefully banked up track, then descended to Tsungtang, where a bare-footed, green-uniformed policeman made us fill in a form. Here the Lachen (big pass) and Lachung (little pass) meet, and the valley opens out to allow of a certain amount of cultivation—chiefly potatoes and barley. There is a fine bungalow here, the house of a forestry official, a post-office and several tin-roofed houses. The path hung precariously over the edge of vast cliffs. We looked down almost vertically 500 feet into the torrent. It came on to rain, so we camped at 2.30, down by the river, where we were much troubled by leeches and all manner of insects.

I went for a walk in the evening and saw my first yaks. They are most terrifying-looking creatures with huge shoulders, no dewlaps, thin necks and heads with sharp, light, upcurving horns. They have great tufts of black hair above the knees and a black bushy tail. They look very fierce but are really quite timid if approached with sufficient resolution.

The next day we left the tropical forest behind us, with its sinister shadows and hungry leeches, and almost reached the snows. We met several parties of yaks coming from the north. The yak herds seemed cheerful and friendly in a dignified way; some of them had huge Tibetan mastiffs with them, black, and black and tan, and often with great red ruff-like collars of wool to protect them from the bites of wild animals. These dogs were very aloof; they did not bark, but they gave us a wide berth. Our mules overtook us that morning; they too were taking it easy.

Looking up we could see only conifers—mostly deodars, on the hillsides above. Soon we started climbing in earnest. I noticed a lovely red maple with spear-head leaves not yet fully out. Down in the forest it seemed to be summer or autumn, but up here it was early spring, and the snow was just down to the tree line, about 12,000 feet. On the grassy paths between the deodars were masses of mauve primula (*denticulata*). After a sharp ascent through pine trees we came out on to a bare open fell-side and I experienced a great sense of liberation and joy after the unnatural gloom of the forest. The heady smell of exotic plants and rotting vegetation was giving way to the purer scent of grass and pine trees. The ground was carpeted with primulas and we saw several huge magnolia trees, leafless, but with fantastically large, waxy, cream-coloured flowers. Around them bloomed rhododendron trees, scarlet, pink and mauve, and below were reedy ponds from which I put up some teal and a snipe. I saw some Himalayan pies with long streamer tails, and a chough with orange beak. The path returned again to the coniferous forest, and suddenly we turned a corner and came upon Lachen.

Lachen is like a Swiss village built on a steeply sloping bay of the hill. The village consists of about a hundred unpainted wooden houses with roofs of grey shingles weighted down with stones. Above, the steep slope, carpeted with bamboo scrub and smaller and smaller pines, eventually met a snow-clad summit of about 18,000 feet. Dominating the village is a monastery with golden ornaments on the roof. The lower walls of the houses are made of beaten mud and they have beautifully carved woodwork round the windows and doors. The bungalow at the foot of the village was a fine building with panelled rooms and a great open fireplace. The headman, a young and rather effeminate-looking Tibetan, came down and greeted us. Some of the women were very good-looking, but dirty. After tea, Pallis and I went up to the monastery, the finest building in the place. We entered it barefooted. It had a floor of mud beaten to the consistency of cement. Inside it was very dark and smelt strongly of incense and dirt. At the far end of the room was an altar with hideous images in glass cases and on either side pigeon-holes filled with the pages of holy books pressed between carved wooden covers. Everywhere grotesquely carved faces leered down at us, and on the walls loomed weird paintings in rich colours of different deities and devils of the lama pantheon. Then we went up a crazy ladder and found other shrines above. In one room were stored all the properties for the devil-dances—hideous, grinning masks, some with horns attached, robes, swords and stiff boots. A Swedish woman missionary has been in Lachen for about fifteen years; we visited the austere little tin chapel, and remembered it was Easter Sunday. We stayed in the bungalow instead of camping and found it very comfortable.

The next day we paid off our muleteers and they set off back to Gangtok early in the morning. I saw many new birds here: vivid-coloured varieties of sun birds, robin-accentors, pipits, whistling thrushes, doves, cuckoos and brain-fever birds. The latter sits up in a tree all day saying deliberately, " Ouee—ouee-ou " or " brain *fee*-ver " at monotonously regular intervals, but it is almost impossible to see him.

After breakfast we went up to pay our respects to the abbot of the monastery. He sat cross-legged on a couch in a little room about nine feet square, a fat cheerful, intelligent-looking man, more Mongolian-featured than most of the Lachen people. The room was packed with painted scrolls, silver teapots, holy-water vessels, drums, carved and painted furniture, leopard-skin rugs and even paper Christmas-decorations and tinsel balls. Pallis talked to him in Tibetan, chiefly about the French traveller, Madame David Neel, who came through this way and got everybody into trouble because she had not a pass into Tibet.

We spent the afternoon packing the loads. The headman came in and arranged for twenty-seven local porters to carry our gear up to the Base Camp on the Zemu Glacier, and for a man to bring up our mail and fresh eggs twice a week. We were going to try to reach the Green Lake where Bauer's base camp was in 1931. Roaf and I did a ten-mile walk in the evening. Pallis was still not very fit; it is difficult to throw off a cold or the remains of 'flu at such high altitudes. The next day when we sorted out the porters we found that only half of the Darjeeling men had boots, though they were all given three shillings in advance of their wages at Gangtok to buy Tibetan cloth boots with rope soles; these boots were not available at Lachen. We decided to take on our twenty-one Darjeeling men and twenty-seven Lachen men as far as the Green Lake. We had forty-eight loads, including food, tents of all sorts, skis and high-climbing equipment. We had already chosen the three Darjeeling men who would go high with us: Ang Nima, the man with Everest experience, Rinchen Sherpa and Rinchen Bhutia (the handsome rickshaw walla). These three were given their nailed boots, wool helmets, gloves and green windproof suits, also ice-axes. They immediately put them all on in spite of the warmth of the day. A certain amount of money was also paid out through Ishwar Singh, who was a very responsible head porter though I think the Sherpas rather resented that he was not one of them.

I watched the women planting potatoes in the fields. They have small plots of ground enclosed by low walls to keep the yaks and ponies away. All the work is done with big hoes. In the village I met a blind Tibetan being led along the track northward. He carried an enormous load and felt his way with a stick. Roaf and I walked up to Zemu Ram and then up towards the Tangu La, one of the routes taken by the Everest expedition. Up there the cedars suddenly give way to pines, with occasional larches and birch trees. In one place the trail had been swept away for 100 yards by a landslide. We noticed a number of mouse-hares scuttling down into their burrows, little tailless rat-like animals resembling guinea-pigs.

Pallis had a long talk with the abbot, who asked him why we wanted to visit the high snows. Pallis replied that it was to find solitude. " Surely ", the abbot replied, " you can find that best in your own heart."

The day before we left, the whole expedition went up to the monastery to be blessed by the old man, over fifty of us, a formidable procession. It was a remarkable ceremony. A dais covered with a leopard-skin rug was placed out of doors for the abbot, with a table in front of it and a gay curtain hung between poles behind it. Soon a grubby acolyte appeared with a little green dish of what looked like bread pellets, and an old whisky bottle full of a clear yellow liquid with a reddish sediment. Then the abbot appeared in a yellow silk robe with orange sleeves and red socks and a peculiar hat, something between a boater and a bowler, covered with yellow silk. He removed this and sat buddha-like on the dais. The porters then filed past, each one prostrating himself three times so that his forehead touched the ground; when they had finished, he touched their heads with one hand. A few presented him with white muslin scarves. Then Pallis presented a large and beautiful Chinese painting which they hung up on the monastery wall. Some silk scarves were then brought and we went up one at a time and knelt before him. Each of us was given a small pellet of dough, which we had to eat, and some liquid from the bottle was poured into our hands (I was very relieved to find that we were not expected to drink it); with this we anointed our heads, the abbot mumbling blessings all the time. Finally he put a scarf over our shoulders. The porters were given smaller red scarves, and I noticed that they snuffed the liquid up their noses. At the end of the ceremony, he replaced his hat and went inside the monastery.

When we descended the hill we found there was some sort of marriage ceremony in progress. In front of a gay canopy a row of padded cushions and a low table were set out and a procession appeared, led by two beautifully dressed girls in green and scarlet cloth boots, striped homespun aprons, green silk blouses and high peaked fur hats. They had rich turquoise and gold charm-boxes suspended from large necklaces of agate and coral beads. The bride-to-be appeared very downcast and shy. They sat round the table and tea was served in delicate jade or china cups on tall lotus-pattern silver saucers, then a man read aloud a long proclamation, and barley beer was served from a jar which had three ceremonial pats of yak butter on the spout. I tried to take some films but found it difficult owing to the crowd. The expedition presented the bride with a large plate of sugar and sweets.

In the evening Roaf and I went for a walk and met Finch and Hamblin, two young climbers who were going to attempt Lama Anden (19,250 feet), the peak just behind Lachen. We came upon a troop of about fifty langurs, great Himalayan monkeys with black faces surrounded by white ruffs and very long tails.. We approached quite near before they trotted away, every now and then climbing cedar trees to get a better look at us. They had some very tiny ones in the troop, but the largest stood as tall as men and we were a little afraid that they might turn upon us; however, they seemed very shy.

We left Lachen on April 16th, going up to the Zemu Ram bridge, and then leaving the Tangu La track and following the Zemu Chu by a small winding path. Many wild flowers were coming out, including coltsfoot, and a vetch with a single bright blue flower; I saw swallow-tail butterflies, also comma, painted ladies, clouded-yellow and small tortoiseshell. The birds and flowers and butterflies were all much more like the English varieties than the ones in the lower forest, and the climate was like spring in the Lake District. The path led up and down over very broken country and soon we were in a forest of rhododendron trees, most of them with red scaly bark and pendent spearheads of huge shiny leaves. As there was hardly any path we had to make our way through a tangle of rhododendron branches. Not many were yet in flower. We crossed a huge pile of avalanche snow and several clearings made by man; the Lachen people come up here to plant crops in the summer. We were obviously the first party up the Zemu Chu that year, for we found a bridge broken over a torrent, a relic of last year's monsoon, and had to cross precariously by a tree trunk. The porters walked straight across it in spite of their loads though a misplaced foot would have meant certain death.

At last we came to an open clearing called Tsetang, where all the pine trees were festooned with hanging bunches of pale-green lichen. There were masses of mauve primroses here and soft green moss and pine needles underfoot. We all stripped to the waist and sun-bathed.

It was very cold in the night with hoar frost over everything. I saw an eagle with a white tail, and a cinnamon woodpecker. We decided to stay over the next day because it was such a lovely place. I climbed the hill behind the camp and found a number of plaited yak-hair nooses set for monal and blood pheasants. The going was terribly steep and the earth completely overgrown with tangled bamboo, rhododendron, juniper and thorn scrub. Sometimes I travelled for several hundred yards entirely in the branches without touching the ground at all. It was very difficult going and I was glad to get out on to the snow at last. I came down a snow couloir, sometimes having to lower myself hand over hand down the rhododendrons. When I got back to camp I found Finch and Hamblin were passing through on their way to their base camp for Lama Anden, another six miles on, but over on the Talung side. They had several women coolies, who looked tougher than most of the men. In the evening several woodcock flew over on their ' rhoding ' flight. We sat round a log fire after supper and watched fitful lightning in the distance.

It snowed in the night and Pallis' tent collapsed; luckily Cooke and I had gone out and loosened our guys. We were off by nine after letting things dry. Flocks of snowfinches were passing, and grey and white Sikkim pigeons. We lunched by the Zemu Chu and watched a tufted duck. Later we followed an ill-defined path over very rough country, often having to climb over branches of rhododendron and use our hands on steep places. A path came in from the Talung monastery away on the left, crossed the Zemu Chu by a stout bridge and went up over the hill to Lhonak where Cookie and I had thoughts of climbing later on. More and more snow was lying, but some of the porters still went barefoot to save their boots. The bridge over the Lhonak Chu had collapsed, so we rebuilt it. No one who fell into one of these torrents would have a hope of getting out alive. The Lachen porters wanted to stop and they kept on telling us that each clearing was the last possible camp-site; but we intended to push on to the snout of the glacier so that we could reach the Green Lake in one march. This side of the valley was still heavily wooded but on the west side it was snowy, and only a little rhododendron and juniper scrub protruded. At 3.30 we found an open place where there was just room to pitch the tents. This was fortunate as it started to rain and soon turned to snow with low clouds and a bitter wind.

There was a sudden gleam of sun at 6 o'clock the next morning, so we got up and were away at 9. The track, after winding up and down among patches of snow and rhododendron scrub, suddenly emerged through a final patch of fir trees and we saw the glacier snout blocking the valley. The ice was almost completely hidden in moraine deposit of earth and stone, but there was one steep grey wall of dirty ice festooned with icicles which looked like a Blake picture. The Zemu Chu emerges from beneath the snout. We climbed rapidly up to the right and kept between the moraine and the steep juniper and thorn-clad slope. The high peaks, up till now hidden from our sight, gradually appeared as we rose higher, but we could not distinguish them yet.

There was much more snow than we had expected, and we were not sure if the Lachan men would brave it, but once they started they went well. What a gang of thugs they looked! At last we found a place between the moraine and the hillside where there was level snow for the tents and juniper wood for fuel up above. A truculent, squint-eyed Lachen man had tried to bully Pallis into stopping earlier, but without success, for Pallis hides a good deal of determination behind his mild manner. It tried to snow, then dazzling sunlight dispersed the clouds which hung in hazy bands round Siniolchu and the shoulder of Simvu, which we could now make out across the glacier. All at once the sunshine won and the mists were banished and the beautiful needle of Siniolchu was revealed, fluted with delicate ice couloirs at a formidable angle above hanging glaciers and long avalanche-swept snow slopes. It is one of the most beautiful and terrifying of mountains. Simvu was not clear from here; it seemed to have several summits connected by ice-ridges, and neighbouring Kangchenjunga blocked the whole of the top of the valley. Heavy cumulus clouds hid Lama Anden and Lachen. No wonder the natives worship Kangchenjunga, it dominates the whole glacier basin and seems to control even the weather. The porters spread piles of scrub at the foot of some steep rocks and lit a fire on the snow and sat round it gossiping and playing cards until the mist descended and it came on to snow again.

It was bitterly cold the next day till the sun reached us and made a lovely dappled pattern on the snow. Ishwar Singh read the list of loads out from the other end, thus causing much consternation among the porters, who get attached to one load and do not like changing it; the squint-eyed Lachen man was particularly rebellious. The view was splendid across to Siniolchu and Little Siniolchu and down the valley to Lama Anden. It was 9 o'clock before we had dug out everything and got under way. The porters agreed to leave their sleeping gear at this camp and to come up to the Green Lake and then return in the evening. Cooke and I went ahead to make a track for the porters as there was a foot or two of soft snow. We came to the conclusion that their best route would be along the ridge of the moraine, where they would have either hard snow or rock. However, almost all of them preferred the level strip between the moraine and the hill, although they sank in knee-deep at every step.

Along the hillside there was first rhododendron scrub, then above it only juniper, and snow in the gullies, but as we rose higher snow covered most of the country. Cooke and I walked ahead of the porters making a track, though we often went over our knees in snow. I felt very fit and enjoyed the responsibility of going ahead. The Lachen men kept on refusing to come any further and it did not look as if we would reach the Green Lake, but as there was so much snow about we thought it would probably all be covered, and as we wanted to camp on bare ground it appeared better to stop fairly soon. Pallis nursed them on, mainly by joking and ragging with them in Tibetan. The squint-eyed man was the ringleader but luckily he had a sense of humour, though he and Ishwar Singh nearly came to blows once or twice. At 2 o'clock we reached a south-facing level bay in the hillside. It was free of snow, and as the Lachen men were giving trouble again and it seemed to be the last chance of a snow-free camp-site, we made up our minds to establish our Base Camp here, and as soon as this decision was made known everyone was very cheerful. We gave all the porters biscuits, butter and cheese. Jun Singh was feeling very sick and headachy and lay on the ground moaning. I started to feel the same; carrying a rucksack and making steps over new snow were probably too much at this height—we were now at 14,500 feet.

We paid off all the porters who were going back and then raffled one of the empty ration boxes and three empty tins. The Tibetans delight in any form of gambling and were very happy. Oddly enough, the four prizes all went to Lachen men and the truculent squint-eyed grumbler won the box. It was sad to part with our Darjeeling men. In addition to our original three, Pallis took Kipak, a little man who was by way of being a wit, and one Ang Babu, a very enthusiastic young porter who had several times come with tears in his eyes and begged to be kept on. So there were twelve of us altogether: we five, Ishwar and Jun Singh, Ang Nima, Rinchen Sherpa, Rinchen Bhutia, Kipak and Ang Babu.

When the porters had gone I was overcome with violent nausea and headache; my one desire was to lie down, and as soon as the tent was up I crawled miserably into my sleeping-bag. This was my first attack of mountain sickness—it was exactly like an acute attack of sea-sickness—and was brought on, I suppose, by my having done too much before getting used to the height. I felt much better the next morning but still had pain behind the eyes.

The weather for the next fortnight was very bad. We had intended to wait for a few days to acclimatize, and then to move our Base Camp up to the Green Lake as soon as the snow should melt there. But the weather did not improve and it was twelve days before we left the camp for good. Each day it snowed; the clouds came right down over the surrounding peaks and we could merely sit in camp, nursing our impatience and listening to the snow whispering on the sides of the tent and to the sinister sound of avalanches pouring off the mountains with a noise like trains crossing distant viaducts. It took us some time to acclimatize even though we had moved up so slowly from Gangtok. I found difficulty in sleeping and my appetite was uncertain. To turn over in bed or to dress required a definite effort which left me breathless and exhausted; we were all rather short-tempered, and an air of disappointment pervaded the camp, partly because we were held up by the weather, and also because Pallis had been refused permission to enter Tibet. The expedition doctor made our lives a burden by carrying out a series of bloodthirsty and wearisome experiments: he examined our hearts and carefully felt our pulses after different degrees of exertion; he pierced the lobes of our ears with a bodkin and compared the colour of the blood produced with a card showing all shades of sanguinity— it was interesting to see how much darker it had turned as we climbed higher—and our hearts were apparently slightly larger and our pulses more rapid since leaving Lachen. The intelligence tests were the most exacting, though, oddly enough, my mental reactions seemed to improve with altitude.

I grew increasingly impatient during this fortnight's waiting; I was longing to get on to the high snows, but afraid that I might not acclimatize and still more afraid that my standard of climbing might not be adequate. Although I knew I could last as long as anybody, I was not much good on really difficult rock, my experience of step-cutting and ice-work was small and I was afraid I might impede the party. The most difficult part of a Himalayan attempt is choosing a route and deciding just what slope is practicable and safe under given conditions, and at what stage one can no longer risk the porters' lives and at what stage one's own. These more difficult decisions I would not be called upon to make, but nevertheless I had a continual sense of apprehension and foreboding.

On our first day at the Base Camp I noticed two animals grazing on the grassy slope above the camp. These turned out to be burrhal, the big-horned mountain sheep, and I am ashamed to say that I, having a great desire for some fresh meat, was rash enough to deplore the fact that we had no firearms with us. Pallis and Nicholson were simply horrified to think that I could even contemplate such an act of sacrilege in such a place : I suppose they were right, but the hunter's instinct dies hard. However, I consoled myself by stalking them with a camera. One day when, as usual, the mist was down over the tops, I stalked a small flock which I picked out about a thousand feet above the camp; using the cover provided by a rocky gully, I crawled to within a hundred yards of where they were grazing just on the borderline of the mist, with the help of which I was able to get even nearer. However, a young burrhal sheep which seemed to be on guard became suspicious and we indulged in a staring match which lasted the best part of an hour. The rest of the herd were grazing placidly, two were even lying down. Several had enormous horns curling down on either side. They had barred faces and black patches on the front of their legs and conspicuous white backsides, made still more noticeable by black scuts. At last the sentry disappeared over the ridge whither the rest of the herd had gone. After a few minutes I advanced, but the old busybody returned and I had to lie still for another half-hour. An Apollo butterfly settled on my face and a lammergeyer with great spade tail and ten-foot wing span came swooping over me with a shrill whining noise like the wind in telegraph wires. Again the mist came right down and I ran to the side and then upward, making a wide detour. But I had forgotten to allow for the height and had to wait some minutes for my breathing to recover: one must not hurry uphill at 16,000 feet, for at that height there is only about half the normal amount of oxygen in the air. I went on again as soon as I could so as to be just above the flock as they grazed uphill. Without warning, the mist rose and I found myself right in the middle of a flock, not of seven or eight as I had imagined, but about thirty. The nearest one, a great heavy-horned ram, was only ten yards away; he saw me at once and with shrill bleats of alarm raced up the hill. The rest of the flock panicked and, not knowing where the danger was, raced past me to disappear in single file over the shoulder of the hill. It was one of the most wonderful sights I have ever seen and luckily I had the presence of mind to film them as they went.

There were all kinds of birds on the Zemu Glacier, many of them species I had never seen before. Choughs flew over the camp every day, and beautiful grey and white Sikkim pigeons came up each morning from the woods below to feed on the snow-free slopes above the camp, and returned each evening. On the steep rocks above the Green Lake I saw Hodgson's Grandula, a bird the size of a starling but with vivid powder-blue plumage. The many varieties of snow and mountain finches defied identification.

The day after we reached the Base Camp we unpacked the skis and went up to the Green Lake. The skis were of ash, six inches shorter than is usual and with *alpina* toe-irons. The ski-ing was very disappointing, for the snow was slushy and in any case was fast disappearing. We found the Green Lake was still hidden by snow, but there was a south-facing slope near by, which we thought would be ready for our tents in less than a week's time. We started carrying loads up the glacier, and continued until we had a substantial depot there. The Zemu Glacier is unlike any other I have seen. Between the steep hillsides and the moraines marking the edge of the glacier there were level grassy belts several hundred yards wide. In some places these were formed by alluvial fans brought down by the many streams which broke up these level bands. The lateral moraine, about a hundred feet high, ran the whole length of the glacier, the top, already bare of snow, being marked by patches of heather, especially on the south side; the steep northern slope, which faced our camp, was still snow-covered and provided excellent nursery slopes for ski-ing. The actual glacier was about a mile wide from moraine to moraine and was a maze of old ice, great boulders, heaps of earth and sand, and even frozen lakes and vertical walls of ice fifty feet high. To cross it one had continually to climb up and down incredibly steep and irregular mounds fifty to a hundred feet high. At this time the moraine was rendered still more impassable by a treacherous covering of snow, so that one could not see whether one's feet were on loose or firm stones, and often the whole thing would crumble away beneath one and roll to the bottom of the hill—most unpleasant when one was carrying a fifty-pound load.

Our days were spent either in carrying loads—with the porters—to the depot we had made on the moraine near the Green Lake, just where the Nepal Gap Glacier meets the Zemu at 16,200 feet, or in making short expeditions into the mountains to the north of our camp. In the evenings we used to sit round an open fire of juniper logs which the porters brought from farther down the valley. We lived on *chupatties*—pancakes made from flour and water—potatoes, eggs, rice and dahl, porridge and occasional tins of sardines or tongue.

On April 25th, Nicholson, Cooke and Roaf left the camp to attempt a 19,500-foot peak on the north-east. Pallis and I set off up the Zemu Glacier with a view to making a reconnaissance of Simvu. We had decided that Siniolchu was beyond our powers, and even Simvu with its five summits and ice-fluted ridges might well turn us back, and seemed quite likely to do so if the weather did not improve.

## CHAPTER FIVE

### SIMVU

THE pioneers of exploration and climbing in Sikkim were Sir Joseph Hooker, that energetic botanist and traveller; Sir Douglas Freshfield, the distinguished Alpine and Caucasian mountaineer, and Dr. Kellas, an amazingly enterprising climber who for many years conquered more peaks in a single season than most people attempt in a lifetime. Dr. Hooker spent most of 1848 and 1849 in Sikkim. In April of the latter year, in spite of the immense transport difficulties of those days, he found his way up the Teesta to Lachen and made several attempts to climb Lama Anden (19,500 feet). From here, he followed the south bank of the Zemu Chu (we kept to the north) and endeavoured to reach the Zemu Glacier. Being unsuccessful in this, he crossed over to the Lachung district and made unsuccessful attempts to climb Kang-chenjau (22,700 feet) and Pauhunri (23,180 feet), in the extreme north-east of Sikkim, returning over the Dongkya La (18,130 feet) to Lachung. On his return to Darjeeling he and his companion, Dr. Campbell, the Superintendent at Darjeeling, were taken prisoners and detained at Tumlong, a few miles to the north of Gangtok, by Namgay, the influential native Prime Minister of Sikkim. Long negotiations were necessary before the explorers were released, and as a result of this outrage the district to the south of the Great Rangit River, including the Darjeeling district with its rich tea gardens, was annexed by the British Government. Darjeeling itself had been ceded to us by the Sikkim Raja in 1817, after the Gurkha war, when this whole district had been conquered and annexed by the Nepalese. Further exploration of the district was prevented by the open hostility of the inhabitants until the famous " Pundits " took up the work. These romantic figures were Bengalis, trained by the Survey of India. At great personal risk they would penetrate in disguise the forbidden parts of Sikkim and Tibet and return, possibly years later, with the data from which the earliest maps of these districts were compiled. But the Pundits did not visit the Zemu district.

The Survey of India Records next tell of "the Lama ", a mysterious hillman who was at one time a schoolmaster at Darjeeling. In 1883, he travelled by the Teesta Valley and Lachung route to the Dongkya La, after which he reached the forbidden city of Lhasa. In the same year other native surveyors explored the Zemu and Talung valleys and reached the northern frontier of Sikkim. Between 1889 and 1902, Mr. Claud White, then Political Officer of Sikkim, made some exploratory journeys in the Zemu Glacier district. First he crossed the Guicha La and descended the Talung Glacier to the Teesta River, an adventurous journey, for up till that time no one had visited the gorges between Pandim and Simvu. In the following year he worked up the Talung Chu, from its confluence with the Teesta near Singhik, and then past Talung Monastery on the Ringbi Chu and over the Yeumtso La, between Lama Anden and Siniolchu, into the Zemu Chu. He even ascended the glacier to a height of 17,500 feet (about level with the Green Lake), but was forced to return by bad weather. From the Zemu Glacier he went northward into Lhonak.

In 1899, Sir Douglas Freshfield made the expedition to this district which is so well described in his book *Round Kangchenjunga*. Leaving Darjeeling in early September, his party ascended the north bank of the Zemu Chu and camped a little above 15,000 feet, just short of what he called the Green Lake. His plan was to ascend the glacier and explore the possibilities of the Zemu Gap and Nepal Gap approaches to Kangchenjunga. Bad weather, however, drove him over to Lhonak to examine the northern approaches of the mountain. In 1907, that amazingly enterprising and reticent climber, Dr. Kellas, who died at Kampa Dzong on his way to Everest in 1920, spent a season in the Zemu Glacier district. In May 1907, Kellas visited the Zemu Glacier via Lachen and reached the Simvu Saddle (16,570 feet) and the Zemu Gap (19,300 feet) for the first time. In September of the same year, assisted by Swiss guides, he made three attempts to reach the top of Simvu but was driven back by new snow and bad weather. In 1920, just before starting for Everest, he is supposed to have climbed—though this is not absolutely certain— Lama Anden (19,250 feet), the peak near Lachen. In 1920, Harold Raeburn, accompanied by Colonel Tobin, examined the south-east approaches of Kangchenjunga. Crossing the Guicha La, they approached the Zemu Gap by the Talung and Tong-shyong glaciers, but the narrow entrance of the gap and the bordering mountain sides were raked by such a continuous hail of rocks and debris that they came to the conclusion that an approach by that route would have been suicidal. (This was in July and August.) In 1925, Mr. N. A. Tombazi made the first ascent of the Zemu Gap from the south, via the Talung and Tongshyong glaciers. He pronounced this approach to be unsuitable for laden porters. In the following year, Major Boustead reached the Zemu Gap by the same route and stressed the danger of this region owing to frequent avalanches and thick mists.

In 1929, after the monsoon, the German Kangchenjunga Expedition—under the leadership of Dr. Paul Bauer—visited the Zemu Glacier by way of the Teesta River and Lachen; it was probably their track through the rhododendron and bamboo scrub that we followed beside the Zemu Chu. One party was driven back three times in an attempt to climb the Simvu Saddle with a view to making a long-distance reconnaissance of Kangchenjunga from across the Zemu Glacier. They concluded that the Simvu massif was in reality quite different from its appearance on the maps, and they also discovered that it was quite impossible to reach the main peak directly from the saddle. Meanwhile, Bauer, having decided that the glacier valley between Kangchenjunga and the Twins was an impossible approach, set about the assault of the north-eastern arête with characteristic German thoroughness, while another party attacked the eastern approach from the Zemu Gap. The last week of August was spent in strenuous attempts to reach the arête, but the party was driven back by almost insuperable difficulties. At last, in early September, by developing an entirely new technique of ice-work, the ridge was reached. This technique consisted in hacking and tunnelling through the great ice pinnacles and gendarmes which guarded the arête, so that it could be made safe even for porters, and ice caves were hewn in which the climbers and porters could pass the night out of the wind and safe from avalanches.

At last, by September 26th, the last 200-foot ice gendarme had been passed, by the remarkable expedient of cutting a 25-foot tunnel—a task which took two whole days—and by October 3rd they camped at 23,400 feet, ready for the final assault, with a party of six Germans and four porters. Then the weather broke and for four days a blizzard raged. The party made two assaults and reached a height of 24,450 feet, but the bitter wind and six feet of fresh snow forced them back. On the way down they marched through a lane of snow the height of a man and the route was intermittently swept by frightful avalanches. That the return journey was completed without any accident more serious than one member being badly frost-bitten was a wonderful achievement. Although the attempt was unsuccessful, it set up a new standard in Himalayan mountaineering, for up to this time no one had attempted to climb one of the steep fluted ice-ridges so characteristic of the Himalaya.

In 1931 the Bavarians returned to the attack. This time a height of about 25,260 feet was reached by following the same bold tactics. When the end of the N.E. spur was attained, it was discovered that the main N.N.E. ridge of the mountain—of which the N.E. spur is but a tributary—was at a higher level, and the steep 300-foot wall separating them could not safely be climbed owing to dangerous snow conditions. On their retreat from Kangchenjunga in late October 1931, Dr. Allwein and Herr Pircher crossed the Zemu Glacier and ascended the Simvu Saddle (16,570 feet). From here they made for the first time a descent on to the Passanram Glacier 2600 feet below. After a week's very arduous travelling through completely unexplored country they reached Talung.

It will be seen from this short summary of previous expeditions to the Zemu Glacier district, that considerable reconnaissance was necessary before we could start the actual attempt on Simvu. On April 25th Pallis and I, accompanied by Ang Nima, Rinchen Bhutia and Kipak, set off for the Zemu Gap to examine the south-western approach to the Simvu massif. Following the level going between the moraine and the mountain, we reached the Green Lake and found a camp site on a snow-free platform at the foot of the great rock-face to the north. The porters made a fire of juniper and azalea scrub and we sat round it enjoying the aromatic fragrance of the smoke until long after dark. We had pemmican, rice and potatoes for supper, followed by tea. During the night avalanches frequently roared down in the distance and fitful flashes of lightning lit up the inside of the tent. I had never camped as high as this (16,500 feet) before, but seemed to be well acclimatized after our gradual ascent, and slept fairly well. In the early morning I awoke to hear the extraordinary bubbling note of snow-cock and the querulous call of choughs from the hill above the camp.

C

Ang Nima and Rinchen (Kipak having returned to the Base Camp after carrying up a load) rose early and got our breakfast of tea and biscuits ready, having previously prepared their own. It was a clear, cloudless morning with little wind. The porters took our rucksacks, about 35 lb. each, while we carried the skis, hoping to be able to use them higher up the glacier where the surface was more regular and the snow deeper. We walked round the Green Lake, which still belied its name, though it was by this time thawing into muddy brown pools. We crossed the Nepal Gap Glacier and fought our way up and down the rough surface of the glacier whose dirty ice was covered with moraine debris and discoloured patches of snow. After two or three hours we reached the comparatively level area of snow which runs down the middle of the glacier. Here we put on our skis and took the rucksacks from the porters, who were to return to the Green Lake, pick up their tent and bedding and return to the Base Camp. It was necessary to be a very good ski-er to work over such rough ground, carrying rucksacks of 30 or 40 lb. in weight. After a time we put sealskins on our skis and made better progress and found it less exhausting, though also less exciting. We enjoyed good views up to the snowy dome of the Sugarloaf, then to the Twins and on to the several summits of Kangchenjunga. Straight in front of us as we advanced up the glacier was the Bavarian's formidable ridge. Looking at those broken, icy pinnacles set at so steep an angle, it was amazing to think that Bauer's parties had climbed so high. I wrote in my diary : " The Tent Peak looks quite impossible from here : the last 1000 feet is of snow-plastered rock set at an impregnable angle. The Twins look possible, if only one could get on to the ridge. They would have to be approached from the Nepal Gap. Siniolchu might yield to the Bavarian technique; it is certainly beyond us. I think Simvu is climbable; being a complicated massif, like Kangchenjunga it may be attacked in so many different ways; but it is no easy matter : even if we reach one of the summits, it will be a terrific task to cut along the icy knife-edge ridges and complete the traverse. I shall be petrified with fear if I ever get up there."

We camped beside an enormous boulder just opposite to where the Kangchenjunga Glacier comes in. In the middle of the ice-fall of this glacier was an island of rock where lies the grave of Schaller, one of Bauer's 1932 party. We noticed that the ridge coming straight down from Simvu towards our camp looked quite possible, and though the rolling snow slopes of the Upper Zemu Glacier were most tempting, we decided to examine this ridge on the morrow. After all, everyone who has been up to the Zemu Gap says that the Simvu ridge is unclimbable, though I have an idea that it might be possible to descend the far side of the Gap and approach Simvu from behind—from the south-west. We had Ovaltine and sardines for supper and were asleep by 7.30. On the ice we were using small Li-lo air mattresses about 3 ft. 6 ins. by 2 ft. as insulation. These were excellent, but were on the short side. In double eiderdown sleeping-bags, and still wearing most of our clothes, we were as warm as we could have wished to be. As usual it clouded up in the evening; this phenomenon is probably due to the fact that this district is between the low moist Teesta and Talung valleys on one side and the high wind-swept Tibetan plateau on the other, consequently there are usually high winds until after the monsoon, when the warmth of the valleys is brought up to the level of the Tibetan plateau, thus eliminating convectional disturbances. On April 27th we were woken up at 6 by the sun, which blazed on to our tent. The view of Kang-chenjunga, with the sun reddening its high snows and casting purple shadows into every icy couloir against a background of translucent blue, was majestic in the extreme, almost terrifying. After strong Ovaltine and sardines for breakfast we left our tent standing and set off at 8.

I was very reluctant to abandon the attractive-looking ski-slopes of the Zemu Gap, but even from here we could see that the arête of Simvu to the east of the Gap was quite unclimbable, as all previous climbers have reported, and Pallis was very much excited by the possibilities of the ridge which ran down between two glaciers. We walked across and examined the magnificently turbulent ice-fall to the south of the ridge. The left of the ice-fall was possible but was rather badly crevassed, so we kept to the right, climbing up very steep rock to avoid the crevasses. We succeeded in getting on to the ridge about 1550 feet above the glacier by working our way up a gully and then out over some very exposed rock. We found a suitable place for the big tent on a wide ledge, and Pallis seemed to think that it would be possible to force a way up to the top of the ice arête which connected our buttress with the main massif. We glissaded straight down a steep, snowy couloir between the rock and the ice-fall. I had found it very exhausting climbing uphill at 17,000 or 18,000 feet, but descending was as easy as at sea-level; going up, it seemed essential to get into some sort of rhythm, so that one moved mechanically, otherwise one soon became exhausted; indeed, I soon discovered that this matter of rhythm was the whole secret of high altitude climbing. We decided to return to our tent and to set off back to the Base Camp the same day, in order to make the most of the unusual spell of good weather: it had not snowed for two whole days. We packed up the tent and were away at 1.30. The ski-ing was good but rather slow, as the afternoon sun made the snow sticky. Getting up again after falling with a 30-lb. rucksack on one's back was terribly exhausting. At 4 o'clock we reached the place from which the porters had returned; I could not face the prospect of carrying both rucksack and skis for two hours over the rough moraine, so I suggested that we should ski right down the far side of the glacier, where there appeared to be plenty of snow, until we were level with our camp, and then dump our skis and walk home across the glacier. This turned out to be a very bad plan and we got into some terribly rough country. Pallis, who was not a very experienced ski-er, became very tired, and as the going on the far side was impossibly rough we left our skis there and wearily crossed the glacier again to the Green Lake, which we reached at 6.30, just as it got dark. It was a terrific walk, up and down the interminable ridges of the moraine, and as the sun had melted the snow we often sank in waist-deep, and twisted our ankles between boulders hidden in the snow. It took us two hours to get back to the camp from the Green Lake and we were tired out. Often we sat on boulders and rested, and sometimes fell asleep. There was just enough light from the crescent moon and stars for us to find our way. We were utterly exhausted by the time we reached the camp and had reached the stage when we were walking like machines, scarcely aware of the very still night and the fact that the clouds had lifted. Orion's belt and Sirius shone with unnatural brilliance over Kangchen-junga; Regulis and the great sickle of Leo were straight above us; Arcturus and Virgo hung low across the valley. The brightness of the stars in the clear mountain atmosphere is one of the greatest joys of a Himalayan expedition. The others were asleep, but they soon turned out and cooked us some supper. Cooke and

Nicholson had failed to get up their peak, being turned by very steep ice near the summit.

Next day Cooke and Nicholson climbed the Lagerberg (18,977 feet) from the camp. They found that one of Bauer's party had previously climbed it and left a cairn on the summit. The porters were sent down to Lachen for more food, as with two more of them than we had originally intended to keep, supplies were running short. On April 29th it snowed most of the day, so Roaf and I walked across the glacier and collected the skis which Pallis and I had left there. How I grew to hate that Zemu moraine! On April 30th, Pallis and Cooke attempted the peak to the north of the Green Lake. The rest of us went up with them, carried loads to the dump, camped there and returned to the Base Camp next day. Pallis and Cooke returned in the evening, having made a first ascent of the 19,500-foot peak overlooking the Nepal Gap Glacier. They were surprised to find that the top part of the peak, which was of snow and ice, had crevasses right across the summit. They had had a wonderful view down on to the Hidden Glacier which separated us from the Lhonak district.

In the evening we boiled up a Christmas pudding and, having put in a rupee, gave some to each of the porters. Ang Nima found the rupee and later brought it to Pallis to ask if he was really allowed to keep it. It seemed to him too good to be true. Next day it was overcast and snowing. Roaf and I went up to the dump to collect some food as we were running short at the Base Camp. Ishwar Singh and the other men whom we had sent down to Lachen to bring up more food and mails returned, together with half a dozen Lachen porters, on May 3rd. There were about a dozen letters for me, some of which brought exciting news, as will be explained in the following chapter. In the meantime, now that the Base Camp was restocked with provisions, we were ready to start up Simvu as soon as the weather improved, and we thought it would be as well to move across the Zemu Glacier and establish a higher camp on the Simvu Glacier, so that we should be ready to take advantage of any fine weather there might be.

On May 4th, Cooke and I, with Ang Nima and Rinchen Sherpa, set off to carry the skis across to the foot of the Simvu Glacier. We took an hour to the Green Lake—a record with heavy loads—and worked our way across the glacier, carefully cairning a route for the benefit of later parties. The going was terribly rough, as all the boulders and steep slopes of stones seemed to be most precariously balanced and were ready to slide down like a moving staircase the moment one touched them. Once I fell down a crevasse up to my armpits, but none of the crevasses on this part of the glacier goes very deep and we could see the bottom. It is not really necessary to use a rope on the Zemu Glacier, though most of the tributary glaciers and the Upper Zemu Glacier, being much steeper and more active, are dangerously crevassed. Once across the glacier we had to get over the south moraine and then climb up the right-hand (or easterly) moraine of the Simvu Glacier. It was extremely difficult to find a route here, as the moraine was very steep and there was a crevasse parallel to it with waist-deep snow everywhere. As usual, it came on to snow in the evening and we were glad of our row of cairns to find the way back. While we were crouching for shelter behind a rock near the Green Lake, I suddenly heard a familiar note and saw three terns flying overhead. I wonder if they had lost their way, or if the Zemu Glacier is used by them as a regular migration route, and, if so, where on earth were they off to? When we reached the Base we were completely encrusted in snow, like snow men.

May 5th and 6th were overcast and it snowed most of the time. We could do nothing except send more loads up to the Green Lake. Everything except our personal gear was then ready for the attempt at Simvu. On May 7th it again snowed practically all day. We were getting depressed and even talked of moving down to Tsetang and waiting until the weather should improve; we were not high enough to be actually deteriorating, in fact we were all extraordinarily well acclimatized, but we were getting stale, and some of us found that living on eggs, porridge, rice, dahl and potatoes was not having a good effect on our digestions. Personally, I longed for meat.

On the evening of May 8th, Ishwar Singh put up a prayer flag on the summit of a large boulder near the camp and burnt incense before it. This seemed to have the required effect upon the weather, for that evening the stars gradually appeared through the mist and in the middle of the night I awoke to hear a rushing wind and the tent flapping furiously. This must have marked the exodus of the devils, for next day, May 9th, it was gloriously fine, and we got up at 6 o'clock in glorious sunshine. We sorted out all the gear and were ready to start by 10 o'clock. Just before we left the camp the porters lit more incense on the top of the boulder and, all wearing their green windproof suits, waved their arms and shouted invocations. We all went as far as the Green Lake depot and then Ishwar, who carried only an umbrella and Pallis' ruck-sack up to the dump, returned alone to look after the Base Camp, while the rest of us sat down with field-glasses to have a final look at Simvu and to plan our route. We would go to the upper Simvu Saddle and attempt the arête running from there up to the north-east summit; if all went well, we would traverse the summit ridge and descend by the route that Pallis and I had dis-covered on our reconnaissance trip. The mountain looked most formidable, and I remember wishing that the assault were behind and not before us. A Himalayan peak has the odds heavily in its favour. Its defences are varied: it can drive back a party by the difficulty of its approaches, by the effects of altitude, and above all by the many vagaries of weather.

We crossed the Zemu Glacier and climbed up the Simvu Glacier moraine to our camp-site at about 800 feet above the Zemu Glacier. Roaf and I ski-ed, but it was very steep and the snow was patchy and uneven. There was a slight wind and clouds were forming over Kangchenjunga, the Twins and the distant Tent Peak. We put up three Base Camp tents and a two-man bivouac tent. Pallis and Nicholson shared one, Cooke and I another, the four porters the third, and Roaf had the bivouac tent. (Jun Singh and Kipak had returned to the Base Camp from the foot of the Simvu Glacier.) It was a heavenly starlit night and we could see the Simvu Saddle, a wide col like a Swiss pass, only a mile or two up the glacier and not at a very much higher level than ourselves. The Pole Star, which was obscured at the Base Camp, was visible, and Arcturus, Spica and Corvus; Orion was hidden, but we saw Procyon, Castor and Pollux, and Regulus straight above us with Leo like a great question mark. Should we get up Simvu or not? It was good to smell a primus in a tent again. I had a slight altitude cough, but none of us had sore throats; Pallis' cough was still very bad. There was a strongish wind in the night and fine snow pattered mournfully on the tent and ran down the canvas with a steady soft swishing noise like the sound of a boat's gunwale. I had cold feet all night and an icy patch between my shoulders. Cooke put his feet on a coil of rope and was warm. Cooke and Pallis were to be on the first rope and Nicholson and I on the second. Roaf was to hold the camp.

Cooke and I got up at 6.30 and made tea for the porters so that they could go down to the foot of the moraine for the rest of the gear. Pallis did not like them using a primus in their tent, so we had to prepare all their meals: a strange inversion of services. We were going to take half the gear up to the Upper Saddle so that we could move on the next day with all the rest of it. It was overcast at 8 A.M., but blue sky showed over the Upper Saddle; by 9 it was snowing. We all had tea, biscuits and butter and cheese, in our tent and had to lie up for the day. A long discussion about the War and the merits of different nations as colonists led to a violent argument about the Public Schools; as we represented Harrow, Winchester, Shrewsbury, Liverpool Grammar School and Sedbergh between us, we had a fair variety of experience. The porters returned at 10. We found one primus stove had no spanner and the spanner to the other one did not fit it: a proof that one should always attend to every tiny detail and leave nothing to the porters. I spent most of the day learning Tibetan. Our voices had practically gone with talking so much. It snowed hard in the afternoon and then blew a blizzard.

The next morning we were up at 6 to find a marvellous day: clear sky except for a wisp or two of cloud wreathing Kangchenjunga. I had slept very well once I got to sleep, but Cooke was breathing very queerly in the night, panting five or six times, then giving a great sigh; this is called Cheyne-Stokes breathing and is usual at high altitudes.

The primus gave trouble at breakfast so we were not away till 7.30. The steep slopes at the top of the Upper Saddle would not be safe for a few days after the new snow, so Roaf, Cooke and I decided to ski up to the Simvu Saddle to see if there was a possible way up from there. We could see that the alternative route which we looked across to from the camp was steep and badly crevassed. We had a splendid trip; there were five inches of new powder snow and very few open crevasses and ice-falls; it was just a good steady climb with a splendid view across to the towering Tent Peak. The ascent looked almost impossible from this side, but the Twins seemed much more possible. We could see the Pyramid Peak over the Nepal Gap Glacier and thought it, too, looked possible and that we might attempt it when we went to Lhonak. From the top of the Saddle we looked straight down on to the Passanram Glacier, 2600 feet below. I cannot think how the Germans managed to force a way down there. Away beyond the glacier stretched the purple-shadowed valleys of Talung and the wooded hillsides of Sikkim.

The approach to the Upper Saddle was obviously impossible from here. Our ridge up to the north-east peak of Simvu looked difficult but not impossible. The difficulty would be to get on to it. We had a good view of the long north-west arête of Siniolchu leading up to the final needle which bristled with jagged gendarmes. Two griffon vultures sailed over the Saddle. We had a good run down to the camp, though we were just an hour late, as the snow was starting to get sticky. I think climbers underestimate the value of skis in the Himalaya. Roaf and I were the only ski-ers of the party and we gained tremendously. It is so much easier to maintain a rhythm on skis than on foot, and the delight of a good run down is ample recompense for any amount of slogging.

The others were taking loads towards the Upper Saddle. We noticed heavy solid-looking columns of cumulus cloud forming over the Pyramid Peak and a wisp of cloud on the Saddle. Soon after they had started it came on to snow and was soon blowing a blizzard and they had to find their way back to the camp by compass. Roaf came into our tent and we discussed the future of farming in England and read the whole of the Epistle to the Galatians aloud. I slept well that night but was rather cold. In the morning we had the usual trouble with the primus. We sat in the sun and breakfasted at 8 o'clock on boiled eggs and cheese and biscuits. Eggs needed six or seven minutes up here and tea had to be stewed for some time, as the water boils far blow 100° C. It was a hot, windless, cloudless day. We packed up everything and were away at 10. Small tortoise-shell butterflies kept on coming down from the Saddle. I counted 21 that morning, and one dark clouded yellow, and I also saw several vultures and a lammergeyer. Perhaps they use this route over to Lhonak and Tibet.

We ski-ed down from our moraine, then across the Simvu Glacier and up a long gradual climb to the ice-fall. It was absolutely no effort on skis, in spite of 40-lb. loads. We had special skis about 4 feet long and 6 inches wide with plush below for the porters, but they resolutely refused to wear them; they will not try to learn anything new and preferred to carry them. We climbed well, zigzagging across with frequent rests. At midday it clouded over and became oppressively warm and we suffered from what is called " glacier lassitude ". The sun, especially when shining through thin cloud, blazes up from the snow. Any part of the face that is exposed gets burnt in spite of Anti-Lux and other devices to protect the skin. One's lips and the edge of the nostrils suffer most, and usually these places are skinned and agonizingly raw after a few days on the glaciers. The application of grease of any sort merely makes the skin fry in the hot sunlight, though it can be put on safely at night.

The straps of our rucksacks cut into our shoulders and the weight of the load upset the balance in the most infuriating way. In spite of snow-goggles, our eyes ached and the glass misted up so that it was impossible to see. The snow was sticky and piled up on our skis; swing-turns were impossible, kick-turns were infinitely exhausting and life became a burden. Snow was pouring off all the couloirs on either side with a swishing, roaring noise. There was a fine view back to Siniolchu and Little Siniolchu and across to the Sugarloaf, Twins, Nepal Peak, Tent Peak and Pyramid Peak. At 2 o'clock, clouds suddenly blew across from the north and we camped at once; and not a moment too soon, as it came on to blow and snow. We put up the four tents, having dug platforms for them just below some bad crevasses. The sun must have been terribly powerful; I had sore places behind the ears where I had forgotten to put any Anti-Lux; my beard protected my face, but my nose was sore and my lips painfully dry and cracked.

The weather soon cleared but the valley remained full of cloud. We had pemmican and tea for supper—it is extraordinary how important meals become on an expedition. There was a fine view in the evening down on to the billowy top of the clouds out of which the peaks rose grandly. The slanting sun lights up and reveals details not visible in the clear light of day; there was a queer violet reflection on the glacier, and flurries of snow-smoke blew across. A fiery glow lit up the western sky and deep purple and coppery shadows gave a strangely solid look to the rounded heads of cumulus : a cold, frightening, beautiful world.

We were away next morning by 8, only Roaf and I wearing skis. I carried 35 lb. We roped up at the crevasses but found a safe way through. The lips of the crevasses curled over treacherously but the bridges seemed safe. The bare walls of ice showed irregular stratification, probably indicating the amount of annual snowfall; it was impossible to see to the bottom—just sinister blue and green shadows.

We were all past the crevasses by 11, when a sudden enveloping mist crept over the Upper Saddle from the south. What vile weather we had ! I was ahead and went on till we came to a level place where we camped. All at once the mists swirled aside and we caught a momentary glimpse of Simvu towering majestically above us, and the amazing summit of Siniolchu away to the east with its south ridge now visible. It was a superb position, but I could not see how we were going to get on to the ridge of Simvu.

In the evening we held a council of war. Pallis favoured the ridge and two of us would go ahead and prospect it the next day. The porters were going well, with heavy loads on steep going. Roaf measured our hearts and pulses, tested blood-coloration and made us do intelligence tests. According to them, my brain certainly works better higher up. It snowed most of the afternoon. We seemed always to have had the best of the weather by 11 or 12, which made a very long night. Pemmican for supper with *tsamba* (*tsamba* is parched barley-meal; mixed with buttered tea it is the staple food of most Tibetans). I did not like the mixture. One is very conservative at 19,000 feet.

The next day was fine. There was a wonderful view down into Sikkim, with blue ridge paling into blue ridge and a bank of cumulus clouds in the far distance. Frightful pinnacles showed on the Siniolchu ridge and on the Talung Peak, which was just visible. Looking at Simvu, only ice and snow appeared, hardly any rock. Pallis and Nicholson set off to investigate the northern arête, Roaf and Cooke went down the route of the day before to collect various things we had left behind, and I took the three porters to find a new way down to the dump which Pallis and Nicholson had left three days before. I avoided the crevasses so that there would be no danger if the porters had to use it alone in the future. I went straight across the top of the ice-falls to the rocks, then over some big grey slabs and down a steep snow-gully between the rocks and a frightful maze of crevasses. Two cols in the rock-ridge gave glimpses of the Zemu Glacier far below. We collected the loads and set off back at a breakneck speed. I kept in the rear. The porters decided when to stop and rest; I decided when to go on again. The mist blew over the col from Talung as we returned to camp. We could see Pallis and Nicholson now and then through the mist. They seemed to be making very little progress. Roaf and I had some most enjoyable ski-ing on a little snowy mound which lay to the east of our camp and was really an offshoot of the rocky mass separating us from the lower saddle. Running downhill was just the same as at normal altitude, but one had to climb very slowly indeed. Pallis and Nicholson returned late in the evening with the news that they thought we could force a way on to the ridge from the east.

What an age it took to do anything at that height! The primus wouldn't light, boots were frozen like iron, clothes took hours to pull on, and if one tried to hurry at all one lay back panting and exhausted. I slept with my boots in my sleeping-bag to keep them from freezing; but it is not worth the discomfort if one can afford time and fuel to thaw them out in the morning. One night I used them as a pillow, but then they were not only frozen but squashed flat and it took a quarter of an hour to thaw them out. The best thing is simply to bulge them out as much as possible and then leave them; once you can get your feet into them they soon get supple.

Our plan was for us all to go up and establish a camp at the foot of the arête, leaving Pallis, Nicholson and Cooke in one tent to try to force the ridge. Roaf and I were to return with the porters and come up again the next day. We did not get off till 10 o'clock; tatters of clouds were already blowing up from Talung and a heavy bank of cloud was settling down on the glaciers. We wore skis to begin with, then abandoned them and followed a difficult track between crevasses and below a formidable row of ice serracs, roping up over crevasses. At last a fairly level camp-site was found after we had plodded up through deep soft snow at a precarious angle. The whole place was dangerously overhung by the arête but the actual camp-site was on a small saddle and reasonably likely to be clear of avalanches. We levelled a place for the tents and left the others at 3.30. There was a thick mist,

but we managed to follow our tracks. Rinchen Sherpa was completely exhausted and Roaf had to steady him over the steep
places. There was still no visibility when we reached the skis
and we had a strange run down in the mist with crevasses suddenly
appearing on either side. It is very difficult to ski when one is
tired, especially in diffused light, and terribly difficult to get up
again, once down.

For supper we scrambled some cracked eggs and made Ovaltine; I had a great craving for salad and smoked salmon; one's
appetite became very capricious at this height.

We left one tent standing when we went up again the next
morning. Ang Nima, Ang Babu and I were to stay up at the
top camp, while Roaf was to take the two Rinchens back to this
camp, sleep a night, then next day go the whole way back to the
Base Camp. We were going to try the arête, and if we could
force that we were going across the glacier to the west to attempt
the second peak. We got away at 7 and reached the top camp at
12 and had brilliant sunshine all the way. We saw a great
avalanche go down the north-east side of Simvu into the Talung
Valley. It roared away down like thunder, and delicate white
heads of snow-cloud were formed in its wake. Across the
Passanram Glacier, just this side of Siniolchu, is a remarkable
needle of rock about a thousand feet high. It is quite unlike a
Himalayan formation and closely resembles a Chamonix aiguille.
From the top camp we could see down into the blue jungle of
Sikkim and also away beyond the summits of the Nepal and
Pyramid Peaks across to the snow-free uplands of Tibet. There
were great rolling amber-coloured hillsides with dark violet
shadows and only occasional patches of snow. The others had
already returned when we reached the upper camp. They had
cut steps up to 700 feet or so above the camp, then reached very
steep dangerous snow overlying ice. They could work no
further round to the left, and it was too steep to cut straight up
to the arête, and impossible to traverse round to the right, so they
had to return. Ang Nima was completely incapacitated by a
violent headache, so he was to go down with Roaf and the
Rinchens the next day, leaving only Ang Babu with us. I felt
rather heavy behind the eyes (we were now at 20,000 feet) and
my lips and nose were very sore, but I was fairly cheerful and still
full of energy. We spent a long time making tea for two thermos

flasks so that Pallis and Cooke could get away very early and have one more attempt at the ridge, while Nicholson and I worked further over to the right. During the night it snowed again.

I slept well, though I once or twice awoke panting, with an awful feeling of suffocation caused by the lack of anything I could use as a high pillow. It is essential to get one's head as high as possible.

The next day Pallis and Cooke got away at 5.30, the right time of day to start, and Nicholson and I were off half an hour later. I wore my big felt-lined climbing-boots, three pairs of socks, puttees, woollen underclothes, grey flannel trousers with windproofs over the top, a flannel shirt, two thin jerseys and windproof jacket, Terai hat [1] and goggles, wool mitts and windproof outer gloves, and took with me a wool helmet and spare sweater. Pallis and Cooke cut across level with the camp until they reached very dangerous snow. Then they returned a short distance and traversed across again. Once more they were forced off the ridge. We caught them up just as they were making tea in a windsheltered hollow. From here I could see Roaf going down the glacier with the two Rinchens. After tea Nicholson and I traversed across beneath some vertical ice-falls and followed a narrow level ledge round a corner. From here it became apparent that we had discovered a possible way up. There seemed to be just one weak spot in the formidable defences of the mountain : if only we could get up an extremely steep nose of ice we could be on the arête. We returned for the others and they too thought it might be a possible way, and Pallis started cutting up it. It was a most horrible place, a vertical corner to be negotiated and then twenty feet of extremely steep ice which dropped at an increasing angle to the glacier below.

Pallis spent a long hour cutting both foot- and hand-holds up the corner. He was panting and groaning with the exertion. I watched Roaf still ski-ing down the glacier and felt more and more frightened lest I should completely fail to climb this formidable ice-wall. We all wore crampons, except Nicholson, who had left his behind. When at last I had to climb I found it very exposed and airy but not extraordinarily difficult. There were

[1] The Terai hat is a double felt hat with a wide brim ; it is worn by tea-planters.

adequate steps, and it was simply a matter of control and balance, but for all that I should not have liked it much without the moral support of the rope. The glacier simply fell away beneath us. One was tempted to cling against the ice instead of standing well away from it and finding one's own balance. At last we were all on the bulging arête and it seemed as if the summit was ours. In front of us the ridge gradually rose to the final pyramid, nothing ahead of us appeared half as steep as what we had just done. We were all exultant and stopped in a sheltered hollow to eat sardines and prunes. Crystals of snow were forming in the air and gusts of wind blew up from the Talung Glacier. We hurriedly finished our meal and advanced up the ridge. If the weather kept fairly fine and our luck held, we should be able to reach the summit peak and return to the camp before dark. In any case there was a full moon. But it was not to be; we had advanced but a few yards when suddenly we saw to our horror that between us and the arête above there was a great gash right across the ridge; none of us had ever seen such a thing before; it was a huge crevasse or bergschrund 20 feet wide, 30 feet deep and open at each end. We examined every possible means of crossing it, then realized that there was no hope.

It started to snow as we returned and clouds formed rapidly. I could see Ang Babu watching us beside our two tiny tents perched among jagged serracs down below. It took us some time to negotiate the steep corner all on the same rope, weighed down, as we were, with a bitter sense of disappointment. I hated the climb coming down and leant in too far, with the result that one step broke under me; however, my axe held, and I was able to cut it out again. At last we got off this perilous place, and by the time we were back in camp it was snowing and blowing a blizzard. We decided to return to our Base Camp the next day. Simvu had won. Oddly enough we all felt vastly relieved. We were no longer in a state of suspense, and although it would have been more satisfactory to have got up, still, we had been turned back by a most unusual obstacle after a prolonged and not dishonourable siege. There was no talk of trying the second peak, though Cooke and I were very keen to attempt it. But we had not enough food, the weather was vile, and the party was not really up to it. Pallis still had a bad cough, Nicholson had been suffering from headaches and it was Cooke's and my first climb

at this height.    It was obvious that we must return to the Base
Camp and then decide on our next move.

Just as we were going to start breakfast the next morning there
was a terrific thud and the whole tent floor shook as if there was
an earthquake.    I thought it was an avalanche starting above us
and was expecting to be swept away into Talung at any moment;
however, nothing happened, but when we got outside we saw a
ridge of snow about twenty feet from the tent which had not been
there before, and a crevasse, which had previously shown only as
a warning hollow in the snow, had opened up to a great fissure
several feet wide and many yards long.    We soon packed up all
our gear and in high spirits set off down the glacier.    There was a
feeling of tremendous relief in all of us.    We could get off the
mountain with a clear conscience.    We passed the camp-site on
the Upper Saddle, had a fine ski-run down the glacier, and soon
reached the moraine camp, where we left all the gear except our
personal possessions and set off for the Base Camp.    Most of the
snow had gone from the moraine in our absence and it seemed that
summer had come too.    Birds were singing, butterflies flew past,
and I found a minute pink primula and a red vetch in flower.
Here we came upon a stream of melted snow water and had a
long drink.    At the Green Lake Ishwar Singh, Kipak and Roaf
were waiting for us with the news that there were letters for us at
the camp.    Life seemed too good to endure.    The Green Lake
was thawing to a muddy pond, nearly all the snow had gone
except on the north side of the moraine; everywhere birds were
singing and insects flying about in the sunshine.

A very odd thing happened the next day.    Jun Singh with the
two Rinchens, Ang Nima and Kipak were sent across to the Simvu
Glacier moraine to collect the rest of the gear.    Soon after they
had started, Jun, in his blue jersey, returned blubbering and
staggering down the moraine.    Apparently there had been
terrible jealousy in our absence between Jun and the others.
Having been with Pallis before, Jun gave himself airs and ordered
them about.    They did not mind Ishwar so much as he was older
and had authority, though the Darjeeling men accused him of
faking the accounts.    Jun's explanation, between tears, was extraordinary: apparently the porters had decided that we would all
die on the mountain, and Jun and Kipak agreed that when this
happened they would settle a long-smouldering quarrel and fight

until one of them was dead. Now, although we had all returned safely, Kipak was not going to be done out of his fight and had taken his revenge, although he had luckily stopped short of killing.

Then another remarkable thing happened. Looking down the glacier, we saw two figures approaching the camp without loads of any sort. As they got nearer one turned and ran back, but the other, whom we soon recognized as Kilo, one of the youngest of the Darjeeling men whom we had paid off a fortnight before, came up grinning sheepishly and vigorously scratching his tousled hair with both hands, a habit of his when self-conscious. He produced some strange tale of a Sahib further down the glacier, and another Sahib having returned to Lachen after being taken ill, and Pallis went off with him to investigate.

Soon he returned with a tall young Englishman, one Jock Harrison, a subaltern in the Punjabis. Apparently he and a Captain Sams had started off together for the Zemu Gap but the latter had fallen ill and had had to return, so Harrison was left alone with an efficient little Sirdah and some Sherpa and Lachen porters. As will be seen in the next chapter, our meeting with him greatly simplified our somewhat complicated plans.

# CHAPTER SIX

## PLANS AND COMPLICATIONS

I HAD planned when the climbing was over to go across country to Shanghai, and then to return by Trans-Siberian railway to England. I had worked out a very interesting route by Manipur to Bhamo, then across the great river gorges to Yunnan-Fu, and down the Yangtse to Shanghai, and had even gone so far as to get permission from the various Residents concerned. But at the beginning of April, when I was staying with Mr. Gould, the Political Officer in Sikkim, he called me into his office one morning and said, " I don't want to make any sort of promise, but if by any chance a job turned up in Tibet, would you be interested? " At any time there could be only one answer to such a question, and it happened that at that time I was very depressed because I had

just heard that various plans I had made for the future before
leaving England had gone completely awry, and I felt that there
was nothing I would rather do than spend the rest of my life in
the practically unknown country of Tibet.

It appeared that the last Dalai Lama, the priest-king of Tibet,
had been a man of very advanced ideas, and had shown a high
respect for European education. In 1920 he had actually sent four
boys to be educated in England. Mr. Gould, who was then
British Trade Agent at Gyantse, had been responsible for taking
them home, where they spent three years at Rugby School and
elsewhere, and had since returned to Lhasa. The Dalai Lama had
also supported the establishment of a school, run on British lines
and with a British headmaster, at Gyantse, but owing to lack of
support from the local Tibetans and the fact that the Lhasa families
were reluctant to be without their children for so long a period,
the school was abandoned in 1932, in spite of the efforts of Mr. F.
Ludlow, the headmaster.

The last Dalai Lama had died in 1933, and those in power at
Lhasa had not yet revealed their intentions, but the Government
of India had told Mr. Gould that the Lhasa Government might
ask him to reopen the school at Gyantse or to start one at Lhasa,
and they had told him to look out for a likely headmaster. A
man was needed who knew something about English educational
methods and who would not find it intolerable to be the only
European living in Lhasa.

This project was at that time both secret and indefinite, but
Mr. Gould told me that he was going to Delhi in a few days' time
and it was probable that the Government of India would be sending him up to Lhasa later on in the year should an invitation
arrive from the Tibetan Government, and that he might be able
to take me as his Private Secretary. Even if the school did not
materialize, I would have a chance of visiting the closed city of
Lhasa and of seeing all sorts of new birds and plants on the way.
I was wildly excited about this and could scarcely keep the good
news from the others, but Mr. Gould had made me promise not
to say anything to them until he had been to Delhi, when he would
write to me and say how the land lay. Unfortunately it affected
the expedition plans, in that I might have to join Mr. Gould before
the expedition was over, in which case Cooke might be left in the
lurch as far as our Lhonak arrangement was concerned.

On May 3rd, when we were just preparing to start up Simvu, Mr. Gould wrote to Pallis telling him that he had offered me a job and asking when I would be free.  He also wrote in more detail to me : the Government had approved his suggestion and it now remained for the invitation to come from Lhasa.  He would know better in a few weeks' time when we would actually be starting, but he wanted me to come to Sikkim and get used to the office work and also to start learning Tibetan.  It seemed that the best thing was for me to go down to Gangtok as soon as we should get back from Simvu and then, if time allowed, to return and climb with Cooke in Lhonak before joining the Political Officer for good.  If I could not get back again, then Nicholson would climb with Cooke, while Pallis and Roaf went to Tibet— if permission were forthcoming.  But this plan was upset when Mr. Gould wrote to Pallis and told him that owing to the Kaulback incident and for other political reasons he could not give him permission to enter any part of Tibet except to follow the normal trade route to Gyantse.

Here was a fantastic situation : Pallis, the leader of the expedition, who knew as much about the language and customs of the Tibetans as almost any man in Europe, was not allowed to enter the country, while I, who knew nothing whatsoever about Tibet, had been invited to go up to Lhasa itself.  Pallis was violently opposed to the idea of starting a British school in Lhasa ; thinking, as he did, that the Tibetan way of life and Tibetan culture were incomparably superior to Western civilization, he considered it would be a most presumptuous act on our part to start teaching them how to live.  It says something for Pallis' magnanimity that in these circumstances we still remained on the best of terms, even above 20,000 feet.  Antagonisms, if they exist, working obscurely in the back of one's mind, can completely wreck a Himalayan expedition, and as, in my opinion, the conquest of a high peak is much more of a mental struggle than a physical one, a subconscious grudge might make all the difference to the success, and certainly to the enjoyment, of an expedition.

It was decided that as soon as we returned from Simvu, even if the others renewed the siege, I would make a flying visit to Gangtok to see Mr. Gould.  The opportune appearance of Jock Harrison on May 19th took a great weight off my conscience, for it meant that even if I had to stay at Gangtok, Cooke would be able to climb with Harrison and I would not have the feeling that I was letting him down. That night, after too large a meal, I was unable to sleep, and soon after midnight I went out to look at the stars. Cooke, who also could not sleep, heard me and crept out of his tent and we went for a walk down the moraine in the moonlight. Cooke was pleased to have a certain climbing companion for Lhonak, but three is a much better number than two, and I agreed that if I possibly could I would join them, for we had already discovered that our ideas of how an expedition should be carried out were remarkably similar. Meanwhile they would return to Tsetang to recuperate, and if I did not appear after a reasonable interval they would set off for Lhonak without me.

On May 20th I got up at 5 to find hoar-frost over everything, but it was a clear, cloudless morning full of promise. Everyone turned out to say good-bye, and I set off down the glacier feeling very forlorn and lonely. There is something very melancholy in parting with friends whom you have been camping and climbing with on an expedition.

But my sadness soon evaporated. It was a perfect morning and I determined to try to reach Lachen the same afternoon and to get the whole way to Gangtok on the following day. Actually this was a forlorn hope, as I was in very poor condition after the climb and needed a rest, and the track from Lachen to Gangtok is the longest fifty miles I know in the world; not only is there a general fall of 7000 and a climb of 4000 feet to the Penlong La, but the track twists and turns continually and the surface is very uneven. I was carrying only about 20 lb., just my camera, sleeping-bag, a few extra clothes and some food. Looking back I could see the early morning sun turn the snows from delicate shell-pink to a hard and dazzling white. There was elegant Siniolchu, the immense mass of Kangchenjunga, the Twins and the formidable Tent Peak, against a foreground of dark, heather-clad moraine and patches of juniper scrub on the hillside above our camp. As I followed the stream beside the moraine I had to dodge from one side to the other. Soon it fell steeply and there was no more snow. I had some difficulty getting off the end of the moraine, as it was very steep, and the precariously balanced stones were ready at the least touch to roll down to the bottom.

As soon as I got away from the glacier I was among azaleas and scarlet tamarisk flowers, and soon there were whole hillsides covered with pale yellow rhododendrons and occasional pink and white ones. At this altitude they were three or four feet high and covered the level part of the valley like a carpet. On either side great expanses of heathery ground led up to rocky pinnacles and alcoves full of snow. It was a glorious prospect, especially after the experiences of the last few weeks.

The track was elusive. Sometimes I followed the bank of the Zemu Chu, only to be forced to the undergrowth when the stream entered a gorge. When I was two hours out from the camp I reached the pine trees and suddenly I came upon a mass of deep claret-coloured *primula Royalei*, and a few minutes later I saw a blue poppy, my first, a most beautiful thing, with its clear sky-blue petals and yellow sepals, *meconopsis simplicifolia*, not *Baileyi*.

The track led on to various marshy clearings where the going was easy, but the path was nearly always lost on the far side. I wasted a great deal of time searching for the track in such places. How different all this seemed from the journey up! It was winter when I had last passed that way, now it was full spring.

At 10 o'clock I crossed the bridge over the Lhonak Chu and saw the track winding up to Talung. When I reached a fork in the track I was not sure which way to go, so I took the upper route and climbed up to the edge of the trees again. Soon I reached Tsetang, the clearing with the lichen on the pine trees. Once again I was conscious of the strangeness and beauty of the place, with delicate banners of green swaying in the wind like seaweed floating from the timbers of a wreck.

The next stretch was very laborious; I worked my way through tangled rhododendron thickets until I found the tree-trunk bridge, which I crossed gingerly on all fours, for the torrent had increased with the melting snow-water. I often followed a path till it lost itself in the forest, and then had to fight my way through until I came on to another track. As I went lower the heat of the forest became oppressive, and I stripped to my shirt. At last, soon after midday, I met the Tangu La track and crossed to Zemu Ram. I walked very fast along the good track and reached Lachen at 1 o'clock.

On the way down I had felt ill, and so had eaten nothing, but now I was ravenous and ordered six boiled eggs and some tea from the man in charge of the dak bungalow. Lachen, also, seemed

quite different from what it had been a month before; it was
strange and impersonal then, but now it seemed familiar and
homely; the air was warm and fragrant, the people smiled as they
passed. Later in the evening, when I returned to the bungalow
after a visit to the headman, I found two Englishmen there,
Waller and Acaster. They had been up to the Dongkya La and
had tried to cross it with yaks, but two feet of new snow had
defeated even these hardy beasts and they had been forced to
turn back. I had a good supper with them and was delighted
to have real bread and jam again and, above all, the luxury of a
hot bath.

On May 21st a few late stars were still shining when I left
Lachen at half-past four. The brain-fever bird was already noisy
in the fir trees above the village, and choughs were calling querul-
ously to each other. Near some outlying chalets I surprised a
party of langurs who were digging up potatoes in the fields. On
this winding stony track I found I could only just keep up four
miles per hour, even running down all the hills.

It was not until 8 o'clock that I reached the barley-fields of
Chungtang. It grew unbearably hot as the path took me down
and down, and my gym shoes started to fall to pieces on the
rough, cobbled track. Once I stopped to eat some delicious
yellow raspberries and discovered a leech on my fingers and found
the disgusting creatures crawling all over me. At 1 o'clock I
reached Singhik and after a meal of tea and eggs—all I could ever
procure at the bungalows, where they do not normally provide
food—I lay exhausted on the veranda of the bungalow with
aching muscles and blistered feet. I realized I could not get to
Gangtok that day. I could have carried on down to the malaria-
infested bungalow at Sikchu, but would not have had the strength
for the long climb over the Penlong La to Gangtok.

The garden of the bungalow at Singhik was some compensation
for staying. All along the veranda were tree orchids swaying
in wire baskets, and in the garden were sweet-scented camellias,
trim orange trees, roses, the long trumpet-flowered bush, and
masses of magenta bougainvillaea. There is much competition
among the bungalow-keepers to produce the best garden. After
the usual tea and eggs I read an old *Illustrated London News* that I
found there and went to sleep early, feeling rather lonely in the
empty house.

At 4.30 next morning I was on the road again; my feet were terribly blistered and I could hardly move at first, but it was an exquisitely fresh morning and I soon livened up. There is something very inspiriting in the early morning fragrance of the jungle, before the fierce sun and heat have liberated the ranker smells of midday. It seemed a very long way to Ma gan, and walking downhill was most painful. I found it much more comfortable in my gym shoes to keep to the muddy border beside the track and avoid the hard, uneven cobbles. At last I reached Dikchu at 8.30 A.M. and had some more tea and eggs. The man in charge told me that Captain Sams—Harrison's partner, who had been taken ill—had been at Dikchu the night before, going down to Gangtok on a litter. After breakfast I lay back in a deck-chair to rest and noticed blood running out of the back of my gym shoe. On investigation I found nineteen leeches on one foot alone. I had picked them up as my legs brushed against the grass while walking in the soft track beside the path. It was such a revolting sight that I did not dare to examine the other leg. There is nothing more loathsome than to see bloated leeches staggering drunkenly away from one, leaving a track of blood on which the flies cluster.

I left Dikchu bungalow at 9.30 and reached the top of the Penlong La after four hours of climbing. It rained hard on the way and I enjoyed getting soaked to the skin. All the Nepalis and Babus I passed on the road stared hard at me; they must have thought me a very low-caste sahib, for it is rare to see a sahib on foot at all, and his worth is judged by his clothes and the number of servants he has with him. An hour later I was climbing the steep path through the Residency garden and wishing I were a little less disreputable. There I found Mr. Gould, also Colonel Bailey, the well-known naturalist-explorer who was at that time British Resident at Katmandu, the capital of Nepal. A few years before that he had been Political Officer of Sikkim. There also was Miss Audrey Harris, whom I had last met at a cocktail party in London, and the genial Rajah Tobgay Dorje, a Bhutanese who is the connecting-link between the P.O. Sikkim and the Maharajah of Bhutan. His charming wife, Ranee Chuni, a sister of the Maharajah of Sikkim, was with him. I had met them both at Kalimpong, where they have a house; they both speak perfect English and are as delightful a couple as one could meet.

After a bath I was provided with an old grey suit which H. W. Tilman, of Everest and Nanda Devi fame, had worn only the day before when it was found that his climbing clothes were also too disreputable for the Residency. Tilman had called in to make arrangements for visiting the Zemu Gap from the west, before joining the rest of the Nanda Devi party. Later in the afternoon the Maharajah of Sikkim arrived, and then General Sir Douglas Baird with Brigadier Philip Neame, V.C., who was to accompany the Lhasa Mission—if it materialized—as military adviser. At dinner, having borrowed some of the P.O.'s evening clothes, I had to start my duties as Private Secretary by helping to entertain the company. It seemed incredible to be sitting there in a dinner-jacket making small-talk to Generals and Maharajahs after the vicissitudes of the last few weeks, or even of the last few days. The P.O. told me that he would not really need me until the beginning of June and that we would start for Lhasa at the end of July. So I decided to stay two more days at Gangtok and then take advantage of his offer of a pony and return to Lachen as quickly as I could and join Cooke and Harrison before they reached Lhonak.

The same day a present of two beautiful cloisonné jars arrived from the Tashi Lama, who was up near Jyekundo on the borders of Tibet and China. It appeared that the Tibetans were in a very difficult position and would almost certainly invite the P.O. up to Lhasa to give them the advice of the Government of India. The late Dalai Lama had died in 1933 and the next incarnation had not yet been found. The Tashi Lama, the next most holy of the lamas who are the ruling force in Tibet, had quarrelled with the Dalai and had fled to China. The Tibetans implored him to return, as the spiritual life of the country was crippled in the absence of the two highest lamas. But the Tashi, perhaps fearing for his personal safety, would only return if he was allowed to bring with him an escort of Chinese soldiers, and the Tibetans, having had bitter experience of the treachery of the Chinese, and fearing another foreign domination of Lhasa, refused to allow this escort into Tibet. There was just a chance that both parties might agree to the Political Officer's going up to Jyekundo and escorting His Serenity back to Lhasa. The future was full of exciting possibilities.

Next day there was a garden-party at the Residency. That was a most remarkable spectacle. By way of entertainment, music was provided by the local talent. First there was a Nepali band : all the performers were dressed in tight-fitting black suits like professional skaters, and one played an enormous trumpet which curled round his body and emitted the most fearful noises. Then there was a Sikkimese band : these men wore the uniform of the old Sikkimese militia, which is now used by the servants of the P.O. and the Maharajah of Sikkim, and which consists of a short scarlet jacket with black facings, a striped home-woven skirt, puttees and bare feet. The hair is worn in a long pigtail, and on top of the head is a wickerwork hat with a bunch of peacock feathers at the side. The chief feature about this band was a drum which was carried on the back of one man and beaten by another who marched behind him. Then there was a smart drum and bagpipe band played by the Gurkha police in green uniforms. Finally there were five serious-looking Tibetans who stood in a line on a wood plank and performed a solemn dance and sang a quiet broken little song, while a brigand-like Tibetan kept time with a strange stringed instrument. The men wore wide scarlet hats tasselled like lampshades, and long homespun robes. Another group did a dance arm-in-arm which was the very image of the Palais Glide. The four other white residents of Gangtok were there as well as all the Kazis, or high Sikkimese officials, dressed in magnificently coloured silk robes. Then the brother of the Maharanee arrived, having just come down from Lhasa, where he had an official post. He wore in his left ear the single six-inch-long turquoise and gold ear-ring, the badge of office of all Tibetan officials. His hair, instead of being in a long pigtail, was tied up with red ribbon into two buns on the top of his head, with a coral and turquoise charm-box between them. He was a very distinguished-looking young man with a pale complexion and fine, rather effeminate, features. The party was a great success. After tea and ices, decorations were presented to two Sikkimese officials, and the entertainment was over.

In the evening we all went down to the Maharajah's palace for dinner. His house is a curious mixture of the old and the new; the dinner was European and quite excellent, but the furniture was largely Tibetan, and there was a set of very beautiful *thankas* or Tibetan holy paintings. After dinner, the Maharajah showed us some films he had taken of this year's Everest party, Colonel

Bailey ran through some of Bhutan and Nepal and I finished up with some of Greenland.

On May 25th I left Gangtok for Lhonak. The P.O. had so many guests at the Residency that he could not spare one of his own ponies, but he produced a minute white beast from the village, also a Nepalo groom on a brown pony, and a coolie for my rucksack. I managed to slip out by the back gate, avoiding the Nepali band which was at the front door waiting to give the General—not me—a suitable send-off. We made good progress, though my saddle, being a native one, made me terribly sore. The coolie with the rucksack held on to the horse's tail and kept up even when we were galloping. We reached Singhik that night and I was so saddle-sore I could hardly move. When we got to Chungtang next day I went to the post office and bought all the stamp paper available and stuck it on to my seat, which was rapidly becoming completely skinned. Unfortunately, post-office gum cannot be very antiseptic and it was some time before I could sit down with any comfort.

On horseback I was much more conscious of the way the path overhung the river. The ponies are used to carrying loads and they walk on the very outside of the track to allow for an imaginary pack. In the afternoon I reached Lachen and was delighted to see two of our green Base Camp tents on the field below the bungalow. Pallis, Nicholson and Roaf were there, having arrived from Tsetang only an hour or two before, and they told me that Cooke and Harrison had set off that very day for Lhonak, having given up waiting for me.

I spent most of May 27th at Lachen, as I had to wait until the expedition reserve supply of boxes could be unpacked before collecting my gear together. I helped Pallis to pay off the Lachen men who had brought all the equipment down from the Base Camp. It is melancholy to see what a demoralizing influence the passage of several large expeditions has had on the inhabitants of Lachen. In the first place, seeing sahibs apparently possessing boundless wealth and giving away or discarding articles of value along the route, they have entirely lost their sense of values. The Lachen men, knowing that no other local man-power is available, expect twice as much wages as porters in other localities, and worse than that, they make an agreement, then under various pretexts refuse to carry on unless the wages are increased. They will also try to curtail each day's march by stopping about midday and declaring that there is no fuel further on, or no possible camp-site ahead. Then they try to shout down any opposition from their sahibs, relying on their superior knowledge of local conditions. Yet they are thoroughly good fellows at heart and excellent porters. We have only ourselves to blame if they have been corrupted.

After paying the men we were invited up to the headman's house, which was a very fine one with stables on the ground floor in which the cows and horses were kept, and wooden balconies above. The painted carving round the windows and doors was especially beautiful. There was even glass in the upstairs windows instead of the more usual cloth stretched over a trellis-work of wood. The living-rooms on the first floor were entered by an outside staircase. On the balcony skins of sheep and goats were drying. The main living-room was also the private chapel of the house; one complete wall was occupied by a high, painted and carved shrine in front of which were rows of holy-water vessels and an incense burner, and there were also racks for holy books, and several fine *thankas* hanging on the wall. On low, carved wooden tables were china tea-cups on high, beaten-silver saucers and with beautifully carved lids. There was a plate of *tsamba* (barley meal), a dish of puffed rice and another of cakes made from maize meal. A man-servant brought tea in a copper and silver tea-pot. The moment we drank any the cup was filled up again : luckily it is the custom to leave the cup full, or the process would be interminable. Tibetan tea is very different from what we call tea in Europe. In the first place the leaves come down from China in compressed bricks containing stalks and all kinds of impurities. The leaves are boiled for a considerable time and then the infusion is mixed with salt, soda and butter. This is poured into a section of hollow bamboo and churned up with a plunger. As long as it is drunk hot, and as long as the butter is fresh, it is an excellent drink. It is better still if one can forget that one is meant to be drinking " tea ". At the end of a long day spent in the cold there is nothing better than buttered tea with a handful of barley meal stirred into it.

This was only a preliminary to the meal, and soon a big shallow bowl of beautifully boiled rice was brought to each of us, an omelette, a bowl of curried potatoes and meat, and a bowl of

spinach and meat. We found chopsticks rather difficult to mani-
pulate, but it was quite easy once we got the knack. It was as
good a meal as one could have had anywhere. Our host wore his
long ear-ring of office, a superb violet brocade robe held in with
a scarlet sash and high black boots ornamented with green appliqué
work. The effect was spoilt by the addition of a ghastly cheap
European felt hat with a band of gold brocade round it.

After this meal I said good-bye to the others. Their plans were
still undecided. They might return to England or go up to
Gyantse, or visit the Gangotri district where Pallis and Nicholson
had been in 1933. I left Lachen at 3.30 with Rinchen Sherpa and
Kipak. I also took one Lachen man who went on ahead to
Tsetang where we intended to spend the night, and an extra tent
and food and gear to eke out what Cooke and Harrison would
already have. It took us four hours in thin rain to reach Tsetang,
where I found the Lachen man sitting in a primitive shelter stripped
to the waist in front of a huge fire. The porters boiled up a great
dish of dried mutton, putting in lumps of red marsala bean, and
each produced a leather bag of *tsamba* and mixed it with tea
to make a sort of dough cake which tasted very good. They
were all very cheerful and the Lachen man seemed to be rather
a wag.

Next day I woke the others at 6 o'clock and made porridge.
They had the same meal as on the evening before, so it was 8
o'clock before we got away. We went straight up the hill from
here, following a fair track. As we got higher the flowers were
wonderful. There was a delicate green fritillary spotted with
magenta, and all kinds of new primulas, poppies and saxifrages.
Higher up the rhododendrons were even better than those I had
seen beside the Zemu Chu. The whole mountain-side was a
blaze of colour, from pure waxy white blooms to the deepest
of scarlet. There was a small dark-leaved bush covered with
huge saffron-coloured flowers, and one with enormous trumpets
of the softest shell-pink, another the colour of lilac, another bright
crimson. The most lovely of all had long thin trumpets, ver-
milion-flame at the base, shading irregularly to orange.

We soon rose above the trees and followed a deep valley with
a furious rushing torrent in the bottom of it. I found I was
perfectly acclimatized and could walk just as fast as at sea-level. I
talked to the porters as we went along and learnt new Tibetan

words. At midday we found a small lake surrounded by sandy bays and rested there in the sun while the porters lit a fire and made the inevitable tea. On each side steep rhododendron-covered hills ran up to bold rock peaks flecked with snow silhouetted against a deep blue sky. Soon after we had passed the lake the valley widened out and we had to cross the torrent. I managed to get over first, then I found a place for the porters to cross after hauling the loads up a vertical ten-foot wall of rock with a yak-hair rope. Not long after this the track became more distinct and the valley opened out on to a wide grassy plain. This might have been an entirely different country from the Zemu; ahead of us was a vast, open, rolling plateau quite clear of snow, the ground an amber brown colour, dotted with black grazing yaks, and beyond that the level grassland. This happy valley was surrounded by bare rounded hills leading up to a distant circle of snowy peaks. Halts became more frequent, although the path ceased to rise so sharply, and at 4 o'clock we reached a level grassy place and the men were very anxious to camp. I had hoped to get right on to Lhonak, but gave in on condition that we should get away really early in the morning. I had agreed with them on a definite wage for the whole trip (4 rupees from Lachen to Lhonak and back), so they were less anxious than usual to stop before half the day's journey was done. I had been terribly itchy all day, so I had a hunt in my sleeping-bag and on my clothes, where I found fourteen fleas, five ticks and two leeches, and was very gratified that there were no lice. I suppose I collected this assortment while sitting in the shelter at Tsetang the night before. The porters cooked rice and mutton, then tea and *tsamba*. We all went to sleep early.

On May 29th I got up at 6 o'clock, but as the porters insisted on cooking rice and mutton again, it was 8 o'clock before we started. It was a bleak and windy morning but the sky was clear. We passed many beautiful patches of the claret-coloured primula and smaller rhododendrons and azaleas. Up here they were only a foot or so in height, but all the more beautiful for that, after the almost excessive exuberance of the lower valleys. There was also a minute blue gentian growing beside the path, a yellow ranunculus and a scarlet vetch. It distressed me very much that I could not put a name to all these plants, but I made a collection of all I found and, though they suffered from the damp as we returned through the forest, they eventually reached Kew Herbarium, when they were identified.

A considerable descent brought us to the river, a pale-emerald glacier torrent running between rust-coloured rocks and steep grassy banks dotted with dark patches of juniper scrub. We then crossed the branch stream coming in from Chomiomo and the north. It was over knee-deep and we had to hold on to each other to avoid being swept off our feet. A track followed this stream by which one could cross the Lungnak La to Tangu. We followed the main river, now the Langpo Chu, westward until we came out on to a parched stony plain, which nevertheless seemed to afford some pasturage here, for great herds of yaks and sheep appeared ahead. Soon we saw a crowd of men approaching us; these were the twelve Lachen men that Cooke and Harrison had taken up to their camp. They told us we still had about five miles to go, and as it was midday by then we went across to some yak-herds' shelters to make tea. Near by were two solid dome-shaped buildings of stone and sods, about eight feet high, presumably of some religious significance. In a rough stone shelter was a shepherd looking after a motley flock of brown and white sheep. His face was burnt almost black by the sun, and his tousled hair was tied into innumerable tiny plaits which united to form a thick pigtail, heavily ornamented with silver rings, coral and turquoise. He had a heavy gold ear-ring in one ear and a plain piece of turquoise in the other. As he walked he was spinning a thread from a roll of yak hair round his wrist. On his back was a six-stringed fiddle.

We made a fire, and a large bowl of yak's milk was produced. It had a sweet and smoky flavour, but was very good. We also bought a hollow bamboo full of curdled yak milk which was very similar to Icelandic *skyr*. I ate some of this, though the Lachen man indicated that it would make me giddy. While we were eating, a man passed on his way to Tangu. With him was an enormous black Tibetan mastiff, very superior and stand-offish. The man was driving four yaks which were heavily laden with bags of butter and were literally festooned with prayer flags tied to branches of bamboo. They also had scarlet tassels hanging from their ears. Many of the yaks here had calves which grunted like pigs and scampered round like excited dogs. The people accepted chocolate and biscuits but never ate them in my presence.

One yak-herd was sewing a yak-hair boot-sole as he walked, using a very practical cylindrical thimble with slots in it for the needle head. They nearly all have very finely worked brass plaques, not unlike the old-fashioned horse-brasses, about three inches in diameter, hanging from their belts.

A little further on we could see the La, which runs southward straight over to the Zemu Glacier, but our way led still westward over a spur leading into another wide valley where we could make out the black hair tents of the yak-herds. Their real home is the Chang Tang, the high central plateau of Tibet; they only come down here for the summer. The porters wanted to stop and said it was too far to the camp. However, I took the load of the Lachen man, who was grumbling most, and offered the others an additional rupee if we reached the camp that night. The Lachen man was then furious and wanted to take his load back, but I would not give it to him.

We crossed the Langpo Chu, over knee-deep again, and visited a big yak-hair tent built up on sods. There were two very aged but friendly women inside. They gave me some yak milk and *tsamba*. I stirred the meal into the milk with one finger, in proper Tibetan style. It was excellent. There was an open fire of yak-dung fuel in the middle of the tent and bundles of wool and striped bags of *tsamba* all round. I gave the old women some tobacco and they seemed very pleased. Soon after this I saw the green tents of Cooke's Base Camp at the junction of the Langpo Chu and the Podong Chu. It was at an altitude of 16,000 feet in a beautiful place which was entirely different in character from the Zemu Base Camp. I shouted as we approached the tents and soon Kilo emerged, scratching his tousled head, and said vaguely that the sahibs had gone off for ten days up the valley. It was essential that I should find them at once before they got too far away, so I put my sleeping-bag in a rucksack, took some food with me and set off in the direction Kilo indicated. Rinchen Sherpa, who had been going extremely well all day, asked if he could accompany me and carry the rucksack, so I put his sleeping-bag and more food into it and we set off at once. I intended to sleep at their camp if we found it, and if not, to return to their Base Camp. It was then 6 o'clock and would soon be dark.

I followed the hill to the south of the Langpo Chu, then crossed an awkward moraine and descended into the wide horse-shoe valley of the Langpo Chu and climbed a rocky hill which dominated the valley. From here there was a superb view from the Tent Peak round to the Pyramid and Langpo Peaks and back to the graceful Fluted Peak a short distance to the north. I yodelled and yodelled but there was no reply, nor could I see their tents. By this time it was dark and Rinchen, who had been going very slowly, was nowhere in sight. It was a beautiful night with a half moon and clear stars. I thought that I might see the lights in their tents when it got darker, so I sat on top of this hill waiting for Rinchen. He did not appear, however, and I got rather tired of " chanting faint hymns to the cold fruitless moon " and returned to the Base Camp, getting there at 10 o'clock. Rinchen was not there, but I was not much worried, because it was a wonderful night and he had both sleeping-bags with him and plenty of food.

It was cold without a sleeping-bag, so I got up as soon as it was light and set off with Kilo to find the camp. It soon became clear that he had been up there already and knew the way perfectly : it was only laziness that had prevented him coming up with me the evening before. I realized once again that one cannot get the most out of porters unless one can speak Tibetan. The going was very easy, first up a grassy hillside where a deep violet primula was in full bloom and cushions of androsace with white or forget-me-not blue flowers. We then reached some stony ground where there were several lakes. I had come this way on the night before but then had kept level, whereas Kilo went up over a stony moraine where we soon found their tents, only 1½ hours from the Base Camp.

I yodelled loudly and they tumbled out of their sleeping-bags vastly surprised to see me after having quite given me up. It was good to see the grinning faces of Ang Nima and Ang Babu again, and Harrison's busy little Darjeeling sirdar. After eggs and bacon with them, I returned to the Base Camp as I had not brought up any gear, being ignorant of their plans, and I was rather worried about Rinchen. Meanwhile they were to go on and prospect the approaches to the Pyramid Peak, which was our immediate objective. After that the plan was to attempt the Fluted Peak, the graceful mountain I had seen the night before, and finally to visit the almost unknown district to the north towards the Chorten Nyima La.

SINIOLCHU FROM THE LANGPO-LA

RECONNOITRING THE FLUTED PEAK

CLIMBING THE SPHINX ARETE

When Kilo and I reached the Base Camp at 10 o'clock there was still no sign of Rinchen. I did not think it possible that he could have lost himself, but set off to search, thinking that he must have sprained an ankle in the dark. The four of us started out in different directions, but the other three soon returned saying that a snow man (*mi-go*) had got him and it was no good looking for him. Although this seemed the only possible explanation, I once again climbed my look-out hill, blowing a whistle as I went. I reached the top camp again anxious for their advice, but found they had already moved up to the glacier. By the time I returned to the Base Camp I was extremely worried and tired, but there, thank goodness, was Rinchen. It was difficult to follow his story, but apparently he had gone right over the hill to the south-east and, finding himself alone in the darkness, had lost his head and started wandering in circles. Then, according to the others who took up the story, he had been overcome by fear of encountering a snow man and had wept and started hurling himself about among the stones. He was thus engaged, apparently, when Kilo found him a few miles from the camp; it was a very mysterious tale and I still do not feel that I got to the bottom of it.

By 3 o'clock I was ready to start up to the top camp again, but then it was discovered that Rinchen had left my ice-axe and the rucksack containing the sleeping-bags somewhere up in the hills, he did not know where. This was very serious indeed, as I could not possibly go any further without a sleeping-bag. I went in the direction where Kilo had found Rinchen, and after an hour's search succeeded in finding the rucksack and ice-axe about two miles from the camp; the sleeping-bag had not been used but most of the food had been eaten. By the time I reached the camp again it was 6 p.m. and clouds were low over the hills. I paid off my three porters and was not sorry to see the last of Rinchen Sherpa.

Kilo and I left for the upper camp at 6.30. When we reached the moraine it came on to snow hard and there was no chance of finding the new camp, so we put up in the small tent I had brought with me. As we had relied on reaching the others' camp we had only emergency rations with us and no stove to warm ourselves. It is only when one shares a minute tent with an over-heated Sherpa that one becomes aware of the fact that they do not believe in washing and that garlic forms a considerable part of their

D

diet. Although I had walked the better part of a hundred miles in the last 48 hours I found it very difficult to get any sleep. It snowed all night, but the clouds lifted in the morning though it was still dull. Kilo and I left our tent at dawn and followed the barely discernible trail of Cooke and Harrison, and reached their camp just in time for breakfast. We were now all ready for our attempt at the Pyramid.

# CHAPTER SEVEN

## THE PYRAMID AND THE SPHINX

THE Pyramid is a cone-shaped mountain, 24,000 feet high, on the long ridge that runs from the Talung Peak to the Langpo Peak; this ridge dips down to 20,000 at the Langpo La and rises to an unnamed mountain of 23,500 which we called the Sphinx, and again to the summit of the Pyramid before running southward past the Tent Peak to the great mass of Kangchenjunga. So far as I know, the Pyramid had never previously been attempted by any climbing party.

It was on Sunday, May 31st, that I joined the others at Camp 2 on the Upper Lhonak Glacier in the shadow of the formidable-looking wall of the Langpo La. It snowed steadily all that day and I was glad of the rest and a chance to acclimatize after my recent exertions. We spent a very pleasant day, eating, sleeping, reading and doing a *Times* crossword puzzle. Harrison, being used to the ways of the East, had his cook-sirdar, Mahn Bahadur, extremely well trained. We lay comfortably in our sleeping-bags and, in answer to our shouts, cups of tea and excellent meals appeared as if by magic. Pallis had such a horror of reducing his servants to a state of servility that he erred in the other direction and spoiled them unreasonably.

Four or five inches of new snow fell during the day and avalanches were continually roaring down the semicircle of steep rock and ice slopes which encloses the Upper Lhonak Glacier. Some of these avalanches were near enough to shake our tent, and occasionally there would be rending and explosive noises from the belt of crevasses near our camp. Cooke and Harrison had chosen this site in diffused light, and not until one of them put his foot through a frail bridge was it discovered that they had started to pitch their tent right over a hidden crevasse. The three of us were sleeping in one tent and there was very little room to move, especially as drifts of new snow had piled up against the sides. A thin spray of snow came from the ventilator at the top until we blocked it up with a sock. Mahn Bahadur, Ang Nima, Ang Babu and Phintzu (one of Harrison's Sherpas) were in two smaller tents near by. All night it blew and snowed, and we awoke occasionally to hear the straining of the canvas and the swish and patter of dry snow on the sides of the tent.

Next morning it was still snowing but the wind had dropped completely. The black line of the moraine stood out above a sea of cloud, and the fearsome-looking Tent Peak was, as usual, half-obscured by a snow-storm. In spite of the inauspicious weather we decided to send the cook and Phintzu down to Camp 1, and to push on with Ang Nima, Ang Babu and three or four days' food to try to establish a camp on the summit of the Langpo La. The rock face was so steep that all the new snow had avalanched off it, and by the time we were ready to attempt the arête running up to the Sphinx and Pyramid we hoped that it would also be safe.

One hour's walk took us to the foot of the 1000-foot rock wall leading up to the Langpo La, but it was much steeper than we had anticipated, and after a couple of hours' work we were still unable even to get on to the rock. The holds all seemed to slope outwards, and every ledge was filled with snow or loose gravel. Each of us in turn attempted to force a way up the rock while the others stood shivering below with the new snow running down their necks and soaking through their clothes, listening apprehensively to the roar of small snow avalanches crashing down the couloirs and pouring over the rock faces. Once a rather larger avalanche came down quite near where I was standing and I was knocked flat by the wind of its passing. Until then I had never realized the force of the draught produced by the displacement of air as an avalanche descends.

At last Harrison, with his prodigious reach, managed to find a way up the rock, and we hauled our heavy rucksacks after us on the rope. In spite of a line held by the man at the bottom to keep the rucksacks away from the edges, they were considerably torn and damaged. A crampon hurtled down, narrowly missing one of those waiting below, then a porter's load burst and a thin stream of *tsamba* poured down the rocks, and a cooking-pot leaped the open bergschrund and crashed to the glacier below. The climbing was extremely difficult and the porters continually declared they would not be able to follow.

As the rock seemed to be just as steep above and it was snowing harder than ever, we realized we would have to return to the Base Camp and wait until the weather was more settled. The porters welcomed this decision with enthusiasm and we set about lowering the loads that we had hauled up with so much difficulty. After a weary trudge down the glacier we reached the Base Camp, where the cook and Phintzu were comfortably ensconced, although they had been told to go only as far down as Camp 1, Mahn Bahadur's excuse being that he had come down to buy milk from the yak-herds and to make toffee and that he had had every intention of returning to Camp 1 on the following day. We also found that Kilo was suffering from snow-blindness after his visit to Camp 2 in diffused light. Snow-blindness, which is caused by the inflammation of the minute capillary blood-vessels that serve the eye, is extraordinarily painful; it feels just as if one's eyelids were filled with red-hot sand. Any exposure to light causes additional irritation and watering of the eyes. One is more prone to become snow-blind while straining to see objects in a diffused or hazy light than in bright clear sunshine. The only remedy is to remain in the dark, although the application of cocaine or adrenalin may dull the pain and cause the blood-vessels to contract. The best preventive is to wear snow-glasses, which eliminate the harmful rays.

June 2nd was a pleasant day of rest at the Base Camp. Having drawn lots as to which of the porters should act as butcher, we killed a sheep which Harrison and Sams had led with them from Lachen and had kidney and mutton chops for lunch. This method of ensuring one's supply of fresh mutton, though somewhat painful—for one gets rather attached to such a camp-follower— is strongly to be recommended. In the afternoon it stopped snowing, but there was still an icy wind. I had fired the others with my enthusiasm for natural history and we spent the afternoon collecting flowers and watching birds. Our chief find was a curiously attenuated-looking pink primula with round mealy leaves. It grew only in dark hollows among boulders, and had an exquisite hyacinthine scent. We also visited a yak-herd who had pitched his tent at 17,000 feet, while his yaks and sheep grazed another thousand feet higher, right to the edge of the snow line. I asked him if he had seen any snow men around this way. He admitted he had occasionally seen their tracks, but so far this year he had not encountered any. Lhonak, he said, was one of their favourite haunts.

On the way back to our camp we stalked some marmots who sat up on their hind-legs outside their buries looking like a cross between a kangaroo and a beaver. They are of a light reddish-brown colour, have blunt rodent-like faces and sit up with their front paws in a begging position. They have a shrill bird-like whistle, and whenever they make this noise their paws and bodies twitch like a squirrel's. We saw several Elwes' horned lark, some comic little ground choughs, a willow warbler, a very lovely rosefinch, a spectacular black, white and scarlet redstart (Hodgson's) and several varieties of snow and mountain finches. Most impressive of all was the huge lammergeyer vulture who used to sweep over our camp, his gigantic wings making no visible motion. The sound of the wind in his pinions was like the whine of a bullet. In the evening I pressed the fifty different wild flowers we had collected and then we supped off mutton broth, liver and onion and chips, followed by caramel pudding.

I find that my expedition diaries are very largely filled with descriptions of what we had to eat, but this is inevitable when food plays such an important part in one's day. Not only is one exceedingly hungry—until higher altitudes are reached—but on an expedition meals acquire an almost sacramental significance. A good cook is an essential to a successful expedition. After dinner—it was too good a meal to be called supper—we lit our pipes and had one of our usual abstruse and all-embracing discussions. It is very easy to put the world right when you are lying in your sleeping-bag at 17,000 feet after a good dinner. On this occasion we decided that the teachers of the young were to blame for everything that was wrong, and that if the schoolmasters could reorganize their methods and teach the spirit of Christianity, without such deadly emphasis on the ritual, and could implant an abiding horror of war the world could be changed in ten years.

The next morning we decided to move up to Camp 1, and all set off with small loads, lazing up in the warm sunshine, watching birds and collecting flowers. We spent a delightful hour sitting at lunch beside a small rock-girt lake. In the afternoon it came on to blow and snow again. The next day we were at Camp 2 once more, although a clammy mist came up from the valley and the mountains were still hidden in cloud. All five porters stayed the night at Camp 2, though the cook and Ang Babu complained of headaches.

June 5th was a more successful day, though the weather was still unsettled. The valleys were full of monsoon-like billows of cloud and the Tent Peak struggled with its habitual snow-storm. After waiting an hour for the snow to stop, we left the tents with Ang Nima only, while the other porters returned—with evident delight—to the Base Camp. We took only one tent with us, food for four days and two 70-foot lines. Even so, our loads were uncomfortably heavy when it came to climbing. All night long avalanches had continued to pour down the steep face of the Langpo La, but there had been none since the early morning and we thought the mountain safe enough to justify another attempt.

After the initial steep face, which had troubled us the last time, the angle became easier though the rock was unpleasantly rotten. The snow in the couloirs had been so compressed by the recent passage of avalanches that it afforded good, if steep, going; one or two kicks with the toe of the boot gave an excellent footing. Once when we were spread across a patch of snow we heard the terrifying roar of an avalanche above us. We instinctively pushed our axes in and hung on to them, but it was too late to move. We could hear the ice and rocks crashing down and the evil hiss of the snow and the violent wind that always accompanies an avalanche. Luckily it thundered down the next couloir and with a deafening noise and volumes of white wind-cloud it ran far out across the glacier, perilously near our tent, which we could still see as a black dot on the dazzling whiteness. It came on to snow again and Ang Nima, with his heavier load, found the climbing difficult. His load was attached to his forehead with a scarf as head-strap, and we had to steady it for him as he climbed. We

were all on the same rope, taking it in turn to lead. Cooke or
Harrison usually led up the rock while I went ahead on snow or
ice. The face was exceedingly severe and was only justifiable
in that we could get perfect belays in the hard-packed snow. As
we cut steps up the final ice couloir we were in the track of a
fine stream of snow which poured off the rocks above and to the
left. Sometimes it went down our necks and piled up round our
legs but more often it was whirled into the sky before it reached us,
like a lakeland stream in a strong wind. The ice couloirs led
straight up to the top of the La, but the final pitch became impossibly steep and we were forced out on to some towering
serracs of ice on the right. We managed to cut across tangled
blocks and gaping crevasses at the snout of this hanging glacier
and then found ourselves on a gently sloping shelf which seemed
to lead up diagonally to the La.

We had been climbing vigorously for 8 hours with only a
short halt for sardines, biscuits and chocolate, but so difficult
was the going that we could not have been much more than 800
feet above the camp. The small platform on which we found
ourselves appeared to be poised between two long bergschrunds
which gaped so widely that it seemed as if the whole shelf would
break away and crash down to the glacier beneath. However,
it was the only possible camp-site, for a gale of wind was howling
over the top of the La 200 feet above us, whereas here it was
sheltered. Our shelf was at such an angle that we had to excavate
a platform two feet deep at the back to hold our tent. Using a
'Tommy' cooker we made several lots of tea and divided a tongue
and fruit cake among us. We all felt very fit except for Ang
Nima, who complained of a headache. After a fruitless attempt to
complete our *Times* crossword, we went to sleep, all four of us
packed with difficulty into one small tent, where we had a somewhat disturbed night, as pieces of ice kept breaking away below us
so that our shelf shivered and rumbled.

At 4 o'clock we breakfasted off tea, bath olivers, butter and
marmalade. At that grey hour of the morning it is difficult to
eat anything at all, and getting dressed requires an almost intolerable exertion of body and will-power. The valleys were still
full of a level sea of solid-looking mauve cloud, but the Langpo
Peak was in dazzling sunshine against an Italian-blue sky. Plumes
of snow trailing from the summit warned us that we must expect

trouble on the top of the La. Only the western arête of the Tent Peak was visible, the rest of the mountain being hidden in a banner of cloud. The rounded head of the Sphinx obscured the main summit of the Pyramid. Having struck camp, we set off in high spirits at 6 o'clock, hoping to get on to the La and follow the arête to the top of the Sphinx, camping just this side or beyond the summit in a position from which we could attempt the Pyramid on the following day.

I kicked steps straight up for the ridge 200 feet above us, but was soon forced to the right by a wide bergschrund. This route was easier, although we were being driven away from the Pyramid. The last 50 feet were perilously steep, though the snow was firm; I had to kick steps, dig my ice-axe in above me and then pull myself up on it. This method of progress depended on perfect balance and would have been impossible in a strong wind. As we climbed, we could hear the wind whistling over the La above us, and great pieces of snow and ice were broken off and hurled far out over the glacier. Now we met its full fury, and before I was far enough up to see over the top I had to crouch flat and hang on to my ice-axe to prevent myself from being blown away. Several times Cooke and I were nearly torn from our holds as we flattened ourselves into the snow. A few feet short of the La my nose and cheeks went dead with frostbite, and we realized that life would not be possible there until the wind dropped.

Reluctantly we returned, and sat by our camp-site in boiling sunshine until the snow that was blown over us from the ridge above made us re-pitch our tent for shelter. At midday the wind dropped and we retraced our steps to the summit of the La and made a reconnaissance from there. The Pyramid could be seen from this position, much further away than we had expected. The route up the Sphinx looked fairly straightforward, but it was impossible to get on to this arête from our present position because of a vertical wall of ice which barred our way. The final part of the Pyramid arête seemed to be a knife-edge ridge, but it was not unduly steep. There was a good view over the side of the La on to the Jonsong Glacier, and to the right to the first and second Langpo peaks and to the gently sloping mass of the Jonsong Peak. We returned once more to our camp-site and lunched off tunny fish and biscuits. Ang Nima again complained of a headache. Our food supplies were running short, the wind was increasing again—no wonder we talked of returning. We simply had not the porter-power to lay siege to a peak of such magnitude as the Pyramid. At last we decided to return once more to the couloir up which we had climbed the day before and to try to reach the La on the far side of it, thus short-circuiting the *mauvais-pas* we had seen in our reconnaissance; and then to attempt the Sphinx from there.

Travelling without loads we crossed the couloir and worked our way up 100 feet of steep rotten rock. This led to a final 100 feet of steep snow above ice and then, after tunnelling through a formidable cornice, we were on the La and had found a way to the summit. This took about two hours. We returned to the camp intending to start at dawn on the following day and to push our next camp as far on as possible. We all felt rather headachy, so took two aspirins each and went to sleep. Personally I slept for nine hours with only one short break; in all my clothes and a double eiderdown bag I was as warm as I could wish. The great secret of being comfortable on snow is to make a depression which more or less fits the body.

On June 7th we woke to hear the dismal sound of snow pattering on to the tent and to see the valleys full of cloud. But the sun soon appeared and after a few violent gusts of wind it became calm. Owing to the inevitable slowness of movement at this height, it was 6 o'clock before we had put on our boots, packed up the tent and loaded the rucksacks. To save time we climbed on two ropes, Cooke and I on the first rope, and Harrison and Ang Nima on the second. We carried loads of 15 or 20 lb. each. As we came over the top of the La we were welcomed by one of the most remarkable views I have ever seen : far away to the west, Everest, Lhotse and Makalu appeared over the top of the clouds, like a rim to a flat world, and nearer at hand Longridge, the Jonsong Peak and Langpo hid the highlands of Tibet. On the other side of the La, over the precipitous eastern shoulder of the Langpo Peak, a sea of blue hills, including Chomiomo, Pauhunri and distant Chomolhari, stretched right round the eastern horizon to Siniolchu and across the gap to Simvu. The great oasis of Lhonak showed brown and green among all these snowy peaks and glaciers. The Chanson Glacier terminated not far below us in a line of great pointed ice pinnacles, looking like the sails in a yacht race. We could see our own tiny tent on the Upper Langpo Glacier and the track wandering down to Camp 1. The Podong La and Tent Peak La showed very clearly, the Tent Peak itself looking as formidable as ever with its customary plume of snow. The Nepal Peak, though visible from the La yesterday, could not be seen today. Siniolchu stood up as the ideal of mountain beauty. It appeared from here to be standing alone and we could the better appreciate its exquisite form. From here the ridge running up from the Zemu Glacier showed in high relief, also the Simvu Saddle and the ridge we had failed to get up a month before.

Our arête sloped very steeply down to the west, so we kept almost on the crest of the ridge to avoid the danger of avalanches. Twice Harrison slipped down a crevasse but was held by the rope and easily pulled out. At last we reached a difficult place where there was a break in the ridge and we had to cut steps up the edge of a triangular block of ice which was almost vertical. We all got up this except Ang Nima, who said it was no good, and after falling twice on to the rope, he refused to try again. He explained that three of his Darjeeling friends had been killed on a similar place on Nanga Parbat and that he would never be able to pass it. We decided to return to a camp-site we had passed a few hundred feet lower, to camp, at once, as the wind was increasing again, and to leave Ang Nima behind while we made a final try for the summit on the following day.

We had pemmican for supper, followed by tea and *tsamba*. There was a most uncomfortable crush in the tent and we were all feeling the height. We felt heavy and depressed and without much desire to eat or to do anything else. However, we all slept well, though breathing was difficult. When I woke up in the night I could hear the others breathing heavily several times as if they were just going to dive into deep water, and then later their breathing would cease altogether for some time, as if life had suddenly been suspended, then the gasping would start again.

At 3.30 next morning it was blowing a gale and snow was lashing the tent, but it stopped snowing soon afterwards, and when we staggered out of the tent at 7 it was still bitterly cold and blowing an icy west wind. The view was as wonderful as on the day before, but as we got frostbitten if we lingered to admire it, we hurried on, leaving Ang Nima groaning quietly in the tent. I wore my felt-lined climbing-boots, four pairs of socks, puttees, grey flannel and windproof trousers, a flannel shirt, three sweaters, a ski-jacket, windproof coat, wool helmet, wool and leather gloves, and snow-glasses. I carried my crampons, a scarf, some food—chocolate, biscuits, butter, raisins and sardines—a compass, map and camera.

The awkward gap was passed without difficulty, and after circumventing several more unpleasant corners we reached the summit of the Sphinx (23,500 feet) at 11 o'clock. There was a hollow near the summit where we could have camped had we been able to push on as far the day before. Now there was hardly time to descend to the La between the Sphinx and the Pyramid, to climb the Pyramid and then to return to the camp before nightfall, especially as the last part of the Pyramid arête seemed very difficult. Two of us were in favour of attempting it, but the third thought it was suicidal and his counsel prevailed. He was probably quite right, for we had only half a day's food left and we might well have been held up again by bad weather.

We returned without adventure and reached the camp at 2 o'clock. Ang Nima had come to life and had melted large quantities of drinking water on the flap of the tent in the sun. For this we were most grateful, as we had had nothing to drink for eight hours. We then packed up the tent, finished our last scraps of food and said good-bye to the Sphinx. The descent was difficult for tired men—personally I am always more frightened when descending—but we were back at Camp 2 by 5.30. The others wanted to camp, but I was in favour of going right on down while the weather was fine, and this we eventually did, leaving everything behind us except our sleeping-bags. The snow bridges on the glacier had melted since we were last there, and several times one or other of us fell through on apparently level going, to be pulled out again with the help of the rope. It was quite dark by the time we passed Camp 1 and I, feeling very energetic, ran on to tell Mahn Bahadur to prepare a supper worthy of the occasion.

I was so relieved to be off the mountains again that my weariness had disappeared. Steering a course on Vega, I reached the camp at about 9 o'clock. The others came in some time afterwards, having lost their way. In the camp we found a parcel from Mr. Gould which contained a large cake and some bread and fresh vegetables. We sat round a roaring fire watching a half moon rising over the shoulder of a hill. The cook produced

an enormous supper but we were disappointed to find how little
we could eat. We were too exhausted. But we felt as happy
as it is possible for mortals to feel, even though we had not reached
the top of the Pyramid.

## CHAPTER EIGHT

### THE ASCENT OF THE FLUTED PEAK

AFTER our return from the Sphinx we spent two idyllic days
resting, collecting plants and eating the large and beautifully
cooked meals that Mahn Bahadur prepared. By this time it was
full summer: Swallow-tail, Apollo, tortoise-shell and clouded-
yellow butterflies flew around in the warm sunshine, new birds
arrived and all the flowers were in bloom. My search for new
plants was always fruitful, for the Himalayan flowers are extraordinarily local: a blue iris grows in profusion in one small
valley, but is found nowhere else; a certain primula flourishes
on one stony hillside, but is replaced by another species on the
opposite side of the valley. We found sixteen species of primula
in the vicinity of our camp, from snowy white to the colour of
vintage port. The blue poppies were the most wonderful of all
the plants; the sudden discovery of those translucent blue petals
and rusty green foliage against a background of snow and bare
mountain peaks never ceases to have something miraculous in it.
The azaleas were coming into flower too, not with the lavish
exuberance of their close relations, the rhododendrons, but with a
more restrained and orderly beauty. A bush which was a foot
at the most in height would be covered with white or pale purple
flowers, while higher up the valleys there were varieties with dark,
leathery leaves and a few single cream or plum-coloured waxy
blooms.

On June 11th we set off up the Langpo Chu with three days'
food, intending to climb the Fluted Peak. We took Ang Nima,
Ang Babu and Kilo to carry the loads and look after the camp.
As the Fluted Peak is only 20,000 feet, we did not mean to take
the porters on the climb. From what we had seen of it from the

neighbouring heights, it appeared to be a rock problem, with snow and ice only on the final few hundred feet. This peak cannot have escaped the appreciative eye of Dr. Kellas when he was in this part of the Himalaya in 1910, but there is no record of his having attempted it. In 1933 Osmaston, Stobart and Lattimer tried to climb it but did not reach the summit. We had a delightfully leisurely walk with light rucksacks beside the Langpo Chu, which meandered peacefully at the foot of a valley whose grassy sides were starred with flowers. In the afternoon we camped on some sand beside a small lake at the foot of the glacier, a mile to the south-east of our peak. We had hoped to climb higher, but it came on to snow and there was no visibility. As usual after a rest day, we all felt very lethargic. After tea the snow stopped falling, the clouds rolled back and the sun shone again. We put on gym shoes and went up the rocks to prospect a way on to the rocky ridge which we intended to attempt. The difficulty of getting on to a Himalayan peak is sometimes as severe as the climb itself; however, we found a possible route between two glaciers which flowed down towards our camp. When we reached the shoulder of the hill above our tent, the clouds cleared on the far side of the Fluted Peak, and we saw the glacier falling in a gigantic tangle of jagged seracs to a milky green lake of considerable size. Beyond that the wide brown valley of the Lhonak Chu rose to the Tibetan frontier—a range of high pointed peaks with the Chorten Nyima La (19,036 feet) cutting down in the centre. We could also see Korayedu's two rounded summits and behind us the Langpo Peak and Tent Peak caught the coppery evening sunshine. It is extraordinary how peaks can change their character completely when viewed from different positions or in an unusual light. We would not have recognized the Tent Peak had we not known it by its position.

In the evening it came on to snow again and a cold mist rose from the valley. After supper of pea soup and fried bully beef, we were just going to sleep when there was a noise as of tins being knocked together just outside the tent and the sound of breathing and grunting. One of the others remarked that it was very late for Nima to be washing up and I said I thought it was a snow leopard. In Greenland I was always expecting to see polar bears, and the consequence was that I did see twice as many as anybody else, and in the Himalaya I was continually on the look-out for snow leopards. That night I dreamt that one attacked the tent and I fought it with an ice-axe and eventually drove it away. Next morning, after a breakfast of porridge with plenty of butter and golden syrup in it, we emerged from our tent at 4.30. The dawn was piercing the low clouds and promised a fine warm day, which might give way to snow in the afternoon. A line of large pad-marks showed in the soft sand beside the lake, and the plate we had fried the meat in had been licked clean and carried some distance away from the tent; the pad-marks were 27 inches apart, and each one was 4 inches wide and 5 inches long: there could be no doubt that it was a snow leopard and an exceptionally large one.

With Ang Nima carrying our rucksack up to the rocks we followed a rocky stream between the two glaciers and climbed a fairly easy gully—which we named Snow Leopard Gully—to the ridge. The gully led up past a rather awkward chockstone pitch to a steep scree shoot which joined the ridge at a spot conveniently marked by a pillar of brown rock. Here we roped up. The clouds gradually lifted to give us a wide view over to the Chorten Nyima La. The colouring of the mountain-sides there was reminiscent of Corot's earlier paintings, Avignon Castle for instance. Warm beech and bracken colour contrasted with the deep violet and indigo cloud shadows on the far side of the La. Snow squalls intermittently swept up the Lhonak Valley to the pass, but we had fine weather and only a light wind. It seemed as if the vanguard of the monsoon swept up the Lhonak Valley to be vanquished by the frowning frontier wall of Tibet.

The climbing on the ridge was straightforward, over easy rock which afforded plenty of variety and good belays. Occasional descents were needed to avoid the gendarmes which guarded the ridge. At one point we were held up for half an hour by a difficult place which Cooke tried to avoid by traversing out to the right; but we found ourselves on steep and holdless slabs and were forced to return to the *mauvais-pas* which we turned by following a steep chimney pitch to the left of the ridge. It was on this section of the climb that one of the others knocked out a loose boulder the size of my head; luckily I was looking up at the time and was able to avoid it as it whizzed past to crash once or twice against the mountain before it buried itself in a snowfield below. It was 10 o'clock by this time and we stopped for a hurried lunch of sardines, cheese, biscuits and chocolate, realizing that we would only just have time to get to the summit and return to the camp before dark, especially as it looked more difficult ahead, where the rock gave way to an undulating fluted ridge of snow and ice. We all agreed that so far it was one of the finest rock-climbs we had ever done.

After lunch we had some trouble with the rope. It became soaked from the melting snow which adhered to it and then froze like a wire hawser. The weather was deteriorating; it grew colder and the clouds frequently swept right down over us. We reached a horizontal snow ridge of exceeding sharpness from which as we climbed along we could look down on either side into the open crevasses of the glaciers below, while the snow and ice that we hacked off the ridge started miniature avalanches which rattled over the icy slabs into the gaping bergschrunds. The ridge was so rotten, after the mild sunshine of the morning, that it would not bear us, and the leader had to sit astride it and demolish with his ice-axe the top 2 or 3 feet of rotten snow; only then was it possible to stand upright and to push the ice-axe into the firmer snow and ice beneath.

Once again the time-factor intervened and we held a council of war. Earlier on we had decided that even if it kept fine we ought to turn not later than 2 o'clock if we were to regain our camp before dark, and even this was allowing only half the time for the descent that the ascent had taken. It was now after 2 o'clock and was starting to snow, we were still some distance from the summit, and it looked very much more difficult ahead. As had happened on the Pyramid climb, opinion was strongly divided and it was left to me to give the casting vote. I thought we could reasonably risk going on; we could descend the ridge at good speed, abseil down the difficult pitches and if necessary do the easier final part of the climb in darkness.

Cooke continued to excavate a route along the snow arête, leaving the debris to rattle down on either side of the ridge. Soon the mist swirled over us and his work of demolition was hidden from us, though the result of his toil continued to pour past us to be swallowed up again in the mist. When Cooke emerged we found that he had made a twelve-foot tunnel to avoid climbing over a awkward overhanging bridge of rotten ice and snow. After crawling through this we came to an unpleasant place where the angle of the ridge became vertical, and after cutting away the looser surface snow and ice, Cooke had to cut both foot- and hand-holds for a perilous ten feet. A final fifty feet of steep but not unduly difficult snow and ice brought us at last to the blunt, mist-shrouded summit. It was then 3.30; it had taken us 10½ hours to get up, and in 3 hours it would be dark. It was now snowing steadily. I was last man on the rope and I joined the others for one moment in the mist on the sharp spade-shaped summit ridge and then turned to descend. Cooke lowered the two of us bodily over the vertical pitch and, once he had climbed down himself, we all moved together, concentrating in silence on all the small details that go to make a rapid descent safe—to lean out on steep slopes so that the steps do not crumble, to keep the rope out of the way of the other climbers, to hold one's ice-axe in such a position that in any moment of emergency one can stop oneself or hastily throw a loop over the axe and hold the others, not with a jerk which would pull the axe out or break the line, but with a gradual tightening like the action of a spring.

Soon the clouds thinned around us and we caught a glimpse of the ridge below and then of the scree slope beyond the ridge. This vision is firmly imprinted on my mind, for at the same moment a disaster very nearly occurred: on one of the more difficult rock faces I was traversing across to get off the rock on to the snow, where descent was safe and more rapid, and was edging past an enormous flake of rock a yard wide, when it suddenly came away and crashed downwards. I was just able to jump to one side, catch hold of another rock and pull myself on to it until I found footholds. Meanwhile the flake rebounded over the rocks below and an acrid gunpowdery smell reached our nostrils. When we left the rock for the snow, we unroped to make progress faster, coiled the rope with difficulty—it had frozen stiff—and ran down the scree into the gully, yodelling to attract the porters' attention. Soon Ang Nima appeared to take the rope and rucksack, and by 6.30, just as darkness fell, we were in the camp, feeling so deliriously happy that our weariness was forgotten. That night we slept for ten hours and if the snow-leopard visited us again we were not aware of it.

Next morning the clouds were over the Fluted Peak as we sent the porters back along the route by the Langpo Chu, while we cut over the hill making a direct line for the Base Camp. It was wonderful to dawdle along watching the birds and looking for new plants. We heard the distinctive bubbling call of the snow-cock and then saw a pair of these streaked greyish birds running like partridges over the rocks. Coming suddenly over the edge of a little coombe we surprised a flock of seventeen burrhal grazing peacefully on the velvety grass a hundred feet below us. The wind was from their direction and as they had not seen us we were able to lie and watch them for half an hour. There were two rams with ponderous curling horns and several sheep, some of which were only half-grown. When we were tired of watching them we stood up and in a moment they were away out of the coombe. Soon their curiosity overcame their initial panic and they stopped, facing us, while one or two even came a few steps towards us, then they turned and disappeared over the sky-line in single file. We saw several marmots on this unfrequented hillside, at one place surprising four outside the same bury. They loped awkwardly across to their holes, like aged over-fed dogs trying to hurry, when they were disturbed.

We were back in the Base Camp in time for lunch of mutton patties and tinned pears; then we lay in the sun and after some discussion decided that our next move would be up to the Tibetan frontier to attempt the two peaks of Korayedu (West Peak, 21,700 feet; East Peak, 21,100 feet), and after that I would race back to join Mr. Gould at Gangtok, while the rest of the party returned in a more leisurely manner. I spent the afternoon pressing plants while the others sorted and packed stores. After an excellent supper of soup, roast chicken (tinned) and chips, semolina and stewed fruit, we sat smoking our pipes outside and looking at the bright stars. We sat in silence as no words could express the great content we all felt.

On Sunday, June 14th, we left our Base Camp for good and started to follow the Lhonak Chu in the direction of the Chorten Nyima La. I cut over the hills to the west as I wanted to photograph the Fluted Peak from the north and to look at some lakes I had seen from its ridge. There were duck on one of these lakes and I was anxious to find out what species it was that lived at 17,500 feet. I crossed an open dried-up plain where several marmots lived, surprised another big flock of burrhal and watched a pair of white-capped redstart feeding their young in a nest among the scree that ran down to a shallow lake. Here I had a swim and was surprised to find how warm it was. The second lake appeared to be very deep and was milky green from the glacier which fed it. There were three tufted duck on this lake, but though I was sure they were nesting, I was unable to find their eggs. After this I hurried over to the junction of the Lhonak Chu and Sayok Chu, where I had agreed to meet the others. I tried, after watching a dipper and a pair of white wagtails, to cross the river alone but was very nearly swept off my feet and was glad when Ang Nima emerged from a large yak-herd's tent which I had seen on the far side and helped me across. If two or more people hold hands and support each other, moving one at a time, rivers can be crossed which would be quite impossible alone.

As it was now raining, we all went into the tent, from which a huge brown Tibetan mastiff escaped into the hills with bristling mane and bared teeth; another dog, which was chained up near the tent, barked steadily the whole hour that we were there. Inside we found a wild-looking but friendly yak-herd with a face burnt almost as black as his coarse home-spun clothes; I don't think he or his wife or small son had washed since they were born. The tent, which was supported on two wooden poles, was made of woven yak-hair with a space between the poles for the smoke of the yak-dung fire to escape. A considerable amount of light percolated through the coarse weave of the cloth, and a fine spray fell inside as the rain splashed against it. Tea was boiled up for us over a metal brazier pierced with holes. It tasted curiously like the silver pellets on Christmas cake, but was none the less acceptable. As it was raining harder than ever, and the mountains were all blotted out, we camped soon after we had passed the yak-herd's tent. It seemed that the great wall of mountains between Sikkim and Tibet stopped the monsoon clouds and caused the frequent rain squalls which we had noticed sweeping across when we were climbing further south. We wore our hooded oilskin capes, but they only reached to our knees and from there downward we were soaking wet.

At this time we were making for the Sayok La (18,000 feet), but as we had not yet seen it or the Korayedu peaks, we were seriously considering returning to Lachen by the Lungnak La (17,500 feet) and Tangu route. However, early next morning, Korayedu cleared, and we saw that just above our camp was a great rock wall with several hanging glaciers and ice-falls above a line of scree slopes. The Sayok La showed as a snowy gap further west than we had expected. A difficult and unpleasant climb across steep rock and snowfields into which we sank eighteen inches, led over an avalanche-swept couloir to the La. The clouds were coming down again and it was starting to rain; it seemed that a spell of monsoon weather had set in, which would account for the fact that we were all feeling very slack and weary. We agreed that we would have lunch on the far side of the La, and if Korayedu did not show herself we would cross the Sayok La and return by Tangu, sending the porters back to collect our Base Camp supplies and bring them across to meet us.

The Sayok La proved to be a strange wind-swept gap almost surrounded by ice and snow cornices. Korayedu became more and more hidden in clouds and the glimpse we had caught of two steep hanging glaciers with an inaccessible rock buttress between them had not been very reassuring. When we looked over the far side of the La into a smiling valley where a stream meandered among meadows where yaks were grazing, our minds were made up and we set off towards a yak-herd's tent which we could just make out in the distance. From the map we could see that this stream, the Sayok Chu, soon met the Lhonak Chu, down which the porters could bring the rest of our gear to meet us at the junction. At this stage a further difficulty appeared in that we could not find any way off the steep glacier which led down from the Sayok La towards our Elysian valley. Three places were tried but each one ended in a vertical ice-wall; at last we had to climb almost to the La again and get off the glacier at the top.

We were still reluctant to give up our attempt at Korayedu in spite of the spell of monsoon weather that seemed to be affecting the heights; and judging by the number of avalanches which, loosened by the warm weather, could be heard crashing down through the mists, it would be several days before the mountains would be safe. We sat down to lunch on the moraine to the east of the Sayok La, having made up our minds that if Korayedu did not clear before we had finished our sardines and chocolate we would at once set off down the valley whose sunlit meadows still tempted us. It did not clear; indeed the mist and cloud descended to the La itself, and soon we put on our rucksacks and turned our backs for good on the high mountains. Our climbing season was over; here was an end of sweating up terrifying rock-ridges, of cutting steps across vertiginous ice-falls, of disappointments, mountain sickness, frostbite and snowburn; now we could wander down the happy valleys, seeing new birds and finding new flowers.

The valley that we were descending was shut in on three sides by formidable peaks whose glaciers could be seen as they emerged from the mist. We soon found a warm lake, where we bathed, the water being about blood-heat in the shallower parts. On its shores we found a new red pendicularis, a pinkish cress, and masses of yellow spearwort and marsh-marigold. The hillsides round about were carpeted with azaleas, a foot or so in height, of a heather-purple colour. As the valley gradually widened and flattened, the wild life became more abundant; a pair of cinnamon-coloured ruddy sheld-duck (or Brahminy duck) rose from a reedy pool and flew round with deep grunting notes; some redshank appeared, giving their familiar alarm note; a dipper shot upstream and two rose-finches sat on a flowering shrub with pink lilac-scented blooms. Harrison found a willow-warbler's nest in a juniper bush. Beside the stream, in the middle of the valley, we saw a curious construction which looked like a grave, measuring about 6 feet by 2, and built of large flat stones. Inside it were many bones. We were puzzling over it when two huge Tibetan mastiffs rushed with a fearful barking from a tent on the hillside, closely pursued by an uncouth-looking yak-herd who was trying to silence them by slinging stones from a yak-hair sling and shouting wild cries. He was an exceptionally ugly man with filthy hair and a much-lined toothless face, but he was most friendly and told us that the stone square was a trap for snow leopards. He accompanied us as far as two very large tents and a stone pen for sheep, of which there were two large flocks on the hillside above. He had the curious Tibetan habit of protruding his tongue as a mark of respect whenever he was spoken to.

Soon after this we reached the junction of our stream with the Lhonak Chu and put up our tents on a level grassy meadow. There were masses of white butterwort in a marshy place beside the stream and a most interesting wader, the ibis bill, which none of us had ever seen before. This bird had a long curved beak and flew round screaming incessantly. We were all feeling the reaction of coming down from the heights and were soon asleep after a large supper of soup, tinned herrings and peaches.

At dawn next morning the porters went up the Lhonak Chu to collect the personnel and gear from our Base Camp while we enjoyed a rest day in a delightful valley. The stream glittered in the morning sunshine, and all the level floor of the valley was carpeted with dwarf azalea bushes rarely more than eighteen inches high, the flowers pure white, a lovely carnation pink, and heather-purple. These fields of delicate-coloured small mountain azaleas which run up to the edge of the snow-line are much more beautiful —to my mind—than the almost overpoweringly exuberant giant scarlet and magenta rhododendrons of the lower valleys.

In the middle of the day our porters returned, accompanied by the Lachen postman, who had reached the Base Camp the day before. He had come by Tangu and the Lungnak La, as the Tsetang route was impassable owing to the bridges having been swept away by the monsoon floods. As well as welcome letters from home he had three dozen eggs and some potatoes for us. He also had news of the Everest expedition : they had established Camp 6, and two climbers were ready there to make a bid for the summit. In the afternoon I left the others and followed the Lhonak Chu to a gorge where the path was forced away from the river and cut across a bare hillside. In this sheltered gorge whose sides were great rock cliffs, hundreds of feet high, I found quite large bushes growing and several new flowers. There were tall white anemones and honesty, pink thistles, yellow jasmine, red tamarisk and suddenly a whole mass of enormous blue poppies with hairy stalks and yellow-green leaves : some the clearest azure, others pinkish-red or cloudy-blue. This gorge was a remarkable place altogether, very unlike anything I had yet seen in the district.

Next morning, June 17th, we rose at dawn—about 4 o'clock— and saw the great snow peaks at the head of the valley in the thin early morning sunshine, though cloud still surrounded their bases. Skylarks were singing and a white-capped redstart with resplendent red and black plumage whistled energetically on a rock. After a bathe in the deep pool where the two streams met, we breakfasted in the sunshine and then struck camp. Having enlisted the Lachen postman as a willing porter, the loads were less heavy, though with all the bedding and tents and empty boxes (the porters' perquisites) they looked enormous. With the postman as guide, we hoped to cross the Lungnak La to Tangu and to reach Lachen on the following day; there we would part company and I would go head to Gangtok, where Mr. Gould would now be expecting me.

Our route led us away from the Lhonak Chu on to a vast honey-coloured open plain where many yaks, sheep and goats were grazing. The sheep had curious curved noses—like flamingoes' beaks—and were mainly piebald black and white. The goats had long curly hair and odd twisted horns like algebraic brackets. Our path led us up a side valley past some ruined stone buildings, possibly forts, now overgrown with flowering currant bushes and stinging-nettles, and over an easy grassy pass into another valley with a large stream flowing from the north. Here we found a settlement of four tents beside a ford. A good-looking woman was washing wool in the stream in a bamboo basket; her hair was arranged round a semicircular framework a yard in diameter, the front of which was studded with coral and turquoise. As we passed, everyone rushed out of the tents to gaze at the unusual visitors and to hold the fierce dogs which strained to get at us.

Here we left the main valley and turned right-handed towards the Lungnak La, which lay to the east, up a steep valley beside an old moraine. Some women were picking the bloom off the small white azalea bushes (for tea, perhaps) and singing a loud harsh song with a catch in it, almost like a yodel. We soon found ourselves in a deep valley shut in by great precipices. The rocky slopes between the foot of the crags and the mountain torrent were overgrown with flowering shrubs and plants. Two miles ahead of us the gorge seemed to be completely enclosed by a rock wall down which snow avalanches intermittently poured from the snowfields above, which were now hidden in cloud. Turning a corner, we came upon a beautiful lake which had so far been hidden by a rocky spur. It was of a jade-green colour with silver ripples, and was surrounded by banks of golden sand. At the far end some yaks stood dewlap-deep, like Highland cattle in a conventional picture.

Passing the lake, we climbed laboriously up a steep scree slope, following a path which was well-defined except when it disappeared beneath the snow. The porters were moving very slowly now, finding some difficulty in balancing their cumbersome loads on the steep going; one or two of them walked barefoot all day in spite of the snow we had to cross. We were now in the mist and, having reached the top of the horseshoe cliffs which surrounded the valley, we were surprised when the Lachen postman, who was acting as our guide, led us across to the left over a stony plateau and up another horseshoe valley whose existence we had not hitherto suspected. Much snow obscured the zigzag path and the porters had to negotiate some very difficult places. At the summit (17,500 feet), which was covered with new snow, we found several large cairns. In spite of the mist there were some Hodgson's Grandula and choughs flying about, but no vegetation of any sort appeared.

The descent was very steep and unpleasant for the laden porters, but soon we found hanging gardens on ledges among the crags, and after an hour we were among rhododendrons again. Harrison found a large mauve fritillary, and I found several minute and very beautiful new primulas. There were also masses of deep-violet *primula Royalei* and blue poppy. By now it was snowing again, and dark was falling, and as the porters were getting slower and slower, we decided to stop as soon as we found any firewood, though we knew that Tangu could not be more than two or three miles ahead. At 6 P.M. we camped on a grassy patch surrounded by pink and saffron-coloured rhododendrons whose foliage was coated with fresh snow.

Although the tent leaked all night we slept well, and awoke next morning to find ourselves on a hillside overlooking a steep and much-wooded valley leading to Tangu, which we reached in a few hours. On the way we found a beautiful white clematis, the four-petalled Sikkim rose and a multi-flowered yellow poppy, like a hollyhock, standing six feet high. More and more new varieties of flowers appeared and then birch trees and cedars as we reached the Tangu–Lachen road in the bottom of the valley. In some places beside the track we found whole fields of primulas in bloom, one primrose colour with an orange centre, another the *primula sikkimensis* that flourishes in English gardens, with hanging cowslip-like flowers, and others mauve or purple.

At Yatung we found a smallish village and saw some men demolishing the mud walls of the best house in the place with picks. Our friend the young headman of Lachen appeared and told us that it was his house and that it was being rebuilt, a porcess which Tibetan houses go though every fifty years or so. He told us that nearly all the inhabitants of Lachen came up to Yatung at this time of the year to avoid the monsoon rains, but promised to send five porters to Lachen the next day to help us down to Gangtok with all our gear.

It rained all day and we found the dank trees and dripping undergrowth most oppressive after the open hills and clean fresh air blowing from the high snows.   Here, instead of the blue poppy and creeping rock plants, we found the multi-flowered Sikkim lily ten feet high, lush purple orchids, and trees with heavy perfume and exotic blooms.   In place of the chough and skylark were noisy babblers and brightly coloured sunbirds.   We reached Lachen in the early evening, but it was four hours before the weary porters arrived.   In spite of the joys of hot baths and a farewell supper we all felt very depressed.   We had had wonderful experiences together, and it was sad to have to part.

Next morning I got up at 2 o'clock, determined to reach Gangtok in a single day.   The last two marches had been heavy ones, and the fifty miles from Lachen to Gangtok, with its winding cobbled track and continual losing and gaining of height, is quite the longest fifty miles I know, especially with the feeling of lassi-tude that attacks one on descending to the fetid jungle from the hills, but for some unaccountable reason I was quite determined that unless I was unable to put one foot in front of the other I would get to Gangtok that night.

I left Lachen at 2.30 A.M. armed with a torch, as it was still dark. When I was a mile or two out from the village I thought I heard something or somebody following me.   Each time I stopped the sound of feet behind me stopped too, but at times I could hear breathing, and once a stick broke with a loud crack.   I did not think it could be a man, and imagined it was an animal—a bear of some kind, or a langur monkey.   Growing rather frightened, I increased my speed, but I could still hear it coming along the track behind me.   Then I started to run, and with the feeling that it was gaining on me, ran faster and faster.   I flashed the light behind me occasionally but could see nothing at all, though I could distinctly hear the padding of feet and loud breathing. Becoming more and more panicky, I ran as fast as I could, flashing the light behind me as I ran and shouting to frighten the beast away.   However, this led to disaster, for when I reached one of the sharp corners of the track I was unable to take it and fell headlong over the banked-up edge of the path and crashed into the bushes below. I landed unhurt, but lost my torch and made a tremendous noise. All at once the situation struck me as funny and I started to laugh, quietly at first, and then more and more loudly. Afraid of leeches, I did not stop to search for the torch, but hurried back to the track, feeling—for some unaccountable reason—quite certain that the animal would have fled. This proved to be so, if indeed there had been anything there are all, and although I could not help looking back occasionally, I heard it no more. I discovered afterwards that bears and langurs do follow people, but more out of curiosity than for any sinister motive.

Once as I came over the top of a rise, treading silently in my gym shoes, I saw a very beautiful wild cat lying sunning itself in the middle of the track. It was of deep orange or flame colour. I stood still for a moment watching it until suddenly, sensing danger, it disappeared without a sound into the jungle. A thing that troubled me very much was that the soles of my gym shoes came unstuck and flapped beneath my feet as I walked. I was able to attach them with the laces, but stones and dirt kept on getting inside so that my feet were badly blistered. The long pull up from Dikchu to the top of the Penlong La was the worst part of the walk. It was pouring with tropical rain by that time and being soaked to the skin certainly gave some variety to the interminable journey. I was so exhausted that I used to climb for a hundred paces and then sit and rest and sometimes even fall asleep. At last I reached the summit some time after dark, and was able to run down the far side to reach the Residency, very weary and dishevelled, soon after 8 o'clock.

# CHAPTER NINE

## CHOMOLHARI : PREPARATIONS

ON the last day of July 1936, the British Diplomatic Mission left Gangtok for Lhasa. At the end of February 1937, we returned, having spent just over six months in the Holy City itself.

I have written my impressions of Lhasa and of the journey through Tibet in another book.[1]

We did not go beyond Lhasa, as at one time seemed possible, because neither the Lhasa Government nor the Tashi Lama directly invited our mediation. There seemed to be a state of stalemate. The Tashi Lama refused to return to Tibet without his Chinese escort, and the Lhasa Government, though they conceded as much as they possibly could, still resolutely refused to allow the escort into the country. The fact that the Tashi Lama's 'luggage in advance', sent ahead from Jyekundo, was found to contain several camel loads of bombs did little to convince the Tibetans of His Serenity's good faith; though it was realized in Lhasa that the uncompromising attitude of the Tashi Lama was due either to the machinations of self-interested officials in his retinue, who would probably lose everything if they returned to Tibet, or to the fact that His Serenity was so indebted to his hosts that he was virtually a prisoner of the Chinese.

In the beginning of December 1937 news reached England that the Tashi Lama had died at Jyekundo, and so far his successor has not been discovered. Only recently, July 1939, has the reincarnation of the Dalai Lama been discovered by the customary process of magic and divination. While we were at Lhasa, power was in the hands of the Regent and the Prime Minister, both very young men who were still uncertain of themselves and their followers, and the Kashag, or Cabinet of four ministers, one of whom was a representative of the all-powerful priesthood. There was also a body called the National Assembly which voiced the opinions of the three great monasteries, Drepung, Sera and Ganden, known as the Three Pillars of the State, which, between them, hold close on 20,000 monks. A powerful voice in this more democratic body was Tsarong Shapé, a retired general and Cabinet Minister who was very pro-British in outlook and represented a more progressive party—if one can talk of progress in connection with such a country as Tibet. I saw a great deal of all these officials in Lhasa and became very friendly with some of them. We attended official banquets, which often lasted for four or five hours, and in return we invited our hosts with their wives and families to dinner-parties, and gave cinematograph entertainments

[1] *Lhasa : The Holy City.*  Chatto and Windus.

which included ancient Charlie Chaplin comedies and colour films of themselves and the local scenery.

On our way to and from Lhasa we had spent the night at the squalid mud-walled village of Phari at an altitude of 14,300 feet on the most bleak and wind-swept part of the great Tibetan plateau. Like every European who has stopped there, I was tremendously impressed by the remarkable peak of Chomolhari (24,000 feet), which lies only a few miles from the top of the Tang La, the pass leading northward from Phari. This peak, which rises 10,000 feet sheer from the dusty Tibetan plain, gives a greater impression of sheer height and inaccessibility than any other I know; it drops in a series of almost vertical rock precipices to the low foothills beneath. To the east, a steep col connects it to Kakapu (22,300 feet) and Takapu (21,429 feet), and to a long ridge of completely unexplored snow-covered peaks which run for 100 miles in a north-easterly direction to terminate in Ning-dzing-zong-ka (23,794 feet), just beside the Karo La (16,200 feet) between Gyantse and Lhasa. To the south a long snow and ice-ridge runs steeply down to lose itself in the unexplored mountains of northern Bhutan. It is thought by many to be the most beautiful mountain in the whole length of the Himalaya on the north and west; that is, on the sides overlooking the plain of Tuna and the Tang La, respectively.

While I was at Phari I went as near to Chomolhari as was possible in the time available and I concluded that the long southern ridge might be climbed if once one could get on it. No adequate maps were available, but certainly it would involve an approach from the Bhutan side, which meant that permission from both Tibet and Bhutan would be necessary, and as Chomolhari, which means literally the Goddess of the Holy Mountain, is even more sacred to the Tibetans than Everest, it was unlikely that such permission would be given. I do not think anyone had previously attempted to climb it, though any mountaineer crossing the Tang La, particularly the members of the three Everest expeditions that have passed this way, must have been attracted by the southern arête. Odell, I know, made a reconnaissance of the mountain in 1924. But, on the way to Everest, climbers would be too conscious of the necessity of husbanding their strength, and on the return journey they probably had not the energy to spare, though I think it was the problem of getting permission to climb which kept Chomolhari for so long inviolate. It seemed to me that I was in a strong position so far as the Tibetan permission was concerned. I knew all the Lhasa officials personally, and my friend Hugh Richardson, the British Trade Agent at Gyantse, was still in the Holy City and would, I knew, do all he could to help me. Bhutanese permission was a more difficult problem; however, I had heard much of the enlightened views of the young Maharajah who ruled at Punakha, and certainly Rajah Tobgay Dorje, the English-speaking Bhutanese resident at Kalimpong, would help me in every possible way as long as he did not think the interests of his country were prejudiced.

It was not until the middle of April that the plans which controlled the date of my return to England were sufficiently settled for me to decide to attempt Chomolhari, and by then it was almost too late to do it with any probability of success. The monsoon would break at the end of May or early June, and at such short notice it would be very difficult to collect a party. However, on April 18th I broached the question to the Political Officer at Gangtok. At first he was rather reluctant to trouble the Lhasa authorities with such a minor matter, which might mean a great deal to them. We had realized when we were in Lhasa how sincere and deep are their religious objections to any violation of their holy places; it was only with the greatest difficulty that we had obtained permission for the 1937 Everest expedition, and Mr. Gould did not want to upset them at a time when they had many important political problems to deal with. As a preliminary, he said I might go over to Kalimpong and see if Rajah Tobgay could give me permission himself, and, if not, what prospects there were of the Maharajah of Bhutan allowing me to go.

I went to Kalimpong next day and met Rajah Tobgay and told him my plans. He was very sympathetic, but said that he could not give me permission himself though he was almost sure the Maharajah would have no objection. He agreed to dispatch a runner up to Punakha the next day, but it would be at least a fortnight before he could return. I then asked Rai Bahardur Norbhu, who had been our interpreter during the Lhasa Mission and knew all the intricacies of Tibetan mentality, whether he thought the Lhasa authorities would grant the desired permission. He said that it would certainly be necessary to get the sanction of the Cabinet, even though I would approach through Bhutan, as Chomolhari is the most holy mountain in Tibet and in so far as Buddhist opinion was concerned no political frontiers could make it anything but wholly Tibetan. So anxious are the Tibetans to propitiate the goddess of the holy mountain that several religious processions go up each year to the foothills, and there are important monasteries on its lower slopes. Indeed, he thought it was quite possible that the Tibetans might refuse permission altogether, even to someone who was well known to them.

As soon as I returned to Gangtok, the P.O. sent a telegram to Richardson at Lhasa asking him to try to secure permission unless he thought it was not diplomatically advisable. Richardson replied after a few days that he thought permission might eventually be given but that he must await an auspicious moment before approaching the Regent or Cabinet. At this stage it seemed so improbable that the expedition would materialize that I very nearly lost heart and returned at once to England in time to start teaching again at the beginning of the summer term. On May 1st I went over to Kalimpong to stay with Mr. and Mrs. Odling and to make as many preparations as I could in the absence of permission either from Lhasa or Bhutan.

I had met a young man called Charles Crawford who was working for Imperial Chemicals in Calcutta, and I wrote asking him if he would be able to join me. At first he thought it would be quite impossible for him to come; a few days later, however, he wrote that he might be able to get leave on condition he was back in time to go up to Lahore before the end of the month. In answer to that I optimistically replied that a fortnight in all would be enough if we were not held up at all by bad weather or unexpected difficulties. Crawford had no Himalayan experience; indeed, except for some scrambling in Skye and in the Pyrenees, he had done no climbing whatsoever. On the other hand he was a person I liked very much indeed, and though he had been in Calcutta for some time he was young, and had kept himself very fit by playing hockey and other games. I thought that three was the ideal number, and I wanted to get somebody who had had more experience of Himalayan work than I had. As there was no one else available in Calcutta I wired to the local secretaries of the Himalaya Club at Simla and Darjeeling, and to R. L. Holdsworth, then headmaster of Islamia College, Peshawar;

we had made a winter ascent of Pitz Kesch together in 1930 (see page 24) and he had been with Smythe on Kamet in 1930. I also wired to J. A. K. Martyn, a master at the new Indian Public School at Dehra Dun. Then I rang up George Wood Johnson on his tea garden near Darjeeling. All these wished me luck but regretted that they could not get away.

The time was getting short: in view of Crawford's return to Calcutta before the end of the month, and the impending monsoon, it was essential that we should start in the first week in May. But still there was no word from Lhasa or Bhutan. I sent another wire to Richardson and he replied that all was going well, but that the Cabinet would not be hurried. Then I persuaded the P.O. to allow us to start. We could go up the Lhasa Trade Route and wait at Gnatong, just this side of the frontier, where there was a post office, until permission came through.

We were also short of equipment. I had my own high-climbing clothes left over from the previous year's climbing, but I had no tents of any description and no clothes or boots for the porters. So I telegraphed to Crawford telling him what equipment I was short of, and asking him to procure tents, ropes, stoves, crampons and high-climbing gear and ice-axes for himself and three porters. Most of this could be borrowed from the Himalayan Club's supply at Calcutta. Then I hired a small car and ran over to Darjeeling to choose the porters. By this time it was May 4th. I had previously written to Mr. Kidd at Darjeeling, the local secretary of the Himalayan Club, asking him to have three Sherpas ready in the event of my being able to secure permission. I told him that, if possible, I wanted experienced men who would be able to do their share of step-cutting and who would know something about route finding.

Mr. Kidd had picked out several. Of these I chose three. Nima Tendrip, the " old soldier " who was familiar to me from Frank Smythe's books: a man now well over forty, a quiet, thick-set, genial-looking man with a wonderful record. He had been up Kamet with Smythe and on two Kanchenjunga and three Everest expeditions. He, if anybody, would be able to give advice when necessary. Then I chose Kikuli, a young man who had been on the 1934 German expedition to Nanga Parbat, and whose record showed him to be a competent ice-climber. Then there was Pasang, a very young and rather dour-looking porter who was obviously so keen to come that I had not the heart to refuse him, especially as the three were friends and anxious to work together. I hoped that Nima, who was supposed to be a tiger for carrying weights, would come a certain way up the mountain and help me to choose the route and I expected that Kikuli would go highest; Pasang, I regarded as the weakest of the three. Just as I had made the final arrangements about wages and the porters had signed the agreement with a thumb-print, who should turn up but old Ang Nima, with whom I had climbed on the Zemu Glacier and in Lhonak the year before. He was terribly disappointed not to be included in the party, but I knew from experience that he failed to acclimatize and suffered badly at altitudes over 20,000 feet, though he was an excellent fellow and a very hard worker. I arranged for the porters to meet us at Gangtok in two days' time, insisting that they should go by Namchi to avoid the malarial Teesta Valley.

Crawford could not get away from Calcutta until the evening of May 5th, as he had to spend a whole day there running about procuring all the odd things I had put down on my list. It was difficult for him getting boots and windproofs for three porters whose size he had no idea of; as it turned out, they already had most of the necessaries from their previous expeditions, but I could not rely on this.

We spent most of May 6th sorting our gear on the lawn of the Odlings' house at Kalimpong. These kind people had put their house at our disposal and gave us all possible encouragement and assistance. It was an odd assortment of equipment. We had one big marquee of a tent, without a ground-sheet, which weighed over 30 lb.; it would do as a base-camp tent or for the extra porters we would have to take on from Phari. Then there were two excellent Mummery tents with ground-sheets sewn in, 7 feet by 5 and 5 feet high, and a tiny bivouac tent which relied on ice-axes for poles. Crawford said there was another of these available in Calcutta, so I wired for it to be sent on to Phari. The crampons were all enormous but we took them. Then we went down to Kalimpong store and ordered our provisions. We could get all we wanted there except pemmican and meta fuel, but luckily Crawford had been able to get enough of these in Calcutta. When we had packed up everything there was nothing more we could do except to work out the expedition's accounts, fortunately a very simple matter, for the actual cost of the expedition was phenomenally low. This was due to the simplicity of our methods and because the equipment was either left over from Pallis' expedition or borrowed from the Himalayan Club. Including the porters' wages and unlimited cigarettes for them, food, transport, photography, bungalow expenses and what little equipment we had to buy, the expedition cost Crawford and me only £19 : 12 : 6 each. I have great satisfaction in the thought that we reached a height of 24,000 feet at a cost of under £20 each, while the Everest expedition which was being carried on at the same time was unable to get higher than 23,000 feet in spite of the expenditure of several thousand pounds. I remember I wrote to Jack Longland that night telling him of our optimistic project : it was with him that I had done my first serious climb— the Meije.

We had a hilarious farewell dinner that night, and Mr. Odling produced an enormous pressure cooker like a diving helmet with a steering wheel and various valves attached; apparently Eric Shipton had left it there a year ago and was reported to have said that he would rather be without his sleeping-bag than a pressure cooker in the Himalayas. However, the thing was prodigiously heavy and we felt it was hardly in keeping with our modestly equipped expedition. Such an apparatus is useful, owing to the fact that at an altitude of over 25,000 feet water boils at about 70° F., so one's food does not cook and indigestion results; but this cooker would have needed a special porter to itself, so we had to leave it behind.

On May 7th we got up at 4 o'clock and after a hurried breakfast packed everything into the car and got away at 6. Crawford was sick most of the way to Gangtok, only recovering when we started the final climb. There was an unusual number of bullock carts on the road, and as it is impossible to pass them except in certain places the journey took us some time. The last part of the journey exerted its usual fascination, and our spirits rose as we climbed higher. Everywhere there were bright colours. The rice in the steeply terraced paddy-fields was of a quick green just ready for planting out. Vivid birds flew across the road, gay butterflies hovered over patches of moisture. The weather was fine, though the snows were invisible and clouds hung low over the Natu La.

As time was so short we had decided to drive to Gangtok and to use the Natu La route rather than the longer Jelep La, although the telegraph line follows the latter pass. When we reached Changu we planned to cross over to Gnatong, where we would await the long-delayed permission. We reached the Residency at 10 o'clock and had much to do before we could get away. All the loads had to be made up both for porters and baggage animals. We found we had to take four mules and an extra one for fodder. There was a detention allowance to pay, as the animals had been ordered for the day before, and Pasang had a black eye from some scrap in the bazaar. We did not make the porters carry much more than their own possessions as we wanted to save them for more energetic work beyond Phari. The mules and porters were off by 2 P.M. but it was two hours later before we were ready to start. Mr. Gould was away, but he gave us the run of the Residency and told us we could take anything we could persuade the cook to let us have. Here we did fairly well; he produced a 15-lb. bag of pulled bread (an ideal farinaceous food for climbing which is made by half-baking dough and then pulling it into fragments and finishing it off in the oven. It is very easy and light to carry and does not get stale; the only objection is that it is rather hard). We also got a cooked shoulder of mutton, two cakes, and some vegetables.

We wore shorts and climbing-boots, and carried our ice-axes, as they are so awkward to pack. We had one rucksack of about 30 lb. between us, to accustom ourselves to loads, as we expected to carry heavy ones in the mountains. It rained hard as we climbed the steep cobbled track behind the Residency on our way to Karponang, the first dak bungalow, a distance of ten miles. On the way we saw an exquisite rainbow with a paler reflection beneath. As a rule one sees only sky through the transparent light of a rainbow, but here we looked through a band of multi-coloured light at the forest, from the top of the pass far above us, to the distant foot of the deep Rongni Chu valley, an effect so surpassingly strange that it almost seemed worth while turning aside to search for the Crock of Gold at the rainbow's end.

The Natu La approach to the mountains is very different from the Lachen one; here we rose almost at once out of the thick forest and as the track traverses high up on the edge of the valley one does not have the sense of oppression and hostility that is so strong

E

in the Teesta Valley. We had under-estimated the distance to Karponang and I was feeling ill, so it was long after dark when we reached the bungalow in pouring rain at 8.30. Just before the final climb to the bungalow we had a wonderful view down to the fairy lights of Gangtok spread along the ridge, and far away to the south-west we could see the twinkling lights of Darjeeling. There were several other people in the bungalow but luckily it is one of the largest and we had a room to ourselves. Nima proved himself a good cook and an excellent servant. That night there was a succession of thunderstorms, and next morning several inches of fresh snow lay on the track. It was a curious day with thin driving mist over the tops, a blue sky directly above and packs of heavy cumulus cloud in the valleys. This most spectacular part of the track crept round vertical rock faces supported on crazy bamboo scaffolding, and zigzagged up to the Lagyap La at the beginning of the pine zone. All day long, mules, donkeys and yaks passed us carrying bales of coarse wool down to Gangtok, and the cheerful faces of their drivers reminded us how far we were away from the depressing plains of India.

As we reached Changu Lake at 12,000 feet, a hailstorm came on and slushy snow covered the ground. Part of the lake was still frozen over and the whole place looked unutterably desolate and cold. We reached the bungalow at 1.30. Up here we were beyond the tree line; only rhododendrons, azaleas and birch scrub covered the hillsides. As it was snowing hard we were very surprised to hear thunder in the afternoon, but in the evening it cleared and there was a grand view from the bungalow down on to the lake, which was clear black where the open water was and opaque where it was still frozen. The dark wooded hillsides ran down to the head of the lake just where it appeared to tumble over into the valley, and beyond was a triangle of vivid primrose light in the sky with almost luminous heads of coppery cumulus cloud showing away down by Gangtok.

At Changu we repacked all the boxes so that three out of the four mule loads need not be unpacked till Phari. In the evening we climbed the ridge to the west of the camp and looked down into a great amphitheatre of rocky hills with a river rising in the centre. Away to the north-west a shaft of evening sunlight lit up an amethyst-coloured hill silhouetted and rising out of a level sea of clouds; later on the sky cleared and before we turned in

we saw Orion slanting across the V of sky beyond the lake and
Sirius preternaturally bright overhead. The reflections in the
lake seemed even brighter than the stars themselves. That
evening some muleteers arrived from the Natu La and we heard
from them that the road across to Kopup and Gnatong, where
we were to await our permits, was under snow and impassable,
so we would be forced to cross the Natu La into Tibet and await
our permits at Yatung, where the Natu La and the Jelep La meet.

We both slept rather badly at Changu. As has often been
remarked, it seems to be at a critical height, and people who come
up too quickly from Gangtok usually pay for it here. After
porridge and an omelette we were away at 6 o'clock, making an
early start because we particularly wanted to get a view of Chomolhari from the top of the Natu La. There was new snow on the
path and for some distance we followed the tracks of a hill fox.
Rhododendron scrub stretched all along the track but it was not
yet in flower; in fact it was still winter up here. The big valley
that comes up to the Natu La from the south was full of swirling
brown cloud. At the foot of the steep climb to the pass there
was a signpost to Kopup, but there was a yard of snow on the
track and nothing had passed that way for some time. On the
way up the pass I felt very ill and had all the symptoms of mountain sickness. If this was so, it was surprising, as I had only recently
spent six months at 12,000 feet and during that time had often
been much higher; Crawford, on the other hand, felt perfectly
fit at this stage, but succumbed later.

There was absolutely no view from the summit of the pass.
We could see only the line of cairns festooned with bright-
coloured prayer-flags marking the frontier between Sikkim and
Tibet. It was bitterly cold, and all the stones and blades of grass
were plastered with ice and snow. Our mules passed us here:
they had come up the pass at a very good speed in spite of their
loads. Near the summit a train of fifty mules laden with wool
met us, and a party of Tibetans with their household goods on
the backs of unfortunate donkeys, one of which was so over-
loaded that it collapsed every few yards. On the far side the sun
shone through, and an aromatic fragrance came up to us from
miles and miles of azalea bushes. The descent was very steep and
I was feeling so ill that I had to stop and lie down every now and
then. I had a terrible pain behind the eyes and suffered from

diarrhœa and vomiting. We stopped at Champithang instead of going straight on to Yatung as we had intended and I crawled into my sleeping-bag at once.

On May 10th we reached Yatung, a village of the same size and character as Lachen, but at the foot of a valley instead of being perched up on the side. The track down from Champithang took us through a beautiful landscape and we had occasional backward glimpses above the lichen-clad pines to the Natu La with a snowy peak on either side. Every now and then there were grassy clearings like Swiss alps where yaks grazed placidly among masses of mauve *primula denticulata* with spherical flowering heads as big as golf balls, and the more sedate *primula sikkimensis* with pendant cream-coloured flowers. There was also a dark-violet primula with a yellow centre and a tiny pink one with shiny leaves. Everywhere the grass was crushed and pressed down, a reminder of the recently melted snow. From the grassy slope above Kargyu Monastery we had a view up the wide Amo Chu: trim fields green with young barley in the bottom of the valley and clusters of grey wooden houses like Swiss chalets; on the west the Jelep La came in to meet our track at Pipitang, where the river is bridged. Just below the monastery we saw some monks chopping wood, and among them I recognized the old Abbot whose acquaintance I had made on the way up to Lhasa; I was surprised to see him wielding an axe. When I told him we were hoping to climb Chomolhari, he roared with laughter and then suddenly became serious and asked me why. My Tibetan was hardly up to this, so I said it was to see the goddess there. He shook his head sadly and said we would have to be very careful or she would throw us down the mountain. Then he said he had been up there often, but I presume he meant only in the spirit.

At Pipitang there is a square *chorten*, or religious edifice, surrounded by cylindrical drums of prayers which the pious turn as they walk round and thus acquire merit. It is important always to have them on the right, otherwise it is very inauspicious. We very nearly passed this one on the wrong side, but luckily an old man pointed out our mistake and made us go back. Just beyond the bridge are some tall prayer-poles with bundles of auspicious yak-tails attached to the summit. In the Chumbi Valley there are many evidences of the Buddhist religion; not only is it on the direct route to Lhasa, but traders about to brave the Jelep La or Natu La like to appease the gods in all possible ways. The Chumbi Valley, quite unlike other parts of Tibet, thrusts its way southward between Sikkim and Bhutan, and as all the trade between Lhasa and Eastern India passes this way the people are very prosperous. Since the trade agreement of 1910 we have had power to keep a British Trade Agent at Yatung and a small detachment of Indian troops as an escort.

Down in the valley there were bronze-winged turtle-doves and hoopoes in the fields and white wagtails and dippers beside the river. Just before we reached Lachen there was a large *chorten* beside the road surrounded by tall prayer-poles; soon after this we crossed the bridge and went up to the dak bungalow. Here I found my friend Captain Morgan, who had been the doctor on the Lhasa Mission, bandaging up the legs of an American bacteriologist who had crossed the Natu La in socks and shorts and was suffering from severe sunburn: all the skin had been blistered off his legs. The next move was to visit the postmaster, who told me there were two telegrams and two letters for me at Gnatong. We waited anxiously while copies of them were telegraphed along the line. It would have been terrible to have had to go straight home having got so far—but all was well: one was from Mr. Gould, wishing us luck and saying that the Tibetans had no objection to our attempting Chomolhari and that we could go on as far as Yatung or Phari and there await Bhutanese permission. The other telegram was from Rajah Tobgay: he also wished us luck and said that the Maharajah of Bhutan had given his consent.

This happened to be my thirtieth birthday and no present could possibly have been more welcome. We wanted to push on to Phari the same day, but Yatung represents the end of the transport stage from Gangtok and our muleteer would go no further, and try as we might we could not get the Yatung muleteers to start until the following morning. This was really a good thing, because we would have been over-tired had we gone any further that day, and it meant that we could go and have lunch with Captain and Mrs. Morgan at the British Trade Agent's house where they were staying. Before turning in we went for a walk up the hillside above Yatung and looked down to the drifting smoke and fluttering prayer-flags above the grey shingled roofs of the village. We wondered what the weather was like on Chomolhari.

On May 11th the sunshine crept down the Amo Chu Valley to the north-east, then suddenly appeared over the summit of the mountains on the opposite side of the valley. Our five ponies appeared at 7 o'clock and after breakfast of porridge and rumble-tumble (scrambled eggs), we were on the road by 8. The track followed the river for some time, past the ruins of an old fort put up by the Chinese and a small hamlet surrounded by very fertile fields where young barley sprouted, then it began to rise through thickly wooded country until we found ourselves at Ling-matan, a wide level expanse of green turf dotted with black yak-hair tents and with a peaceful river meandering through it. Hundreds of yaks were grazing on the level pasture, and all round it the rocky fir-clad hills sloped steeply up to snow-scattered upland pastures. A mesh of alto-cumulus cloud hung aslant a deep blue sky.

.Charles and I bathed in a deep pool of the river, and Kikuli—much to our surprise—followed our example. Nima stayed behind with the ponies to make sure they kept up and that no one tampered with our precious gear. On the 1933 Everest expedition about £100 worth of food and clothing were stolen from the boxes, and stones were cunningly substituted to make up the weight. We had brought absolutely nothing in excess of our needs, and the loss of anything would have been fatal to the success of the expedition. The track soon dived into the forest again and on the left was the old Tibetan Government mint. They had built it down in the forest where plenty of fuel was available, but they found it too remote from official supervision and now the mint is at Lhasa.

We reached Gautsa bungalow at 1 o'clock, intending to push on to Phari, but we were secretly very relieved when Nima came up an hour later with the ponies and said that they could not possibly go any further. We had done twelve miles, mostly uphill, and it was a good seventeen on to Phari, as well as a considerable rise in altitude. The Gautsa valley is sullen and forbidding; it reminded me of the Pass of Glencoe. For the last few miles great rugged slopes had appeared to shut in the valley at each turn so that it looked as if there was no escape for the track, but each time we turned at right angles into another V-shaped opening overhung by rock precipices and boulder-strewn scree slopes. Up above us lammergeyers and grey vultures were soaring in wide circles, surprised at their meal on an unfortunate mule whose carcase lay beside the track.

Gautsa is a gloomy and sinister place, but Nima cheered us up by producing a supper of herrings (tinned) and chips, followed by fried cake and custard. I gave Kikuli some quinine for his cold and the other two porters insisted on having some too. All the people here looked at us with awestruck expressions when the porters told them we were going to attempt Chomolhari, as if they knew that some frightful retribution was in store for us, or as if we were attempting what they knew perfectly well to be utterly impossible. We both slept very badly that night, and Crawford felt ill all the way to Phari.

We left Gautsa at 5 A.M. and soon emerged from the gorge and traversed along the steep side of a wide grassy valley. On the right a great waterfall, still half frozen, dropped from a tributary valley to meet the main stream. On the grassy uplands we could see innumerable yaks grazing, and on the steeper hillsides small parties of burrhal. In the gorge we heard whistling thrushes and sudden bursts of song from a wren. There were white-capped and plumbeous redstarts by the stream and willow-warblers in the thickets. The rhododendrons were not yet out, but there was a pink daphne in flower with a hyacinthine scent, and at least six different kinds of primula.

Suddenly turning a corner, the white pyramid of Chomolhari appeared dramatically framed by the steep green sides of the valley. We stopped and examined the southern arête carefully with glasses. The Sherpas were optimistic; it certainly did not look impossibly steep, but an ominous plume of snow trailing from the summit showed that we must not expect calm weather. Soon the track passed a cairn of stones hung with prayer-flags, and then the valley opened out to the level rolling plateau of the real Tibet, and we were met by an icy wind blowing from the snow-clad peaks that surround the plain. The wild life had completely changed. Here were the Tibetan skylark and Elwes' horned lark with black and white head, mouse-hares and various species of snow and mountain finches. Kites circled overhead and three black-necked cranes were screaming away on the right. In the distance we could see a herd of kiang, the rare wild ass of Tibet, racing across the plain.

The track across the plain to Phari seemed interminable, and Crawford was feeling the effects of the height. In the clear Tibetan atmosphere the great fort of Phari and the mud walls of the village looked much nearer than they really were. It was not until after midday that we reached the bungalow, and never have I been more grateful for a cup of tea and a rest. We remembered it was May 12th, Coronation Day, and as we were sleeping in the same building as the highest post office in the world, I thought of dispatching to Their Majesties a telegram of congratulation, but when we went into the figures we found it would come to almost as much as the total cost of the expedition. After lunch I felt much revived, so I went up the rounded stony hills to the north to see if I could get a view of the approaches to Chomolhari. The maps of the district were only the roughest approximation, and I felt that our chief difficulty would be to get on to the ridge at all. Unfortunately the clouds came down when I had reached about 17,500 feet and I had to return without having discovered anything except that I was better acclimatized than I had ever been before.

Up in the hills I saw a grey Tibetan wolf, several blue hares, and two marmots sitting up outside their holes. There were also several varieties of small mauve and pink primulas of species I had not hitherto seen. I collected some of the seedlings and sent them to Mrs. Odling at Kalimpong, but I heard later that they did not take root, although some of the seeds I sent to the Botanical Gardens at Edinburgh have actually flowered. As I returned I met the women of Phari coming out to fill their wooden water-buckets at the stream that flows from the hills to the village. Phari has the reputation of being the filthiest village in the world, and certainly these black-faced, tousle-haired women did little to belie that reputation. However, they were all very cheerful and friendly. I went across to the village but was so besieged by beggars that I had to retire. I thought of the description of Phari written by Thomas Manning, a friend of Charles Lamb, who passed this way in 1811: "Dirt, dirt, grease, smoke," he wrote, "misery, but good mutton." Changes come very slowly to Tibet, and Phari is just the same today, except that the fort which must have been an impressive building in his day was practically destroyed by the 1904 expedition to Lhasa.

In the evening the village headman came in to present a scarf of greeting, and I arranged that he should provide six stalwart coolies for the next day at 1 rupee each. I hoped that they would carry most of our gear towards the ridge so as to save the Sherpas for more serious work. The summit of Chomolhari is only ten miles in a straight line from Phari and I hoped to get to the foot of the southern arête in a single day. The headman tried to dissuade us from our attempt. He said that the people at Phari had been discussing the matter and they were very anxious—not from any fear that the mountain would be desecrated, for the mountain was quite unclimbable, any fool could see that—no, it was for our safety that they feared. Then he went on to warn us about the goddess—or rather goddesses, I think there were. They would not allow us to approach the summit, and if we were to go too near, he solemnly warned us, they would most certainly hurl us down. Then he warned us about *mi-go* (snow men) who were known to inhabit the northern valleys of Bhutan, and he told us a long story of some Phari traders who had lost their way on the Tremo La (the pass from Phari into Bhutan) in a snowstorm, and how they had seen the tracks of the snow men and two of the party had disappeared in the night and had never been heard of since. These solemn warnings were becoming rather disquieting—what if there were some truth in them after all?

That evening we sent Nima to the bazaar to buy a small mirror, some safety pins and a few yards of tape—the only things we had forgotten; then we checked over the tents, tested the primus stoves, darned our socks and saw that everything was in order.

When all was ready for the morrow, we sat by the juniper-wood fire in the dak-bungalow and examined the Survey of India quarter-inch sheet 78 E, the only available map. According to that, we had only one ridge to cross before reaching our arête. We allowed one day for that, three days to the summit, if it was to be climbed at all, and two days for the return journey: exactly a week, allowing for one day's bad weather. Then the bungalow watchman came in, a handsome Tibetan with a long pigtail and heavy gold and turquoise ear-ring. He bustled about tidying up the room and putting more logs on the fire. Then he turned to us and said very seriously, "You are young. Chomolhari cannot possibly be climbed. You may not return at all. Why not give it up and return to Yatung, where it is already summer?" Why not? I could not answer him.

# CHAPTER TEN

### CHOMOLHARI: THE ASCENT

ON May 13th we got up at 4.45 to find an inauspicious morning with damp, cold mist right down to the bungalow. After fried eggs and porridge for breakfast, we sorted all our gear: the large boxes to be left in charge of the watchman while the rest was made into six coolie loads of 80 lb. each. Nima and I, carrying little beyond my cameras, were to go on ahead to climb a hill from which we should get a view of the approaches to Chomolhari. Crawford was to follow with Kikuli and Pasang, who would carry about 50 lb. each. Just as we started, soon after 7 A.M., the clouds parted and we saw Chomolhari, still in deep, cold shadow, with the sun lighting up a plume of silver cloud trailing from the summit, and rags of ugly-looking cumulus blowing up from the west.

As we crossed the stream, where the women of Phari were already filling their water-buckets, Nima and I saw six Brahminy ducks flying noisily over us from the south, and very high up we saw a buzzard with pale head and tail, several vultures and the usual horned larks and snow finches. We went towards the Chomolhari monastery and followed the stream up from there. I had intended to visit the monastery and to persuade the Abbot to give us some prayer-flags to put on the summit, but such a visit would have cost us more time than we could afford. Up the valley was a small shallow lake of four acres or so, and beside it a nomad's black tent and yaks. Three mastiffs rushed fiercely out, followed by a very black-faced yak-herd, who saluted us with one arm half stretched out and the other supporting its elbow. Leaving a note for Crawford on the top of a pile of stones, we turned left up an extremely steep hill covered with boulders.

It was impossible to see anything of Cholmolhari, so we sheltered in the lee of some boulders, hoping it would clear, then gave it up and descended on the far side of the hill into a big rocky amphitheatre, very similar in size and character to the Crid Goch ridge on Snowdon. Here I was relieved to see the others for the first time since we had left Phari. In the finer intervals we caught disquieting glimpses of pinnacled hills and precipitous glaciers between us and Chomolhari. It was quite obvious that it was impossible to get any nearer from this side; apparently we should have to keep further south. The valley we were in was enclosed by a steep rocky ridge with a difficult high col to the north and another easier one to the east which might prove impassable on the other side, and in any case were rather difficult for laden porters. As there was nothing to be done until it cleared, we camped in hail and mist at 12.30, after putting up the big tent for the coolies and the two Mummery tents for ourselves and the Sherpas. The coolies were very cheerful; they pulled azalea scrub to light a fire, and produced an amazing pair of goatskin bellows which had to be used incessantly to keep it going. As we were both rather weary and disappointed we had some food and went to sleep, to be woken half an hour later by a thunderstorm and gale of wind.

This seemed to clear the weather and the clouds were rising, so Crawford and I put our boots on again and set off to see what happened over the ridge to the south-east. On the way, much to our surprise, we found a *primula Royalei*, protruding through the new snow, and the mauve primula with the white eye, also the dried stalks of *mecanopsis horridula* (blue poppy). There was easy going up scree slopes, then it flattened out above and a faint track led over an easy col. The head of the valley on the far side of the ridge was still full of cloud, but we could see down into a dis-quietingly wide deep gorge, and to the blue wooded valleys of Bhutan. In order to see if there was a more direct route from our camp we climbed to the crest of the ridge and followed it north-ward round the head of the valley where our camp was. As the snow and loose rock made the climbing precarious we did not attempt the last part of the ridge round to the other col, but made a very interesting descent down a snow couloir direct to our camp, which we reached at dusk.

The coolies were chattering and singing shrilly with queer catches of the breath and gasps rather like Eskimo singing. It was perfectly still now and the setting sun shone through a coppery haze which looked as if another storm were brewing. In the stillness we could hear an intermittent roaring noise in the direction of Chomolhari as if the wind was still vexing the higher slopes, or perhaps the new snow was pouring down in countless small avalanches. We decided to leave here the big tent, our trek boots and everything we could possibly do without and send them back to Phari with the returning coolies, who would come half a day's march with us. Then we would try to carry on with five loads. Chomolhari seemed a very forlorn hope at this stage, but we hoped our reconnaissance would be useful to somebody, though it would have been still more valuable, I reflected, if we had had survey gear with us.

It snowed quietly most of the night with a soft whispering sound on the tent-wall. We woke at 3.30, just as dawn was breaking, having slept well. I shouted to Nima, but he had some trouble with the primus and breakfast was not ready until 5, by which time we had packed up our gear. As we worked, a snow-cock was crowing like an old grouse from side to side of the valley, and a finch suddenly burst into song. There was ice inside the tent-wall and three inches of new snow outside, but it was still and clear. The rising sun shone red on the great mass of Pau-hunri, on the other side of the Phari plain where it rose like an island out of a sea of amethyst mist. A few minutes later the vision had disappeared and clouds came down to the tops of the hills around us and swept up the valley from the west.

As we ate our breakfast of porridge, rumble-tumble and tea, the coolies emerged frowstily from their tent and made a fire, then sat round it in the snow and ate tea and *tsamba*, as did the Sherpas. We sorted all our loads and put aside every ounce we could spare—the big tent and most of the pegs, a thermos, an extra ground-sheet, a torch, a few books and some odd clothes—but no food. After this sorting it was 7 o'clock before we got away, the Sherpas very cheerfully with small loads, and the Phari men somewhat despondently because their loads were heavy. I took some cinema film of them going up the steep slope we had reconnoitred previously as I intended to send the camera back with the coolies. There was a foot of snow here, pitted with tiny tracks, probably of mouse-hares, and larger ones of mountain hares and foxes. On the summit we passed a line of small cairns at right angles to our track—the frontier between Tibet and Bhutan. This pass was a fairly easy one, the Sur La they called it, but only two of the Phari men had been over it before. We were in the clouds here, but could make out fairly level going to the right and a small lake covered with wet green slush. Our way led down into a steep rocky gorge. We built a few cairns in case we returned this way and after half an hour of descent came on to a tolerable path with very fresh burrhal tracks on it. Now we were below the clouds and could see across to a steep rocky mountain-side opposite, from which we were separated by a valley less deep than I had feared. Soon we came out on to a level 'grand-stand', so we stopped in the sun to let it clear below. Half left across the valley was a deep high amphitheatre lost in the clouds with the green and blue snouts of two hanging glaciers showing. It seemed that we could either go over these and hope to reach our arête that way, or cross the valley and traverse to the right round the hills on the far side, hoping that there would not be other valleys. We decided to try the former course and to fall back on the latter if it proved impossible.

Suddenly, as the last wisps of cloud dispersed below us, I saw a huge flock of burrhal in the valley bottom. There were about sixty of them, including some huge rams with great flowing horns, black breasts edged with white and black on the front of their legs. Many of them were lying down, secure from fear in this unfrequented place. Unfortunately, before I could prevent it, the porters rolled stones down, and the flock ran out of sight in the narrows of the valley. It reminded me of cinema films of animals in Africa taken from an aeroplane. Below us we could see the valley clad with rhododendrons and further down with pines and deodars where it joined the main valley which came in from the east. Our map knew nothing of all this, and I wished again that we could have done some survey to justify the trip, but we could not possibly have afforded it, nor had we the time. We descended steeply over very rough ground to the valley bottom, then followed the stream up into a side valley on the east side surrounded by bottle-green hanging glaciers and steep bare rock slabs. The path petered out below, but was well marked up above. In the valley bottom I saw an Apollo butterfly and found all sorts of wild flowers—masses of purple primula, and a tiny clustered mauve one, also the red tamarisk and a yellow celandine-like flower. No snow lay here, and we seemed to be in a different world from the snow-covered camp we had left in the early morning. It was only 10 o'clock, but the Phari coolies had a long way to go and were anxious to start home. I paid them 2 rupees each, and 5 annas backsheesh in addition. They set off up the valley to the north where there is a pass, so they say, which

is used by shepherds; it must come out near Chu-gya monastery.
I sent all but one pair of the crampons back with them, as it was skis
we needed for all the new snow. We put up the two Mummery
tents beside a small lake, and after a lunch of sardines, cake, bread
and strawberry jam, we had a short sleep since it was impossible
to make any decision until the visibility improved. In the afternoon it cleared a little and we could see that the glaciers flowed
from a steep and much-crevassed ice-field in the direction of
Chomolhari. If we could only reach that ice it might lead up
on to our arête, otherwise we would have to go still further
to the south.

At 12 o'clock we set off up the steel rock wall above the camp
to reconnoitre and see if we could discover the lie of the country
on the other side. On the way up we noticed dried rhubarb
stalks sticking up among the dry grass like solitary fencing posts,
a pipit was singing on the wing as it volplaned down, some choughs
called as they somersaulted across the sky, and a pair of Hodgson's
Grandula flashed blue and purple as they disappeared into a gully.
After some most enjoyable climbing, we left the rock and for two
hours we worked our way up steep soft new snow until we were
stopped by some rocky outcrops and very awkward holdless
slabs which led to the crest at about 19,000 feet. We kept north
along the summit snow and rock ridge for half a mile. As the
clouds lifted higher and higher, we could see down beneath them
into the brown and purple valleys of Bhutan and across to the dun
Phari plain through the pass our coolies had taken. Suddenly a
rift appeared in the clouds to the north-east, and we saw Chomolhari far above us. The last 3000 feet looked practically impossible :
a series of gigantic crevasses and apparently impassable ice-falls
led to the almost perpendicular final ice slopes. I just had time
to put on a yellow filter and take a photograph before the clouds
closed down again and hid it. So beautiful and unexpected was
this vision that it was not until I developed the film that I was
really sure we had not imagined it.

The ridge running up from the glacier above our camp to
Chomolhari seemed to be quite impossible, as it meets the southern
arête at a lower level and is separated from it by a steep and turbulent
ice-fall. To get on to the arête it appeared that we should have
to coast round about four valleys and approach directly from the
south. To the west of Chomolhari we could see a sharp needle-

like peak of grey rock and ice which seemed surprisingly high. To this we gave the name of Khap-ri, the Tibetan word for a needle. We also caught a glimpse of Takapu, Chomolhari's neighbour to the east. After following a buttress of the ridge straight down, in spite of some difficulty, we reached our camp at 5.30 to find that Nima had supper ready—corned beef and potatoes fried up, followed by chocolate and cake. In the evening the clouds came down again and it started to snow and hail.

Next morning, May 15th, I lit the primus at 4 o'clock and called to the others. There was an inch of new snow over everything, but it was fine and clear in spite of occasional wisps of cloud. We could now see Khap-ri between our camp and Chomolhari, and a better view of the ice-fall convinced us that that route was impossible. Our breakfast of porridge, tea and fried tinned herrings was finished by 5, and we were packed up and away by 6 o'clock, intending to work our way round until we reached our ridge, at the same time losing as little height as possible. We all carried heavy loads. Had I known what was ahead I should have kept the Phari men for another day at least. The Sherpas carried 80 or 90 lb., while Crawford and I had 50 or 60, which is too much before a strenuous climb. We set off on the principle of walking for twenty minutes and then resting for ten, in order to husband our strength. Crawford wanted to go down into the valley and round, but I was opposed to losing any height, so we tried to traverse round the mountain-side, cutting across below the slabs we had climbed on the day before. But it was hard work carrying such heavy loads on rough going, and as after-events proved, we would have done better to have followed the stream down and approached Chomolhari by a track which we only discovered on our return a week later. We crossed our ridge by a low col, but clouds were already streaming over and we had only brief views back to the Crib Goch ridge and the Sur La, and to another pass further south.

It was almost impossible to keep any sense of direction in the mist which intermittently enveloped us, and with such heavy loads every yard was valuable. At last, coasting round three hillsides, without losing much height, we reached a rounded hill with a cairn on the summit. In front of us there was yet another deep valley to cross; but it appeared to be the last, and we could look across to our arête and to Chomolhari, which half cleared now and then so that we could begin to prospect a route. The grassy ridge led up from the south to a rocky projection, which we called the Giant's Fang, marking the transition from rock to snow and ice. From this landmark a sharp but gently sloping ice-ridge led to irregular broken ice and a row of deep crevasses which cut across the saddle, leaving, so far as we could see, but one place where there was any possibility of a bridge. After these formidable defences, it rose in great broken slabs of ice and snow to the summit.

I ran down a little way and saw that the descent into the valley was gentle at first and then appeared to drop vertically. We would have to go yet further south before being able to cross the valley. As we started off down a steep grass slope broken by patches of juniper, we put up three burrhal which dashed across just below us. The lilac-coloured shrub with the sweet scent was common and also several kinds of primula, and a yellow potentilla. Our ridge flattened out to a low grassy col where there was a derelict shelter, and a path could be seen going westward over a low wooded col and then presumably into the valley where the large flock of burrhal were, and up a pass parallel to the Sur La, but south of it. Here, too, the track could be seen going right up over the hill.

From the grassy col in front of us our way fell abruptly through a thousand feet of dense rhododendron and birch trees, at an unusually steep angle. A tiny path wound precipitously downward, so steep that we had to hold on to the bushes as we descended. Shell-pink and pale saffron-yellow rhododendrons were just breaking into flower, and when the track straightened out at the foot of the bluff we suddenly came upon several enormous patches of *primula Royalei* of violet-purple colour—a sight so beautiful that it made us forget the extreme discomfort of carrying heavy rucksacks down such a hill. In the valley, by the remains of an old barn, were three very vacant-looking yak-herds who gaped open-mouthed at us but said nothing at all. The valley flattened out as we emerged from the trees and a lovely trout stream wound through level fields of lush grass starred with flowers. Further up, the valley was at least a mile wide and overgrown with low willows covered with yellow catkins. The mauve primula with mealy leaves and mass of bloom the size of a golf ball was very common, also the tiny pink one with shiny leaves. We took our rucksacks off and lay in the sun, thankful that we had reached our ridge at least, but uncertain whether we had the energy left to carry our loads to its summit. The sides of this valley were very steep and at the head of it the green and blue snouts of hanging glaciers showed through the mist.

There were some large juniper trees on the eastern side which, after crossing the stream by a rustic wooden bridge, we started to climb by a steep well-defined trail. Rather surprisingly, we came to a *mané* wall about thirty yards long which we duly left on our right. A prayer-wall is a familiar sight beside a much-frequented track, but on this remote mountain-side it struck an unfamiliar but not incongruous note. After a steep ascent the trees grew smaller and smaller, and we saw masses of the mauve primula and fields of a lovely blue iris with a short stem. Then we came over a ridge, which had the appearance of an ancient lateral moraine, into a horse-shoe valley. In this sheltered hollow there was a great abundance of wild flowers, especially primulas and iris, and well-fed marmots sat outside their burrows in the sun. A steep climb took us up to a spring 200 feet from the top of the ridge—our ridge, at last. We stopped to rest and examine a pale-yellow primula which grew beside the spring and watched a buzzard soaring and mewing. Suddenly there was a tremendous roaring, whizzing noise and a golden eagle rushed down with half-closed wings and the two birds hurled themselves about the sky, chasing each other in play or anger. All at once the eagle swooped off down the valley and the little buzzard had to use his wings vigorously to keep up. When we could first see over the ridge into the valley further east, we noticed a green lake about a mile in circumference, and to my surprise and delight there were four tufted duck on it. Some yaks gazed at us amazedly on the ridge, and a chough came down and settled on the back of one of them. From up here we had a superb view down into a wide pine-filled valley of Bhutan and across to a great pyramid mountain with terraces of brown rock. There was sunshine while we rested beside the spring, then clouds came down, and by 2.30, when we were fairly well up our ridge, we were again in the mist. I had hoped to camp just short of the snow-line, but Crawford was feeling the height and the porters were going slower and slower; Nima especially, having smoked cigarettes incessantly, was scarcely able to walk ten yards without a rest, so we stopped near a stream and put up the tents. Possibly our exhaustion was due to the fact that we had not eaten enough. At that height one's appetite often fails, but it is most important to eat, especially when carrying heavy loads, and even to suck a bit of barley-sugar is better than nothing.

May 16th was a miserably ineffectual day. I woke shortly before 4 o'clock to hear a small bird already twittering, so I started the primus, and shouted to waken the other tent. We had all slept well in spite of the persistent dripping of water through the tent wall. Porridge and tea was all we needed for breakfast: porridge is an excellent high-altitude food; for fit and hungry climbers it provides bulk, and if one feels ill, it slips down quite easily; if made with plenty of sugar and butter, it will keep one going most of the day. There was a powdering of new snow outside and the water in the cooking-pots had frozen but it was a mild and tolerably clear morning, although dirty cumulus cloud was blowing up from the east, looking singularly like the smoke of a great prairie fire as it glowed red in the morning sun. Snow-cock called to each other from hillside to hillside and a faint scent of deodars came up from the valleys below.

From a rocky eminence fifty feet above the camp we had an excellent view of Chomolhari. We looked almost straight up the long southern ridge, and although the perspective was very much foreshortened, we realized once again that we had something very formidable to contend with. After the Giant's Fang— one spur of which looked exactly like the steep side of the In-accessible Pinnacle in Skye—a sharp snow and ice ridge led up to a broken ice hummock. From there a twisted knife-edge ice-ridge led to a long saddle at a higher level, which was scarred as it met the main mountain by a transverse gash of crevasses which we named the Great Divide. After this it rose, evenly but steeply, 3000 feet to the summit. It appeared that once we had passed the Giant's Fang the whole climb would be on snow and ice. Only on the west side of the final pyramid did the rocky foundations of the mountain appear through their icy covering.

Shortly before 6 o'clock we started up the rock-ridge which was still easy but more broken up than it had been lower down. Two lakes could now be seen in the valley to the east, and beyond the valley another ridge became a snow and ice arête and led to Takapu. It struck me that if we could not pass the Giant's

Fang, we might as an alternative cross the valley and try this other arête and then traverse back towards Chomolhari. The approach from the west which we had examined a day or two earlier seemed almost possible from here, although the slope leading from Khap-ri to the main pyramid of Chomolhari looked very broken and steep. Certainly these three approaches to the mountain were the only possible ones, and the central one, which we had eventually chosen, seemed to be the least impossible.

The valleys on either side of our ridge were clear, but ominous brown clouds were continually forming on the mountains to the south, and a quarter of an hour before we reached the Giant's Fang the mist completely enveloped us and did not lift for the rest of the day. We had seen that it was quite easy to climb up the south side of the Fang, but all the other sides were steep, especially the eastern side, which fell away in a series of precipices. We decided that it would be possible to skirt the foot of the western wall of the Fang and reach the snow-ridge in that way. The altitude we estimated as 19,000 feet, and this marked the beginning of the snow-line, although there were a few isolated snow-fields just below the Fang. As nothing could be done until it cleared, we camped rather dismally at 10 o'clock in a snowy hollow to the south-west of the Fang.

All that day it snowed steadily with a gradually increasing wind. The tent leaked badly and we spent a depressing day making dampers (pancakes without eggs), reading poetry aloud, singing and discussing everything under the sun, especially the futility of climbing in the Himalayas. When we looked outside there was nothing to be seen but an intense glare of diffused light and the ice-axe supporting the tent. No sound came from the porters' tent: they seemed to be capable of sleeping soundly all day and night. The outlook was anything but cheerful. The monsoon seemed to have broken, and in any case all the new snow would make the mountain exceedingly dangerous. We had only six or eight days' food; Crawford's leave was running short, and from what we had seen of the mountain, it looked very difficult even for a strong party in ideal conditions.

Next morning, May 17th, dawned calm and fine. After lighting the primus and shouting to the other tent, I crept out of the tent feeling very exhausted, as often happens after a day of inactivity, struggled across the new soft snow and climbed to a point of rock overhanging the eastern wall of the Giant's Fang. The stars shone with unabated brilliance but the eastern sky had paled, and the mountains glimmered with a strange luminescence. Suddenly a finger of light touched the summit of Chomolhari and it glowed like the crater of an active volcano; I hurried back to the tent and took a colour photograph of the light slanting across the eastern face. There was a fine view down one ridge to the shadow-filled valleys of Bhutan and to the great terraced mountain and other unknown hills beyond. To the south-west I could see the mass of Ma-song-chong-dzong-ri, which was also gleaming in the sun. Our view to the west, where all the larger peaks lay, was limited by the high ridge we had climbed a few days earlier.

We did not get away until 6.30, as the porters went to sleep again after I had called them. Retreating a little to get off the Fang, we traversed along, close in under the western wall in spite of broken rocks and a foot or two of soft snow, until we reached a snowy col at the foot of the north face of the Giant's Fang. In a prominent place we left a depôt of everything except the barest necessities for three or four days. This included half the food and paraffin, all books, the cinema camera, and Alpine line, and the remaining crampons (for it was clear that there was so much snow over everything that we should not need them). We roped for the first time here, and I led up an easy ridge between crevasses to the foot of a four-ridged dome we called the Dorjé (the handle of a *dorjé* or Buddhist symbolic thunderbolt is similarly shaped). The nearest ridge of this, though very sharp and steep, led easily to the summit of the Dorjé, about 600 feet above the start at the foot of the Fang. Nima was on my rope—a reliable second—and Kikuli, Crawford and Pasang on the other. The surface was perfect, a few inches of soft powder snow on firm névé. We crossed some wide, safe bridges over a few crevasses which cut the arête, and worked our way along another steep ridge to a flat plateau, the long saddle we had seen from below. Here, unfortunately, though it was only 11 o'clock, we were forced to camp as the clouds came down. In the glaring, diffused light it was impossible to see what lay ahead, and, owing to the prevalence of crevasses, it was obviously unsafe to advance a step until it cleared. It looked as if the next quarter of a mile would be easy, then we would have to cross from our arête to the main mass of the mountain. This might stop us, as several large crevasses seemed to cut right across the ridge at the Great Divide. The next stage after this appeared to be a critical one. On the east side there was a long, very exposed and very steep fluted ridge of bare grey ice running up to the foot of the long slope. This was too severe a test for our party, but it might be possible to turn it on the left : we could not yet see how.

To the east of our tent the ice rose for a short distance, then fell almost vertically to a steep rock wall overhanging the valley of the two lakes. The ice arête on the far side of this valley looked more level, but appeared to be harder to get on to in the first place. The two ice-ridges met just before the Great Divide.

We were still using the Mummery tents, keeping the smaller bivouac tents in reserve. Crawford was going very well, but was unable to eat and felt very exhausted and ill. Nima could not get much higher on account of his age and general unfitness; Kikuli, much to my surprise, was going rather badly today and spitting blood from time to time; Pasang went exceptionally well and made no fuss at all. That night we slept soundly, but I dreamt that Crawford and I were at sea in an open boat and huge waves kept towering over us and we could see the sun through green walls of water, but the waves never actually broke; our food was all in tins and we had no tin-opener; the skin was burnt off our faces and we had practically no clothes.

After breakfast of porridge and tea, I asked Nima if he minded staying in one of the Mummery tents alone while the rest of us made a bid for the summit. He seemed very relieved not to be going any higher and told us to get to the top and come back quickly. Kikuli seemed to be much better so I took him on my rope while Pasang and Crawford followed on the other. Although we started the primus at 3.30 it was 6 o'clock before we said good-bye to Nima and set off across a wide expanse of ice with six inches of newly fallen snow and a further six inches of soft snow beneath it. There was a terrible glare off the snow, but the Hamblin Everest glasses we were using seemed to eliminate the harmful rays without taking away too much light.

We kept right over on the east side at the Great Divide and crossed a narrow strip of snow without much difficulty. But it was the only possible way across from the two southern ridges to the peak itself. From here the ice fell away steeply to the west in a series of broken serracs and tangled crevasses. The steep fluted ridge ahead looked as if it were made of bare hard ice. It was the most direct route, but I decided not even to attempt it. If the rope and ice-axe are used skilfully, one can fall off a slope or even down a crevasse and get away with it, but only once off a ridge of this sort. The alternative was a large, crescent-shaped basin to the west, broken by a bergschrund, or at any rate a prodigious crevasse, across which there appeared to be some flakes forming a precarious bridge, and above this more crevasses and serracs.

We cut steps down a short descent into the basin and crossed it to the foot of the steep surrounding ice-ridge. The snow was over knee-deep in the basin, and what with the altitude (we were now at 20,000 feet) and the ghastly glare of the sun on the new snow we found it very exhausting to move at all. Kikuli went ahead for a short time, but he was spitting blood again and was obviously unfit. Whenever we stopped, he fell asleep. I changed loads with him, but he was practically a passenger, and it was clear that he could not keep going for long. Pasang, who was a trifle over-eager, pushed ahead, so I let him lead. He went like a war-horse, but he had no idea what to do with the axe or rope; luckily he did not object to being told. Hail was falling now, but the visibility was still intermittently good.

The steep fluted ice-ridge formed the eastern wall of this crescent, and we found a way up some enormous flakes which, I presume, fell at some time from the ridge. But there was waist-deep snow at the foot of the ice and among the tangled fragments, as all the snow which had landed on the polished ice-ridge above had accumulated here. One pitch was rather severe, and we had to cut hand-holds up the all but perpendicular side of a gigantic flake of ice. It was just possible. The very middle of the crescent might have been possible, but it was very steep and bare in places and that route would have landed us among crevasses. I noted at the time that it would make a useful emergency descent.

From here we cut along several thin ice-ridges up to a platform, say 800 feet above the floor of the crescent, where we were stopped by a vertical wall of ice. Again we found a way up this by climbing up the side of a sharp flake that had fallen from an exposed ice-wall which showed much stratification. The edge of the flake had knee-deep snow on it which had to be scooped away as we climbed. Ahead of us stretched an even, steeply-sloping ice-field for another 800 feet, then a great, broken ice-fall guarded the approaches to the final arête. This looked impossible unless it could be turned on the right. There was some talk of camping, as we were all completely exhausted, and Kikuli was on the verge of collapse. But it was unsafe to camp where we were, owing to the danger of avalanches, and I was particularly anxious to get a little further as the weather was fine for once, and it would be only just possible to get to the summit and back from a camp 3000 feet from the top.

I led for another hour over a ridge up to the west to avoid a vast crevasse, then up a steep slope of crutch-deep snow till we were among crevasses again, to avoid which I went further east and worked across to a slight saddle only a hundred feet from the drop into two-lake valley. This was the only place on this side of the mountain which was fairly safe from an avalanche, unless the whole of the south face came down, and that seemed almost possible after all the new snow. Wearily we camped at 3 P.M., after a terrific but successful day. I suppose we were at 20,000 feet. Kikuli fell exhausted in the snow and Crawford was groaning and unable to eat anything. After resting for some time in the snow we forced ourselves to put up the two bivouac tents and crawled inside them. They were very tiny and relied on ice-axes for poles. A zip-fastener secured the opening at one end. After supper of herrings, bread and tea, we all took aspirins (actually the brand we used were aspirin-caffein-phenacetin tablets) to cure our headaches, and went to sleep.

On May 19th, I woke everyone at 3 o'clock. We were all feeling the effects of the height and were very, very slow at getting ready to start. Indeed it was 5 o'clock before we emerged from the tents, just as it was getting light. The sun already glittered on the snow and we could look right down our ridge, past the little black dots of Nima's tents and on to the Giant's Fang. Beyond again was the brown pyramid-shaped mountain and then mile after mile of blue and purple-shadowed ridges showing above valleys brimming with violet cloud. It was so beautiful that it almost recompensed us for the feeling of hopelessness that filled us as we looked towards Chomolhari. Crawford's leave was almost up, and he was not in a fit state to attempt the summit. When I called to the porters, only Pasang, with a broad grin, emerged, while Kikuli eloquently put an arm out and emptied a cupful of blood into the snow; as it was only his teeth that were bleeding and nothing internal, we felt it was possible to leave him alone in the camp while the rest of us made a reconnaissance. We still spoke of it as an attempt on the summit, but I think we all realized that we could not hope to get there and back from this camp, considering the intrinsic difficulty of the climb, the unsuitable weather conditions, and the inexperience of the party.

The three of us tied on to one rope, and set off to find the best way up a vertical ice-fall, about twelve feet high, which seemed to prevent us from getting more than a few hundred feet above our camp. The slope was fairly easy and there were not many crevasses, but the snow was over knee-deep, so at this height progress was unbelievably slow. With the terrible glare from the new snow our faces were very sore, in spite of the use of Anti-Lux, which affords a certain amount of protection; our lips were very raw and swollen, and most of the skin was burnt off our nostrils and the lower part of the nose.

We worked steadily up to the right, only occasionally having to cut steps. Gradually it grew steeper and we realized that it was impossible to get over the ice-fall on this side. Crawford was completely used up, and Pasang, who had started off too fast, was moving more and more slowly. It was obvious that it was only a waste of time to attempt the vertical ice-wall at this end, and the best we could do was to return to camp and get a good night's rest before attempting the western end of it on the following morning. With indescribable relief we turned in our tracks and returned to camp. At this height, especially under such conditions, any exertion is intolerable, and great will-power is needed before every upward step is taken; progress is so slow that it is necessary to breathe several times for every step forward. Climbers are apt to wonder why on earth they ever set out on such a forlorn quest, and their great desire is to bring the expedition to an honourable conclusion—so long as somebody gets to the top, it need not be oneself—so that the expedition can get back to altitudes at which man was meant to exist and enjoy life.

I suppose we had climbed only 1000 feet from our camp, but it had seemed an intolerable distance. On the way down we were not troubled by the height, and using our footsteps, which made a thigh-deep tunnel through the soft snow, we were back at our camp again in half an hour. It is amazing to me that the new snow did not avalanche off these steep slopes, but we hardly heard a single avalanche all the time we were on the mountain. As we reached the camp, it started to snow again and we held a council of war. Crawford's leave was practically over; even if he returned at once he would only just be able to get back to Calcutta in time, and he was suffering from severe mountain sickness. It seemed very hard luck that, having got so far, he could not make another attempt on the summit, but in any case it was very improbable that if Pasang and I attempted it alone we would be able to get beyond the ice-fall. It was also questionable whether it was a justifiable risk to let Crawford and Kikuli return by themselves. I left the final decision until the following day; what we really wanted now was a long drink of tea and some aspirin tablets for our headaches.

It was a depressing afternoon. Snow pattered incessantly against the tent walls, which sagged in so that one could not avoid them, and then water poured in and also melted up from the ground-sheet which was designed to be light rather than water-proof. Crawford was dozing with his mouth open; his swollen face looked like a death-mask, except that it was skinned and burnt scarlet by the sun. Kikuli groaned aloud in the neighbouring tent. There was nothing for it but to go to sleep and hope that things would seem less black in the morning.

May 20th dawned superlatively fine. I got up at 3 o'clock and made porridge and tea for breakfast. Kikuli was quite cheerful at the prospect of getting off the mountain and said he was capable of leading. Crawford, on the other hand, was feeling little better, but was sure he would recover once he was lower down. We had much sorting of gear to do before we could start, and as the two tents were frozen into the snow, it was not until 5.30 that we parted company. Pasang and I took one ruck-sack each, our ice-axes, a 100-foot rope, the better bivouac tent, two pitons, a double eiderdown sleeping bag each, and a small li-lo, my Contax camera and telephoto lens, a primus, a cooking-pot, mugs, plates, spoons, two boxes of matches and a tin-opener. For food we took three tins of sardines, a tongue and a tin of herrings, two pounds of pemmican, three-quarters of a pound of sweets, four half-pound slabs of chocolate, some oatmeal, sugar, butter, tea and pulled bread. Pasang also brought a bag of *tsambo* and a brick of Tibetan tea. I wore my felt-lined climbing-

boots, four pairs of ordinary socks, cotton pants, shorts, grey
flannel trousers, a flannel shirt, a high-necked jersey with sleeves
and a smaller sleeveless pullover, an imitation-leather wind-
jacket (this had a zip-fastener which had gone wrong, and was
attached with safety pins), a single Grenfell-cloth windproof suit
with a fur-edged hood, wool mitts, horse-leather mitts, a balaclava wool helmet, and snow-glasses. Of medical supplies we
took only a tube of Anti-Lux, some sticking-plaster and an enve-
lope of aspirins. Although we hoped to be off the snow in a
couple of days, this outfit was designed to last us for as much as a
week in case of necessity. We were carrying about 20 lb. each.

We followed the tracks of the day before, although at first
they were already filled with snow. About 800 feet above the
camp we struck left and made for what appeared from below to be
the only gap in the impregnability of the ice-wall. If this turned
us back our last hope was to follow the ice-wall yet further left,
and to try to force a way where it met the rock wall. We were
lucky: there was one weak spot in the defences of the mountain
where a huge flake of ice leant against a 20-foot vertical ice-wall
which overhung a gaping bergschrund.

For two hours I cut foot- and hand-holds up the edge of this
flake and then, standing on the top of it, I was just able to get on
to the slope above where the ice was less tough and glutinous.
Every now and then when I stopped to rest I looked down
below to see if I could see anything of Crawford and Kikuli,
about whom I felt extremely anxious. There was no sign of
them, but I could make out Nima's two tents far away.

Having passed what I considered the worst obstacle our spirits
rose, and we made further over to the left, where the going was
better, though rather steeper. Here we found much less snow, as
most of it seemed to have blown off the mountain. There
was no distant view, as clouds were forming all around us, though
the sharp top of Khap-ri still showed disconcertingly high above
us. Once again the slope steepened, and we had to use our ice-
axes for every step, instead of having to cut one only now and
then.

About 1 o'clock a blizzard came up very suddenly from the
west. Perhaps we ought to have noticed its approach, but we
were concentrating on the work of step-cutting, and before we
had time to do anything but plunge our ice-axes into the snow and

crouch over them, we were blinded by swirling snow and a maniac wind. It was impossible to move up or down, and we could only wait motionless, getting colder and colder as the minutes dragged by. In spite of my windproof hood, my nose and cheeks were frostbitten, and I dared not take a hand out of my glove to thaw them out. Several times it thundered, but no lightning lit up the gloom of the blizzard, for which I was glad, remembering an experience of a friend of mine on the Eiger, when an electric storm was attracted to his ice-axe and he was hurled off his foothold to find himself dangling on the end of the rope.

After two hours of this, I realized that we would have to do something to avoid being frozen to death where we stood. In lulls of the storm, I had made out the shadow of a dark serrac just above us, and others to the right; to descend over our flake in this wind was out of the question; our only hope was to make our way up to this serrac, and at the foot of it to excavate a platform on which we could pitch our tent. The slope was dangerously steep, but the vertical wall of ice above would probably throw any avalanches clear of the tent.

Making the most of the few lulls in the storm, we fought our way to this place and started to cut away the ice. Pasang at first seemed to regard the situation as hopeless, but when the wind, as if quelled for the moment by our endeavour, died down a little, he joined me in the work of excavation. At last we had hewn a crazy platform big enough for the tents, which we put up as best we could. Unfortunately the zip-fastener was faulty, and whenever the tent ballooned with the wind, the opening tore apart and snow blew in, although we did our best to hold it together with safety pins. Taking off only our windproofs and boots we crawled into our sleeping-bags and fell asleep, feeling that we were lucky to be alive at all. It had been impossible to fix the side-guys at that angle, and the snow which piled up on the outside of the tent was soon melted by the heat of our bodies and soaked into our sleeping-bags. When the excessive moisture made us too cold we awoke and made some Tibetan tea, with this we ate a mixture of *tsamba* and sugar, our first meal since breakfast. As usual, we had been so preoccupied that we had forgotten to eat, a very stupid mistake.

That night I, at any rate, slept well, although snow continually poured over the protruding ice-wall above us and piled on to the tent so that we could hardly move. However, it was wonderfully warm, though I wondered what would happen if a real avalanche came down : perhaps it would be thrown clear. There was little inducement to sleep on, and at 2 o'clock I struggled half out of my sleeping-bag, threw out the pile of snow that was piled up round our heads, and lit the primus. For breakfast we had porridge with plenty of butter and sugar, followed by Tibetan tea and *tsamba*. This camp was at about 21,500 feet, 1500 feet above our last camp and 2500 from the summit. If all went well and there were no long pitches of excessive difficulty, I thought it should just be possible to reach the summit and return in a single day. Accordingly we left our tent standing, though when once we had crawled out of it, it collapsed forlornly from the weight of snow on top of it, and took only one rucksack between us with my camera, two pitons, and some odds and ends of food for lunch.

In spite of our early awakening it was 4.30 before we emerged from the tent. Our buffeting by the wind on the day before had left us somewhat demoralized, and at such an altitude that means exhausted. There was no room to move inside the tent, and before we could put them on, our boots had to be thawed out over the primus. During the night a pile of snow had blown in through the makeshift fastening of the tent, and though most of this had been scooped out before I lit the primus, what was left now melted with the heat of the stove.

It was light enough to start at 4 o'clock, and when we came out of the tent at 4.30 we found a beautiful morning, and ourselves perched on an appallingly steep ice-slope, which seemed to be totally disconnected from the rest of the awakening world. There was no wind, and the going was perfect. For several hours, with only short rests, we cut and kicked steps up the 2000-foot snow-slope. The warm flush of dawn faded from the snow and gave way to hard bright daylight. After an hour we had passed the summit of Khap-ri to the west-south-west; this peak is actually much higher than it appears to be from below. At first we kept well to the left and worked our way across to a reddish outcrop of granite separating the snow-slope from the tremendous rock precipice that seemed to fall almost sheer to the Phari plain. We tried the rock, but it was easier to keep to the snow, where the going was ideal. Up here all the loose snow had blown off the mountain or was packed by the wind into a consistency between ice and snow. Only occasionally, where exposed ribs of hard ice protruded through the snow, was it necessary to cut steps. As a rule a few scoops with the axe or a good kick with the boot was sufficient, and most of the time we could move together, only stopping to belay over a particularly steep or difficult part. This was very different from the heart-breaking surface we had experienced lower down, where we sank in to the knee and even the fork. On this going we could achieve perfect rhythm—a kick, a pause, a step; a kick, a pause, a step—and thereby husband our strength and move at much greater speed. We took it in turn to lead, and Pasang went magnificently, his cheerfulness, determination and speed never flagging. Just before midday we reached the top of the long slope, after seven hours of most exhilarating and enjoyable climbing.

The view on the way up had been superb. When we left the tent we saw to the south a sea of level clouds with peaks rising from it, and as we climbed higher and worked more over to the western ridge, we could see down into the wooded valleys of Bhutan, separated by massive mountains of brown rock which only occasionally raised their heads above the snow-line. Then we looked into the dun-coloured Tibetan plateau where we could make out the mud-walled village of Phari with a white track threading the plain on either side. I hoped the good people there were watching us, though I supposed they were so certain that Chomolhari was unclimbable that they would not even trouble to look.

Gradually, as we approached the western ridge, all the mountains of the Eastern Himalaya that I had ever heard of swung into view, and we felt as if we were on the very top of the world: isolated Ma-song-chong-dzong-ri to the south-west; Pauhunri, westward across the Phari plain; the great mass of Kangchenjunga, with a cloud system all of its own; Siniolchu, Chomiomo, Pandim, Kabru, and 150 miles away to the west, yellowed by vast distance, unconquered Everest and Makalu.

At the top of the slope, Pasang was disappointed to see that the actual summit still lay another 500 feet above us to the north, though I had been prepared for it by my examination of the mountain from the plain. We were separated from the summit by a curved, undulating ridge of extreme sharpness which marked the culmination of the steep couloirs on the west. An error of judgment on this side would have resulted in a fall of thousands of feet down almost vertical rock to a frozen and ice-covered lake we could see far below. To the east one would have fallen over ice and snow, but the result would have been much the same.

Pasang asked me if it was necessary to go to the farther summit. It was a pertinent question. My body certainly had no desire to go on, and as the wind was blowing up from the west accompanied by tatters of cloud, the wisdom of further advance was questionable. But I knew it would not take us long to get downhill again to our camp and we should not have much difficulty in finding it unless another blizzard struck us. So we went on. Luckily the snow was fairly rotten up here and we could kick away the top of the ridge and travel fast. Further gusts of wind made us crouch over our ice-axes, realizing that it would be impossible to get back if the gale developed. The last 300 feet up a snow-slope which only became steep at the very end, was the easiest part of the whole climb. Soon we were shaking hands on the summit, which was a three-pointed snow dome, slightly corniced on the south and east. From here we could see towards Kampa Dzong and the rose-coloured hills of Tuna. When we reached the summit, the clouds were drifting up with icy breath from the west and dispersing again before they reached us. But they became more persistent, and as the wind had increased I realized we must hurry back over the exposed ice-ridge before the weather grew worse. At Pasang's request I took a photograph of him on the summit, then, at 1 o'clock, we started the descent.

# CHAPTER ELEVEN

## CHOMOLHARI : THE DESCENT

EARLIER in this book I quoted a remark of the great explorer Stefansson to the effect that the story of a successful expedition makes dull reading, because, if all goes according to plan, there should be no exciting adventures to relate. If this is true, then our descent of Chomolhari would make an epic of incompetence, for one mishap followed hard upon another.

As we left the triple snow-ridge of the summit, shreds of cloud were racing over from the west, and I was anxious to get back over the exposed knife-edge ridge before the wind increased. At the top of the long slope we stopped to eat some barley-sugar; we had had no food for ten hours, except some sweets and chocolate which we had sucked as we climbed; we ought to have stopped to rest and eat something more substantial, but I was determined to return to our camp without delay, especially as it was now beginning to snow. I utilized a momentary clearing of the weather to take some more photographs, and we were ready to begin the descent.

The Tibetans had told us repeatedly that the stronghold of the goddess was impregnable. They also warned us that if we presumed to set foot among her solitary snows, she would make us pay dearly for our temerity. This, and my desire for haste, must account for the disaster that so nearly befell us at the moment we began the descent. I have no clear recollection of how the fall started. We were standing together at the top of the long slope preparing to descend. I had finished my photography, and, while putting my camera away, told Pasang to go ahead, for when descending the leader goes last. A moment later he shot past me on his back. I managed to slip the camera into my windproof pocket and tried to throw my weight on to my ice-axe, just as the rope whipped tight, and the next instant I was falling on my back head-first down the slope. We fell fast, sometimes flying through the air, sometimes bumping and somersaulting over outcrops of ice. Several times I dug my axe point in, but before I could get enough weight on to it to stop us I was pulled on by the more rapid acceleration of Pasang, on whose Buddhist mind the spells of the goddess had such power that he let go his ice-axe and did not even attempt to retard our descent.

I was completely winded, my goggles were filled with snow, I could see nothing, and I knew nothing, except that we were falling faster and faster and that further down the slope became so steep that we would not be able to stop before rolling over the edge of the rocks, to drop 3000 feet into Tibet. I remember wondering if Crawford and the other porters were watching our descent from some point on their way back to Phari; I hoped they were not. I recollect also hoping that my camera would not fall out of my pocket; actually it did, but I recovered it further down, though half the film was ruined. I suppose we fell 300–400 feet before my axe point cut home and I gradually stopped. I felt a tug at my waist. Pasang too had stopped— or had the rope severed? Lifting my snow-clogged glasses I could see him lying motionless, head downwards, within a few yards of the edge of the precipice, his ice-axe having come to rest above him. There I lay in agony for several minutes, choking, gasping, fighting for breath. At that height even moderate exertion is intolerable, and I had resisted the fall with every nerve and muscle in my body; now a black mist hid everything and I thought my lungs and heart would burst. Pasang was unhurt, but the fall had completely demoralized him, and until we were off the mountain and away from the influence of the goddess, I could no longer rely upon his nerve and judgment.

Keeping carefully to our upward tracks, we were back at our camp by 3 o'clock. A blizzard was threatening, and tired as we were I felt it essential to move our tent from its precarious ledge so that we could sleep soundly away from the danger and dis- comfort of falling ice and snow. But we had eaten nothing except barley-sugar and chocolate for twelve hours, and although we did not feel hungry I knew we must have a hot meal before any further exertion. We made some Tibetan tea, but one of the tent guy ropes was hidden under some snow beneath the primus, and when Pasang rummaged in the tent to find a mug the guy tightened and the tea was spilt. We had not the heart to boil up any more though we ate some sugar, prunes and sardines. Then we began to move the camp, the desire to lose no time in getting off the steep part of the mountain overcoming our bodily exhaustion. Wearily we dug away the snow debris, rolled up the tent and repacked our rucksacks. If only we could reach the sanctuary of the easier slopes below the ice-fall we hoped to rest thoroughly and then get off the mountain in a single day.

We had descended only about 300 feet, however, when the wind, which had died down while we struck camp, suddenly increased to blizzard force, and we were held up again in almost exactly the same spot where we had been stopped for two hours by a storm on the ascent. The ice-fall was immediately below us; we knew that there was only one certain way down it, a way which

NORTHERN FACE OF CHOMOLHARI (the peak on right) FROM THE TUNA REST-HOUSE

THE AUTHOR AFTER CHONG BARI

APPROACHING THE RIDGE OF THE LANGPO LA

in ideal conditions it would be difficult to see from above, and which in a blizzard we could not hope to find, much less descend. We waited for an hour, getting colder and more miserable, then the wind dropped a little, and we began to retrace our steps to the camp-site we had just left.

As soon as we started to climb upwards I realized for the first time that I was utterly exhausted. I had no strength left at all. That climb of a mere 300 feet back to our ledge is one of the most dreadful memories I have. Each single step required a concentration of will-power I was scarcely capable of exerting. The idea of just letting go and sliding over the ice-fall into the oblivion of the gaping bergschrund below was terribly attractive. I seemed to have lost all resistance to the biting cold of the wind. My rucksack was intolerably heavy and upset my balance. I found difficulty in breathing. I felt sick and had a dull ache at the back of my eyes.

It must have taken us well over an hour to regain those few hundred feet, and as soon as we reached the platform where our tent had been, we collapsed and fell asleep. Some time later, I do not know how long, we roused ourselves and put up the tent, which was now frozen stiff and intractable. Then we crawled into our sleeping-bags, wearing windproofs, helmets—everything except boots—and again went to sleep. Later on we melted some snow over the primus and forced ourselves to eat some *tsamba* and sugar mixed with water.

The night was most uncomfortable, as our sleeping-bags were soaked by the snow which had been melted by the heat of our bodies. The wind had gone round to the east and blew quantities of snow through the faulty opening of our tent, and the wall, with the weight of wet snow above it, pressed upon us from above. Everything became drenched, and when the temperature fell during the night, we were too cold and miserable to sleep. In the morning I found that the matches in my inner trouser-pocket had disintegrated, and the other box in my rucksack contained only half a dozen. Snow was still drifting gustily on a biting wind but the sun was shining coldly and I decided we must make a move. Pasang, however, seemed to be suffering from concussion and refused to eat or do anything but lie on the floor of the tent, watering at the eyes and moaning. He had broken one of his snow-glasses in the fall, and had groaned and sobbed all night

F

long. He was more comfortable when I had covered up his bad eye with a handkerchief, but in no fit state to travel.

Breakfast of Tibetan tea and *tsamba* put more life and warmth in us until we found that Pasang's boots were frozen; he had slept with them under his head instead of taking them into his sleeping bag, and now they were quite flat and hard. Before he could force his feet into them, I had to use one of our precious matches in order to relight the primus and thaw them out.

At last we left that miserable camp, but there was no sign of our track of the day before, and fine snow blew along the surface. Pasang seemed to have lost his sense of balance, and kept falling, so I had to go ahead, knowing that he would not be able to hold me if I slipped, cut the steps and then return to him and steady him while he descended, almost lowering him on the rope. Once when he fell, his rucksack burst open, and our only cooking-pot as well as most of our remaining stores went bouncing down the glacier. It is extraordinary how difficult it was to find the route above, and, as we failed to find the flake by which we ascended, we had to force a way down the ice-fall, and by the time we had accomplished this in safety it started to snow heavily and we had to camp about midday. If there had been any sign of our upward tracks we could have gone on in almost any weather and got off the mountain in a single day. As it was, the frequency of wide crevasses made it quite unsafe to move in a diffused light, especially as many of them were hidden by snow.

All night snow pattered dismally against the tent wall and we shivered so much in our wet sleeping-bags that it was almost impossible to sleep. Next morning, May 23rd, when we eventually packed up and got under way we found that we had to plough through snow thigh-deep, and in our exhausted state could make little headway. The glare from the new snow was worse than it had been before, our rucksacks were heavy with all the moisture our tent and sleeping-bags had absorbed, and Pasang was no better. It was impossible to move through the soft deep snow with any rhythm; all joy of progression had gone, only mechanical drudgery remained. We passed the camp from which Crawford and Kikuli had returned and approached the amphitheatre which had caused us so much trouble on the ascent. From above everything looked so different that it was impossible to follow our earlier route, but I had noticed then that a party could probably, if pressed for time, get down in the middle of the ice-fall; it was steep and exposed, but at the bottom there was a deep drift into which one could, if necessary, make a forced landing. To reach this ' shoot ', however, we had first to cross a belt of about six crevasses, but before we could reach them the snow came on again, and, as we could see only about ten yards, we were again forced to camp, though it was not yet 11 o'clock.

Our position was becoming serious. Pasang, though he had climbed magnificently on the ascent, was now only a passenger. I was still well, but my face was terribly raw from the effect of the burning rays of the sun thrown up by the glare of the new snow. In spite of every precaution all the skin was off my lips, which clotted together when I slept and bled profusely when I forgot about them and suddenly opened my mouth. It is curious how much more liable one is to snow-blindness and sunburn in diffused light; though, fortunately, through using amber glasses as supplied to Mount Everest Expeditions, I was not troubled by blindness or sore eyes in spite of most trying conditions. We were too miserable to bother what we ate, especially as our matches were now finished and we could no longer use the primus for cooking food or to warm the tent and dry our clothes. We occasionally ate a little *tsamba*, sugar and snow mixed together, or some sweets and raisins, but I did not feel in the least hungry and in any case the *tsamba* tasted strongly of paraffin. On the other hand, we were tortured by thirst, though we could always melt a certain amount of snow on our boots for drinking-water (snow melts rapidly on a black surface which absorbs heat, and remains unmelted on one's white windproofs), and when we had to lie up during the day we could melt a certain amount of water on any dark object we put outside in the snow. Our chief discomfort was the fact that our socks and sleeping-bags became sodden wet, though we laboriously wrung them out each night and morning.

The nights were dreadful. We were usually forced by the bad weather to camp before midday, then we would get into our sleeping-bags and, being exhausted after the morning's exertions, would fall asleep at once. After a time I would be woken up by the cold and wonder if it was yet morning, to discover it was only just after midday. This would continue during the afternoon, so that by the time night came and the temperature had fallen below zero, I was no longer tired and could hardly sleep at all. We used to shiver as if we had the ague, and our teeth chattered loudly and uncontrollably. I consider myself rather a connoisseur of uncomfortable nights. I have had my tent blown off me by a hundred-mile-an-hour gale on the ice-cap of Greenland; I have, while camping far out on the Arctic pack, as related elsewhere in this book, known the sea-ice break up in a storm, and watched the water welling up through a widening crack across the floor of the tent, but for sheer, interminable, shivering misery, I have never known anything like those six nights passed in our bivouac tent on the snows of Chomolhari.

On the morning of May 24th, it was some time before I could get Pasang moving, and I was feeling sick and ill myself. More new snow had fallen in the night, and progress was slower than ever. Before we could descend the shoot into the amphitheatre we had to cross the crevasses, which were so shrouded in snow that they were almost impossible to find except where they were wide and gaping. When we reached the first one, which was twenty feet wide in some places, I made for where it narrowed and was bridged by a level covering of snow. Probing carefully with my ice-axe, I found that it was here four or five feet across. It might have taken us half a day to go round and I decided that it was less of a hazard to jump it than to risk the bridge breaking under me. In so great a depth of snow the ice-axe becomes insensitive, and I could not tell how strong the bridge was. Now Pasang had a tiresome habit of letting out the rope rather jerkily, as if he had tied a clove-hitch round the handle of his axe, so I told him I was going to jump and that he must let me have plenty of rope, and to make sure he understood—for we always conversed in Tibetan, which neither of us spoke very fluently—I went back to him and loosened the rope.

But Pasang was not very intelligent these days, and when I was in mid-air over the crevasse there was a violent jerk on the rope and down I went, crashing straight through the frail snow bridge. I fell about thirty feet, but was unhurt, for the rope cut into the snow on the lip of the crevasse and that, combined with the weight of Pasang, dragged like an anchor through the deep snow towards the crevasse mouth, brought me slowly to rest. Not that there was much rest in dangling in an apparently bottomless crevasse with my face full of snow, my rucksack pressing on the back of my head and the rope squeezing the life out of me. At first Pasang simply hauled on the rope, to my extreme discomfort, while I tried to swing far enough to one side to get a footing on a ledge which protruded from one wall of the crevasse. After several attempts I managed, as I swung by, to grapple the ledge with my ice-axe and then to hold myself there by jamming the fingers of one hand into a crack in the ice, while I cut away the top of the ledge to make a place large enough for me to stand. Only then, after many Tibetan oaths, could I persuade Pasang to loosen his stranglehold on the rope.

When I had recovered from this frightful exertion, I realized with horror that the crevasse was nowhere narrow enough to bridge in the normal way, *i.e.*, by cutting steps up both sides, and I remembered having read somewhere that it is quite impossible to get óut of a crevasse by cutting steps up one wall—however, there was no alternative but to try. Having made myself as secure as possible on my ledge, I undid the rope, removed my ruck-sack, almost falling off the ledge during this complicated manœuvre, tied the rucksack on to the end of the rope, and, after much shouting, persuaded Pasang to haul it up to the top. When the rope came down again he had tied his red scarf on to the end of it—perhaps as a subtle hint to me that I was in danger.

Then I roped again, and set about a task which I suppose is the most difficult I have ever attempted. While Pasang hauled vigorously on the rope, I started cutting hand- and foot-holds up the vertical blue wall of ice. It was desperately hard work : I could rest a little by leaning on my axe, which I dug into the opposite wall of the crevasse, but even then I had to descend to my ledge several times for every step I cut, and holds which were shaped for my fingers to grip soon got broken by my clumsy boots and had to be recut before I could use them again. And the ice was that peculiar tough, glutinous kind so often found in the Himalaya. Another difficulty was that I could not make Pasang understand when to steady me with a pull, and when to let go so that I could descend to my ledge. It was only after three or four hours of most exacting work that I at last put my head over the lip of the crevasse, where I saw, to my horror, that Pasang was sitting in the very middle of the frail snow bridge, not six feet away from the gaping hole through which I had recently disappeared. However, he seemed quite pleased to see me.

The next obstacle was the amphitheatre, which we reached after threading our way through the rest of the crevasses. We came down the 200-foot shoot in the middle of it without misadventure as the ice was hard and exposed and I could cut huge platforms from which I could safely lower Pasang to the full length of the rope and then cut steps for my own descent. The snow was waist-deep at the foot of the shoot and we could only just plough through it, taking two hours to reach the Great Divide, which we crossed without incident. The sun was terribly hot and the glare intense. Our progress became slower and slower until we had to stop and rest after practically every step and whenever we sat down in the snow we immediately fell asleep.

Not far below us, only two or three hours' going in normal conditions, we could see a small lake just beyond the Giant's Fang, where the snow gave way to grass, azaleas and primulas. That vision soon vanished, however, as it came on to snow again, and we had to stop as there were crevasses ahead. We waited for an hour in the hope that it would clear, but the weather grew worse and there was nothing for it but to camp. I dreaded another night on the snow, and had we been less exhausted we would have been greatly tempted to risk the crevasses and push on along the crest of the ridge.

The night that followed was the worst of all and we were lucky to survive it. In the periods of fitful sleep that alternated with bouts of uncontrollable shuddering, I had strange dreams in which I seemed to separate from my body and could return to pity the poor wretch fighting there for his life. In one of these dreams, which I still remember vividly, the Political Officer of Sikkim and all our Lhasa party were visiting the abbots of one of the large Tibetan monasteries. As usual they provided buttered tea and small ceremonial cones of rice piled high on silver saucers. As a rule we did not eat this, but took only a few grains between the thumb and second finger of the right hand and scattered them as an offering to the gods. But on this occasion I surreptitiously collected the rice from all the party in the loose blouse of my Tibetan robe and slipped out to give it to the two miserable men who, I knew, were lying half dead from exposure and starvation in a tent on the glacier outside. Just as I wakened 'myself' up and offered the rice I woke. In the other dreams I was always trying to escape with warm dry blankets or hot drinks to two people whose welfare was a matter of life and death to me, but always before I was able to help them I woke up to find the wet tent wall clinging to my back or the tent flap beating against the frozen end of my sleeping-bag.

The next day, May 25th, we determined would be our last on the snow. We ate a few prunes, had the usual difficulty in pulling on our iron-hard boots, and got away at 6. Plodding painfully through very deep snow we passed the camp where Nima had waited for us, and crossed the Dorjé and final snow-ridge to the Giant's Fang. Here for the first time we found the track of the others and followed it to the dump, where we left the rope and everything we could do without.

By 9 o'clock we were lying on the rocks by the lake while our bedding dried in the sun. We ate some sardines, bread and cake and made some cocoa, and watched a pair of cuckoos which flew past, noisily chasing each other, and a small tortoiseshell butterfly fanning its wings in the sun, and saw a bright scarlet vetch among the grey boulders. Life was very sweet. It was as though we had just awakened from a nightmare; already our adventures seemed scarcely credible. The others, hurrying back to Calcutta, had added to the dump at the Giant's Fang, and although we left behind a Mummery tent, two ropes, and everything else we could spare, we were still carrying about 30 lb. each, but we had only to drift downhill, snatching an occasional sleep where we rested.

When we reached the spring, where the yellow primula was now in flower, we slept again, to be woken up by the singing of two women in pointed straw hats who came out of the wooden chalet and wandered over the hill to call the yaks in. We went into the chalet and found a benign lama sitting cross-legged on the floor droning the Buddhist scriptures, while a dishevelled but hand-some Bhutanese girl wove a bamboo basket in the sunshine. They gave us some sour yak curd and fresh yak cheese and Tibetan tea. Although it was only 11 o'clock we determined to stay with them and rest, for we could hardly walk with our heavy rucksacks. Presently an old yak-herd returned with his animals, which were bringing juniper wood from the forest below, and the two women came in after picketing about sixty yaks outside the hut. To the music of their bells, we all ate boiled rice and drank hot yak milk. Never have I been so conscious of the change from cold, hunger and despair to comfort, safety and content. We had achieved our object in spite of the goddess, and my only regret was that Crawford had not reached the summit with me. Had it not been for his return with Kikuli, the assault must have failed. We had dried our clothes and sleeping-bags in the sun, and that night slept soundly for twelve hours.

In spite of our long sleep, we were utterly exhausted, and the twenty-mile walk to Phari was a nightmare. We crossed two high passes to the south of the La which we had used on the out-ward journey, and at last, after being soaked by a rain-storm, we came out, just as it grew dark, on to the wide Tremo La track, a few miles short of Phari. Here we stopped to drink Tibetan tea with some yak-herds, and in darkness and driving mist started up the final climb to the top of the Tremo La. It was snowing as we passed the summit cairns at 7.30, and we wandered down the far side in a stupor until we lost the track where it crossed a river. In the distance, near where we expected Phari to be, we saw strange lights flitting about like fireflies, appearing, moving slowly along, and then disappearing. I have never been able to account for these will-o'-the-wisp-like lights. After an hour's walking across the plain, when I was beginning to think we had missed the village, I heard a familiar noise—the barking of a dog with a very cracked voice. It guarded one of the monasteries on the out-skirts of Phari, and I knew at once where we were. Soon after this I made out the outline of the fort, and then a faint but constant light—Phari, at last! The dogs all started barking and we stumbled into the dak bungalow to waken the watchman, who came out and gazed at us in amazement, having thought we were long since dead. He kept putting his hands together in front of him and then raising them reverently to his head and heart as if in prayer.

When we went to the post office to collect our letters we dis-covered that our continued absence had caused much concern. Friends at Gangtok and Kalimpong had organized a search party and Crawford had returned to Yatung and was coming to Phari with another climber. Although we had agreed that whatever happened there should be no search parties, he had felt very anxious; knowing the bad weather we must have experienced and being the only person in the world who knew our whereabouts, he could not rest until he had found out what had happened to us.

As we left Phari next morning on two mules with high Tibetan saddles, we saw that all the yaks working in the fields were gorgeously caparisoned with flags and scarlet tassels. It was the first ploughing day of the year, and this ceremony was to implore the goddess of Chomolhari to give them a good harvest. I hoped she would treat them better than she had treated us. Looking back we caught our last glimpse of Chomolhari with snow clouds surrounding the base of the mountain and only the sharp summit showing, trailing its warning plume of wind-driven snow. We pushed right on to Yatung that day, sending our mules back from Gautsa. At Lingmatan we were met by some saddle-ponies that Rai Bahadur Norbhu had most kindly sent out for our use.

We rested for a day at Yatung, where a dinner-party was given to celebrate our safe return. Here I received several telegrams of congratulation, including one from His Excellency the Viceroy, with whom I had had the honour of staying at New Delhi; and an offer from the *Daily Mail*—heaven knows how they had heard of our success—for the exclusive rights of the story. The three-day journey over the Jelep La to Kalimpong was very exhausting, though we carried only the barest necessities, sending most of our gear by mule. The lower valleys, where primulus and blue poppies were now in full flower, seemed amazingly beautiful after our recent hardships, and in the comfort and peace of the Odlings' beautiful house at Kalimpong my health and spirits were soon restored. Pasang, when asked by a Nepali-speaking friend of mine what he felt like on the descent replied, " I lost all love for my body, but the sahib brought it back safely, and I hope we shall climb another mountain together ". I hope we shall.

I lost fifteen or twenty pounds' weight on the climb and both Pasang and I found that we had no feeling at all in our feet. I was afraid that they had been seriously frostbitten, but though this numbness lasted for several weeks it was only superficial. Another curious effect of the climb was that a deep groove appeared across my finger-nails and toe-nails, marking the time, I suppose, when my life was at so low an ebb that its customary supply of calcium was cut off.

The late General Bruce, in an after-dinner speech to the Fell and Rock Climbing Club of the English Lake District, referred to my safe return from Chomolhari as the Eighth Wonder of the World. As his other remarks were almost embarrassingly complimentary I trust he did not mean to imply that I had broken the unwritten law of British mountaineering by stretching the margin of safety beyond justifiable limits.

Had the diabolical stratagems of the goddess prevailed, I could have been blamed—posthumously—for my rashness and temerity in laying siege to so formidable a stronghold with a small and inexperienced party; but not, I think, for my reluctance to turn back when I had once accepted her challenge. For, having decided to go on, I took all possible care, and the evil that befell us had no connection with our weakness but was caused by a series of misfortunes which might have happened to the strongest party.

The season following our ascent of Chomolhari was remarkable for the richness of the harvest, especially in the plain of Phari. By this gift of fecundity the goddess condoned our violation of her virgin snows.

# GLOSSARY OF MOUNTAINEERING TERMS

*abseil (to)*—to descend by a fixed rope which is passed round the shoulder and thigh.

*aiguille*—a needle-like peak of rock or ice.

*arête*—the crest of a ridge.

*avalanche*—a large mass of snow, often mixed with earth and ice, loosened and descending swiftly down a mountain-side.

*belay (to)*—to secure the rope round the ice-axe or round a projection of rock or ice.

*bergschrund*—the great crevasse separating the top of a snowfield or glacier from the mountain-side.

*brèche*—a narrow gap in a ridge.

*buttress*—a rib projecting from a rock or ice face.

*cairn*—a pile of stones.

*chimney*—a vertical narrow rift in a rock face.

*col*—a pass (*La* in Tibetan).

*cornice*—an over-hang of snow or ice formed on a ridge by the wind.

*couloir*—a steep gully in a rock or ice face.

*crevasse*—a fissure in a snowfield or glacier.

*flake*—a flat piece of snow or ice partially detached from the main body.

*gendarme*—(literally, a policeman)—a pinnacle on a ridge.

*glacier*—an immense mass or river of ice in a high mountain valley, formed by the descent and consolidation of the snow that falls on the higher ground.

*glissade*—a method of descending snow-slopes by sliding.

*gully*—a steep ravine in a mountain-side.

*ice-fall*—a much-crevassed part of a glacier formed by irregularities beneath the ice.

*moraine*—a pile or line of stones carried down or deposited by a glacier.

*pitch*—a section of a climb, often from one suitable belay to another.

*piton*—a spike, usually with a ring attached, which can be driven into ice or a crack in the rock for fixing a rope.

*scree*—steep slopes of loose rock.

*serrac*—ice pinnacles formed by intersecting crevasses.

*traverse (to)*—to make a more or less horizontal passage across a mountain-side; also used to describe a climb up one side of a mountain and down the other.

# LHASA: THE HOLY CITY

THIS EDITION OF "LHASA: THE HOLY CITY" IS SLIGHTLY ABBREVIATED. THE CHAPTER NUMBERED FOURTEEN IN THE ORIGINAL VERSION HAS BEEN OMITTED.

# LHASA : THE HOLY CITY

## CONTENTS

| CHAP. | | PAGE |
|---|---|---|
| I. | Preparations | 175 |
| II. | To Phari | 183 |
| III. | To Gyantse | 198 |
| IV. | To Lhasa | 213 |
| V. | Lhasa Officials Come to Call | 234 |
| VI. | We Return Their Calls | 256 |
| VII. | Historical Interlude | 278 |
| VIII. | Lhasa City | 297 |
| IX. | The Potala | 319 |
| X. | The Norbhu Lingka | 329 |
| XI. | Monasteries | 340 |
| XII. | Festivals and Processions | 356 |
| XIII. | Our Life in Lhasa | 367 |
| XIV. | Christmas Holiday Interlude | 391 |
| XV. | Tibetan New Year | 409 |
| | Conclusion | 432 |
| | Index | 435 |

# CHAPTER ONE

## PREPARATIONS

THE train left the sweltering heat of Calcutta at nine o'clock in the evening of July 27th, 1936, and reached Siliguri, the terminus of the full-gauge railway, at six-thirty the following morning.

When I woke up at six, we were still crossing the interminable plain of Bengal. But already, with a growing excitement, I could see ahead of us the misty blue line of the Himalayan foot-hills. In the early mornings and late evening the plain has a strange nebulous beauty which vanishes in the cruel heat of day. In the uncertain light of approaching dawn shadowy forms gradually reveal themselves: groves of graceful olive-green bamboos like bunches of Prince of Wales' feathers, big-leafed banana trees slashed and torn by the recent monsoon rains, a village of thatched mud huts, groups of clumsy water-buffaloes, and everywhere paddy-fields separated by low walls of mud. They say that so fine is the alluvial deposit brought down from the Himalaya to form this immense plain, that the whole way from Siliguri to Calcutta there is found no stone bigger than a child's fist.

At Siliguri there was an infectious holiday spirit abroad, and in the air a sweet tang of the hills. How good it was to see the smiling, oblique-eyed faces of the hillmen again after the impenetrable sly hostility of the Bengali Babu! I felt that one had so much in common with these virile, cheerful folk; they smile, and are obviously glad to see one. The narrow-gauge Darjeeling line starts at Siliguri, and most of the way to Teesta Bridge plays hide-and-seek with the road. There is something very romantic about these Lilliputian railways: possibly because of their resemblance to the clockwork trains of one's childhood.

After eggs and bacon at the station, I chose a spacious open car and, with all my luggage in the back, set off for Gangtok, a journey of about fifty miles in which we would have to climb 5000 feet. My driver was a lithe, yellow-skinned Nepali, wearing an embroidered black hat like a small fez. Unfortunately we had no common language.

The village of Siliguri, set about with mango trees and dingy fly-infested roadside shops, is depressingly squalid; but soon the road crosses an open stretch of country where the houses are raised on stilts—presumably because of floods—and where heavy-horned water-buffaloes plough the dark rich soil. Here a big roadside tree was clustered with vultures somnolently replete after some loathsome feast; exquisite azure-blue jays sat sunning themselves on telegraph wires and long-tailed emerald or white parrots flew screaming from tree to tree. For several miles the road crosses the level strip of jungle between the plains and the Himalayan foot-hills known as the Terai, a belt of swampy fever-haunted forest, the home of countless elephants, rhinos and tigers. Between the pale, straight tree-trunks I could see for a long way, but near the ground the undergrowth flourishes with such luxuriance that it would be almost impossible to force a way through, except along the occasional tracks.

Soon after this we entered the forbidding gorge of the Teesta River, appropriately called by the natives "the Cleft of the Winds". The Teesta, a wide and turbulent river at this stage, is famous for marseer (the Indian hill salmon), but in its lower reaches has an evil reputation as a haunt for cerebral malaria. Rising from the glaciers of Kangchenjunga and the great mountains along the Tibetan border, the Teesta flows down the centre of Sikkim eventually to join the Brahmaputra just as that mysterious river takes its final southward bend five hundred miles north of Calcutta. The valley becomes deeper and deeper, and the road is forced to follow the tortuous gorge of the river, occasionally making long detours to cross by suspension bridges the steep-sided valleys that tributary streams have carved out of the rocky mountain-sides. The road is very narrow here, and seems to consist of an endless succession of blind corners and hairpin bends.

My Nepali drove well, but like most Indian drivers seemed to have a violent prejudice against changing gear, and an obsession for blowing his horn whenever he could see less than a hundred yards ahead.

Above the road the forest-clad mountain-sides rose steeply for thousands of feet; below they led, often in a series of precipices, to the turbid torrent below. The forest was tropical in its luxuriance: tree-trunks were shrouded in ferns and creepers; parasitic tree-orchids with sprays of white or magenta flowers sprouted from branches; palms, tree-ferns, and banana trees strained to reach the sunlight through the choking dim-day undergrowth. The trees themselves grew to a surprising height. Their straight ashen trunks looked as thick above, where, reaching the sunlight, they suddenly burst into exuberant foliage, as they were near the ground.

In one place a landslide had recently blocked the way, and as stones were still falling from the scarred cliff above the road, a protecting wooden shelter had been built. As we went beneath this, a shower of boulders and earth crashed on to the roof above us, and hurtled away beyond us to fall into the river below. A cone of debris containing uprooted trees and tons of earth spread steeply below the road down to the waterside. During the monsoon such disturbances are frequent and whole sections of the road may disappear into the river; on little-used roads cars may be held up indefinitely. Thirty-two miles from Siliguri we crossed the Teesta by a magnificent single-span concrete bridge. We were now about seven hundred feet above sea-level. Had we gone straight on past a ramshackle village of dilapidated tin-roofed huts, the road would eventually have climbed through prim tea-gardens and then coniferous and rhododendron forest to Darjeeling. Above the bridge was a string of multi-coloured bunting stretched from side to side of the river. A closer scrutiny showed that each was covered with fine Tibetan characters. They were Buddhist charms and prayer-flags, put here to ensure the safety of travellers crossing the river—a strange contrast to the ferro-concrete bridge!

Soon after this we passed a signpost pointing up to the right, which read " Kalimpong 9 miles ". Ignoring this we continued to follow the Teesta, whose valley opened up sufficiently to allow a certain amount of crazy cultivation: here an alluvial fan of rich soil, deposited for centuries by a mountain stream which now wound peacefully through its handiwork, was lined with concentric steps of mud-walled paddy-fields; here a clearing in the forest showed a fine crop of maize with lush green stalks ten or twelve feet high; and further up were groves of trim dark-green orange trees like overgrown privet bushes. In some places the mountain-sides, too steep for trees, overhung the river; and sometimes a causeway, little wider than the breadth of the car, was precariously supported on wooden props a hundred feet above the water. It was at just such a corner that we met a bullock-cart plodding slowly down the middle of the road. The driver, a low-caste Hindoo, was fast asleep or drunk on top of his load, and no amount of horn-blowing would wake him. I wanted my driver, after passing the cart, to turn it round and leave the Hindoo, still asleep, progressing in the wrong direction; but the man, though quite deaf to our clamour, woke up the instant his cart stopped, and as the bullocks wisely refused to go backwards we were forced to reverse to a place where the road was wide enough for two-way traffic.

At Rangpo we passed from Bengal to the State of Sikkim; and my permit to enter the country, issued by the Deputy Commissioner at Darjeeling, was examined by two Nepali policemen. I also had to sign my name together with innumerable particulars in the police book.

One of the first things that struck me in Sikkim was the extraordinary profusion of large brilliant butterflies. Twenty or thirty scarlet, green and blue swallow-tails, settled or hovering above every patch of moisture in the road, would rise like a flock of iridescent humming-birds as the car approached.

The road continued to climb. The undergrowth became less exuberant. The air grew cool and fresh. Suddenly, above the high forested ridges, there was a glimpse of the far snows. We had reached Gangtok, the capital of Sikkim, a large village which straggles along a ridge running out from the centre of a great horseshoe of densely wooded hills. The sides of this ridge, wrinkled with steeply terraced paddy-fields, drop precipitously to the rushing torrents at the valley foot; while at the lower end lies the Maharajah's palace and his private temple. From here a wide concrete road, lit by electric light and bordered with carefully laid out trees and flower-beds, runs past the rest-house and up to the Residency, which is hidden in trees a mile from the main part of the village. The native bazaar—full of strange people and stranger smells—lies just below the ridge.

The Residency is a most attractive house, solidly built of stone, and roofed with red felting instead of the hideous corrugated iron so common in India, while the entrance hall and rooms are panelled with attractive local woods. The garden, with its well-kept lawns, rustic lily-pool, and flower-beds of Sweet Williams, asters and hollyhocks, forms a pleasantly trim oasis in the tangled undergrowth of the encroaching forest with its graceful tree ferns and orchid-festooned branches. The only Europeans in Gangtok besides the Political Officer, who is frequently away on tour as he is responsible for our diplomatic relations with Tibet and Bhutan, are a lady missionary, the schoolmaster and his wife, and the wife of the State doctor.

The population of Gangtok is about two thousand, and of the whole of Sikkim, eighty or ninety thousand. The ruling family is related to many of the leading Lhasa families. The people are Lepchas—the original inhabitants of the Sikkim forests—Nepalis and Tibetans. In recent years the aggressive and more enterprising Nepali has gradually driven back the easy-going improvident Lepcha, so that nowadays, except in the more remote valleys, the pure Lepcha is rarely seen. He is a guileless gnome-like person with a great knowledge of the trees and plants of the forest.

From Gangtok the mule-track starts for the Natu La, and from Kalimpong the longer and more difficult road leaves for the Jelep La. By these two passes the road from Lhasa crosses the main range of the Himalaya on its way to India, consequently Kalimpong and Gangtok are the great centres for the Tibetan trade, especially in wool. In each of these places many Tibetans reside, and there is accommodation for the muleteer and his animals.

The personnel of the 1936 Mission comprised seven; it was thus the largest Diplomatic Mission ever to visit Lhasa. Of these, all except two were assembled at the Residency on the last day of July, ready to set off for Lhasa. H. E. Richardson of the Indian Civil Service, British Trade Agent at Gyantse, and Captain W. S. Morgan of the Indian Medical Service, both recently appointed, were already at Gyantse, about half-way along the road to Lhasa, and we were to pick them up there on our way north. As well as the Political Officer, who was in charge of the Mission, Brigadier P. Neame, V.C., D.S.O., Royal Engineers, accompanied us, since he was going to give the Tibetans advice upon military matters. He was at that time Brigadier, General Staff, to General Sir Douglas Baird, at Eastern Command Headquarters, and could be spared only until October. The Brigadier, in addition to his distinguished military record, is a well-known big-game hunter and " trekker " and a keen photographer.

When making our plans for the journey we had absolutely no idea how long we would be away. We had been invited up to Lhasa to help the young Regent and his Cabinet to solve several exceptionally difficult problems which had arisen in the last few years. The chief of these was to persuade the Tashi Lama, who had fled to China in 1923 as a result of a quarrel with the late Dalai Lama and who refused to come back to his monastery at Tashi-lhünpo without an escort of 300 Chinese troops, to return to his native country. As the Dalai and Tashi Lamas are the two most revered pontiffs of the Buddhist church, the continued absence of the latter virtually paralysed the religious life of a country where religion is always the primary consideration. The peaceful and speedy return of His Serenity (the title by which the Tashi Lama is usually known) was especially imperative at this time, as the Dalai Lama had died in 1933 and his successor had not yet been found. We were therefore prepared when we left Gangtok to travel to the Chinese border, perhaps as far as Jyekundo, to meet His Serenity and to escort him back to the Holy City on his way to Tashi-lhünpo.

There is a telegraph line from Kalimpong to Lhasa. This was laid to Gyantse by the 1904 Expedition, and continued to Lhasa by British engineers in 1921. As far as Gyantse it belongs to us, but from there onwards it is under Tibetan control. There is also a wireless transmitting station at Lhasa, but this had been left, not entirely with the consent of the Tibetans, in charge of a Chinese operator, by General Huang Mu Sung, after the Chinese Mission of 1934. As it was necessary for Gould to keep in touch with the Government of India, he had asked the Royal Corps of Signals to lend him two young officers who would be able to do the necessary wireless work, and also enough equipment for us to be able to establish and maintain an independent transmitting station should we go far beyond Lhasa. Lieutenants E. Y. Nepean and S. G. Dagg were chosen for this work. I was attached to the Mission as Private Secretary to the Political Officer in order to help him with cipher and other work which could not be done by his staff of Sikkimese clerks. As I had been trained as a surveyor and had had experience of cinemaphotography, these would be useful; the former especially so if we were to cross the little-known upper reaches of the Salween and Mekong rivers on our way to Jyekundo. I was also to undertake natural history work, especially by collecting pressed plants and seeds, and by making notes on the birds seen.

Owing to the uncertain duration of the Mission, and the fact that the official invitation from Lhasa had come through only at the last moment, Gould had had the greatest difficulty in making preparations. We knew that mutton, eggs, potatoes and butter could be obtained at Lhasa and at the various rest-houses, but otherwise we should have to rely entirely on what we ourselves brought from India; and as we would have to do a great deal of entertaining this meant that our supplies of food and drink alone were enormous. After Gyantse—roughly half-way to Lhasa— there were no rest-houses, and we would have to rely on tents. Though most of us were used to travelling light and living simply, and would probably have preferred this, nevertheless a certain amount of display was necessary to impress the Tibetans, whose own officials travel in magnificent style with many mounted servants and an immense quantity of baggage. In a feudal country such as Tibet these outward forms are very important, especially on a Diplomatic Mission.

For a few days at the end of July, while preparations for our departure were in full swing, the yard at the back of the Residency was a scene of great disorder and activity. Nepean and Dagg were packing things that had arrived at the last moment, and trying to reduce charging motors, accumulators and wireless sets into loads suitable for mules. I struggled with theodolites, cinema cameras and flower presses, and tried to make up my mind what I would need on the journey and what could be sent ahead.

July 31st, the day chosen for our departure, dawned inauspiciously enough. At daybreak the clamour of the muleteers and their animals in the Residency yard made further sleep impossible. A thin rain was falling. The stately tree ferns at the foot of the Residency garden were silhouetted against a valley full of billowing white mist. On the opposite side of the valley, thickly wooded spurs, dank and forbidding in the early morning light, led steeply to an undulating crest which was half obscured in cloud. Beyond this should have been visible the far snows of Kangchenjunga and its satellite peaks, but on this drab morning they were totally hidden from view. The boom of a trumpet and a confused throbbing of gongs came up from the monastery below, but was almost lost in the clatter of mule-bells nearer at hand.

The tumult in the Residency yard increased tenfold. The mules were picketed in lines to yak-hair ropes held to the ground by staples. They were small animals, but strong and with that air of sleek well-being that mules seem to maintain under conditions that reduce donkeys and ponies to mere skin and bone. Some of them had terribly sore backs, and all showed the white scars of former galls. A crude wooden pack-saddle was put above several layers of felting, and to this the loads, usually a couple of boxes each of about eighty pounds weight, were attached with thongs of yak-hide. Most of the mules were gaily decorated. Several had strings of bells round their necks or a large single bell, of the type associated with Swiss cattle, hanging on their chests. Another favourite form of embellishment was tassels of yak-tails dyed a brilliant scarlet, and hung about the head and neck of the mule. All had on their foreheads a star-shaped piece of brightly-coloured carpet material, in the centre of which was occasionally a small circular mirror.

It surprised me to see how docile these animals were; even a stranger could thread his way through their close ranks with no fear of being bitten or kicked. The muleteers themselves were a ruggedly handsome crowd of vagabonds with scarred, sunburnt faces, who clearly did not believe in too much washing. They had long pigtails usually finished with a scarlet thread or tassel. Often the plait was brought round over the front brim of their dilapidated felt hats, to prevent them blowing away. The better-dressed ones wore a large single ear-ring in the left ear and a plain piece of turquoise in the other. This ear-ring took the form of a fluted gold ring about two inches in diameter, with a turquoise mounted in the front. As this ring is very heavy, it is supported by a loop of red cotton over the top of the ear. Covering a very dirty shirt, a homespun robe was worn hitched up at the waist to leave the knees free. Very often only one sleeve was used, the other hanging loose and leaving one shoulder bare. Homespun trousers were tucked into cloth knee-boots with thick yak-hide or rope soles. All had a wooden whip-handle with a short lash thrust into the belt. Many of them also carried swords.

Even more striking than the muleteers were the orderlies of the Sikkim Residency who were helping to arrange the loads, and many of whom would accompany us as servants. These men, in common with the servants of the Maharajah, wear the uniform of the old Sikkimese militia. A robe of brightly striped woven material comes almost down to the knees. Over this is a very short jacket of bright scarlet with black facings. Puttees are worn, but the knees and feet are bare. The hat is of conical wickerwork, like an upturned waste-paper basket, on the summit of which is a bunch of peacock feathers. From the back of this hat protrudes the inevitable pigtail. A broad Sikkimese sword in an open bamboo scabbard is usually worn.

Most of the mules set off in advance of us, one driver being in charge of eight or nine animals. Occasionally their loads became entangled, or a mule took the wrong turning, but beyond ruining the appearance of a part of the lawn which seemed to attract them, they were persuaded without undue difficulty to take the steep zigzag track that led from the garden to the roadway above.

# CHAPTER TWO

## TO PHARI.

THE main Lhasa–India trade route, together with the telegraph line, goes to Kalimpong in the extreme north of Bengal. This route crosses the southern ridge of the Himalaya by the Jelep La, a pass slightly higher and much more difficult than the Natu La, which descends directly to Gangtok. Kalimpong is connected by a ropeway to the Darjeeling Railway, whereas any merchandise arriving at Gangtok has to be carried by car or bullock-cart beyond Teesta Bridge before it can be brought to the railway. Thus it is that the bulk of the Tibetan trade, more especially the wool traffic, goes to Kalimpong, leaving the shorter Natu La track comparatively free.

Taking a steep short-cut straight up from the Residency garden we passed the Sikkim State gaol with its cheerful-looking prisoners and met the Tibet road on the further side of the spur on which Gangtok is built. For the first few miles the road is possible for motor traffic, though I have never seen a car there. The track zigzags steeply for a thousand feet, then, having gained the requisite height, contours precariously around the steep wooded curve of an immense horse-shoe valley carved during centuries by the upper waters of the Rongni Chu.

It came on to rain soon after we started, and became oppressively hot. The atmosphere of the forest on the lower stretches of the road seemed to be a combination of the Tropical House at Kew and the Parrot House at Regent's Park. Every leaf and twig scintillated with drops of moisture; the brooding silence was punctuated by the monotonous dripping of sodden foliage; a heavy fragrance hung everywhere—the fetid smell of decaying vegetation mingled with a hot-house perfume of orchids and other sub-tropical blooms. At intervals birds would start to shriek, continually repeating some haunting clarion call; and if they showed themselves one saw the vivid colours associated with tropical forest and jungle—the lapis lazuli blue of a verditer fly-catcher, the peacock iridescence of a king-crow, the gold and scarlet of elegant minivets.

The scenery was magnificent; but, to me, depressing in its dank luxuriance, especially so in the silent drizzle. The track occasionally led across level clearings where hump-backed cattle, reminiscent of the plains, wandered knee-deep in the lush grass. Here would be frail huts walled and roofed with strips of woven bamboo, and occasionally a more substantial house of wood. Their occupants, heavy-featured Nepalis or effete sallow-faced Lepchas, watched us with expressionless faces as if they had long since been overcome by the leaden spirit of the forest.

The track was about nine feet wide and very well constructed, with large cobbles neatly aligned at the edge. This surface provided a good footing for the pack-animals, and successfully withstood the monsoon rains without becoming a quagmire. On the left there was a steep grassy bank of a few feet, on which flourished all sorts of flowering plants; but immediately above this the impenetrable forest started, and sloped steeply upward to be lost in lowering clouds a thousand feet above the track. On the right the wooded mountain-side dropped thousands of feet to the river in the valley bottom, invisible among the tree-tops and shreds of cloud. From the other bank of the stream a similar mountain-side, with never a patch of grass or earth showing through the trees, ran straight up to disappear far above in the same sullen clouds.

As we climbed, the character of the forest changed. At first there were semi-tropical trees with straight pale trunks and large leaves, while the undergrowth consisted of flamboyant bamboos and tree ferns. Gradually the big trees became fewer, partly owing to the increasing height, but also because the hillside inclines ever more steeply, leaving insufficient subsoil for the nourishment of any but the most hardy trees. It seemed incredible that vegetation could cleave to such vertiginous hillsides; indeed in many places the very earth had peeled away, leaving long scars of naked rock like the ribs of an ancient wreck half choked in moss and seaweed.

We soon noticed rhododendrons, not the stunted bushes of the tree-line border-land, but great trees with scaly red bark and leathery emerald-green foliage. One variety had leaves a foot in length hanging in the form of a spearhead at the summit of each gnarled twig. Their flowering season was long over but there were still a few belated and bedraggled clusters of pink or scarlet blossom.

The ponies were in excellent condition, and we reached the rest-house of Karponang, nine miles from Gangtok, at one o'clock. These rest-houses have been put up every ten or fifteen miles along the way from Gangtok to Gyantse. They were originally built soon after the Younghusband expedition of 1904, but most of them have been enlarged or rebuilt since. They are intended for the use of Government officials, but are also at the disposal of tourists, a limited number of whom are each year allowed up the trade route as far as Gyantse.

Karponang is the dog-Tibetan name given to the place by a British subaltern who was attached to the escort at Gyantse. It is a literal translation of the words White House; but in the first place the two words would be the other way round in the Tibetan language, and in any case they are not the right words. The bungalow is built on a steep ridge overlooking the track. It is made of wood, and has half a dozen rooms furnished with beds, wooden arm-chairs, tables and large open fire-places. Visitors provide their own bedding and food, but, from the watchman, paraffin for the lamps can be bought, and an unlimited quantity of firewood. At one time an enterprising Political Officer ornamented the walls with menus of sumptuous dinners from most of the best-known eating-houses of London and Paris. But one of his successors, thinking these too tantalizing for an exile living on eggs and tinned food, had them removed. In each bungalow there is a collection of literature, including, inevitably, venerable bound volumes of *Punch*, *Blackwood's Magazine*, *Vogue*—for lady travellers—and a mixed collection of cheap thrillers, Victorian novelettes and obsolete text-books on the most abstruse subjects under the sun. Karponang bungalow was exceptionally large and imposing. A glass-fronted veranda enclosed one side of the building from which doors opened to the rooms. As the cook and his mate had gone on ahead, a hot lunch was ready for us on our arrival.

When the pack-mules came in I collected all my gear and sorted it, leaving out the boiling-point thermometer so that I could estimate the exact altitude of the bungalow. Some difficulty was experienced in carrying my cameras so that they would be available at a moment's notice, especially as some of them were so bulky. No saddle-bags were available at Gangtok and I had not had time to have any made. In the end I packed most of the cameras in a large rucksack which was carried, not without some complaint, by one of the grooms (the word groom is rather flattering: most of the *syces*, as they are called in India, know little about the care of horses, relying on their masters for instruction).

After lunch I went out to collect plants. The forest flora is fairly well known, as botanists since the time of Sir Joseph Hooker have collected in Sikkim. I did not really intend to collect and press specimens until we reached the highlands of Tibet, but there were many plants entirely new to me, and I could not resist making a collection of these. So engrossed was I in blue campanulas, new primulas and other exciting flowers that I forgot all about the leeches, those insidious pests of the forest that for me, at any rate, take all the pleasure from forest travel at this time of the year. Suddenly, as I stooped to pick a flower, I saw two of these slimy slug-like creatures moving over my hand trying to secure themselves in their favourite place for blood-sucking—the soft flesh between the fingers. They were impossible to shake off, and plucking at them merely transferred them from one hand to the other. Desperately wringing my hands to get rid of them, I saw another, an enormous one, looping its hideous way from my stocking to my bare knee; several were disappearing over the tops of my shoes; another, anchored firmly to my shorts, blindly waved its body as it searched for my flesh. All around me through the wet grass I could see them undulating their way towards me relentlessly, their eyeless senses telling them that here, at last, was the smell of living blood, the meal of a lifetime—for how many of all the millions of leeches can ever get the chance of a good drink of warm red blood? Leeches always fill me with an inordinate fear, and I was paralysed with terror. Was it better to stay there desperately plucking off the creatures while more and more surrounded me and crawled on to my shoes, or should I allow many of them to get a hold while I bolted for the open path where I could keep pace with their attacks? The latter course prevailed, and I charged precipitantly through the clinging undergrowth and half ran, half slithered to the track a hundred yards below. I pulled off those that had not already attached themselves, and then ran back to the bungalow where I could get salt, which instantly makes them release their hold. I knew that there were a good many already sucking, and to be without salt (or a cigarette-end, which is equally effective) and to watch these loathsome creatures gradually bloating themselves, and knowing that if you pull them off not only will it hurt, but the wound will go on bleeding for hours, is a horrible predicament. Even when the replete leech lets go of his own accord the small puncture will bleed for several hours and will itch terribly for days, because the insect injects some chemical which prevents the blood from coagulating. Leeches have a way of lying in wait on the extremities of twigs, so that as the victims brushes past they can attach themselves. Some say they drop from trees. But most of them come from the ground, clinging to your shoes as you pass. This can be prevented if you wear two pairs of socks or stockings, and smear them well with a solution of areca nut. The natives sometimes go about with a small bag of damp salt on the end of a stick and one touch with this makes the leech drop off. The above may sound rather exaggerated seeing that these forest leeches are a mere couple of inches in length at the most; but it is an understatement of the paralytic terror that seizes me when I find myself among them.

After dinner we sat round a roaring log fire, and for the first time I could really believe we had started. Though I had gone to Dehra Dun to take a " refresher " course in survey, and though for some time I had been practising cipher work and trying to learn the Tibetan language, it had not been certain until only a week or two previously that we would actually go to Lhasa; and since the official invitation came through I had been so busy making last-minute preparations and not thinking beyond the matter in hand that I had scarcely had time to realize that I was about to satisfy a life's ambition—to visit the Holy City of Lhasa; that once more I was embarking on an expedition—leaving civilization (as we smugly call it) with a few chosen companions in order to undertake a difficult enterprise.

There is always a feeling of overwhelming liberation in setting off on some carefully planned expedition that has occupied your mind, possibly for years; but there was something essentially dramatic in the beginning of this journey to Lhasa. One day we did not know if we would even start : a day later—as it seemed— we were on the road.

That night, after spending some time pressing plants and writing up my various logs, I went out to look at the weather. I could hear the laughter of the muleteers as they sat—probably gambling —round the fire in the hut a hundred feet below, through the frail walls of which the lamplight feebly glowed. The mist had rolled away. The clouds had vanished. It was a clear starlit night. Far, far above me I could make out the broken line where the summit trees were silhouetted against the sky. And the Great Bear, who usually rides so freely in the heavens, appeared to be shut in and almost surrounded by the encroaching sides of a bay in this high horizon.

Next day, the 1st of August, we left soon after five o'clock. It was cloudy, but the hills were clear. Their wooded slopes cut by deep gorges rose right up above us; and coasting across them, disappearing only to follow the contours round the edges of hidden ravines, could be seen our track until it disappeared among pine trees over the Lagyap La, a pass just over 10,000 feet, the lowest exit from the great amphitheatre formed by the head of the valley. The track here was in a few places really steep, but was far more spectacular than the day before. In some places, supported only by crazy scaffolding, it cut across precipices. On many stretches an iron railing was necessary to protect the animals from a vertical drop of hundreds of feet on to the tree-tops below. There were still a few large rhododendron trees beside the track, but higher up the steep slopes were covered with scrubby bushes of an exquisite blue-green colour, a contrast to the yellower green of the dwarf hill bamboos.

The flowers increased in number as we approached the pass, and

I grew weary of getting on and off my pony to collect them. In one place, turning a sharp corner, we came upon a waterfall pouring down on to the track. There was just room to splash across a narrow platform, where the water ran level, before plunging over the edge and falling in a series of cascades to be lost in the tree-tops below. The ponies were imperturbable, having been bred to forest tracks and passes. Just as we reached the Lagyap La, looking back, we had our last view of Gangtok: 4000 feet below us on the end of a wooded spur we could see the Maharajah's palace, and the golden roof of the temple shining in the sunlight. Above the ridge, hill behind hill paled into distance.

Beyond the head of the pass we seemed once again to be in a different world. Here were only coniferous trees; and the track at first followed a clear mountain stream, occasionally crossing it by wooden bridges. The fir-clad hills sloped steeply to bare hill-tops over which the clouds hung low. The aromatic fragrance of pines, the clear cold air blowing off the hills in front of us, the bright primulas growing out of the moss beside pellucid springs, the sound of yak bells falling sweetly from the upland pastures, and the houses roofed like chalets with ash-grey wooden tiles weighted down with stones, all carried an atmosphere of Switzerland.

We passed a wayside monastery where a surly monk stood at the entrance gate and watched us with expressionless face. The track zigzagged steeply for several miles through the lichen-covered fir trees, then suddenly, in company with a fair-sized cascade which tumbled down the rocks, it emerged above the final wooded ridge and entered a cup-shaped valley filled with a still grey lake. The trees stopped abruptly. On the right of the lake a steep slope clothed in birch and rhododendron scrub ran down to the water's edge. On the left a bare rocky hill-side just left us sufficient room along the margin. A mile ahead of us the lonely bungalow of Changu overlooked the lake, and beyond it the track led over a low ridge covered with dwarf rhododendron and azalea bushes. The scenery reminded me of the north of Sutherland, especially as the clouds had descended again and low mist swept across the hills.

Changu has a bad reputation. Hardened travellers feel ill here and blame the water, which they say is poisoned by the rhododendrons. But the explanation is simple: being at an

altitude of just over 12,000 feet, it is high enough to bring on a
temporary attack of mountain sickness, especially in those who
come up from Gangtok, more than 6000 feet lower down, in a
single day. We had lunch at the bungalow, and a much-needed
rest. Though none of us felt ill we were all rather weary.
Through the window of the bungalow we looked out on to a
border of tall *Primula Sikkimensis* and wild blue iris. Below us
lay the lake, sombre and grey. At the far end, just at the outflow
of the water, the mountains fell back on either side so that the
sky appeared to meet the lake in which it was reflected. Beyond
there seemed to be a great void.

After lunch we climbed the low hill behind the bungalow
and contoured round the head of a deep but narrow valley to
the foot of the Natu La. On this stage of the journey there were
open meadows covered with gay flowers like an Alpine pasture.
Just at the foot of the pass lay a shallow lake, and near this a track
came in from the right, and there was actually a signpost. Had
we turned to the right we should have reached, after seven or
eight miles, the village and bungalow of Kopup on the main
Lhasa–Kalimpong trade route, just south of the Jelep La.

Our own track climbed the rock-strewn grassy slopes to the
summit of the Natu La (14,300 feet) in a series of carefully graded
zigzags. Unfortunately there was thick mist on the top, and we
were deprived of a magnificent view across to the highlands of
Tibet. From here we should have seen the distant peak of
Chomolhari (pronounced Cho-mo-lha-ri) rising in majestic
isolation to a height of 24,000 feet. Near the summit of the pass
we met a herd of yaks picking their way carefully down the stony
pathway. Grotesque, with their matted coats hanging like plus-
fours to their knees, they are, in spite of their formidable horns,
as docile as domestic cattle. At the very top of the pass were
several large heaps of stone surmounted with bunches of many-
coloured prayer-flags tied to sticks. These were not only used to
afford spiritual protection to travellers, but to mark the frontier
between Sikkim and Tibet. Some of the muleteers threw
additional stones on to the cairns, and one of the more pious
attached a scarlet flag covered with black writing. I could hear
the querulous note of choughs coming through the mist, and once
the deep croak of a raven. On the far side we soon got clear of
the mist, and here the whole hill-side was carpeted with rhodo-

dendron bushes three feet or so in height. It was indeed a pity they were not in bloom. Once more we descended from the upland meadows to the belt of birches and flowering shrubs, then to the woods of deodar, silver fir and pine. When we stopped by the roadside for a picnic lunch we were intrigued by a great number of spikes, four to six feet in height, standing like candles on the bare hill-sides above us. At that distance they seemed too straight and regular to be any kind of flowering plant, but on investigation we discovered that they were giant wild rhubarb.

The road was no longer paved with stones, and henceforward it deteriorated into a treacherous muddy track with puddles up to the horses' knees. At four o'clock we reached the bungalow of Champithang (13,350 feet), having covered a double stage of about twenty-five miles. This bungalow has three rooms—a small dining-room and two bedrooms—but that night I think we would have slept anywhere.

I now make more direct use of my diary:

*August 2nd, Sunday.*—Stayed up till midnight pressing flowers and drying their paper before the fire; in this damp country it has to be changed almost daily. Called at five. Feel dull and heavy owing to the height, but not really ill. Porridge, tinned herrings, scrambled eggs, bacon and potatoes: the height doesn't affect our appetites! Arranged my camera gear into a coolie load and two saddle-bags. The big tripod is awkward to carry on horseback. Away soon after seven. Raining intermittently and lowering clouds. The track is vile here: alternate ridges of clayey mud and water, as if the foundation were railway sleepers. Tree-trunks were put down in the worst places to lead across the mud. Neame, who had a headache last night, rode; Gould and I walked all the way to the monastery. I collected flowers. Two new primulas today: a deep violet variety with grape-like bloom on it, and a cowslip-coloured one with the flowers in several whorls. The periwinkle gentian is common and a new blue one. Very few birds. Saw two blood pheasants and a monal. The path ran gently downhill among pine trees for several miles, then quite suddenly came out at the top of an open bank sloping steeply down to Kargyu monastery.

This south-facing slope was a veritable flower-garden. There was a wild red rose in flower, and two varieties of the single waxy azalea, deep cherry-coloured and cream. Several kinds of orchid grow here, including a vivid pink one I haven't seen before. Away down below we can see the winding river of the Chumbi valley set among a chequer-work of fields, green and gold and brown. Villages of grey-roofed chalets cluster at the foot of the heavily wooded hill-sides; and up above, intermittently visible through a hanging curtain of mist, are clearings of open pasture where yaks graze.

Took some cinema shots of our baggage mules descending the hill. Met a few travellers: women dressed in brightly striped homespun, carrying immense loads of grass and bamboo shoots for fodder; vagabond men with square turquoise ear-rings, untidy pigtails tied round their heads, and unkempt straggly beards; itinerant monks, with shaven heads and deep-set unfriendly eyes, wearing dirty mulberry-coloured robes; and always trains of mules and donkeys carrying wool. The muleteers and yak-herds are often accompanied by large black mastiffs with heavy red woollen collars, worn as protection against wolves. Often they are kept on chains. They are very independent and aloof, but not aggressive.

The monastery of Kargyü, on the spur of a hill commanding the Chumbi valley, looks lovely from above with its ash-grey shingled roof and brightly painted walls. The monks of the monastery belong to a special sect of Buddhism called Kargyü, which is prominent in Bhutan but rare in Tibet. On the hill-side above, and just beside the monastery, are a number of *chortens* (curiously shaped monuments of stone usually erected over the ashes or relics of a holy man; similar to the Indian *stupa*). As we approached we heard the deep resonant boom of the long trumpets, like a buffalo in pain. Just outside the monastery entrance was a *mane*, or prayer-wall, overgrown with moss and ferns. Religious custom demands that the traveller leave these on his right-hand side. Just here we were met by a lama [1] band of drums and cymbals, which preceded us to the monastery. As in Sikkim, one man carries the drum on his back while another walks after him and beats it. The musicians were cheerful grubby youths with deep terra-cotta robes and close-cropped hair.

[1] The word lama means " superior one " and is correctly applicable only to monks who are the incarnations of certain Buddhist saints, or to those who, by their devotion and learning, have raised themselves to that status. It has now come to include any Buddhist monk.

CROSSING THE YAMDROK LAKE IN FEBRUARY. NINGDZINGZONKA (23,000 ft.) IN BACKGROUND.
NAN-GARTSE VILLAGE IS VISIBLE BEYOND THE WHITE PONY'S HEAD

THE OLD ABBOT OF SERA
MONASTERY

THE LORD CHAMBERLAIN
(CHIKYAK KHEM-PO)

LHASA : WE ENTERTAIN VISITORS, NORBHU, TRIMON, TSARONG

We followed them through a most attractive wooden gateway into a large cobbled courtyard where a crowd of monks welcomed us. Behind carved pillars there was an ambulatory right round the yard with ancient-looking frescoes on the walls, depicting fierce gods embracing, meditating Buddhas, multi-headed Buddhas, Buddhas with blue, green or red skins—hundreds of Buddhas, and all different; also the wheel of life depicting man's vicissitudes through endless cycles of existence. A fine pony was tied to a pole in the centre of the court; many dogs prowled round.

We climbed a rickety wooden stair, up and up till we reached the Abbot's room. Here we were presented with blue, instead of the customary white silk scarves of greeting, which were collected again before we left. The Abbot (he has held that position for twenty-seven years) is an aged man with a benign yet lively face; unlike the other monks we had met, he wore a grey robe, and had a great mass of hair tied in a bundle on top of his head. We were told that never during his life had he cut his hair. He wore flat discs of spiral-curled ivory in his ears and rings on his fingers—surely unusual for a monk. He also wore steel-rimmed glasses. A very striking figure, but that of a man of the world rather than of an ascetic. When we asked him if it were going to be fine, he replied that it was bound to rain for three days as the Holy Pig had just risen from Mansorawar Lake (near Mount Kailas) and that three days of rain were necessary to consecrate it.

He was extremely affable and gave us tea, cakes made with maize-meal, and russet apples grown in the valley below. The room was painted everywhere with vivid colours, and on the two walls were richly coloured religious paintings hanging in frames of silk brocade. One side of the room was filled with holy books and innumerable images of Buddha in gaily coloured pigeon-holes. (A Tibetan book consists of rectangular unbound pages of manuscript held between two carved wooden boards; the whole is usually wrapped in a cloth to preserve it.) The tumult of bright colours was bizarre but effective. Before going outside again we followed the Abbot into a long musty-smelling room where we walked between rows of huge gilded figures. We then wandered round the outside of the monastery, and returned to the yard, where we took photos of the monks. They enjoyed this thoroughly. Some of them looked intelligent, others

G

degenerate and criminal. They were all very dirty. Gould gave them the customary present of 50 rupees (nearly £4)—an expensive tea! Escorted by our child band, we followed the track downhill. Here we were met by Captain Salomons, of the 2/7 Rajputs, who is in charge of the escorts stationed at Gyantse and Yatung. A cheerful Scot who is very fond of Tibet, both people and country.

Below the monastery the track dropped steeply through fir woods to the village of Pipitang. The Tibetan Trade Agent, usually a fairly senior Lhasa official, lives here. It looked like some Tyrolean village with its wide-eaved roofs almost meeting over narrow streets. There were some fine houses, built of stone up to the foot of the gables, with beautifully carved wooden window-frames and huge frescoes on the walls. In the middle of an open space is a building encircled by a row of wooden cylinders containing prayers written on tightly rolled paper. These are carefully fixed on axles so that the pious can set them revolving, and thus be so many million prayers to the good. Some of those who turned the big wheels were spinning their own little prayer-wheels with the other hand to make doubly sure.

The Jelep La track comes in here, and from now onwards we should have the company of the telegraph line  We crossed a bridge and passed a number of chortens surrounded by fluttering prayer-flags on enormous poles; on the flags were charms and invocations to various divinities. As there was a good wide track by the river we rode again, rejoicing in the contrast to the steep forest. I saw several bronze-winged turtle-doves in a field of pink buckwheat. A pair of hoopoes crossed the river, and a white wagtail. Many crows too, and orange-billed choughs. The river is twelve or fifteen yards wide and very green and swift. It should be a wonderful wet-fly stream, but I don't think there are any trout here. Passed several small water-mills, then a shed containing an enormous water-driven prayer-wheel eight or ten feet high, and nearly twenty feet in circumference, a prodigious cylinder of prayers painted brightly, and with gold lettering on the outside. Passed more chortens and prayer-flags; then rounded a corner and saw Yatung, a prosperous village of stone houses with grey shingled roofs nestling at the foot of a narrow valley. Steep fir-clad hill-sides rise all round to open grassy meadows.

Gould and Neame inspected a platoon of Indian troops stationed here for the benefit of the British Trade Agent; fine-looking men and well turned out. Then we inspected a group of tiny school-boys, each with a Union Jack. After that we walked up to the Agency, which overlooks the village—a lovely long low red-roofed bungalow with a glass veranda in front. It possesses a most heavenly garden : the drive bordered by riotous masses of nasturtiums, green lawns, a pergola of rambling roses in full bloom, a paved garden with huge pansies, lupins, antirrhinums, esch-scholtzias and petunias—all you could wish for. I should have liked to live there. There are *burrhal* (wild sheep) in the hills, and many bears, which come down from the woods and raid the crops. The rest-house is very comfortable and lies on the other side of the river. On this side are the village, the barracks, the Agency, and Post Office. Yatung is almost 10,000 feet above sea-level, but being so shut in by mountains it cannot get much sun in winter, though in the summer it is delectable.

The Chumbi valley, wedged in between Sikkim and Bhutan on the southern slope of the Himalaya and therefore geographically outside Tibet, has played an important part in our relations with the Tibetans, as it holds the shortest and most practicable route from Lhasa to India. The prosperous natives, who make the most of their position on the trade route, have frequently been disturbed by reminders of the outside world. After the return of the 1904 Mission the British occupied the Chumbi valley until the indemnity had been paid. In 1910, when large numbers of Chinese soldiers suddenly appeared in Lhasa, the Dalai Lama fled from the Holy City. Closely pursued by Chinese officials he made his way down the Chumbi valley and reached the sanctuary of the Agency at Yatung. Next morning, at earliest dawn, he took the Jelep La route to Kalimpong, where he stayed for a few days before proceeding to Darjeeling, where His Holiness was to spend three years as a guest of the British Government. Eight years later the tables were turned : owing to internal strife con-nected with the overthrow of the Monarchy and the establishment of the Chinese Republic, the soldiers at Lhasa found themselves without pay and without orders. It was through the Chumbi valley again that these disarmed Chinese soldiers fled on their way to seek temporary asylum in India.

The valley holds many monuments of the decay of Chinese

power in Tibet.    Where Yatung lies, the valley is comparatively
open; but a mile or two above the village the rocky walls close
in, and in one place almost block the valley.    Just here we noticed
the crumbled remains of a wall built by the Chinese in the eighties
of the last century to strangle any trade between Tibet and India.
A little to the north of this lie the ruins of Chinese barracks and
official residences.

*August 4th, Tuesday : to Gautsa* (12,400 *feet*) : 15 *miles.*—Left
Yatung and followed an eastern tributary of the Amo Chu between
mountains 15,000 feet high.    The river became a rushing mountain
stream overhung with thickets of wild rose, daphne and jasmine.
The stony track, driven to the bottom of the valley, was forced to
follow the stream, and rose with extraordinary steepness.    Up
among the bare crags on our left were a number of desolate
hermitages connected with the monastery of Tungkar, which
overlooks the plain of Lingmatang.    As we rose higher, snowy
mountains appeared above the fir-clad slopes.

This level tract of country set among the surrounding hills
forms one of the most striking changes of scenery I have ever
encountered.    The whole valley has been blocked by some
ancient landslide, and the resulting lake has gradually silted up and
dried.    The track, shut in by steep hill-sides, comes suddenly to
the crest of the heaped-up landslide débris, and as if by magic the
mountains fall back, leaving a dead level expanse, several miles in
length, of lush green grass starred with flowers.    The river,
reminiscent of the Usk in its peaceful meanderings, wanders
through the verdant pasture which in most parts is carpeted with
the cowslip-like blooms of *Primula Sikkimensis* and other flowers.
We lunched beside this pleasant stream which in places forms
deep pools.    Gould put his rod together and tried for a fish, but
though we saw some fry nothing bigger showed itself.    Many
yaks grazed on these meadows, and several of the dark yak-hair
tents of the herdsmen were pitched upon a ring of bales of wool.
They seem to travel in the early morning and let their animals
graze for the rest of the day.

From Lingmatang to the bungalow of Gautsa the scenery
became increasingly wild.    The road climbed steeply at the foot
of the bare mountain-sides broken with desolate crags and huge
detached rocks.    At each turn the valley was so shut in that it
seemed impossible that there could be any escape for the boulder-

strewn track; yet always another gorge appeared with beetling walls or naked tumbled screes—the wildest and most formidably beautiful valley I have ever seen. Crossing a primitive cantilever bridge, we reached the bungalow of Gautsa in a tiny village of wooden houses roofed with shingles. There was a big shed here for the mules and accommodation for the muleteers, who were heard making merry far into the night.

*August 5th, Wednesday : to Phari* (14,600 *feet*) : 23 *miles.*—An amazing day. Filmed the laden mules with a rushing torrent in the foreground and a savage rock-strewn mountain-side behind. A vile track as yesterday. Uneven boulders sticking out of mud, and more mud on each side. Awkward for the ponies. Wonderful flowers. The lavender-coloured campanula still here, and the periwinkle gentian; also several varieties of pedicularis, including the deep magenta one. Much ragwort too. In one place the track ran just beside the stream along the foot of the gorge. Here were prayer-flags on sticks, and a great heap of stones to which every mule-driver added as he passed.

Met three begging monks. The chief one, a gaunt old man with a lovely copper prayer-wheel bound with silver, had a large religious painting which he explained to us in a queer chanting voice. Filmed him. Many travellers on the road today; and always wool, load after load of it. We left the bottom of the gorge with its hard-bitten trees, and climbed up and up past scrubby slopes, seeing new plants all the time, so that I got left far behind trying to collect them. Found a wonderful sky-blue poppy with yellow sepals and prickly stem (*Mecanopsis horridula*); fields of pale mauve cranesbill, smiling blue gentians, and tiny china-pink primulas with yellow centres.

Gradually the country became transformed, and we entered the real Tibet of my imagination. The gorge opened out until we were among rounded hills, grassy low down and marked with scars of scree and ancient landslides, but quite bare and stony on top. There was now not a tree or bush in sight; only a great waterfall dropped from a cleft among some rugged hills on the right. Hundreds of yaks grazed on the fertile valley bottoms or up in the hills, while the blue smoke rising from their dung fires showed where the herdsmen had pitched their tents. Often we would pass a cheerful group of them in the open, naked to the waist, sitting round a fire and eating tea and *tsamba* (roasted barley meal), scooping it out of their polished wooden cups and cramming it into their mouths. They all turned to stare at our cavalcade, but not unkindly. The track passed another great heap of stones surmounted with fluttering prayer-flags, and entered a wide grassy valley which gradually opened up to form a rolling plain about ten miles in length bounded at the sides by rounded hills and sloping gently uphill to the summit of the Tang La. Turning a corner we saw Phari Dzong (fort) away in the distance, and the track going straight across the plain towards it.

## CHAPTER THREE

### TO GYANTSE

*August 5th (continued).*—We have entered another world. A world of immense distances : the dun plateau slopes up to meet the rounded sienna-scarred hills, and behind them the far snows are dominated by the ethereal spire of Chomolhari rising alone into the clouds. In the distance the flat-roofed village of Phari looks like an excrescence on the barren plain. Around it there seems to be a lake of blue water several miles in extent, though we know that this is not so. As we approach we find to our amazement that certain parts of the plain are thickly carpeted with blue forget-me-not and darker aconite. One of the most beautiful things I have ever seen in my life—the sober olives and browns of the plain, then suddenly these exuberant splashes of cerulean blue running up to the massive keep of the Phari fort and the mud boundary-walls of the village.

The plateau, austere and lifeless at a casual glance, is actually full of life. Tiny blue gentians and a minute yellow flower like a celandine smile up at one. I saw several kinds of snow and mountain finches, and Elwes' horned lark with its black and white face like a ringed plover. Soaring above are many birds of prey—lammergeyers, Himalayan vultures, kites and a solitary harrier. Hundreds of mouse-hares, attractive little rodents of the shape and size of guinea-pigs, sit up and watch us, only scuttling into their burrows at the very last moment. At one time I could count over two hundred baggage animals—ponies, mules, donkeys, yaks and oxen straggled along the track between us and Phari, and away beyond where the track sloped gradually up to the summit of the Tang La. I was far behind the rest of the party, having often stopped to collect plants and watch birds, but I could see various officials riding out to present the traditional white silk scarves of greeting.

On the right, coming down from a pass between two rounded hills, can be seen the Tremo La, the main route between Bhutan and Tibet. There are a good many Bhutanese traders here, including the representatives permanently stationed at Phari. They are bigger, wilder-looking men than the Tibetans; they wear their hair short, and their kilt-like robes, usually of a characteristic striped weave, come only as far as the knees. Nearly all of them carry straight swords in beautifully worked silver sheaths. The Bhutanese are inveterate raiders, and up till quite recently they would terrorize the less virile inhabitants of the Phari plain and the Chumbi valley by suddenly crossing the frontier hills and attacking mule-trains and even plundering private houses and monasteries.

The Phari bungalow is flat-roofed, as are all the buildings here, and faces onto a cobbled courtyard together with the Post Office and the rooms of the Postmaster, who is a Nepali, and the hut-keeper, who is rather a superior-looking Tibetan with a long plait, and a heavy gold ring in his left ear. The Post Office, at 15,000 feet, is supposed to be the highest in the world. Soon after our arrival the local headmen, four or five in number, came round to make arrangements for supplying transport for the next stage of the journey. To see them clustered round Gyaltsen, the clerk in charge of the department, was very entertaining. Tibet is a completely feudal country, and except from those in the highest positions there is a great show of obsequiousness. The headman, successful traders and middlemen, stood there with bowed heads nodding in unison as each order was given. In Tibet to obtrude the tongue is a mark of respect, so is a sharp suck-in of the breath so that it will not pollute the air that the honoured person is breathing. As the servant takes orders he continually says the word *la-les*, which means " yes, sir ", in a high-pitched sobbing voice, sucking in his breath at the same time.

The effect is most ludicrous. The result of these negotiations was at any rate successful, for later in the day there were about 200 yaks and *dzos* (cross-bred yaks and cattle) picketed outside the bungalow wall.

The *Dzongpön* (fort commander) of Phari came in for tea. Even fairly minor officials seem to have perfect natural manners. This man wore a long silk robe of a very lovely violet colour with a pattern woven into the material. It was held in at the waist with an orange sash. A white silk shirt was folded down over his collar and cuffs. From his left ear hung a turquoise and gold ear-ring with a single pearl in the middle. (This type of ear-ring is about five inches in length and is worn by Tibetan officials of any standing. The strict sumptuary laws of Lhasa insist that the large tear-shaped stone at the end of the ear-ring shall be of blue porcelain and not turquoise.) His black hair was parted in the middle and arranged in two plaits which were brought up to the crown of his head, where they were held in place by scarlet ribbon tied into a double knot. Thus it has been said that in Tibet the officials even have their hair tied up with red tape. He wore a conical hat of white parchment covered with red tassels which hung down over it like a lamp-shade.

Most writers agree that Phari is a bleak and filthy place with no redeeming feature except its superb surroundings. In the afternoon I went to look at the fort. The roads are deep in mud and dung and no one seems to trouble to remove dead and decaying dogs and mules. There are great piles of dung on all sides. Lean curs wander disconsolately round corners. The streets themselves are so choked with the accumulated garbage of centuries that they are many feet higher than formerly and in most cases actually obscure the ground-floor windows; when leaving the road to enter the courtyards round which most of the houses are built one steps down a considerable distance.

The people are dressed in very dirty robes of dark homespun. The women look cheerful but disfigure their faces by smearing blood onto their cheeks and noses as protection against the sun and wind. Some wear the high hooped head-dress of the Tsang or Gyantse province, while others favour the triangular Lhasa style. Most of them wear turquoise charm boxes. Just east of the fort there is a street of bazaar stalls containing a surprising variety of merchandise: mirrors, ribbons, cheap jewellery, cooking vessels, bricks of Chinese tea, iron and copper goods, spices, china, and wooden tea-cups—all sorts of things. Here innumerable beggars sit cross-legged beside the road spinning prayer-wheels and importuning passers-by for charity. They stretch out and shake their arms with fists clenched and thumbs in the air, at the same time protruding their tongues and whining. Several are maimed and deformed, but many seem young and capable of work.

The walls of the fort are solidly built and in good repair, but no one seems to live there. I went up some steps and through a massive gateway into a cobbled yard, on the far side of which, at the top of more stone steps, was a great double door beautifully carved and painted. Outside this door were stocks, pillories, wide wooden collars that lock round the neck, iron fetters, and several thong whips, all prominently displayed to remind the people to behave themselves. A rickety wooden stair led up three floors to a flat roof. All the doors that I passed were locked with heavy padlocks of local design and workmanship. The whole building seemed to be deserted, but from the roof a low droning complaint could be heard, accompanied by the inter-mittent beating of a deep-toned drum. I traced this to a dark cell-like room opening off one corner of the flat roof, where a solitary monk was praying. He took no notice of me what-soever, looking straight through me as if I were not there.

There was a cold wind blowing, and Chomolhari was hidden in scudding storm-clouds. In winter Phari must be unutterably bleak and desolate, a target for all the winds that blow. The roofs are flat and surrounded by parapets, from the corners of which flutter white prayer-flags on branches of bamboo. I took some photos, then returned. That evening was spent sitting round a blazing wood fire. The wood, juniper and pine, is carried from Bhutan, for yak-dung is the usual fuel here. The wireless made queer noises, Gould composed telegrams, Neame made corrections to the military route book of Tibet, while I changed some films and wrote up my bird diary.

*August 6th: to Tuna* (10,000 *feet*): 21 *miles.*—Slept well. Woke at four to see Chomolhari a forbidding black cone sur-rounded by a wreath of nebulous cloud. An incredible moun-tain—for impression of sheer height and grandeur it surpasses any I have ever seen, except the Matterhorn.

Across on the other side of the plain rises the great snowy mass of Pauhunri with no very striking peaks. Got back in time to photograph our yaks being loaded up. They don't like the smell of Europeans, but are most placid with their own drivers. Their horns and shaggy coats resemble those of Highland cattle, but they are much larger and have long thin faces. Went down to film the forget-me-nots in colour. Rai Sahib Tondup, the Sikkimese doctor from Yatung, is staying with me to interpret to my camera men. I practise my Tibetan on him as we ride along. He is going up to Gyantse to take charge while Morgan and Rai Sahib Bo Tsering, the other Sikkimese doctor, go up with us to Lhasa.

A vast crowd of beggars and other people lined the road as we cut through a corner of the town. Crossed several streams, then got into the open plain again. It is very dusty and reddish coloured. Long stretches are covered with stones. On the south and west of Phari there is considerable cultivation, but I gather the barley never ripens up here, but is cut for fodder. The local officials escorted us for a considerable distance along the track, then before returning they presented Gould with more white silk scarves. This scarf technique is complicated. A senior official accepts a scarf from a junior but does not give one in return; sometimes he places the one he has received over the donor's shoulders like a stole. With officials of equal rank scarves are simply exchanged, and the art is, as you hold out your hands with the scarf, to receive yours underneath. The scarves one receives can be passed on again so that one does not accumulate them.

I am getting very sore from all this riding. Gould's pony, like all the best Tibetan ponies, is an ambler; that is to say it moves like a camel, using the two legs on each side together. He progresses at a slow amble of about six miles per hour, a tireless pace for man and animal. My pony only trots. Going fast is comfortable, but a slow trot throws me up and down intolerably.

We passed fairly near a red-walled monastery and then through the cheerless hamlet of Chu-gya, which means " frozen stream ". It is at a height of 15,000 feet. Just a few houses with mud walls and a square chorten from which a couple of old ravens cursed us. A great many nettles growing here.

Our party of about fifty horsemen looks most impressive. The track gradually rises to the summit of the Tang La. It means "level pass", and certainly presents no difficulty to horse or man. Were it not for the line of cairns it would be difficult to locate the summit. We are at our nearest to Chomolhari here, but though the rocky foot-hills were visible, the snows are hidden in cloud. It is most amazing the way the peak rises suddenly from the level grassy plain. Saw two red foxes skulking along near the top of the pass. Hoped to see some *kiang* (wild asses) but there are none, only great herds of sheep and yaks.

From the top of the Tang La the plain falls only a little to Tuna, our next halt. The country is very barren and stony; only a few scrubby vetches and the sere plateau grass survive. In front of us is a range of low pinkish hills with the village of Tuna at their foot. To the left, the plain continues towards Kampa Dzong, one of the routes taken by Everest expeditions. Our way lies to the right beside a great lake which is hidden in stormy clouds. Lunch was ready for us when we got in just before a heavy rain-storm.

Later I walked up the cindery red hills behind the bungalow, and found a surprising number of flowers, including a magnificent blue poppy. The barrenness of its surroundings emphasized the beauty of its transparent blue petals and yellow sepals so that one literally gasped to see it. There was also a blue allium, arenaria, several androsacae, a pink saussurea, and some mauve asters. For the rest it was very wild and lonely, the more obvious vegetation consisting of nettles and thistles. On the far side I could see for miles and miles; there the wide level bay of the plain rose to another range of scarified red hills paling to amethyst in the distance. I have never seen such colouring. The salmon pink of the Tuna hills; the rich shades of bracken and russet where the sun lights up the grassy foothills; the deep violet of the cloud-shadows chasing each other across the plateau; the clear blue of Dochen Lake, and the white snow-clad peaks beyond.

I saw six burrhal in the distance, and a grey animal which might have been a wolf or a snow leopard. I tried to stalk it but lost sight of it. There is plenty of water at Tuna, and the squares of green barley-field look dark against the olive-coloured plateau. From up here the track can be seen plainly all the way back to the top of the Tang La, twelve miles to the south.

I ran down the scree slope to the bungalow, much to the amazement of the muleteers, who had probably never seen anybody run before. I had a long talk with one of them, but I don't think either of us understood very much. He was telling me about the Gods on Chomolhari. He had tied his pigtail right over the top of his battered felt hat to stop it blowing away. What magnificent teeth many of these men have!

Some monk beggars appeared at dusk. One had a black beard and a curious frilled eye-shade of stiff black hair. The chief one had a drum made from two human skulls, and a *dorje* (symbolical thunderbolt) bell. They chanted a mournful prayer.

Nepean and Dagg fixed up a couple of amplifiers and persuaded some of the muleteers to sing Tibetan songs. A great crowd collected. Their singing is curiously harsh and broken.

*August 7th : to Dochen* (14,950 *feet*) : 13 *miles.*—Got up at five and ran up the hill behind the bungalow. I seem to be fairly well acclimatized, as I climbed a thousand feet in forty minutes and took seven to get down again. The pyramid of Chomolhari is clear but does not stand out, for from here it is no longer isolated but forms the western peak of a magnificent line of mountains. Dochen Lake, the Hram Tso or Otter Lake, can be seen running up to the foot of them. All the photographers were at work taking the Chomolhari range and our yaks moving off. We had changed transport at Yatung and again at Phari, but we keep this lot as far as Gyantse; these stages are carefully regulated, as different types of country require different animals.

The track led round the corner of the Tuna hills and away across a wide level plain. There were tufts of vetch, occasional thistles and a sedum-like plant, otherwise it was barren and stony. Still no wild asses, only Tibetan gazelle seen dimly in the far heat haze. There are solidly built square milestones along the track, but many have been razed, and the mileage is only written in Tibetan.

I like to walk and then canter, but we go along at a slow trot which causes a stitch and a sore backside and makes me bad tempered. Met some craggy red hills on the left and soon reached the hot springs of Guru, where General Macdonald had to fight the Tibetans in 1904. There are still traces of the wall which the Tibetans built between the hills and the marsh. A great many birds in the warm water—mallard, redshank and some new wagtails. Very wild, broken country away to the left.

Soon we met David Macdonald returning from Gyantse. We had hoped he would accompany us to Lhasa to teach us Tibetan, but he has not been well. He is an old man now, an interesting character. His father was a Scot, his mother Sikkimese, and his wife a Nepali; and as he was for twenty years British Trade Agent at Gyantse and Yatung, and was at Lhasa with the 1904 Mission, he has a wider knowledge of the Tibetans than any other English-speaking man. A little later we met a woman and two children with their faces completely muffled up, but for the eyes. Their importance was shown by the number of their retinue. This was the wife of Tsa Serkang, one of the high Tibetan officials with the Tashi Lama. She was coming down to Calcutta to collect her husband's baggage, which had come from China by sea. She had a frank conversation with the Political Officer, and told him that the Tashi Lama had already left China for Lhasa; but one has heard that story for many years and he has not arrived yet.

Soon we reached the lake. Between it and the bare reddish conical hills is a mile of fertile grass where gaze innumerable sheep, goats, donkeys, mules, ponies and yaks. Passed a village of flat-roofed houses built of low mud walls striped vertically with brown paint, and reached Dochen bungalow, which is built round a cobbled courtyard. No trees grow up here, but the grazing seems good and the black tents of nomads are dotted about the pasture-land.

After lunch I walked for several miles back along the lake, then returned over the hills as it got dark. It was a fascinating walk. I watched a pair of red foxes playing like puppies. The lake is very wide, about eight miles across; on the far side the mountains rise steeply to be lost in the clouds. I saw Pallas' fish-eagle soaring above the lake; first I've ever seen. Hundreds of redshank here. There are many flowers in the hills, which at first sight look completely barren. Watched some bright-coloured redstarts and rose-finches. On the way home I suddenly saw two kiang walking past and keeping a careful eye on the people in the fields down below. There was no cover, but I lay flat and they came within thirty yards before they saw me and cantered away. They are most beautiful creatures, not like donkeys at all, but more like zebras. They have cream-coloured legs, belly and chest, and rich chocolate-brown back and flanks with curious diagonal markings on the shoulders. A black line runs from the mane down the back and tail. After cantering away they turned several times to look at me, and each time advanced a few paces as if overcome by curiosity.

Behind the village are many fields of barley and potatoes. As I walked round from the back of the rest-house a big mastiff, which was chained in a niche on the corner, shot out with fierce growls and very nearly got me. Luckily he was firmly chained, but my heart almost stopped beating.

Pressed flowers; had a Tibetan lesson; listened to a German concert on the wireless. Neame developing photographs; Gould studying mysterious files. I am sleeping in a tent now, as the bungalows are small. A vast tent designed to impress the natives of Bengal, but the coldest, draughtiest marquee of a tent I have ever lain awake in.

The evening sunlight illuminates the blue smoke of our yak-herds' fires as it drifts through the black roofs of their hair tents. There are prayer-flags fluttering over each; these too are transfigured by the setting sun.

*August 8th : to Kala* (14,850 *feet*) : 12 *miles.*—Fearful noise of dogs and muleteers from three o'clock onwards, so got up and wandered down to the lake. Some large calandra larks here with an unusual melodious whistle; innumerable terns, gulls and ducks. Clouds down over the mountains but sunny and warm. Neame, Nepean and Dagg went over the hills to Kala to see if they could stalk an *Ovis ammon* (big-horned wild sheep) or gazelle.

We rode along the shores of the lake in blazing sunshine. Several black-necked cranes standing far out: so it must be shallow. They were perfectly reflected in the still water. Hundreds of yaks and dzos coming south, mostly loaded with wool: yaks go at a steady three miles per hour, mules a mile faster. Many of the men carry antiquated flint-lock guns with two projecting prongs of antelope horn to use as a rest when firing. Others carry swords, often with silver scabbards set with coral and turquoise. They are grand-looking men, swarthy and independent as Bedouins. They are very cruel to their animals; I watched donkeys being beaten along with huge loads dragging on the ground. Often when the donkeys stop they lie down and have to be hauled up again by their tails, ears and loads. The foals of many of the animals run alongside while their mothers work.

All along on the left are bare rounded hills of reddish earth. We reached a corner of the lake where a river overflowed into a narrow valley. Crossed the river by a causeway gay with flowers, and followed the valley down to Kala. There is a ribbon of luxuriant cultivation along the foot of the valley, then barren rocky hillsides go up to meet the sky. Excellent crops of barley and mustard with wonderful wild flowers—red and yellow pedicularis, forget-me-not, wild asters and primulas. Passed a bare fort and the small mud-walled village of Chalu. Very biblical scenery: parched white sand, rocky track, ochrous boulder-strewn hill-sides, flat-topped houses with grain and straw stored on the roof, and a blazing sun. Reached the wide Kala valley and saw the lake over to the left; and to the right an immense grassy plain running up to rounded foot-hills and higher mountains to the north.

The low flat-roofed rest-house is surrounded by fields of wonderfully rich barley. Walked down to the lake and watched a man ploughing with two yaks. Followed a winding stream to the lake, and put up a pair of goosanders. There are thousands of animals grazing on the pasture-land here. The lake is very shallow and muddy with sandbanks running far out. Some large fish rippling the surface. Many different kinds of waders and ducks here. Returned by the village. It has turned cold now and is overcast. My face is very sore from the sun. The others returned in the afternoon having seen only one gazelle in the distance.

*August 9th : to Samada* (14,100 *feet*) : 14 *miles*.—Up at five, and down to the lake before breakfast. It is cool and peaceful in the early morning, but too hot later on. The Tibetans are all out at dawn. Set off at eight o'clock. Passed a village where all the inhabitants came out and begged. The women wear a strange hooped head-dress with tousled pigtails hanging from the horizontal base of the hoop; they are all very dirty and ragged, but I dare say they have everything they want of life. The plain is eight miles wide here, and in many places is only sand, parched and cracked. There are flocks of hundreds of piebald goats and sheep tended by ragged boys. Lammergeyers and kites soar above us. Saw a good many kiang and gazelle. Nepean and I tried to photograph them, but they were as wild as could be. I hid behind a sandbank, and Nepean and two grooms drove five gazelle and some kiang quite close; I was so overcome by the grace and beauty of the kiang's movements I almost forgot to use the camera.

Soon we left the plain and met the Nyang Chu, which flows to the north and takes us all the way to Gyantse. It eventually flows into the Tsang-po (the Tibetan name for the Brahmaputra) at Shigatse; so we are really getting on. To the south-east across another plain I saw a remarkable range of snowy mountains which run from Chomolhari north-east to the peaks beside the Karo La; I don't suppose anyone has ever even tried to climb them, except perhaps some lama hermit plodding to his desolate cave. All along the sides of the stream there is lush marshy ground abounding in flowers, while tall yellow senecios and blue delphiniums grow on steep banks carved ages ago by the river. While we rested, the six coolies carrying the charging motor walked past chanting the most weird and haunting dirge to keep in step: four double notes repeated over and over again with variations. Then came a coolie carrying on his back a basket containing three black-and-white cocker spaniel puppies which are going up to Lhasa as a personal present from the Viceroy of India to the Regent of Tibet.

Innumerable ruins here of ancient Tibetan forts and houses. Some say the earlier inhabitants were wiped out by smallpox, others say Bhutanese and Tartar invaders. Certainly the population and cultivation have decreased, for along the lower slopes of the hills are the scars of aqueducts and terraced cultivation which are no longer kept up. Reached Samada, at the junction of two valleys, just before a heavy hailstorm and thunder. Across the river are beautiful rounded hills; on this side there are dry ridges of parched red rock. Near the camp is a massive chorten.

Beside the bungalow is a field of dark-blue aconite, in others yellow mustard grows. The barley is beginning to ripen. Turnips, potatoes and peas are also grown up here. Skylarks are singing, and there are hoopoes and yellow wagtails. A few willow groves here, the first trees since Chumbi.

There is a monastery up the side valley with walls painted

GYANTSE TOWN AND MONASTERY (across background) FROM THE SUMMIT OF THE FORT

THE LATE DALAI LAMA
(FROM A PHOTOGRAPH SEEN IN LHASA)

THE PRIME MINISTER WITH
HIS WIFE AND DAUGHTER

red and ochre. I wish I could like these hostile inscrutable monks, but I cannot see what good they do either to themselves or anybody else. The word charity means nothing to them: they do not heal or minister to the people. They have secured the material detachment advocated by Buddha, but they use it to aggravate and exploit the superstitions of the layman.

*August 10th : to Kangma* (13,900 *feet*) : 14 *miles.*—From 3 A.M. onwards a fearful noise of donkey-bells and shouting people. The rains have worn great gorges down the hill-sides, leaving vertical walls fifteen or twenty feet deep. Soon after starting we passed a very fine monastery on the roadside. There were cylindrical banners and brass ornaments on the roof. A few monks stared insolently as we rode past.

In some places there are low broad walls built right down the middle of the road. Along the sides of these are flat stones carved with Buddhas and with the mystic formula *OM MANE PADME HUM* ("Hail to the Jewel in the Lotus!"; referring to the Buddha, who is often depicted sitting cross-legged upon a lotus bloom). We have always to keep to the left of these.

Followed the river downhill all day to Kangma (red house). Dried-up hill-sides covered with emerald-coloured artemisia scrub and empty watercourses. Except near the rivers the country is intensely parched and desert-like. Many ruins again today.

Some fine villages with gaunt fortress-like houses, whose walls are painted in horizontal stripes of red, brown and white. There are rows of thorns along the parapets surrounding the flat roofs, and prayer-flags built up at the corners. The river falls steeply, and on each side aqueducts lead from it along the sides of the valley to water the barley-fields. The Tibetans are most skilful irrigators. Many blue delphiniums by the side of the track, also a big white gentian and a trailing clematis.

Two miles short of Kangma we met Norbhu, who had come down from Lhasa to meet us. Resplendent he was, in orange silk robe, purple sleeveless jacket, pink, white and blue striped boots, and a hat with a multicoloured braid crown almost hidden by a high brim of black velvet, and with a scarlet tassel hanging down behind. He rode a dun horse with a black tail and flowing mane, gorgeously caparisoned, and with two scarlet tassels hanging from its chest. As soon as we came in sight Norbhu dismounted and presented a scarf to the Political Officer.

[Rai Bahardur Norbhu Tondup is the confidential adviser to the Political Officer of Sikkim. He holds the very high title of Dzasa in Tibet, which is next to that of Cabinet Minister. He has had a most interesting career. By birth he is a Sikkimese Tibetan. When he was sixteen he was at school at Darjeeling when Captain—now Sir Frederick—O'Connor came to choose four boys to accompany the 1904 Mission to Tibet as interpreters. Norbhu, who passed out at the top of the list, was made personal interpreter to Colonel Waddell, who was not only the senior Mission Doctor but a serious student of Tibetan customs and religion. Norbhu witnessed the battles at Guru, Kangma, Red Idol Gorge and the storming of Gyantse fort.

He stayed at Gyantse with Waddell, then went to Phari on a temporary clerkship, and later looked after the 200 Indian drivers of the mule and yak carts there. When the Mission left Tibet, Norbhu, who was engaged to a Tibetan girl, refused to leave and was treated as a deserter. A year later, when the Tashi Lama visited India, Captain O'Connor took Norbhu as interpreter, and afterwards sent him to the office at Gyantse for training. In 1906–7 Norbhu was doing survey work in the Punjab. After this he became Trade Registration Clerk at Pipitang (Yatung) and then Tibet Clerk at Gyantse. He was there in 1912 when the Chinese were driven out of Tibet. In 1913–14, when Gould, as British Trade Agent, Gyantse, was acting Political Officer, Norbhu went to Gangtok as his Confidential Clerk.

In 1913, as the Tashi Lama returned from his visit to India, the Dalai Lama was on his way home after his exile in Darjeeling. They determined to meet and settle their differences. Gould and Norbhu met the Dalai Lama at Phari and escorted him to Gyantse. From 1915 to 1919 Norbhu was Confidential Clerk to the British Trade Agent, Gyantse, and to the Political Officer, Sikkim. In 1920 he accompanied Sir Charles Bell to Lhasa. In 1923 he became Rai Bahardur and that year visited Lhasa with Lieut.-Col. Bailey, having previously gone there alone with a present of ponies for the Dalai Lama. In 1927 the Dalai made Norbhu a Depön (military rank equivalent to a general).

In 1928 Norbhu went up to arrange Lieut.-Col. Weir's visit to Lhasa, and later accompanied it. Both visits were repeated in 1930, when the Dalai Lama conferred the rank of Dzasa on

Norbhu. In 1934 he went alone to Lhasa to counteract the Chinese Mission of General Huang Mu Sung and remained there in considerable danger for eight months. In the following year he accompanied Mr. Williamson to Lhasa and, after the tragic death of the latter, went to Gangtok to be Confidential Clerk to Gould. In May 1936 he went up to Lhasa to make the necessary arrangements for our Mission. He has recently been appointed British Trade Agent, Yatung, a post that for many years has been combined with British Trade Agent, Gyantse. At the end of the Mission he received the O.B.E. For the last thirty years, therefore, Norbhu has been in very close touch with Tibetan affairs and people; he has a wife at Kalimpong and another at Lhasa. From a former wife he has a son of sixteen who is at school at Darjeeling.]

· In the afternoon heavy rain came on and there was a thunderstorm. Had champagne for dinner in honour of Norbhu. Lhasa seems much nearer now that he has joined us.

*August 11th : to Saugang* (13,000 *feet*) : 15 *miles.*—To begin with we followed the river along the foot of a deep grassy valley where there was little cultivation. The chief object of interest was some hot springs on the right of the track. Suddenly the mountains steepened and closed in. We had reached Red Idol Gorge, the scene of a battle in 1904 and certainly the most marvellous place for an ambush. The river falls more steeply here, and for several miles is forced from side to side by immense rocky spurs running out from the all but perpendicular sides of the gorge, which tower a thousand feet above the track. The slopes are a chaos of enormous reddish boulders, many of which almost block the way through. The track is paved with slabs of granite, and is continually forced aside by boulders. White quartz crystals have been heaped together by the pious, and there are Buddhas carved on the rocks and often protected from the weather by side walls and an overhanging lintel. The sacred prayer is also cut in the rocks and there are splashes of dull red paint and innumerable prayer-flags. An awesome and forbidding place, wilder than Glencoe or Killiecrankie.

At the foot of the gorge is a huge carved and painted Buddha about twenty feet high. In front of it is a pile of stones collected as an act of piety. At the end of the gorge a valley came in from the north and we looked down on to fields of barley, mustard and peas. Here were several fine houses surrounded by groves of willow trees. Soon afterwards we crossed the river by a cantilever bridge resting on an enormous central pier, and reached the rest-house of Saugang.

This is a delightful place : groves of willows and a few poplars surround the bungalow; magpies, sand-martins, rose-finches, willow-warblers and partridges abound nearby, and I found a new deep-purple primula. A wonderfully fertile valley carefully irrigated and tended. Was much pestered by beggars. Just above the village and bungalow on the far side of the river many Buddhas have been carved and painted on the vertical walls of rock.

After dinner worked at Tibetan. The man in charge of the rest-house produced a 1½-lb. fish which he had caught in the river; it looks like a kind of char.

*August 12th : to Gyantse* (13,120 feet) : 14 *miles.*—Rai Sahib Tondup and I went on an hour ahead to photograph the officials who will come out to receive us. He wears lovely silk robes but spoils the effect with a Homburg hat. A parching hot day; clear blue sky above and heavy cumulus clouds over the hills. More and more trees. One poplar growing in a village was as big as I've seen anywhere. Passed donkeys carrying loads of rice sewn up in skins. Magnificent scenery here : a great pyramid of rock with a fort on the summit; hills running up for thousands of feet on either side, and in one place overhanging the track in huge vertical rust-coloured cliffs.

Soon the valley opened out and I saw tall delphiniums and aconites as well as wonderful crops of barley and potatoes. Up in the hills on the left was a tiny monastery approached by a precarious track. Suddenly, by a chorten, we saw a group of horsemen, and I dismounted to be introduced to a dark-complexioned man wearing a conical hat with a jewelled ornament, and heavily flowered silk robes. This was Rajah Tering, the half-brother of the Sikkim Maharajah, who had some trouble with the British Government many years ago and now lives on his estates near Gyantse. We exchanged compliments in Tibetan, and I photographed him. The Sikkimese doctor and servants bowed down to the ground three times to him, as he is of their royal family. Soon afterwards we met a platoon of Mounted Infantry, drawn up with Captain Salomons in charge

Richardson, the British Trade Agent, Gyantse, Morgan the doctor, and Guthrie, from whom he is taking over, were also there. I filmed Gould arriving and inspecting the escort. The clerks were all there in brightly coloured silk robes and the Agency orderlies in short scarlet coats—all mounted, of course.

Soon afterwards we met the Eastern and Western Dzongpöns of Gyantse, who had come out to present scarves to the Political Officer. Then a little further on we were stopped again by the Tibetan Trade Agent and the Abbot of Gyantse monastery. All these were fantastically clad in gorgeous silks and jewels. The last two are very high officials; for the more senior a Tibetan is, the less distance he rides out to meet a superior.

All these gaily-dressed officials and their servants fell in at the back of our procession, so that by the time we crossed Gyantse bridge and clattered up to the bungalow we resembled some brilliant scene of Elizabethan pageantry.

## CHAPTER FOUR

### TO LHASA

*August 12th (continued)*.—Gyantse at last! The third biggest town of Tibet, it owes its importance to the trade routes from India, Bhutan, Nepal, Ladakh and Shigatse meeting here on their way to Lhasa.

Immediately after crossing the massive pier bridge yesterday we saw Changlo, the 1904 Mission headquarters, where they were attacked by night and besieged. Half a mile nearer the town, in a grove of willows and poplars, is the rest-house. The dzong is at this end of the town, on the summit of a volcano-like rock 600–700 feet high : a magnificent situation. At the other end of the town, on the southern slopes of a rocky amphitheatre, are the various buildings of the Parkor Choide monastery surrounded by a twenty-foot wall which runs along the top of the rocky spur. The dzong and the monastery, from the summits of the only two eminences of the plain, completely dominate the low white-walled houses of the town, which lie on either side of a rocky saddle connecting them.

These spurs are offshoots of a ridge forming part of a 17,500-foot mountain, the highest in the district, which shelters Gyantse on the north-west. Each hanging valley of this mountain has a white monastery or nunnery secluded in its clump of willows. The plain is wide and of great length, full of fields of barley, wheat, oats, peas, beans and potatoes. Dotted about are little farms and villas, each in its grove of willows. There is much flood-water at this time of year. Mountains rise on every side, but only on the north are they near at hand. We have put up our tents on a beautiful lawn surrounded by willows and poplars. We expect many guests tomorrow, so leave the bungalow free for entertainment. Spent the evening doing cyphers.

*August 13th: at Gyantse.*—Left bungalow at 4 A.M. to climb the high mountain to the north-west. I cut along the edge of barley-fields, through the end of the town, by a vilely muddy street full of barking dogs, and across an open stretch of plain covered with vetch, artemisia and thistles. The foot-hills are seared by great gorges as from torrential rain. Lovely white buildings in the hollows of the hills with trees and shrubs round about, and the inevitable chorten in front. On a spur of the hill some people were chanting and beating drums, and the white smoke of incense drifted up. I presume they were cutting up a dead body because, one after another, twenty-eight vultures whizzed from the hills above me and settled in a circle round the group. I was too far away to see much, and it was only just growing light.

Wonderful flowers here. I found white roses in bloom at 15,500 feet, blue and yellow poppies, several new vetches and a • scabious. As I came over the col on to the final ridge I saw twenty burrhal in the mist on the far side. There is quite a good track up to the summit, on which there is an immense square cairn and bundles of prayer-flags of all colours. A line of smaller cairns goes off to the north.

I reached the top, 17,500 feet, at 6.30 A.M., that is 4000 feet in two and a half hours, including taking photographs and collecting plants. Pulse 104 to the minute. Stayed half an hour on top. I saw a hundred laden yaks and a man on a pass to the north-east. A party of eight large burrhal stags just below me took no notice of the man's shouts. It grew cold as clouds scudded across the summit. The country has a marvellous relief-map appearance: the ridge far below me with the dzong and monastery; the wide chessboard plain with its winding waterways and clumps of dark willows; and then the parched ochrous mountain ranges, ridge behind ridge visible for an unbelievable distance. Some snow peaks still visible to the south-west, probably the range that runs from Chomolhari to the Karo La.

Ran down a vile way over rough screes and dry watercourses. Saw several blue hares and a weasel. From one of the villages half a dozen huge black and yellowish mastiffs came at me; after keeping them at bay for some time with stones, they pressed me so hard that I had to climb up a chorten for sanctuary. A most terrifying experience. They would have finished me in no time if they could have got me. After a time a man came out and rescued me. He was very friendly and thought it the hell of a good joke. Got back at eight-thirty.

Spent morning pressing flowers and changing drying-papers. The Brigadier went outside to inspect the barracks and lines. Wireless officers tried in vain to start the charging motor; a bad show if it won't run at this height, even though it doesn't at the moment look as if we shall go beyond Lhasa. But it limits our entertainment programme. Gould received visitors all day. The first was the Tibetan Trade Agent, who is a very important lay official; he is a wizened little man with a pock-marked face. The last Trade Agent was a monk official. He was a great friend of the late Dalai Lama and used to supply him regularly with news. But he was degraded because he forgot the words of a prayer while he was officiating at some important ceremony. At least that is what we are told. The present man lives in a building which used to be the English school run by Frank Ludlow. It lasted from 1923 to 1925, but was closed down, as the Tibetans did not really support it.

The Eastern and Western Dzongpöns also called. One is tall and has very aristocratic Mongolian features. The other, Ten-dong, who is coming up to Lhasa as our guide, speaks English, having been at Ludlow's school. He is a younger brother of one of the Cabinet Ministers; a shy and very attractive man. The titles Eastern and Western refer to the location of their houses, not to the districts which they control. They work together and watch each other's step.

After the Nepalese representative had called, a monk, Tering Rimpoche (*rimpoche* means " precious one "), came to see us.

He is a brother of the Maharajah of Sikkim, and was at one time in charge of all Sikkim monasteries. He has the wisest and most expressive eyes in all Asia. His brother Tering Rajah came too, with his son, another pupil of Ludlow's. All these officials have the distinguished bearing and perfect natural manners of an ancient and proud civilization.

In the evening we had a dinner-party. The guests were Richardson, Salomons, Morgan, Guthrie and Norbhu. After dinner each of us in turn had to sing a song or tell a story. I sang an Eskimo folk-song, and Norbhu said it was exactly like Tibetan music—a doubtful compliment, but interesting, seeing that the Eskimos and Tibetans are, ethnologically speaking, fairly closely related.

*August 14th : at Gyantse.*—All very busy. Charging motor still only spluttering. Nepean and I sorting big film for the entertainment of Lhasa audiences, with Norbhu as censor. We have Douglas Fairbank's round-the-world trip, a selection of news reels and my Greenland films. The first is a series of shots showing Douglas dancing with dazzlingly beautiful girls of innumerable different nationalities; it won't do for Lhasa. The news reels are too disjointed, and as the subjects are mostly unfamiliar to Tibetans, and the shots all very short, they will be incomprehensible. Probably we shall leave the big projector here and rely on the smaller one.

We rushed round returning calls and drinking Tibetan tea. This is made from Chinese brick-tea. Norbhu says they spread it in the road for several days to let it acquire the strength and flavour demanded by Tibetan palates; certainly we cannot grow it in India, which is a pity, because every year thousands of loads of tea come over the high passes several months' journey from China. Any good Tibetan drinks fifty or sixty cups of tea every day of his life. The leaves are boiled for several hours, then the infusion is poured into a section of hollow bamboo, where it is churned up with a plunger, together with a handful of salt, a pinch of soda and a good lump of butter—usually rancid. The result is a purplish liquid of unusual taste for tea, but as soup excellent. The great thing is to blow aside the floating scum of butter before you drink. The moment you put the cup down, even if you have only taken a sip, it is filled up by a servant who stands ready with a silver or earthenware teapot. Custom demands that one drinks at least twice, but however much one has, the cup is always left full. To eat, we were offered dried apricots, sweets and biscuits.

In the late morning we went to a local race meeting organized by the British Trade Agency. The "Fort" is a solidly built two-storied building surrounding an open square. The rooms seem very comfortable, which is probably necessary, since in winter Gyantse is a grim place, the most frightful dust-storms raging almost every afternoon for months on end and the temperature below zero at nights. In the old days there was considerable trouble here because it was never quite clear who was the senior, the British Trade Agent or the officer in charge of the escort. As the latter was often a major and the former a captain, the position was further complicated. Later it was pointed out that as it is the British Trade Agent's escort, the B.T.A. is obviously in charge. It must be a terrible place in winter for the men's nerves, in spite of the peacefulness of the hills and the people. No English women are ever stationed here. At present it is delightful, with a wonderful vegetable garden (at 13,500 feet) and lines of pollard willows all round to act as wind-breaks.

The polo-field near by had been arranged as a race-course with a smallish track, and tents for grandstands. A pony race came first, then a yak race. Actually they were all cattle or rather under-sized *dzos*. They were ridden bareback with a single rein running from the nose-ring. Most of them ran wide, but three finished. Then there was a pacing race, in which all but one broke into a canter and were disqualified. After this came tent-pegging by the Mounted Infantry of the 2/7 Rajputs, finally egg-and-spoon races and pillow fighting on a greasy pole. It was terribly hot. Clear pale sky above, the ring of dun and olive hills shimmering in the heat, and very heavy cotton-wool clouds like stage scenery. Several hundred of the inhabitants came. The better-class ones brought tents where they drank tea and *chang* (the local beer brewed from barley). The others were incredibly dirty but very cheerful. We then lunched in a big marquee behind the Fort. All the local worthies were there in resplendent silks and brocades. To drink we had chang, which I found to be excellent. It is flat and yeasty and of the colour of cloudy lemonade. Tibetans also have a remarkable liking for crème de menthe; perhaps the colour appeals to them. I sat next to Rai Sahib Bo Tsering, the sub-assistant surgeon, who works under the Agency doctor. He is coming to Lhasa with us. A red-faced genial Sikkimese in loud checks, he is a famous horse-coper and is liked by everybody. His pony won the open race today.

*August 15th: at Gyantse.*—Neame and I visited the dzong. Passed through the bazaar on the way. It lies beside the road leading to the monastery. The goods are on trellis tables or simply on the ground under umbrellas. Queer roots and vegetables, rice and grain, wool, dyes, carpets, dried and fresh fruit, cups, jewellery, swords and all sorts of odds and ends. An open sewer runs the whole length of the street, which is absolutely filthy. Most of the women have red pigment smeared on their faces to protect their complexions. Innumerable scrofulous and clamorous beggars. The walls and doors are covered with lucky signs—swastikas, stars, crescents, and above the doors are intricate devices of rams' horns and coloured wool in geometric patterns to divert the visitations of evil spirits. Lean and hungry dogs everywhere. To reach the dzong we rode up and up a rough roadway. Massive wooden gates with crudely stuffed wild yaks and mastiffs hanging in the rafters as emblems of ferocity.

Tendong showed us round. The dzong is full of small monasteries. Saw six huge Buddhas in one room and a gigantic seventh in a room below. Drank Tibetan tea with the monk in charge. The dzong, which is half ruined, is built tier upon tier to the summit of the steep rock; not unlike Mont St. Michel. Went right up to the top. There are no staircases, so we had to pull the ladder up from roof to roof. In a tiny dark room at the very top sat a monk, muffled up in a heavy red cape, beating a huge gong and praying to the spirit of the dzong. He seemed to be in a trance and appeared quite oblivious of our presence. I felt an unaccountable terror, as if in the presence of something deeply sinister. Superb view: green barley-fields, blue winding rivers, russet and sienna hills. The big monastery of Tse-chen lies on the southern side of a rocky hill a mile or two to the north-east. The monasteries here are more like fortified cities than the abode of peaceful monks. One wonders exactly what goes on inside them.

Had tea with Tendong and watched his carpet-weavers working on the balcony outside. Three of them work on one carpet. They use wonderful vegetable dyes of local preparation and rather a coarse weave, but their colours and designs are good.  Gyantse is famous for its carpets.

Spent afternoon sorting entomological and survey gear. Tremendous discussion about the wireless.  Nepean is to stay here and get things going while Dagg returns to Calcutta to obtain a hand charging machine.  We wired to Kalimpong to see if we could get the Everest Expedition charging motor, but it has been sent back to England.

In the evening Dinka Depön, the Shigatse Dzongpön, appeared to call on Gould.  He is an important official, being the most senior of all the dzongpöns.  A very stout man, he had ridden over at great inconvenience to discuss important matters with Gould.  It appears that the Shigatse Tibetans are increasingly anxious to get the Tashi Lama back.  In their eyes he is more holy than the Dalai Lama, and without his presence at Tashi-lhünpo their religious life is crippled.  A cheerful dinner-party at the Agency Fort.  Wonderful how the ponies know the way home in the dark.

*August 16th : to Gobshi* (13,800 *feet*) : 17½ *miles*.—Couldn't get away early as we had to receive scarves and were lunching with Rajah Tering on the way.  Dull and raining.  Followed the Nyang Chu valley.  Very dried-up this side, with queer barren hillocks sticking out of stone and sand deserts.  The hills are parched and seared by dried-up watercourses.  It's like a land-scape on a dead planet.  A few lammergeyers and kites circling high up over the hill-tops.  Down on the right is a fertile strip of cultivation by the river, and then the same desolate hills beyond.

Tering has a beautiful country estate—which bears his name—about six miles from Gyantse.  He is noted for his hospitality and the excellence of his chang.  His wife, a large cheerful woman, is a wonderful hostess.  We had seen women wearing the hooped head-dress, but hers was incredible.  The hoop was about two feet in radius and was held together with wide bands consisting of strings of seed pearls.  The horizontal part of the hoop was studded with large stones of turquoise and coral.  From a necklace hung a diamond-shaped charm-box inlaid with tur-quoise and other gems.  "Daisy", the son's young wife, is very pretty, and has a beautiful complexion.  She has her black hair brushed back and plaited, without adornments.  The room was spoilt by European furniture and inferior Chinese hangings.  We had a good Tibetan lunch: a dozen small dishes—eggs, curried beans, meat, etc., then five or six big bowls of such delicacies as mince and peas, boiled mutton and mushrooms. Finally, as many bowlsful as we could drink of vermicelli soup. Chopsticks are very difficult at first, but soon yield to practice. Chang was poured out by a beautifully dressed girl. The chang jug was of silver with embossed designs picked out in gold. A magnificent and cheerful party; got away at one o'clock.

Soon after Tering the road enters a stony valley and the river rushes down below in a gorge. Further along it becomes a muddy turgid river crossed by unfenced cantilever bridges. The water coming down the side valleys is led off in aqueducts to water the fields. Gobshi is a desolate half-ruinous village at the junction of several barren valleys. It is guarded by a derelict fort on the summit of a rocky pinnacle.

Just managed to get one of the tents up before deluges of rain came down. There are no more rest-houses now and we rely solely on our tents, of which we have one each. There are also two mess tents, one of which is sent ahead.

Now that we have left behind the thirty loads of wireless and projection gear, we have 200 pack animals—ponies, mules and donkeys. A third of them have gone ahead. The arrangement is for the majority of the gear to set off at daybreak (about four o'clock); our own tents are packed up at six o'clock and, with an hour's start, get in soon after us. Of the two mess tents, one goes on at earliest dawn and is ready when we arrive, and the other is left for breakfast and for us to use after our own tents are packed. The muleteers are very careless. Each is in charge of nine or ten animals, and they let them get too far ahead, when they are apt to knock their loads against the rocks. They continually encourage their charges with loud cries. Yaks seem to respond to whistling rather than shouting. The drivers also have a wild ululating cry which they use to signal to each other at a distance: for instance, when approaching a stretch of one-way track to see if anybody is already on it.

Many flowers here in spite of the apparent barrenness of the country. Tall delphiniums and monkshood by the track, and in the hills a small deep-violet delphinium and a large blue gentian growing from a rosette of leaves. Much edelweiss and deep-red rhubarb. Many choughs and magpies here and innumerable small birds, mostly larks, wagtails, redstarts and rosefinches. Did one cypher after dinner, then pressed plants till midnight.

*August 17th : to Ralung* (14,800 *feet*) : 155 *miles*.—We are called at five, breakfast at six, away at seven. We crossed the Nyang Chu gorge by a high and precarious cantilever bridge, and then struck up a side valley to Ralung. Soon the gorge opened out to a narrow fertile valley. Side streams continually come in, providing irrigation water for a cone of cultivated fields. Barley does well at 14,000 feet, but the upper limit for oats seems to be 12,000 feet, and for wheat 11,000 feet, though this depends upon the amount of shelter. Along the river are dark-green twisted willows exactly like those in willow-pattern china. Just as the road cut round a projecting spur of rock I saw a clump of white spiraea. Pale emerald of artemisia up in the hills, tall yellow senecio, marvellous blue delphiniums and, for the first time, masses of an orange poppy with glaucous leaves. On each side of the valley red and orange volcanic mountains scarred with scree slopes and crags run up for 3000 feet. The houses, with their mud walls and flat roofs with dung-cakes on top, are like Egyptian villages. The desert scenery and houses make the strangest contrast to the wonderful crops and flowers in the valley bottom.

Got in at 10.30 A.M.—a fantastic time to finish the day's march. Ralung is a squalid little village at the junction of two streams. There is a walled Chinese posting-house here, still in a good state of preservation. Our camp is on a great level stretch of turf. In one place some stone paving has been put down with a square of white stones for the Dalai Lama's or Tashi Lama's tent and a pathway. They use this route when travelling to and from Lhasa.

The local headman came and presented a scarf, the dried year-old carcase of a sheep, and a box of eggs. Unfortunately practically all the latter were bad. Climbed a hill behind the camp. There is a magnificent view over to the peaks and glaciers by the Karo La, which we cross tomorrow. These mountains run up to 23,500 feet, and no one has ever tried to climb them though they do not look at all difficult. Many small tortoise-shell and blue butterflies here, and an astonishing variety of beetles and flies. The country ahead is exactly like the north of Sikkim. There is no cultivation, just wide rolling valleys with winding streams in the centre of them, and grassy foot-hills going up to 18,000 or 19,000 feet. The dark tents of nomads are conspicuous again, and immense herds of yaks, sheep and goats. The nomads have black mastiffs with them, but dogs are never used to round up the animals, only for protection against wolves. Over the other side of the hill I could see Ralung monastery where monks and nuns are housed together. This sect are permitted to marry and the children follow their parents' calling. Ralung means " the valley of the goat ".

Carefully following Nepean's directions I joined up innumerable different-coloured wires to aerials, batteries of all sizes, accumulators, earths, and a portable wireless set. As I have never touched a set before—except to turn knobs—we were all very surprised when it worked and we could get the news. An ibisbill and several redshanks are calling down by the stream.

*August 18th: to Dzara* (15,700 *feet*) : 16 *miles.*—Followed Ralung valley for a time, then crossed a wide level plain of wonderful pasture-land. Terribly hot sun. Saw a buzzard. Filmed a party of wild-looking herdsmen sitting round a yak-dung fire eating barley-meal and tea. Innumerable mouse-hares on the plain but no kiang or gazelle. Magnificent view of the glaciers and snows ahead. Soon we turned to the right and followed a narrow valley to the summit of the Karo La (16,800 feet). Met a big party of yaks coming down with wool. They prefer to walk on the rocky broken land by the stream rather than on the track, and are in fact, in spite of their efficiency, the most wayward and grotesque of animals. Saw a wall-creeper, my favourite bird; last one I saw was on the Grepon at Chamonix. The track follows a rocky river-bed with steep pudding-stone rocks on each side leading up to precipitous snow-clad mountains with hanging glaciers. Heard a snow-cock clucking up on the right. Extraordinary luxuriance of plants : even juniper, roses and jasmine grow here up to 15,000 feet, as well as the usual delphiniums and saxifrages. Near the summit are wide level valleys as if the gorge has at some time been dammed up by landslides. Crossed a river of glacier water by a bridge—not many bridges at 16,000 feet! On the summit are two cairns joined by festoons of prayer-flags. All the muleteers raise their hats and shout *Lha Gya-lo* (God be praised). A continuous stream of baggage animals over this pass. On the descent we noticed wide subsidiary valleys of rolling grassland up to 19,000 feet, without any snow.

Soon came to our camp on a stretch of level ground beside the altogether desolate village of Dzara, which has a Chinese posting-house as protection against the brigands for which this valley is famous. On the far side of the stream I saw several large marmots sitting up like kangaroos. They are brown and cream, and have faces like otters. The largest stand three feet high. They have a loud shrill whistle like a bird, and when disturbed run awkwardly along the ground and disappear down their burrows. They hibernate all the winter.

After lunch Richardson and I climbed a mountain behind the camp. The top thousand feet consisted of enormous granite boulders piled together. Among the rocks we found the skull and most of the skeleton of a Tibetan. A little farther up we found the pigtail, rotten but still plaited, caught between two rocks. Probably one of the casualties of the 1904 battle; for there are still the remains of walls here put up by the Tibetans to stop the British Mission. A heavy snowstorm is sweeping over the pass, which is spread below us like a map. There are two lakes here surrounded by glaciers and snowy peaks. Several parties of burrhal in the hills. Found a new striped blue gentian and a pale delphinium with sticky foliage and a nauseous smell of cheap scent and sweat; we are going to call it *Aconitum Barmaidiae.* Had tea in Richardson's tent and discussed books while a sleet-storm raged outside. Dzara in this weather is the bleakest and most unfriendly place in the world.

*August 19th : to Nangartse* (14,500 *feet*) : *14 miles.*—Bitterly cold morning with new snow on the ground and a chilling wind. Sun not up yet, so we walked on ahead of the ponies to get warm. This side of the pass is unutterably wild and desolate with bare scree slopes leading up to overhanging rocks and snow-sprinkled stony summits. The gorge narrowed occasionally and there was only just room for the track between the stream and the rocky spurs. Soon we got out of the gorge into open pasture-land. There are several forts on conical hill-tops, long prayer-walls beside the track, and Buddhas and prayers carved and painted on the rocks. Many burrhal up in the hills and gazelle on the wide plain beside the lake, which we can see in front of us. The rounded mountains on the left run down to a massive fort on a spur above Nangartse village, which is separated from the lake by a mile or two of very green grass. Thousands of animals grazing on the level turf. The lake is intensely blue, and rounded green hills rise on the far side of the water. The fort is most impressive, with grim bare whitewashed walls, and a line of dark red along the summit.

On the far side of the plain is the famous monastery of Samding, which is the home of Dorje Phagmo, the " Thunderbolt Sow ", the only female incarnation in Tibet. With the Dalai and Tashi Lamas (and in former days the Chinese Ambans) she shares the privilege of being allowed to ride in a palanquin.

Our camp lies at the foot of the dzong. After lunch and some cypher work Richardson and I walked down to the lake. A fresh wind now raising white and angry waves on the pale emerald waters of the reedy shallows. Out in the middle are deep-blue spray-flecked strips of water, and beyond, the purple hills are greyed by passing snowstorms—for all the world like a stormy Scottish loch.

This is the Yamdrok Tso, " the lake of the upper pastures ". It is about fifty miles long and almost as wide. In the centre is a piece of land twenty miles across, which would be an island were it not joined by an isthmus near Samding. This peninsula itself contains a lake of considerable size. The water is very slightly brackish and has recently receded, judging by the wide plain which is only a foot or two higher than the lake. It is at a height of 14,500 feet above sea-level.

Small waxy pink primulas, yellow pedicularis and mauve asters flower profusely beside the lake, and there are hundreds of bar-headed geese, Brahminy ducks (the same as our ruddy shelduck) and other wildfowl. On the south-facing hill-side beside Samding is a grove of large willows—surely one of the highest in the world; juniper, wild roses and clematis also flourish.

The two dzongpöns came to present scarves. One is a monk, the other a layman. They seem to work very well together; often one would start a sentence and the other would finish it. They brought the usual presents of dried sheep, eggs and peas.

At four o'clock there was a thunderstorm followed by heavy rain. We have about forty tents on the plain and resemble a small army. I hope the Tibetans are duly impressed !

*August 20th ; to Pede (14,500 feet) : 16½ miles.*—Off early in spite

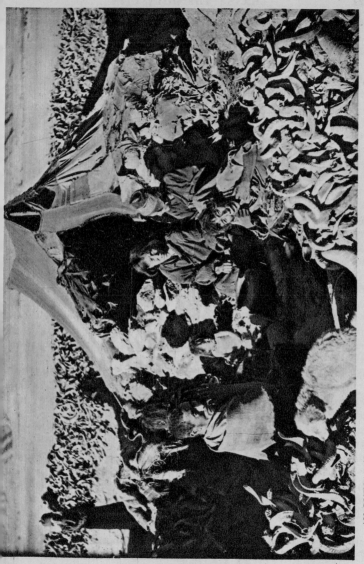

AN OUTCAST'S TENT SURROUNDED BY A WALL OF BONES FROM ANIMALS HE HAS SLAUGHTERED

A NOMAD HEADMAN—BANDIT

A NOMAD WOMAN

A DISPOSER OF DEAD BODIES

A VILLAGE HEADMAN

of the rain. The dzongpöns rode out a mile or two to present scarves. There are many chortens and massive prayer-walls in the road, while rock frescoes increase in number as we approach Lhasa.

All day we rode along beside the lake. I kept a rough check of the pack-animals going south: about 1250 passed us today, of which nearly half were yaks. It is extraordinary how the yaks avoid the track and choose the roughest sort of country. Very often grassy flats lay between the track and the lake, and we could cut across. Saw a grebe's nest floating, and hundreds of sand-martins on the telegraph wire. Many goosanders on the lake and snow-finches and mountain-finches hopping about in the roadway. A pair of black-necked cranes strutted about in a marsh. When I went to photograph them I was attacked by hungry mosquitoes. The birds here are quite tame: I can get within forty yards of goosanders on the lake and even nearer to the cranes. An old fish-eagle sitting (most unsuitably) on a telegraph post allowed me to walk right up to the foot of the post. There is also a strange little bird called a ground-chough that allows me to get quite close; he seems to share burrows with the mouse-hares.

A causeway cuts off a mile of the road just where the Shigatse track branches away to the east. Here we saw innumerable fish, some up to 3 lb. weight. They looked like char. The wild flowers were surprisingly beautiful. On the upper side of the path was the most superb natural rock-garden, while the boulders themselves were carved with exquisitely coloured Buddhas. Deep-blue and violet delphiniums three feet high literally covered the rocks for hundreds of yards. It was just like one of Sutton's seed fields. There were also several kinds of gentian, yellow marigolds, a lavender-coloured mint and clumps of yellow asters. The grass beside the lake was carpeted with bright-yellow pedicularis.

Soon we saw Pede Dzöng on the end of a point running out into the lake. It is just like an old Scottish castle. Unlike Nangartse Dzöng, it is now ruined. The village lies behind. In the valley nearby barley and peas grow very well in spite of the height. We finished our ride in pouring rain and camped on a flooded field beyond the dzong. There are prayer-flags even here in the water, tied to bamboo poles which are stuck into the

H

bottom of the lake. Spent two hours doing Tibetan, and stayed up till eleven pressing flowers.

*August 21st : to Singma Kang-chung* (11,700 *feet*) : 11 *miles.*—Set off at dawn. Overcast. Crossed Nyapso La to Tsang-po (Brahmaputra) valley. Followed the lake for a few miles, then rode up a fertile valley to the left past some square buildings like blockhouses. I suppose these isolated farms and villages must be capable of withstanding the attacks of bandits.

A superb view over the arms of this fantastic lake. It looks more like a Scottish loch every day except that there is no heather on the hills. There are fertile valleys and villages on the far side, but many signs of a decreasing population. Today we must have passed dozens of ruins in small valleys where the terraces of former cultivation and aqueducts still show. The ancient buildings seem to have been taller and even more strongly built than the modern ones.

The top of the Nyapso La is 16,000 feet above sea-level. The ascent was fairly easy. Drifting cloud spread over the top. I left my pony with my groom and started to walk down. Suddenly the mist started to clear, and I found myself gazing through a hole in the clouds into the mysterious Brahmaputra valley, 4500 feet below me. Through this I saw a wide silvery river winding its way among the sandy waste caused by its annual floods. On the far side were areas of rich cultivation and groves of willows on the lower valleys of high mountain ranges. For years this great river flowing at 11,500 feet from east to west beyond the Himalaya was known, but it was not till the adventurous boat journey of Morshead and Bailey that this was proved to be the same as the Brahmaputra of Assam.

The track here descends in a series of steep zigzags. As we got lower the vegetation became more and more luxuriant, and I found many new flowers. A wine-coloured primula, a blue gentian two feet high, periwinkle, and the usual delphiniums and asters. This valley is riotously fertile. Saw a partridge near our camp, which is in a field beside a willow grove.

After lunch I went down to pay my respects to the river, and found a turbid brownish torrent surging past at great speed, never breaking into waves—nothing so undignified—but with fearful power in its writhing eddies. At this time of year, with the melting snow-water from the Himalaya augmented by the torrential monsoon rains, the Tsang-po is at least 400 feet wide even where it is constricted into a single channel. Up to the east are two pointed rock mountains covered in snow. They should just be climbable.

Found clumps of iris here; it has long since flowered, but I got some seeds. Found a new blue flower. Watched an ibisbill by the river. Blackbirds are fluting in the willow groves, and turtle-doves cooing. Again we are in a different world. The barley here is golden ripe and as fine a crop as I have seen anywhere. The women cut it with sickles, singing as they work. There are cherry trees here and apricots. Clouded over and came on to rain.

Morgan, as usual, receives patients and administers medicines. They are nearly all cases of venereal disease. Spent evening pressing flowers and doing a cypher. Millions of midges come in round our pressure-lamps.

*August 22nd: to Chu-shur* (11,600 *feet*): 16 *miles*.—A very thrilling day though dull and overcast—the two pinnacle peaks only occasionally showing through. Many butterflies here, painted ladies, tortoise-shell, dark clouded yellows and blues, also hundreds of big black beetles with red markings on their backs.

We cross the river here by coracle as it is too swollen for the Chaksam ferries to be used. Chaksam is twelve miles farther down. Rode for a mile over rough stony ground where extra banking has been built to hold in the river. The coracles are rectangular and made of yak-hide stretched over a framework of willow branches. Each boat is about 8 feet by 6 feet, and weighs 80 to 90 lb. During the crossing they get swept down nearly half a mile, so the boatmen lift the coracles on to their heads and walk up-stream again, afterwards propping the boats up on one oar to dry. They float very high out of the water and are absolutely unstreamlined. Although one boat is fairly steady, for greater safety we used them lashed together end to end in couples. The unfortunate ponies had to swim alongside while one of the boatmen held the head ropes. As the men would insist on taking three or four together, and the ponies plunged about and got very excited, the back ones were apt to get kicked by those in front. Several broke away before we could persuade them to take to the water, but they soon returned when they saw their companions had disappeared. Rai Sahib Bo's best pony, the one that won the race at Gyantse the other day, got kicked on the way across and, having reached the far shore, broke loose and swam back, but it got washed away downstream and was drowned. Two others that broke back succeeded in getting safely across.

The boatmen row furiously with oars like ping-pong bats on the ends of poles, but even then the coracles go ten yeards downstream for every yard across. We changed transport here, so only the loads had to be ferried across and this had been accomplished without loss early in the morning. Actually most of the baggage is going the whole way to Chu-shur by boat; we ourselves are not allowed to go by boat as it is considered too dangerous and undignified.

On the far bank a Tibetan appliqué-worked tent had been put up, and we were given chang and Tibetan tea by the local headmen. Then a procession of wild-looking yet obsequious ruffians appeared with the usual presents: dried carcases of sheep, eggs and grain. We had a grand gallop over the sandy plain, where there are many prayer-walls and chortens. Cinnamon sparrows nest in these. The banks of the river are too high here to allow of any irrigation, and only at the foot of streams coming from the hills are there villages, monasteries and cultivation. The valley is dead flat and the mountains rise straight out of the plain as from the sea. The river has reduced miles of land to sandy wastes with occasional islands of willow scrub. The sand-storms must be terrible in winter.

We can see the Kamba La zigzagging up the hills. This is the pass used when Chaksam ferry is running. We rode by some huge walnut trees, also peaches, apricots, cherries, alders, poplars and willows. The crops—barley, oats, a little wheat, beans, peas and potatoes—look very rich. We also passed a very beautiful monastery beside the track. The windows and doorways were exquisitely carved and coloured, the chortens pierced by archways under which we rode. There were window-boxes full of bright flowers, and very lovely trees.

Had lunch by the river. Saw a cormorant and watched a pair of Tibetan babax making loud fluting notes—the first we have seen or heard.

A very high percentage of the people here have goitres, sometimes of enormous size. Although the valley is so fertile the peasants seem very poor and ill-clad. There are many alternative tracks winding through the willow groves and fields; some are flooded, others are so rocky that the ponies can scarcely use them, and it is quite difficult to find the way.

It is curious that the sand carried down and left by the flooded river has been blown up into the hills by the winter storms so that valleys several thousand feet above the river are completely choked with sand which is formed into dappled drifts by the wind.

Just before Chu-shur a number of rocky spurs come right down to the river, which throws itself against the foot of the hills in a fearsome boiling torrent. The track was, in many places, under water, so dozens of ragged men and boys were waiting to lead our ponies for the last mile or two. Even then the water came up to our stirrups. One false step and horse and rider would have been swirled away for good.

There are two ruined dzongs perched high up on the pinnacles of the serrated spur which protects the village. Bhuddas, prayer-flags, piles of stones and carved prayers are scattered all along this part of the track, and little shrines protected by iron grilles. At the foot of Chu-shur village is a prayer-wall fifty yards long encircled by slates with attractive coloured deities carved thereon. Some prosperous farms here. Our camp is in a grove of stately pollard willows.

After lunch I climbed to the ruined dzong and had an impressive view of the Tsang-po in flood. The Kyi Chu (meaning either " river of happiness " or " middle river "), the stream on which Lhasa stands, joins the Tsang-po at Chu-shur, and it too is flooded. Each of these rivers has innumerable channels which join and part again, leaving scrub-covered island and sand-banks. The river-beds are therefore about two miles wide. In the other direction lay the rich cultivation of the Chu-shur valley, with yellow-gold fields of mustard, dark-green pea-fields and the varying shades of ripening oats and barley.

The sun was setting in tattered storm-clouds above the Tsang-po, and long shafts of light filled the valley with molten silver.

A busy evening packing up film to be sent to India for processing.

*August 23rd : to Nethang (11,600 feet) : 23 miles.*—It is most important to reach the Holy City on an auspicious date, so we are doing a double march today and getting to Lhasa early tomorrow

morning. All day we followed the Kyi Chu, sometimes crossing level arid plains, at other times splashing through water or
following precarious tracks over spurs which jutted out into the
flooded river-bed. Wherever there is any irrigation the land
abounds with rich crops and groves of trees, but in between these
oases the scenery is as desolate and barren as any we have passed.
The more shallow valleys and the hills themselves are completely
smothered in sand; for miles on end nothing grows except coarse
grass and weeds. At the heads of the valleys are red and white
monasteries and small villages. More traffic than ever today,
mostly wool. Many monks on the road; they are usually bare-
footed, but often carry their boots to save wear. In one place
reddish granite cliffs rose for a thousand feet above the track,
which limped along beside the river. It was exactly like stage
scenery—the clear blue sky, hard cumulus clouds as if cut out of
cardboard, red rocks going straight up in magnificent cliffs and
overhangs, and farther up the valley the blue hills surrounding
Lhasa flecked with transient cloud shadows.

About half-way we were met by a monk official who is to be
one of our guides during our stay. He is a fifth-rank official in
Lhasa, but he counts as fourth rank away from the city. He is a
very polished and intelligent man. Oddly enough, his mulberry-
coloured robe, which is quite new, has small patches on it, not
because it is torn but, I suppose, to indicate conventional poverty.
He rides a fine pacing mule and wears a remarkable wide-brimmed
hat of papier-mâché, covered with gold lacquer. I gather he has
travelled in China and other places. Hence his cleanliness and
savoir-faire.

Nethang is a fair-sized village in the middle of the valley. The
tomb of Atisha is here, the originator of the yellow hat or reformed
church of Tibet. He came up from India just before the Norman
Conquest of England. We camped on a grassy field just beside
the river. Watched a pair of ibisbills and some ringed plover.
Many hoopoes here. Heavy rain in the evening. Some coracles
swished by, doing a good ten knots; one was laden with red
earthenware pots, another with skins of butter.

*August 24th : to Lhasa* (11,800 *feet*) : 16 *miles*.—Lhasa at last :
the Holy and Forbidden City. Had anyone told me a year ago
that I should be in Lhasa today, I would not even for a moment
have taken him seriously.

Country similar to yesterday's. Far ahead we can see a grey-green hill-side in the middle of which is a small hermitage some 3000 feet above the river. This, says Norbhu, is exactly above Drepung, the largest monastery in the world. In one place the flooded river forced us to climb a granite spur. The track became a rocky staircase with a sheer drop on the right-hand side into the deep clear pools below. From up there we saw the monastery of the State Oracle at Nechung just beside Drepung. I could see a golden roof in a grove of large trees. This temple is only four miles from Lhasa. A serrated spur coming down on the opposite side of the Kyi Chu shuts off any view of the Potala [1] Palace or of the city. After taking to the rocks again we passed a colossal Buddha carved in low relief on the rock. This figure is seated and faces the Holy City. In front of it is a huge pile of small stones collected as an offering.

Once more the flooded track forced us to take an alternative path over a spur, and this time, at a distance of ten miles, we had our first view of the Potala, the monastery palace of the Dalai Lamas. In the centre of the wide valley, which is thickly clustered with groves of trees, two cones of rock reach up some 700 feet above the plain. The one on the right is the Iron Hill, on which the Medical College stands; on the other is the Potala, seen from here as a white building surmounted by the glittering roof pavilions which cover the mortal remains of former Dalai Lamas. The city itself is completely hidden by these two hills.

The valley here is broad and fertile, though large parts of it are completely inundated or covered with rushes. The villages look more cheerful and prosperous. From the left another valley joins the Kyi Chu and we saw a large monastery in a bay of the hills. There are many country villas in groves of willows; and crops of barley, oats, peas, beans and potatoes.

This tributary river is fifty yards wide and is kept in check with long stone embankments. The old cantilever bridge called Trisum Sampa used to be washed away almost every summer, so now they are replacing it by a modern construction of girders. At present there are two wooden arches and one of steel. The Government refused to have an engineer up from India, so photographs were sent down in charge of a young official who had been at Ludlow's school and spoke a little English. All the girders

[1] Pronounced *Po-ta-la*, with each syllable equally accentuated.

had to be carried right across the Himalaya on the backs of coolies. They followed the instructions and, having assembled all the pieces, which were of course numbered, they put the bridge together. Rumour has it that there were some thirty girders unaccountably left over, but the bridge seems to hold and they are going to build another one with the surplus.

Avoiding more flooded land, we reached a village called Shingdonkar, where there is a disused Chinese fort. The road climbs steeply between the flat-roofed houses to cross yet another jagged granite spur, gay with prayer-flags and wall paintings. Most of the inhabitants came out to have a look at us. They are incredibly dirty and ill-clad, many are goitrous. The children are often stark naked. Everybody seems very cheerful and friendly. Anyone on horseback dismounts as a sign of respect. The whole valley here seems to be laid waste by the river, whose various channels fill the valley for a width of about two miles. The islands between are sandy and bare or else covered with thorn and willow scrub.

Just short of Drepung Monastery we were met by Möndö, a monk official who, by the most remarkable anomaly, is an Old Rugbeian. Many years ago the last Dalai Lama, a man of very advanced ideas, decided, on the advice of the Government of India, to send four boys to be educated in England. Gould took them home in 1913, and after some discussion they were sent to Rugby and were later trained respectively as a soldier, a surveyor, a mining and an electrical engineer. Möndö, who was already a monk when he went to England, is the mining engineer, but having tried unsuccessfully to overcome the prejudice of the monks to his activities, he has returned to more normal work and is here to welcome us on behalf of the Lhasa Government. Möndö is now a man of between thirty-five and forty. He is a large, genial man, with cropped hair and a moustache. He still speaks the most delightful English, fairly idiomatic and perfectly pronounced. We were also met and presented with scarves by our lay guide, a young official in splendid clothes. He wears a flowered-silk robe the colour of fallen beech-leaves, and over it a loose sleeveless gown of the brightest scarlet lined with pale blue. His flat-topped hat of yellow wool balances on top of his head like a porridge-bowl. The monk and the lay guides are to be attached to the Mission during our stay at Lhasa.

Just after this we passed below Drepung Monastery, which lies across the head of a sandy valley running up to the hills on our left. From here it is very much foreshortened, but even so it looks like a large and fortified city with a long white wall running across the front of it, and tier behind tier of buildings, some with golden roof pavilions, others with cylindrical ornaments or fluttering prayer-flags to relieve the monotony of their straight lines. Below the monastery, just beside the road, live a community of butchers who supply the monastery and city with meat, in spite of the Buddhist prohibitions against taking life.

From here to Lhasa, a distance of three miles, the road is built up on a causeway between reed-covered marshes where pink water-lilies bloom.

We were soon met by more officials, who escorted us to a small roadside tea-garden which, being half-way between the Potala and Drepung, was in former times used by the Dalai Lamas as a resting place. It is called the Garden of the Mystics. Here we rode into a walled enclosure where a tent had been put up for our reception. We were then presented with scarves on behalf of the Regent, Prime Minister and Cabinet. After which we sat on low mattress-like cushions in front of beautifully carved and lacquered tables on which Tibetan tea and biscuits were served. The servants wore dark homespun robes and wide flat-topped hats covered with scarlet tasselling exactly like lamp-shades. The officials are all most courteous and friendly, and full of solicitous enquiries about our health and the discomfort of the journey.

On the right of the track a high sand-bank marks the route of an aqueduct; on the left is a level grassy plain, on which was today drawn up a Guard of Honour, consisting of a company of soldiers and another of police, complete with flying colours and two military bands. They presented arms and so on, while Gould was introduced to the officers. The two young army generals were dressed in extremely smart uniforms, but the soldiers gave rather a comic-opera effect, being dressed in khaki uniforms and battered Wolseley topees, from the back of which their pigtails hung down somewhat incongruously. But they drilled and marched better than one would have expected. Perhaps because the Chief of Police is another Rugbeian called Kyipup. Half the population of Lhasa had come down to see us. They looked a cosmopolitan crowd: a few Chinese, several

H 2

turbaned Ladakis, blue-uniformed soldiers of the escort to the Nepalese representative, Mongolian traders, nomad yak-herds from the desolate high plateau of the Chang Tang, and always crowds of sullen monks with shaven heads and bare arms.

Riding along flooded roads between groves of willows we reached the Deyki Lingka (" garden of happiness "), a small house that has been lent to us by the Abbot of the near-by Gundeling monastery.

# CHAPTER FIVE

### THE LHASA OFFICIALS COME TO CALL

OUR first four days at Lhasa were taken up in entertaining an almost continuous stream of callers, varying in rank from the Prime Minister to the lowest Government secretaries. The arrival and departure of this kaleidoscopic procession of gorgeously clad monk and lay officials gave us a unique opportunity, at the very outset of our visit, to make the acquaintance of this privileged class of Tibetan society and to find out something of the peculiar government of the country. On the day before an official intended to call he would send a secretary or servant round to Norbhu to arrange a suitable hour for his arrival. No serious matters were discussed on these preliminary visits; they were simply occasions for presenting scarves of welcome and for exchanging conventional compliments. Gould, as Political Officer, supported by Neame and myself, received visitors in our upper room; while Richardson, as British Trade Agent, Gyantse, received them afterwards in a specially appointed tent at the end of the garden.

No sooner had we finished lunch on the day of our arrival than Yuto Depön, a young general of the army, came to deliver to the Mission scarves of greeting and presents from the Cabinet Ministers. He was dressed in the smartest of British-made military uniforms, but wore the single long turquoise ear-ring and had his hair tied with red ribbon into the usual double top-knot with a turquoise and gold charm-box in the centre. This

ornament is worn by all Lhasa officials of fifth or higher rank,
and by the sons of a few of the noble families who are in Government service.   Yuto, as well as being a Depön, comes from a very
important Lhasa family: one of his ancestors was a Cabinet
Minister at the time of the 1904 Mission.   Neame congratulated
him on the turn-out and drill of the Guard of Honour, but Yuto
disclaimed all credit, saying that owing to lack of practice he had
forgotten all he had learnt in India, and was afraid that the Brigadier
would laugh at the uniforms and drill of the soldiers.

The presents consisted of boxes of eggs, goat-skins of butter,
striped woven bags of peas for our horses, and dried carcases of
sheep.   The latter, still having the black hair on their heads and
being dried in a life-like attitude, looked strangely pathetic
stacked in line against the wall of our courtyard.   The butter
was unfortunately rancid, and in any case goat-skins are not
ideal containers.   When we came to test the eggs, only one in
ten would sink; the others were not actually bad, but having
been kept for so long in the dry Tibetan climate most of the
contents had evaporated so that they floated right on top of the
water like bubbles.

Our next visitors were the three lay members of the Cabinet,
the Shap-pes, who came in their magnificence to pay a ceremonial call.   Although Norbhu had sent round a watch as
requested, so that they would know our time, they arrived an
hour late.   As we had discovered on the journey up, time means
very little in Tibet.   The first sign of their approach was the
arrival of a mounted servant, who came at a rapid amble to see
that everything was prepared.   He was followed by a group of
secretaries and servants on horseback, about two dozen in all,
who came splashing through the flood-water of our drive.   The
secretaries wore long broadcloth robes of an indigo colour held
in at the waist with red and yellow sashes, from the back of
which hung a small holder with chop-sticks and a jade-handled
knife, pockets and other knick-knacks.   Pen-cases, often beautifully worked in brass, were pushed into their sashes.   Curious
flat-topped hats of yellow wool were balanced like basins on top
of their heads.   These looked most precarious but were actually
clipped securely over the top-knot of hair.   The servants, who
were surprisingly dirty, wore dark homespun robes and wide
flat-topped hats tasselled with scarlet.   In the middle of their

long plaits turquoise and gold charm-boxes were worn. Some
were armed with whips with which to control the crowd.

The Shap-pes themselves rode slowly in order of seniority,
one on a mule and the others on fine ponies. A row of wooden
stools covered with carpet had been put out beside the path,
and here they dismounted, the senior official using the highest
step. Two servants held the horse, another steadied the stirrup,
while two more took the Shap-pe's hands and carefully helped
him down the step.

The Shap-pes were splendidly dressed in robes of saffron-
yellow silk, with an interwoven dragon pattern which junior
officials may not use. The robe, held in at the waist by a scarlet
sash, comes right up to the neck, where a white silk shirt folds
down over the collar. Like all Tibetan robes, it folds across
the chest and is fastened by small gilt buttons under the right
arm and down the right side: thus, with the belt, forming a
large breast-pocket. The sleeves are cut very long indeed, while
the cuffs of the inner shirt, unless folded back, come almost to
the ground. The inevitable long ear-ring is worn and a wide-
brimmed gold brocade hat, with coral and turquoise insignia on
the top. From this ornament red tasselling hangs down as far
as the brim, while from this two further strips of braid, united
in a jewelled clasp, hang over the shoulders.

Norbhu, being a Dzasa, was similarly dressed. He came out
to the courtyard to meet them and, putting his hands together
before him, bowed to each in turn. The Shap-pes walked
slowly, with a curiously self-conscious rocking gait, as though
they were not accustomed to such exercise, as indeed is probably
the case. Once upstairs, each bowed deeply to the Political
Officer and presented him with a silk scarf, which he produced
from the fold of his robe; after Gould had returned a similar
scarf, they shook hands. When we had all exchanged scarves
they sat down on the divans, strictly in order of precedence,
while Gould had to take the highest seat of honour, beneath the
canopy, as he is accorded the honorary title of Lon-chen (chief
minister) and is therefore equal in rank to the Prime Minister and
only inferior to God on Earth, at present incarnate in the person
of the Regent. The Shap-pes sat cross-legged with their red, blue
and white striped boots hidden in the skirts of their long robes.
They did not remove their hats, as this was a ceremonial visit.

Langchungna, the senior Shap-pe by virtue of his having served longest, is not a striking personality. He rarely says anything, except to agree with the others, and habitually wears an expression of good-natured complacency. When he smiles his eyes disappear. His skin is completely covered with pock marks. Unlike most Tibetans, his hair is falling out and, in company with his straggly beard, is quite grey. He is very conservative, continually saying that Lhasa is not what it was when he was a boy, especially with regard to the weather, the deterioration of which, he declares, coincided with the installation of electric light. He says that wireless and electric light have made the winters stuffy. Nobody quite knows why he was made a Shap-pe, as he is neither of noble family nor of conspicuous brilliance. The story goes that when there was a vacancy in the Council several names were submitted to the Dalai Lama for choice. His Holiness, for some reason imagining that his Ministers were trying to coerce him to select a certain popular official, asked for more and more names of possible candidates, and at last chose a certain Langchungna, whom nobody had considered and who was at that time commander of Gartok in western Tibet.

Bhondong Shap-pe is a much younger man. He has a fat face, with a ready grin, and a moustache drooping over the corners of his mouth like a Mandarin. As he was for many years Secretary to the Cabinet, and successfully won his way to his present position, he has a great knowledge of the Lhasa methods of government. Being in possession of several estates formerly belonging to the Tashi Lama, he is popularly supposed to be opposing the return of that unfortunate Prelate. But withal he is a genuine fellow and is undoubtedly efficient.

Tendong Shap-pe was Depön in Kham for many years and has the reputation of being a great fighter. He is a large-featured and rather ugly man, of great natural charm and distinction. His skin is deeply pitted with smallpox scars.

To me the whole interview had an extraordinary air of unreality, as if I were watching a play or dreaming. On one side Gould, with carefully trimmed moustache and immaculate Saville Row suiting, smilingly made polite conversation that seemed additionally unreal in that none of the Tibetans could understand a word of it. Then Norbhu, interpreting, swallowing his words with excitement, and the four Shap-pes bowing in unison and smiling deferentially at each remark. The word "lha-les" was continually used by both our guests and by Norbhu, whispered with a swift sucking-in of the breath and a quick bow. It may be interpreted "Yes, your Honour". The conversation followed traditional lines. I wondered how many times old Langchungna had heard it before.

Shap-pe (with Norbhu interpreting): Is your noble self in good health?

P.O.: Yes, thank your honour: and you?

Shap-pe: Very well, thank you. Have you had a pleasant journey? No trouble of any sort on the way?

P.O.: Thanks to your excellent arrangements no trouble at all, thank you.

Shap-pe: I hope you did not feel the cold.

P.O.: No, thank you; it was, in fact, pleasantly warm.

Shap-pe: I hope you will find your house comfortable.

And so it went on.

The Shap-pes also recalled the fact that the Political Officer had a twenty-five-year acquaintanceship with Tibet, having been British Trade Agent, Gyantse, in 1912, when he met the Dalai Lama, and then in the following year having taken the four Tibetan boys to England.

Tea was served meanwhile, with biscuits and cake, followed by liqueurs. Crème de menthe was the most popular and after that Benedictine. It seemed to be the custom to refuse everything the first time and then to accept under pressure. After a time the Shap-pes whispered that the Political Officer must be very busy and that they would now go, but that they would meet again soon. They also declared their gratitude that the Government of India had sent so senior an officer to advise them, and they were sure that subsequent deliberations would be auspicious.

The moment they got up there was a scurrying outside, as servants rushed about getting the ponies ready for their departure. The trappings of the animals were most resplendent. The saddle was padded with scarlet brocade and above this was a piece of brightly coloured carpet material to keep off the dust. The heavy stirrups of finely worked brass were padded with cloth so that they would not damage the rider's boots. Over the horse's forehead was a diamond-shaped piece of gaily woven cloth and from its neck and chest hung two scarlet tassels, which can only be carried by officials of fifth or higher rank.

As each Shap-pe climbed his wooden stool and mounted, servants smoothed the saddle-cloth and carefully straightened out his robes. With much bowing and smiling the Cabinet rode away. It was an unforgettable sight: the rich saffron of the Shap-pes' robes, the wide scarlet hats of the servants, the quick green of the pollard willows, the soft olives and duns of the far mountains against the pale turquoise sky.

In the afternoon the fourth member of the Cabinet came to pay his respects, apologizing that he had been unable to leave his duties in the morning so as to accompany his colleagues. This was the Kalön Lama, the ecclesiastical Cabinet Minister. He wore his terra-cotta monk's robe over the top of his yellow Shap-pe's silk and a square embroidered water-bottle cover hanging from his girdle. He also wore the stiff wide-brimmed monk official's hat of papier-mâché covered with gold lacquer. His boots were of the "Union Jack" pattern, but very much turned up at the toes, in the manner of the usual monk official's footwear. He seemed to be a mild and courteous old man of no special distinction. He said that the political situation was indeed serious, but that he didn't know what to do about it. After all, he said, he was a peaceful monk and what was he to know about Chinese escorts and machine guns? Actually I think he knows more than one would guess.

On the second day we received a call from the Dzasa of Reting Monastery, the chief official attached to the household of the Regent, on whose behalf he came to arrange our formal visit to the Potala to present ourselves to the Regent and Prime Minister. The former being at present the highest person in the land does not call on visitors, and the latter can only do so after they have first called on him.

Dzasa is a title conferred on monks or laymen who have rendered particularly meritorious service to the state. As a rule it is a non-hereditary title, but there are one or two noble houses that always have a Dzasa in the family. At this time there were six. Four were living inside the country, and two—Norbhu and Layden La, the Darjeeling-Tibetan Deputy Commissioner of Police who had come up to organize the new police force some years ago and died while we were in Lhasa—were living outside. The two Commissioners of Kham have also of recent years held this title.

Another Dzasa who came to pay his respects was the owner of our house, the head of the neighbouring Gundeling Monastery; though the incarnate lama, who is the spiritual head of the monastery, resides at Sera. Dzasa Gundeling is a leading power in the National Assembly, a body which will be described later. He is a most impressive man, very tall for a Tibetan and vigorous in spite of his advanced age, and with a deeply lined face full of character and determination. Though he has a charming gentle manner, he is obviously one of the most forceful personalities in Lhasa.

We also received a visit from the Lord Chamberlain (chikyap kempo), a very aged Lama who is the supreme head of the ecclesiastical organization of Tibet. He is also the chief official of the Dalai Lama's household, is responsible for the upkeep of the Potala, and is in charge of all the Lhasa parks. He is a frail and courteous old man who suffers from rheumatism and over-work. Soon after him came the Grand Secretaries for Clerical Affairs (trung-yik chempo), four monk officials who compose what is virtually the Lama Cabinet. One of these is Commander-in-Chief of the army, which seems a curious position for a monk to hold.

The sooner a call is returned the more respect does it reflect upon the caller, and no sooner had we returned from our visit to the Regent and Prime Minister at the Potala (this will be described in the next chapter), than the latter called on us. Usually the Prime Minister is a wise and experienced official from one of the ancient noble families, but the late Dalai went doubly against tradition by appointing a young man of no experience whatsoever and one who was his eldest brother's son. He is of a friendly nature and, being one of the people, is very popular with the townsfolk.

Another very distinguished visitor was the Duke (yapshi phunkhang kung), a title given to the father or brother of the reigning Dalai Lama. As the title is hereditary, there are usually several Kungs living at the same time, theoretically one for each Dalai Lama. As the Dalai Lama's family is normally a poor one and therefore without patrimony, the title of Kung carries with it considerable estates. The Kung used to be the first layman of the land, but the late Dalai made the office of Prime Minister even more exalted.

The Duke, who was dressed in the same way as the Shap-pes, is a tall lean man with such bad sight that he has to hold everything up to his eyes before he can see it. He gives the impression of being completely absent-minded and unpractical in a very aristocratic and charming way. After him came the State Oracle, whose familiar spirit inhabits an ancient tree just below Drepung Monastery. The Oracle himself lives in the neighbouring Nechung Temple. This was the first time the official Sage of Lhasa had deigned to call on a Political Officer. He is a Ta Lama, one of the highest monk officials, and although his profession is to work himself up into a trance, he seemed very much a man of the world and invited us to come and visit his Temple.

The most interesting visitor of all was Tsarong Dzasa, who came on a friendly call with his wife. He holds no official position now but is the leading figure in the National Assembly and, at a time when a general air of indecision and uncertainty prevails, assumes the position of the Strong Man of Lhasa. He represents an extremely rare phenomenon in the feudal oligarchy of Tibet, that of a man of humble birth who has won his way to high position. A monk official can, by his natural genius and hard work, rise to be an Abbot of his monastery with a seat in the Assembly, but for a layman to do this is almost unprecedented.

Tsarong, or Tsensar Namgyal, to give him his own name, was the son of an archer in the Dalai Lama's bodyguard. A Tibetan told me that he first came to His Holiness' notice in the following way. In 1904, when the British Mission reached Lhasa, the Dalai Lama fled northwards towards Mongolia. He took Tsensar's father with him, but the boy, being young, was left behind. A few days later, very early in the morning, the Dalai was walking along, sunk in meditation, when he saw a boy approaching on foot from Lhasa. This was the young Tsensar, who, resenting being left behind, had walked all night to catch up with the party. The Dalai Lama spoke to him and was so impressed by the child that he took him into his own service, where he rapidly gained promotion. Tsensar accompanied his master during his four-year exile, and his mind was broadened by visiting Urga, Peking and even Japan. When the Dalai fled southwards to India in 1910 Tsensar was in command of the escort that was left on the Lhasa side of the Tsang-po to deal with the pursuing Chinese force. Having sent all the coracles to the south side, Tsensar, who was exceedingly brave, waited for the enemy and utterly defeated them. Following his master, he ran the gauntlet of the Chinese in the Chumbi Valley and reached Yatung disguised as a coolie. By this time the Chinese realized he had slipped through their hands, and put a watch on every road, but Tsensar, this time disguised as a post runner, managed to elude them. A few months later he returned again by Kampa Dzong to Shigatse to rally the Tibetan troops against the Chinese.

Tsensar then spent two years in Darjeeling and other parts of India where the Dalai Lama was a guest of the British Government. When His Holiness returned to Lhasa in 1912 Tsensar was made a Shap-pe, and was chosen by the Lama as the husband to the heiress of the great estates of Tsarong, both her brother and father (the Tsarong Shap-pe who dealt with the British Mission in 1904) having been put to death, as they had backed the wrong side in the recent disturbances. Then it was that Tsensar Namgyal took the title of Tsarong. He sold the old Tsarong mansion which had brought bad luck to the family, and built a magnificent new house away from the dust and dirt of the city. He was then made lay Commander-in-Chief of the army, and put in charge of the Mint.

For ten years Tsarong held these important posts, until in 1923 there was a clash between the army and the newly organized and unpopular police force : they had started to fire at each other and things looked serious. Tsarong dealt firmly with the ringleader, cutting off the man's leg (a customary Tibetan punishment) so that he died. Other offenders had their ears removed.

The Dalai Lama, possibly jealous of the increasing power of his late favourite, thereupon considered that he had been guilty of unnecessary cruelty and degraded him from his high position. In the presence of all the other officials he had to remove his Shap-pe's robes. Since that time he has taken no high office, although he was invited to rejoin the Cabinet a few years ago. At present, together with Langchungna Shap-pe, he controls the Trap-je, the Government barracks, arsenal and mint, and is the moving force of the National Assembly. Tsarong also married a widow, the heiress of the Hor-kang family, who lives in a large house in the middle of the city. He is now fairly old by Tibetan standards (that is, getting on for fifty), a short thick-set jovial man getting rather short of teeth and hair.

The Tsarongs called formally on the Political Officer in our upstairs room and then, as another visitor arrived, went into the garden to present their compliments to Richardson. We all of us soon foregathered here and spent a very happy hour laughing and joking and discussing every sort of subject, as if we had known each other for years. This was a pleasant change after the more formal interviews of the morning. Neither of the Tsarongs know more than a few words of English, but, like all intelligent Tibetans, they are very anxious to learn.

Tsarong's wife is not exactly beautiful, bearing on her face the ravages of smallpox, but she is perfectly self-assured and charming and, as we found later, a perfect hostess. She wore a long sleeveless robe of purple silk held in at the waist, embroidered with gold devices, and a green silk blouse which showed at the sleeves and neck. A heavy gold charm-box, ornamented with turquoise, rubies and diamonds, hung from a necklace of large coral and agate beads, so that it was half tucked into the fold of the dress. An apron, striped horizontally with red, green, yellow and white, the top corners of heavily flowered gold braid, was tied round her waist. Her hair, neatly parted in the middle, was brought Madonna-like over the sides of her forehead to form two long plaits, which were looped up at the waist. It is not customary in Tibet to discuss any serious subject until the preliminary calls and luncheon parties are finished, but we gathered from Tsarong that the Tibetans were extremely worried and prepared to discuss things frankly with the Political Officer and to ask his advice. Whether they will take it or not is a different matter.

Another interesting caller was Kusho Chango Pa, better known as Ringang, the youngest of the four boys who went to Rugby in 1913. He apologized for not having come earlier, but he has to be careful not to appear too obviously pro-British, especially since the death of the late Dalai Lama, in whose favour he stood very high. As Ringang was the youngest of the Rugbeians, and as he spent considerably longer than the others in this country, he has profited most from that curious experiment. He still speaks the most perfect idiomatic English, although he gets little practice except when a British Mission is in Lhasa. Being at present only a sixth-rank official, he is not allowed to wear silk—except in the privacy of his own house—or the charm-box which higher officials wear on the tops of their heads, though his hair is bound in the same way with red ribbon. Instead of silk, a robe of dark purple broadcloth is worn, held in at the waist with a red, green, or yellow sash. In his official dress as a city magistrate he wears a scarlet gown with a sky-blue lining and the sponge hat. To look at, Ringang is a short thick-set man, inclined to fatness. Like most of the Tibetans, he grows no hair on his face.

His status as an official reflects many of the weaknesses of the administration of Lhasa. When Ringang returned from his additional course of engineering in England he was given the task of installing electric light in the city and in the Dalai Lama's summer palace. This involved a tremendous amount of work. A hydro-electric power-station had to be built at the foot of a mountain stream some six miles to the north of Lhasa, and the machinery for this had to be laboriously brought up from Calcutta and put into position. A power-line had to be laid to the city and accumulators brought from India and stored in the basement of Ringang's house. After several months' work the Dalai became impatient and could not understand why there was still no light. Yet Ringang had had to do most of it himself, as the Tibetans were not used to this sort of work. Now the power-station is in the charge of a Tibetan whom Ringang has trained and, except for a few months in winter when the stream is frozen, it works perfectly. At the present time, therefore, the Potala, the streets, and many of the private houses are lit by electric light.

Ringang is also official interpreter to the Cabinet, having to give them items of news from the Indian papers and to be present on the rare occasions when any Europeans visit Lhasa. He is, furthermore, a municipal officer of Lhasa and magistrate, or dzongpön, of a district called Purang in southern Tibet. For this plurality of offices he is paid very little in actual cash: that is not the Lhasa system. In Tibet the State owns practically all the land, and farms it out to the noble families on condition that they supply one or more officials, depending on the value of the estate, for Government employment. Bribery is of course rife and is so ingrained in the system that it has become an indispensable part of it. A young official pays a senior one to put in a good word for him. Huge presents are received by those who have in their power the selection of candidates for a vacant post. Bribes are even paid to spread bad reports of rivals, so there is little feeling of security for a Lhasa official. But this system is tacitly accepted by the Government, who find it convenient not to have to pay salaries.

Ringang has never visited the district of which he is in charge, but his wife, an attractive capable woman, went there one winter to see that everything was all right. The work is done by a deputy, who administers justice, manages the farms, and collects the revenues, usually in kind, through the local headmen. Ringang is supplied with practically all necessities from his estate at no cost to himself. His servants and retainers are the children of his tenants; horses, mules, grain, butter, vegetables, and chang come from the farms; metal-work, carpets and clothes are made on the estate. So at present Ringang is a very busy man and has every hope of one day being a Shap-pe; but he has the harassed air of one who is not quite high enough up in the scale of officialdom to feel secure from the calumnious attacks of his rivals.

The career of Ringang's elder brother, who also came to present a scarf, throws another sidelight onto the methods of the Lhasa Government. Some years ago, when the Tibetan troops were driven out of an important district in the eastern part of the country, the four depöns in charge of the army were all removed from office, and Ringang, who was then in charge of the Government granaries, was one of the new generals appointed. He neither knew the country nor had he any experience of military organization or fighting whatever. Being very intelligent and feeling strongly on the subject, he was, nevertheless, able to give us much valuable information of conditions in Kham and of the complete inadequacy of the Tibetan army. He held this position for several years and is now the Government expert on agriculture. Once seen, the elder Ringang is not easily forgotten, being the very embodiment of Falstaff. He is of enormous size, and is perpetually out of breath and perspiring. His face is continually wreathed in smiles, and he is the champion drinker of chang in all Tibet, having the rare and enviable accomplishment of being able to pour a glass of beer straight down his throat without swallowing.

Of the many officials who came to see us, two more must be described, and these are the other two Rugbeians, Möndö and Kyipup. Of the four sent to England, Ghonkar, the soldier, who was perhaps the most promising of them all and who was most needed by his country, died soon after he returned to Tibet. His training at Woolwich should have fitted him for an administrative post at Lhasa, but it is typical of the Tibetan Government that he was sent to the Sino-Tibetan frontier as a subaltern. It is said that he fell in love with an English girl, but that the Dalai Lama would not allow him to marry her, and that he died from a broken heart.

Möndö was already a monk when he left Tibet in 1913. At Rugby he never seemed to learn anything, but his behaviour was always that of the perfect gentleman. He was also a very keen cricketer. After leaving Rugby he was trained as a mining engineer. When he returned to his native country he immediately set about looking for gold and other precious substances; but as soon as he started to dig or to disturb the soil in any way, the abbot of the nearest monastery would complain that all the local spirits were being disturbed, and would implore him to replace every stone he had dug up and to move on to the next district before the crops failed and the people were smitten with epidemics. After this had happened several times Möndö became discouraged and retired for a time to meditate. He then became an important monk-official. Now Möndö had brought a motor-cycle from India and he used to ride this in the streets of Lhasa, much to the consternation of both man and beast. One day a high official was thrown from his mule owing to the sudden appearance round a corner of this terrifying machine, and as a consequence Möndö was degraded and put in charge of a small district in remote western Tibet, where he spent several years. Now he is a fifth-rank official, sharing with Ramba, our lay guide, the charge of Sho, the village at the foot of the Potala. He also has an office in the Potala and is partly responsible for the park-lands of Lhasa. Möndö is a large genial man with a loud ringing laugh and the extraordinary consideration and politeness that is so strong a characteristic of all the official class. He must have considerable wealth, for he is at present building a large and very beautiful mansion behind Muru monastery in the extreme north-eastern corner of the city.

Kyipup was not a great success at Rugby, as he was not the least amused by either work or games. After two years there, he studied surveying with conspicuous lack of success. When he returned to Lhasa he was put in charge of developing the telegraph system, but as he knew little about this, and was given no encouragement by the Government, he retired to his family estates. He is a nervous little man with an apologetic air and a straggly moustache. At present he is a City Magistrate (*mi-pön*), a sixth-rank official, and in charge of the City Police. Having seen numbers of this force sitting dejectedly in their sentry-boxes sewing boot soles or engaged in similar occupations, I asked him one day what would happen if a smash-and-grab raid were carried out in a Lhasa shop. He replied that the policeman would blow his whistle, on which signal others would appear and, having restored order with their truncheons, the malefactors would be handcuffed and taken to prison. Upon enquiry I discovered that the police carry neither whistles nor truncheons, nor have they any handcuffs. Kyipup is married to a very beautiful daughter of the hospitable Tering Rajah with whom we lunched near Gyantse. They live in a small house near the Lhasa Cathedral.

A son of Rajah Tering also came to see us, a young depön, Jigme Tering. He has married a younger sister of Tsarong's wife and lives in a small house beside the Tsarong mansion. Jigme was at school at St. Paul's, Darjeeling, and speaks absolutely flawless English. We saw a great deal of him during our visit and he is as delightful a person as one could meet anywhere. Jigme, like Yuto, was dressed in the very smartest uniform and his whole turn-out would have done him credit in any European army.

Another English-speaking visitor was Surkang-se, whose father is High Commissioner in Kham (south-eastern Tibet). He comes of a very ancient family, so is allowed to wear the charm-box, although he has only a small job under Tsarong at the Mint. He it was who was sent down to Calcutta to arrange for the transport of the girders for Trisum bridge. Having been at Ludlow's school, he speaks good English, though he was only there for a year before, much to his regret, it closed down. Unfortunately he is rather nervous and has a bad lisp, so is not easy to understand.

The Lhasa Postmaster also spoke English, as he was trained in telegraphy at Kalimpong. The postal and telegraph system is most efficient. The line was laid from Kalimpong over the Jelep La as far as Gyantse during the 1904 Mission. After Sir Charles Bell's visit to Lhasa in 1920 it was continued to the city. It is maintained by Nepalese line-men with occasional visits—usually no farther than Gyantse—from British engineers. The muleteers sometimes take the posts for firewood and amuse themselves by throwing stones at the insulators, but during our visit we were always able to telegraph messages to India. The Potala is connected by telephone with the Post Office. Stamps, in five values and colours (green, yellow, blue and two shades of red), are printed at the Lhasa Mint; they are current only within Tibet. Post-runners carry the mails to Gangtok (our letters were re-stamped at Gyantse). Running from dawn to dusk in relays of about eight miles they covered the 330 miles from Lhasa to Gangtok in from eight to ten days. Our record time for getting an answer from Calcutta was seventeen days.

Trimon, an ex-Shap-pe, came to call. He is grey-haired and looks old and worried. He has just married a new and attractive wife, in whose Lhasa house he now lives; but soon he returns to Gyantse to occupy some estates he has gained possession of after a long and expensive lawsuit. They say that when he wanted to retire from his duties as a Cabinet Minister his resignation was refused by the Dalai Lama, so he took off all his clothes and, feigning madness, ran naked through the streets of Lhasa. He is anything but insane now, though he seems saturnine and dis-illusioned. He spoke very sensibly of the gravity of the Tashi Lama situation. So also did Ngagchen Rimpoche, who is the Tashi Lama's chief agent in Lhasa. He is a Ta Lama (a very high monk official) and a famous preacher. Prayers conducted by him are supposed to be more effective than any others. He told us that the real trouble is caused by the Tibetan officials in the Tashi Lama's entourage. Many of these are in Chinese pay, have Chinese wives, and do not want to return to their country, where they may be degraded, tortured, or even put to death. Tashi himself is a very old man by Tibetan standards. A true

Tibetan at heart and a man of most saintly character, he must yearn to spend his last few years in Shigatse, where his own people revere him as the holiest person in Tibet. But he has for so long accepted the hospitality and pay of China that he is virtually a prisoner there, and probably the Chinese escort is being forced upon him against his will. Ngagchen also deplored the vacillating attitude of the Tibetan Government, who have already conceded more than they should. Ngagchen is a small man of great intelligence with a high forehead and bald head. He has a goatee beard and wise twinkling eyes. He has travelled a great deal in India and China, but is now of advanced age. He complains that he has worms in his teeth.

The young and very aristocratic-looking Ra-ka-sha came in one day. A brother of the Maharani of Sikkim, I had made his acquaintance at Gangtok when he was visiting her. He is a member of one of the two Lhasa families who trace their ancestry to the " Religious Kings " who ruled Tibet in the eighth and ninth centuries. In memory of their ancestors the heads of these families are greeted by their tenants with the obeisances otherwise only accorded to high lamas. His wife is another of Tering Rajah's daughters.

Having endeavoured to describe the personalities and positions of various Lhasa officials it will be interesting to see how they are graded; also to see how the machinery of government worked under the dictatorship of the last Dalai Lama and how it is adapting itself to present contingencies.

Alone in the first rank of Tibetan officials are the Dalai and Tashi Lamas. The Regent, or King according to his Tibetan title, is between the first and second, for it is difficult to classify incarnate lamas. In the second rank is the Prime Minister (*silön* or *lönchen*) alone. The third is headed by the Royal Dukes (*yapshi kung*), and the four Shap-pes are of this rank, so also is the Lord Chamberlain (*chi-kyap kempo*), the head of the ecclesiastical party. Finally there are the Dzasas and *tejis*. The Tejis, of whom some are hereditary, are usually members of noble families who give their services to the Government without receiving payment in cash or estates.

In the fourth rank are several grades of officials: the four Financial Secretaries (*tsi-pön*) and the officials in charge of the

Dalai Lama's private treasury in the Potala and of the Government treasury beside the Cathedral. The monk and the lay Commanders-in-Chief of the army are of this grade, so are the Depöns, or "Lords of the Arrow" (the literal meaning of the title). These correspond to generals in the army, or to military commanders of important districts. The four members of the Lama Cabinet (*trun-yik chempo*), which is presided over by the Lord Chamberlain, are of this rank, so also is the Shigatse dzongpön and the Governor of Gartok.

In the fifth rank are several dzongpöns of important districts, City Magistrates (*mi-pön*), and various storekeepers, judges and receivers of fines. The sixth rank consists of the magistrates of smaller districts, and innumerable junior treasurers and secretaries.

These classifications are by no means rigid, and there was considerable disagreement among my Tibetan informers as to the class to which certain officials belonged. If a position that is normally fourth-class is held by a very important official he will rank as third; a post in the Dalai Lama's household that is responsible during His Holiness' life may be much less so during a Regency. One hundred and seventy-five lay officials are usually appointed, and a similar number of ecclesiastics. Very often certain positions are duplicated, a monk and a lay official being jointly in charge. For instance, the small hamlet at the foot of the Potala is in charge of Möndö (the monk Rugbeian) and Ramba (the acting lay guide to the Mission). The dzongpöns similarly work in pairs, so also do the Commanders-in-Chief of the army.

When there is a Dalai Lama he appoints a Prime Minister, a layman, who is in charge of criminal cases, and who is also the medium between the Shap-pes and the Dalai Lama, for it would be unfitting for the Dalai himself to deal with such matters.

The Cabinet, called Kashak (both vowels pronounced long and the last k not sounded) after the building in which it meets, was founded about two hundred years ago; the four members, three laymen and one monk, are directly appointed by His Holiness. After discussing any matter under consideration they draw up a report, which is forwarded to the Prime Minister, who appends his own opinion and submits it to the Dalai or, in his absence, to the Regent. If the Dalai wishes, he can ignore the recommendations of his Ministers, and in fact frequently did so.

There is yet another governing body which is summoned on occasions of national emergency; this is the National Assembly (*tsondu*). The full Assembly, which rarely meets, as it is somewhat cumbersome, comprises four hundred members, including all lay and monk officials above a certain rank, the Abbots of important monasteries, and various others. The inner Assembly, a variable body, consists of the Abbots of Drepung, Sera and Ganden, the Dzases and Tejis, and one or two other officials who happen to be especially powerful at the time. It is through the Assembly that the opinion of the great monasteries can make itself felt. The Prime Minister and Cabinet are allowed to attend the meetings of the Assembly but they may take no part in the discussion. Before the late Dalai took the government into his own hands, the Assembly used to deal with foreign affairs while the other Ministers confined themselves to internal administration. When the Dalai was alive, backed by the adoration of his subjects and by a small but highly trained bodyguard, he ruled absolutely. There was little precedent, as he came to power after a hundred years of Regency, and for the greater part of his long reign the Chinese had no power in Lhasa. The Assembly could only meet when summoned by him, and then only those whose names appeared on the list that he sent round. Questions of foreign policy he settled himself, even the Prime Minister and Cabinet could only advise. And now that he has gone, the officials, so accustomed to being told what to do, have lost the power of initiative. The Regent, a young incarnation lama, knows little of the art of government. The Prime Minister, though popular with the people, knows still less.

When the Dalai Lama died, in 1933, there was something of a crisis at Lhasa. In the first place, his favourites, who held no official status, were in danger. Kumpa-la especially, for he had enjoyed great power and was regarded with bitter jealousy. Some said he should be beheaded, others wanted to imprison him; in the end the monks had their way and he was banished to south-east Tibet. The Prime Minister was at that time a youth; the Cabinet Ministers, Trimon, Langchungna, Tendong, and the Kalön Lama (the last three being still in office), had little power and submitted questions of importance to the National Assembly, who had assumed control of affairs. The first thing they did was to enquire into the death of the Dalai Lama, for there was some suspicion that he had been poisoned. Shortly before his death he had been given some medicine by the State Oracle at Netchung (the predecessor of the present Oracle). It appeared that His Holiness had been ill for some time, although the people did not know it, and Kumpa-la was sent for, and asked why he had not reported the Dalai Lama's illness before. Lungsha, an ambitious fourth-rank official who was suspected of pro-Chinese tendencies and who had accompanied the Rugby boys to England in 1913, was the chief power in the National Assembly. He wanted to become a Shap-pe; he desired lucrative positions for his friends and also wanted to bring about certain reforms, to which end he prepared a petition signed by a hundred influential people. He suggested that for every post there should be a monk and a lay official; that these should be appointed by the National Assembly instead of by the Cabinet; and that the system of one official holding several jobs and enormous estates, while others had neither, should be stopped. He further plotted to ambush and kill Trimon Shap-pe and the Prime Minister as they walked round the Park Circle (a prescribed holy walk) in the early morning.

One of the enemies in the way of Lungsha's ambitions was a fourth-rank official called Kapshupa, who had had an administrative job in the Hor States in Kham, but who, owing to his financial intrigues, had become so unpopular that complaints of his conduct had been made to the National Assembly. As Kapshupa was known to be a great friend of the banished favourite Kumpa-la, Lungsha was doubly anxious to imprison him. Lungsha therefore accused Kapshupa before the National Assembly.

The Cabinet immediately summoned the two enemies to the Potala, where they were questioned. Suddenly fearing that too much was known of his intrigues, Lungsha endeavoured to flee but was grasped by one of the gigantic monk door-keepers. In the struggle Lungsha's arm was broken and a loaded pistol fell from the pocket of his robe. At the same time one of his boots came off and, from the inside of the boot, two small pieces of paper fell on to the floor. Lungsha seized these and, putting

them into his mouth, tried to swallow them; but a monk
throttled him and recovered one piece on which was written the
name of Trimon Shap-pe. Presumably Kapshupa's name was
on the other. It appeared that Lungsha had been endeavouring
to kill his enemies by witchcraft in the same way that the Regent
of Tengye-ling Monastery had attempted to bring about the
death of the young Dalai Lama, as will be described later.

Lungsha was put in prison. His son, who was depön of the
Norbhu Lingka bodyguard, and others, tried to force his release;
but they were unsuccessful. The unfortunate Lungsha had his
eyes put out and was removed to the Government jail at the
foot of the Potala, where he still languishes. Kapshupa was
tried and imprisoned; soon afterwards he secured a reprieve,
though he was still dismissed from Government service. However, a year later he managed to get back again and is now the
chief financial secretary (tse-pön) and is building himself a magnificent new mansion near the Cathedral.

On the whole, the administration of Lhasa, though corrupt,
is efficient. The people are used to a certain amount of extortion,
but if the traditional limit is exceeded their natural independence
asserts itself and there is trouble; higher authority is appealed to,
and the over-rapacious official is punished. Tibet is in the position
of European countries in the Middle Ages—in many ways a position
which we are bound, nowadays, to envy. The country is run by
the monasteries and by the noble families. If the son of a merchant
or farmer is ambitious he enters a monastery, for only there can he
hope to rise to that position of importance to which he feels he is
entitled. But there is no unemployment, no underlying feeling
of insecurity, and—except for those who choose begging as a
profession—no real poverty.

One important caller who is neither a monk nor a lay official
was the trader Pangda Tsang, a short-haired phlegmatic young
Tibetan, who arrived on a magnificent ambler. He lives in a
large house next to the Surkang mansion. There is a romantic
story attached to him. A few years ago his younger brother,
a rupön (corresponding to a captain), rebelled against his general
in eastern Tibet. As Pangda Tsang was suspected of complicity,
the Government ordered his house to be surrounded by the
Tibetan army. The trader, strong in his innocence, armed himself and a dozen servants with rifles and swords, and declared

that the first soldier to cross his threshold would be a dead man.
The army laid siege. After a few days one of the defenders fell
asleep and accidentally let off his gun. The Tibetan army fled,
and never returned. But Pangda Tsang did not have it all his
own way; rumour has it that it cost him a lac and a half of
rupees (£11,250) to make his peace with the Cabinet.

Apart from the Tibetans in Lhasa, there are various com-
munities of foreigners who add their contribution to the character
of the place. In 1885 the warlike Gurkhas from Nepal invaded
Tibet for the second time and, by the resulting treaty, were
allowed to establish an Agency in Lhasa and to have extra-
territorial rights and free trading facilities. In Lhasa today
there are six or seven hundred Nepalese and, as they are of
Newar and not Gurkha stock, many of them are Buddhists and
have Tibetan wives. Although the most artistic of the Nepalese
tribes, they are not popular in Lhasa. Possibly the Tibetans
resent their high-handed attitude, and perhaps also they consider
that the Nepalese have not kept their side of the 1856 treaty,
by which they undertook to come to the assistance of Tibet if
any invader appeared. But there is another reason. As Lhasa
is the Holy City of Buddhism, a religion that sets itself very
strongly against the taking of any sort of life, the birds and
animals there are unmolested by Tibetans and therefore very
tame. Within a hundred yards of our house there lived flocks
of bar-headed geese, Brahminy duck and mallard, and it would
have been easy to have walked up to these and shot them. In
the rivers too there are char and barbel up to eight and ten
pounds in weight, just asking to be caught; but as we were
members of a Diplomatic Mission, we took no advantage—in
spite of great temptation—of these opportunities, out of respect
to our hosts. The Nepalese, however, both shoot the bird
and catch the fish. If there is any trouble, they are tried by their
own courts and invariably acquitted. They are also to be seen
smoking their hookahs in the streets of Lhasa, thereby infringing
another Tibetan prohibition. We saw a great many of them
in Lhasa, where they are shopkeepers, traders and metal-workers.
We were possibly rather unfavourably impressed, because some
of them, usually members of the Nepalese escort, were among the
doctor's most repulsive patients. Riddled with venereal disease
they would be seen hobbling up to his surgery to receive their
injections.

The Nepalese representative, Major Hamal, was one of the first to call on the Political Officer. He rode up to the Deyki Lingka in magnificent style. He wore a suit of dazzling cloth of gold, and a turban of the same material with a large white aigrette springing from a golden ornament. Over his head was carried an enormous canopied State umbrella. With him came an escort of two officers and twenty men clad in bright blue uniforms. The Major speaks good though slow English; he is somewhat portly, has a black moustache, and wears pince-nez. He dislikes Lhasa, finding the climate exceedingly trying. He has little use for the Tibetans and a genius for drinking innumerable liqueurs in the shortest possible time. Being very short-sighted he walks with difficulty, usually supported by the arms of his two officers. He was always very friendly and genial whenever we met him.

Another early caller was the Agent of Bhutan. The relationship between the Bhutanese and the Tibetans is close. They are of the same stock and religion, for the Bhutanese are followers of the Kagyü sect of Tibetan Buddhism. Bhutan, at one time or another in her obscure and mysterious past, has been under the suzerainty of Cooch Behar, Tibet and China. The inhabitants number a few hundred thousand only, and the country is little more than two and a half times as large as Wales, but it marches with the Indian frontier for 250 miles, overlooking the rich tea gardens of Assam. At the beginning of this century, when our relations with Tibet became strained, Bhutan was virtually an independent State inhabited by people of Tibetan stock, who acknowledged the spiritual authority of the Dalai Lama as head of their faith, and, until Bhutan came under British protection in 1910, the Bhutanese sent annual remittances to Lhasa, though they were careful to point out that these were only religious gifts to the Dalai Lama.

Only one or two commercial agents actually live in Lhasa, though parties of Bhutanese traders often visited the city and we occasionally saw these swarthy short-haired men, distinguished easily enough by their striped robes, which only reach to the knee. They seem less Mongolian-featured than the Tibetans and appear to have larger heads. Rice and birch teacups are the chief exports of Bhutan to Tibet.

Gulam Maidin Mahommad and Asatulla Mahommad, who had ridden out a day's journey to meet us on our arrival, came soon afterwards to pay their respects to the Political Officer. These men, together with their two or three hundred compatriots in Lhasa, are Mohammedans from Ladakh, the north-eastern province of Kashmir. Some of them are descendants of the Dogra force that unsuccessfully attacked western Tibet a hundred years ago. They are practically all traders and live in the south-eastern corner of the city, where they have a small mosque. They wear Tibetan dress, with the addition of a turban, and are clever and successful merchants. They approached the Political Officer to ask for extra-territorial rights similar to those enjoyed by the Nepalese, on the grounds that they come from Ladakh, which is part of British India; but as they have all the advantages and amenities of Lhasa and are not in any way oppressed, the request seemed unreasonable.

# CHAPTER SIX

## WE RETURN THEIR CALLS

On 27th August, two days after our arrival at Lhasa, we rode in solemn procession to pay a ceremonial call on the Regent and Prime Minister at the Potala. The Political Officer wore his black diplomatic uniform complete with cocked-hat and decorations. Brigadier Neame and Captain Morgan were also in uniform; Richardson wore a morning-coat and white topee, while I, having no uniform, wore a dark-blue suit and, to show that the occasion was a very special one, a watch-chain.

As we rode between the willow trees and flooded meadows towards the Potala we were a brilliantly coloured procession: Norbhu in his scarlet and yellow Dzasa's dress; our two guides, the monk in his plum-coloured robes and gold hat, the layman wearing his scarlet magistrate's gown over a violet silk robe, and with his curious "basin" hat perched on top of his head; Rai Sahib Bo and the seven Sikkimese clerks in robes of gay-coloured brocade and short sleeveless jackets of another bright colour; ten scarlet-coated orderlies, those from Gangtok wearing basket-work hats ornamented with peacock feathers; and six

CEREMONIAL TRUMPETS ON THE ROOF OF GUNDELING MONASTERY. THE TRUMPET STAND AND TURRET ARE COVERED IN GOLD LEAF

PAGODA COVERING THE LATE DALAI LAMA'S TOMB

IMAGES IN A TIBETAN MONASTERY

grooms in gold-banded Tibetan hats and spotted coats edged with leopard skin. We rode up to the long flight of steps leading to the northern gateway of the Potala and, leaving our ponies, threaded our way along dark passages to an ante-room where the Reting Dzasa and other officials took charge of us.

The ceremonial is strict and carefully laid down. First we met the Prime Minister in an outer room, later we were received in the Regent's Throne Room. It was a small room with frescoes on the walls and a row of religious banners (*thankas*) hanging above the throne, which was a gaudily cushioned seat about two feet from the ground. The Prime Minister, who came in with us, took his place on a lower seat. We presented scarves and then sat on low cushions, while tea, biscuits and dried fruits were handed round by two colossal monks, who are the Regent's personal attendants. The larger was more than 6 feet 8 inches in height and had his shoulders padded to make him appear even bigger.

Meanwhile Norbhu and the Sikkimese clerks were presented. Each in turn kow-towed three times in Chinese fashion, touching the floor with his forehead, then advanced, bowing low, to present scarves, which were taken by an attendant. The Regent blessed each of them with both hands or only one, according to rank, and put over their necks a fillet of scarlet silk. Gould and the Regent had a formal conversation in which the former delivered a message of greeting from the Viceroy of India, and the usual compliments were exchanged. When we went the Regent got up and shook hands in the most cordial way with each of us in turn. The interview was impressive, although the Regent himself has little presence. He is a frail, undersized, almost emaciated-looking monk of about twenty-three years of age, with very prominent ears. He has a receding chin and peculiar creases above the bridge of his nose which when he frowns assume the shape of rudimentary horns. He wore ordinary monk's clothes, with a braided undercoat, stiff pinkish turned-up boots and red habit, leaving his thin arms bare. No hat was worn over his closely-cropped hair.

On the following day we called privately on the Regent at his newly built summer place, which lies about three-quarters of a mile east-north-east from the Potala, on the outskirts of the city. It is situated behind the Shiday monastery, which is

I

affiliated to his own monastery of Reting. To reach this palace we had to ride through flooded streets and narrow muddy alleys smelling strongly of sewage. The windows meanwhile were crowded with inquisitive but friendly faces.

The palace is very small, containing only storerooms on the ground floor and a single sitting-room above; but it is an attractive building and beautifully decorated. There are golden turrets on the roof, and along the top of the wall the usual golden emblems on a matt background of willow-twig walling. The woodwork round the windows is cleverly carved and painted in bright colours. Boxes of gay flowers stand on every window-sill, protected from the sun by awnings of white cloth. More-over, the palace lies in a walled garden with well-kept lawns, and beds full of English flowers in luxuriant bloom. The Regent is extremely fond of pets. He has several cages full of birds, including a talking "mina" and a laughing-thrush that makes the most fantastic noises in the middle of the most serious conversations. He has a monkey, a fox cub, a leopard, a cage of ornamental pheasants and several different kinds of dogs.

We reached the upper storey by a flight of stone steps outside the palace and found a most attractive room full of light and gay colours. The walls were covered with frescoes of lay and religious subjects, and there were glass cases crammed with pieces of porcelain and cloisonné. The only unbeautiful things were the European table and chairs put ready for us. The young Regent was much more natural and talkative than on the day before, and only the friendly Reting Dzasa, a monk-secretary, and one or two other monks were in attendance. His favourite was also present: a very good-looking monk of about sixteen who is one of the Duke's sons.

As soon as we had presented scarves and drunk tea—both the Tibetan and European drink was served—our presents were brought in and given to the Regent. These consisted of a fine silver tea-service and tray, and such things as rifles, revolvers, a gramophone and a thermos flask. They also included the "Kharitz" (letter of salutation) and a signed photograph from the Viceroy of India, and three young spaniels that we had brought up to Lhasa as a personal gift from His Excellency to the Regent. It is not the custom to show any pleasure at the receipt of presents, but the young Regent could hardly conceal his delight with the dogs, which, I regret to say, did not behave very well on this their first experience of the inside of a house. The visit did not last long. Just before we left the Regent asked Gould to talk freely to all officials because the Tibetans particularly wanted our help in a time of unusual perplexity. They were accustomed to leading a peaceful religious life, he said, and were unused to facing problems such as now confronted them.

When we all went into the garden the Regent had no objection to being photographed, and it was all I could do to persuade his huge orderly (whom we nicknamed Simple Simon) to move about when I wanted to take some cinema films; he struck what he thought was an imposing attitude and resolutely refused to move. Before we went the Regent obligingly blessed each of our servants in turn, placing with his own hands a small white scarf around their necks. It is moving to see with what deep reverence all Buddhists regard their spiritual ruler.

As soon as we had left the Regent's Palace we rode right across the western edge of the city to call on the Prime Minister, who lives fairly near the Kyi Chu (Lhasa river). On our journey between the dwellings of the two highest people in the land we had to splash through stinking puddles and past heaps of dung where ravens vied with mangy dogs in searching for the foulest imaginable carrion and garbage. The Prime Minister lives in a large and rather depressing mansion with a pleasant view over the tree-tops of his park to the mountain slopes across the river.

We rode through a solidly built gateway into a large cobbled courtyard which is overlooked on the southern side by his four-storied mansion. Two-storied outbuildings enclose the rest of the yard. Above the door was a room with an open veranda full of flowers. In the corner of the courtyard a group of labourers were grinding up peas with an ingenious stone handmill. On each side of the doorway were two granite mounting-blocks carved with the Swastika emblem.

We followed dark passages up to the top floor, where we found the Prime Minister waiting for us. He was not very easy to get on with, and remained very much the official, seated on a ceremonial divan at a higher level than one he had prepared for Gould. We did not meet his wife as it is not the custom for womenfolk to appear on ceremonial occasions. In his sitting-room, as is so often the case, the natural beauty of the Tibetan style of decoration was spoilt by a few traces of European influence. There was a map with the names in Russian on one wall, there were several framed photographs, a cheap alarm-clock and some tinsel and glass ornaments. After handing over the presents from the Government of India we took our leave, attributing the Prime Minister's stiffness to his youth and inexperience, rather than to any feeling of unfriendliness.

On the following day we called on the three lay Shap-pes, who live in large houses tucked away in obscure corners of the city. They were all extremely friendly and discussed matters freely. The Shap-pes, unlike the Prime Minister, sat with us in European chairs round a table, and gave us Indian tea as well as Tibetan.

For several days we were kept busy returning calls and delivering the presents from the Government of India. We went to call on the charming old Lord Chamberlain in his rooms at the Potala, and on the Yapshi Kung at his Lhasa house. In every case we were most hospitably entertained and were continually delighted by the dignified courtesy and urbanity of each official we met. Each house gave evidence of the highly developed artistic skill of the Tibetans, for though originally all their culture was derived from Mongolia or China, they have developed a characteristic national style both in architecture and interior decoration. Their carving, metal-work and painting is the work of highly skilled craftsmen; exquisite examples are to be seen in every house, for most of the noble families maintain their own silversmith, woodcarver, lacquer worker and fresco painter.

The private chapel or altar-room is usually the best in the house; here are golden images set with turquoise and other precious stones, priceless specimens of porcelain and cloisonné, inlaid chang jugs, and beautifully embossed silver and gold prayer-wheels. In Tibet religion comes first, and it is in the expression of their faith that the finest artistic work is produced.

Richly coloured thankas and lively frescoes ornament the walls. (The word thanka is pronounced more or less to rhyme with " bunker ".) They became familiar to us in Lhasa as perhaps the most remarkable, if not the finest, example of Tibetan art. They are usually in sets of four, eight or sixteen, and are hung in lines, often overlapping each other, in the monasteries or in the altar-rooms of private houses. The actual painting is usually about two feet wide and three feet long. The pigments used are made from various crushed minerals, the majority of which are imported from India. These are mixed with hot thin glue. Flame-red and green are used most, and several peculiarly rich dull blues. Yellows are rare, gold being frequently used instead. The colours, though garish at first, soon tone down in the smoke and gloom of a monastery temple. The canvas, which is of very fine texture, is stiffened with a chalky preparation. All thankas are not painted: some are of fine embroidery, others of appliqué work. One variety is drawn or embroidered in white on a black background; this is usually of a subject so hideous or obscene that, unlike other thankas, it is normally veiled. The paintings are framed with inch-wide strips of scarlet and gold—the former as a rule being on the inside—and then mounted on the finest silk, usually dark blue, so that the complete thanka is about three feet wide and five feet long— though they are sometimes several times as large as this—and has a wooden roller at top and bottom. The projecting ends of the rollers are occasionally of silver most beautifully embossed. A strip of specially valuable brocade is sewn on to the mount below the picture. Fine silk covers, usually three in number, hang over and protect the painting, together with two narrow strips of silk which are left hanging even when the covers are rolled up. Particularly valuable thankas have on their backs the impression of the entire left hand of the Dalai or Tashi Lama.

The subject-matter of the painting varies greatly. As a rule there is a large image in the centre, either of mild aspect and seated upon a lotus-flower, the symbol of divine birth, or fierce, consumed by flames, and terrible with elaborate hideousness. Every corner of the canvas is filled, either by other scenes and images or by trees, flowers and clouds in conventional Chinese style. Very often there is a small likeness of the artist in an attitude of adoration. Always they show a high standard of drawing and rare magnificence of colouring.

We could not be asked out to lunch until we had been officially entertained by the Cabinet, and this was delayed owing to Gould's rather severe indisposition; but one day we were invited to have tea with Tsarong.

The Tsarong mansion lies just beyond that of the Prime

Minister, between the City and the Kyi Chu. Turning out of a flooded stretch of waste-land we entered the usual type of terraced gateway, clattered across a small cobbled yard to another gateway, and then found ourselves looking at the most remarkable house in Lhasa. The Tsarong mansion, like all Tibetan houses, faces south, but it looks onto a skilfully laid out garden instead of onto the traditional courtyard surrounded by lower buildings. The style is a pleasant combination of Tibetan mansion and English country house. The roof is flat, and there are incense-burners and prayer-flags on it, but the windows are of the casement type and are fitted throughout with glass. The door is ornamented in the best Tibetan style, but in front of it are a dozen granite steps covered with pots of flowering plants.

Inside, the combination of styles is still more attractive. A spacious stone hall hung with Landseer and Farquharson prints in heavy oak frames leads by means of a staircase (practically the only one in Lhasa) to the first floor, on which are all the living-rooms.

We had tea in the private chapel, which is the largest and finest room of the house. Hinged casement windows, with a long window-seat below, take up one wall. Opposite are several half-life-sized golden images in ornate glass cases. The images wear golden diadems studded with precious gems, and round their necks are amber necklaces with stones as large as tangerines. On an altar in front are displayed holy-water vessels, cloisonné lions, a pair of priceless porcelain vases in a glass case, several silver teapots and jugs, and a gold reliquary. At the end of the altar is an ormolu clock and a large terrestrial globe. Another wall displays a line of magnificent thankas framed in purple and gold brocade. Beneath a gay canopy is the throne of the master of the house padded with silken cushions heavily embroidered with dragons and flowers. At the top of two of the pillars supporting the roof are large diamond-shaped scarlet boards bearing Chinese characters in black; these are decorations conferred on Tsarong by the Chinese. Another honourable Chinese order consists of two circular pieces of jade joined by a curving piece of dark lacquered wood. It is about eighteen inches long and is kept in a glass case. I have seen a similar emblem in the Chinese Pavilion of the King of Siam's Palace by the banks of Menong river.

The floor of the room is of sand and small pebbles beaten down and polished to the consistency of marble. On it are several carpets of Tibetan and Indian manufacture. The walls are brightly painted in scarlet, green, blue and ochre; round the top of the walls is painted a fluted scroll-work frieze shaded to resemble a pleated valance. Square wooden pillars support the roof beams, which are all painted red and ornamented with brightly coloured designs of dragons, flowers and clouds.

Another room of the house is furnished in English style with a heavy wooden dining-table, sideboard and chairs. On the walls are family photographs in heavy frames. But the majority of the rooms are Tibetan and are furnished with low divans and carved and lacquered tables. In one room is a huge painting in Chinese style of a well-known picture, showing the seven generations of one family all living at the same time. This was actually painted by the Dalai Lama when a young man and shows considerable talent. Tsarong also possesses a well-appointed bathroom with running water.

It was time for tea when we had looked round the house, and we sat round a low table while Mrs. Tsarong poured out the best Darjeeling tea from a silver teapot. We also had bread and butter, cakes, rock buns, and beautifully iced " penny buns "—one of Tsarong's cooks having been trained in India to make European cakes and dishes. The Tsarongs, unfortunately, cannot speak English, but the Jigmes, who live next door, were there and able to act as interpreters as well as Norbhu.

Jigme's wife Mary is a younger sister of Mrs. Tsarong and, having been at St. Joseph's School, Darjeeling, she speaks perfect English. Jigme and Mary Tering are as charming a young couple as it would be possible to find. Certainly we owe the Tsarongs and Terings a great debt of gratitude for their extraordinary hospitality and helpfulness to us in every way. In most Tibetan houses, except perhaps Ringang's, we had to be on our best behaviour, but Tsarong's parties were always completely riotous, especially when his three children came home from school. The Tsarongs are the most perfect natural host and hostess. Tsarong always drank (or pretended to have drunk) a little more chang than his guests; Mrs. Tsarong made us feel completely at home and, having studied what dishes we liked, she was careful to produce them the next time we came. After tea the Dele

Rabdens came in. He is an official in the service of the Tashi Lama. Here in Lhasa he has his hair done in a plait and does not wear silk; though when living at Shigatse he wears his hair in a top-knot. His wife is very distinguished-looking and has a quiet shy manner.

All three women were dressed in the complicated and re-splendent finery of the Lhasa lady of fashion. The glossy black hair is parted in the middle and brushed down at the side to cover the ears. At the back it is neatly tied in two long plaits. The parting divides on the crown of the head so as to run each side of a small patch of hair as big as a penny, then unites again. The hair from this isolated portion is made into a small plait which covers the parting down the back of the head. Two heavy gold ear-rings set with large pieces of turquoise are hung from the hair above the ears, effectively framing the oval face. On the back of the head is worn a concave triangular crown closely covered with strings of seed pearls and further ornamented with a row of corals the size and colour of cherries. False hair is suspended from each side of the crown; it hangs loose to begin with and is then plaited with a red tassel so that it almost reaches the ground. The women are continually putting their hands up to the points of the crown to see that it is straight, which, as a matter of fact, it seldom is. Sometimes strings of beads and pieces of jade are tied across the sides of the triangle to meet in a pendent ornament hanging down the back. Cosmetics are used, but so skilfully, in most cases, as to pass unnoticed. When the Tibetan boys who came to England first saw fashionable English women, they said, " Ah, I see the women over here chew betel-nut !"

The charm-box is perhaps the most beautiful of all the ladies' adornments. In shape it is a square set across a diamond; it is made of dark Tibetan gold and is set in a geometric petal pattern with turquoise and other precious stones, including rubies, garnets, sapphires and diamonds. The charm-box is held by a short necklace of large stones, usually alternate corals and agate or black glass beads with wavy white bands. Strings of seed pearls form a flat band which hangs from the left shoulder down to the waist. In the centre of this is a circular ornament some three inches in diameter made of various precious stones. Other necklaces of large stones hang round the neck and are looped to the bottom of the pearl band. From the shoulder also hangs a bejewelled chatelaine holding a toothpick, tweezers, wax remover and other contrivances.

The dress, which can be with or without sleeves, is usually of rich purple silk with a pattern of dragons and lucky signs in purple and gold. It is held in at the waist with a bright-coloured sash. An apron with corner pieces of flowered gold braid hangs almost to the foot of the dress. This is woven in horizontal strips of red, blue, green, yellow and white, and is made in sections so that the strips do not continue right across. A silk blouse shows at the neck and sleeves. Thick flat-soled boots are worn of scarlet and green embroidered cloth. Although the head-dress might be considered somewhat grotesque, the whole costume is most effective. The jewellery worn by a Tibetan lady of fashion may be worth thousands of pounds.

It was at Tsarong's house that we first met Tibetan children, whom we found most delightful—quite unspoiled, and full of life and intelligence. Although learning is considered in Tibet to be the highest moral quality, education itself is somewhat primitive. The Tibetan child is taught to read and write, to recite prayers and long passages of the Buddhist scriptures, and the elements of arithmetic, which are taught with such elementary paraphernalia as the rosary and small pebbles or fruit stones. Of history, except in so far as it affects his religion, and of the very elements of geography, he has no knowledge whatsoever. In the case of the noble families, a private tutor is kept who is usually a monk. So excellent a mixture of feudalism and democracy is Tibet that the sons of the tenants and servants also attend the classes.

In Lhasa itself there are only two Government schools, and both are for budding officials. There is the college at the Potala for training young monk officials, and a similar one beside the Cathedral for laymen. The latter is reserved for sons of noble families. In the school for lay officials they are taught to keep accounts and to write letters. In a country where specific and high-flown honorific titles are used and extravagant compliments paid this is no easy task. Besides these there are many private schools, and as parents are nowadays very keen that their sons should learn English, such men as the Nepali dentist, the Tibetan postmaster and certain traders having an altogether inadequate knowledge of the languge, are teaching the boys to speak pidgin English. This is the greatest pity, as Tibetan boys

I 2

when properly taught speak the purest and most delightful English.

On several occasions I visited the school kept by the monk telegraphist. One day the children were all reading aloud, but no two seemed to be reading the same thing. Sometimes they repeated prayers. Usually they were sitting cross-legged on the floor writing from memory passages of the scriptures. The more advanced pupils wrote on parchment, the less skilful on blocks of polished wood; in the latter case, as soon as a child had finished, he would bring it up to the teacher, who would look at it, then rub it out. The child would then start again.

Tea was served at frequent intervals. When the postmaster had to attend to his other work the class was left in charge of the senior boy, who by his long ear-ring seemed to be of good family, for other children do not generally wear jewellery.

The last Dalai Lama was anxious that a school run on Western lines, with an English headmaster, should be established at Gyantse or Lhasa. The experiment in 1914 of sending four boys to be educated in England, though successful, had its disadvantages. It was expensive; the boys were separated from their parents for a very long time, and when they returned they were considered by the Tibetans to be uneducated, in that they had almost forgotten how to read and write their native language, and so were not given sufficiently responsible jobs. Tibetans in general are strongly opposed to parting with their children for any length of time and, though one or two are sent to Darjeeling, they have an innate mistrust of the Indian climate.

In 1923, as a result of Bell's advice, an English school was established at Gyantse in the charge of Mr. Frank Ludlow, who had had considerable experience of teaching in India. Although the Tibetans encouraged this school in theory, they did little to support it. Lhasa parents were reluctant to part with their sons and often sent them back several weeks late; and the Abbot of the Gyantse Monastery, saying that their religious education was being neglected, insisted on teaching them Tibetan for several hours each day. Ludlow found the parents and officials exasperating to deal with, though the children themselves were most intelligent and had the charming natural manners of their race. The Tibetans were most delighted with our system of arithmetic, finding multiplication and division far superior to their method of adding and subtracting with stones and beads. Owing to lack of support the school was abandoned in 1926, much to Ludlow's disappointment. We met several old boys of the Gyantse School and found that they spoke English extremely well, had perfect manners, and a fair knowledge of the game of football.

On 13th September the Shap-pes came to the Deyki Lingka for their first diplomatic talk. They arrived an hour late because the Potala clock, on which all Lhasa relies, seemed to have lost an hour.

In view of Neame's impending departure, military matters were first discussed. For three hours the Brigadier gave them his considered advice on the reforms needed in the Tibetan army. The Shap-pes, who wrote down every word, expressed their complete agreement, but added that they would have to refer all suggestions to the Regent and Prime Minister, nor did they know where the necessary money was coming from. It was part of Bell's policy that the British Government should supply arms and munitions to the Tibetan Government and should train a certain number of officers in India. The Cabinet are anxious that we should continue this policy, otherwise they may have to turn elsewhere for help—to Russia, China or Japan. We do not want to encourage the Tibetans to become once more a warlike nation; but in these days a country must be able to defend itself, and it has always been our policy to assist Tibet to maintain her position as an independent autonomous State under the nominal suzerainty of China.

On 14th September we were all invited to Tsarong's for a farewell dinner in honour of Neame; and the following day he set off for India, as the Eastern Command could spare him no longer. The Brigadier, with his extremely quiet manner—I have seldom known a man of his position throw his weight about less—and his uncanny knack of immediately seeing the essentials of a matter, impressed the Tibetans tremendously.

By 18th September Gould felt strong enough to cope with a Tibetan luncheon, so on this day the Shap-pes invited us to lunch in our garden at the Deyki Lingka. Nobody, not even the Regent or the Prime Minister, could invite us to a party until the Cabinet had given us this luncheon. As usual the Shap-pes' time and ours did not agree, and on this occasion they arrived an hour too early. From the first moment the party went with a swing, possibly because Tsarong and Ringang had also been invited together with our monk and lay guides. Music was provided before, during and after the meal by an orchestra of three curiously fashioned stringed instruments, and a flute played by a bearded Ladaki with a red fez. The band was led by a blind man who is in such high favour that he enjoys the rare privilege of being permitted to smoke even in front of the Cabinet. One of the instruments was remarkable in that the bow passed between the strings. In time with the music, which was to my ear Chinese in character, danced three " girls ", one about fifty, the other two somewhat younger. The dancing consisted in stamping on a plank in time with the music, and occasionally swinging one foot forward. After dancing in silence for some time they would burst into song, a shrill, harsh cacophony, swinging their arms from side to side. It was not very exciting for us and certainly did not appear to give them much pleasure. Their silk sleeves were worn right down over the hands out of respect; for the same reason they dared not look openly at such high officials as the Political Officer and the Shap-pes.

The menu started with the usual innumerable snacks, including sea slugs, sharks' fins and fish stomachs, and ended up with bowls of rice into which one put a selection from the various dishes. Most of these succulent delicacies seemed to be especially designed to elude the unpractised chop-sticks, but if one of the Shap-pes saw us struggling with a particularly slippery slug or an intractable slice of stomach he would deftly catch the morsel with his own chop-sticks and convey it to our plates.

The food was excellent and most skilfully prepared; our only criticism was that, as usual, there was too much of it. One of the many remarkable features of this party were the activities of three of the famous chang girls of Lhasa. Normally they are servants of leading Lhasa families, but they are commandeered on occasion by the Tibetan Government. Their duty is to pour out the chang and to see that it is drunk. The chang girls are of better family than the dancers, and their dress and ornaments are similar to those worn by the highest ladies of the land. As the girls are remarkably pretty and the chang delicious, they start with a distinct advantage. The girl fills the glass and hands it to the guest; if he puts it down she repeats the invitation; if he only drinks a little she is still not satisfied and returns it to him with further importunity. Before moving on to the next victim she refills his glass. In obstinate cases she is permitted to nudge his arm and use any form of coercion. The phrase " *Tunda nang-ro-nang* " ("empty it, please"), spoken in persuasively sweet but compelling tone, was an invitation not to be lightly ignored. They say that the chang girl is allowed to stick pins into the arms of guests, even into the Prime Minister himself, if they are slow to drink; but as I liked the beer I never experienced this myself. Usually one girl would pour out the chang from an enamel teapot while another kept her supplied from a larger container. We could usually keep pace with one pair of chang girls moving round the table, but when a rival team worked in the other direction we were forced to protest. The Doctor was even seen to threaten one of the girls with a soda-water syphon. The chang is excellent, but its potency depends upon its age, and until you have drunk a good deal you do not discover how old it is. Sometimes it is very old. Chang is the colour of rather milky lemonade; it tastes of fermented yeast and barley and it is very nourishing. The Shap-pes used to make us drink with each of them in turn, and later we would return the compliment. Their favourite trick was to make us drain our glasses while they only took a sip.

The upper-class Tibetans, unlike the poorer people, do not drink much chang and, except for the Gargantuan Ringang, we could usually outdrink them, from which we gained very greatly in prestige. The Doctor especially, apart from the fame attached to his professional knowledge, will go down in Lhasa history as a champion drinker of chang. I may say I made a considerable name for myself as a trencherman, and as a drinker (purely out of bravado) of a certain spirit called Mongolian whisky, which tastes of burning rubber and rotten goat-skin (from which it is probably distilled), but which is comforting some time after it is swallowed. The Shap-pes luncheon party lasted from midday until six o'clock in the evening, and was said to have been much more intimate and lacking in restraint than the usual Government lunches; I can well believe it.

Now that the close season for luncheon parties was over, we

found ourselves inundated with invitations, and Gould had to make a rule not to lunch with people under the fourth rank, though this limitation did not bind the rest of us. We lunched with each Shap-pe in turn, with the Duke, Trimön, the Prime Minister and the Regent.

The embodiment of God Incarnate (the Regent) gave us a very good lunch at his summer palace. As his greatness did not permit him to eat at the same table as ourselves, he sat on his throne and had each course brought to him in very beautiful silver bowls embossed with designs in gold. At the end of an extensive Chinese luncheon a huge tray of traditional Tibetan foods was brought in; this was for display and not, we were relieved to find, to be eaten. There were joints of aged dried mutton, raw meat in chillies and a towering mass of barley-meal paste decorated with coloured ornaments of butter.

We found the Regent most unaffected and simple, and rather wearied by the greatness that is thrust upon him. He complains that he can get no exercise, as on the rare occasions that he leaves his palace he must be carried in his palanquin.

Having heard reports of various forms of entertainments that Nepean and Dagg had ingeniously fitted up at the Norbhu Lingka, and being unable, owing to his high position, to come and see for himself, we were requested to bring a selection with us. Accordingly the wireless officers rigged up a public-address amplifier. The microphone was set up in one corner of the garden and the amplifiers near the house. Norbhu and Tsarong then carried on a mock quarrel in front of the microphone, and the Regent, sitting in his room, could hear every word. This simply delighted him and he was as excited as a schoolboy. Then some gramophone records were played. Nothing but the loudest possible noise would satisfy the Regent, who made us play record after record at full blast. After this he went over and spoke into the microphone himself, at first rather self-consciously, but gradually finding great amusement at the sound of his own words and laughter booming back at him.

Langchungna, who gave us an unexpectedly excellent lunch, provided a new sort of entertainment. During the meal we had heard distant singing and afterwards, on climbing up to the flat roof as a necessary digestive exercise, we found three men singing and dancing with phenomenal animation. The dance was based on the sedate performance we had often seen given by the women, but these fellows were singing at the tops of their voices, stamping, and swinging their legs in rapid time and throwing their arms from side to side as if demented. Another attraction in Langchungna's house was a prayer-wheel which rotated by radiation. The heat from a butter-lamp was led through a spiral cylinder of parchment, on which thousands of "Om Manes" had been written, so that it gently revolved. It was curious that his menials and their children were allowed to gaze at us through the window all the time that we were there.

One day we lunched with the old Lord Chamberlain and, as we took the trouble to discover what each dish was and to write down its name, I shall describe this lunch, as being typical of many others. We were entertained in the living-room of a large house in the city which had at one time belonged to Kumpala, the Dalai Lama's banished favourite. The room was decorated in Tibetan style, but there was glass in some of the windows and we used the European type of table and chairs.

Arriving soon after midday, we exchanged the usual compliments with our host and then sat down to Indian tea with Jacob's biscuits and dried apricots. The latter are grown in Kham, in south-east Tibet; they are so hard that the teeth make little impression on them. When the tea had been cleared away small china bowls were brought in, each containing three sweet rose-flavoured dumplings in warm sugary milk. Chop-sticks, and squares of Tibetan paper on which to lay them were provided, and renewed after this course.

After another interval the following small dishes were put on the table together: stewed mutton in gravy with onion and carrots, tinned herrings, dried prawns, halved green peaches, stewed peaches, tinned pineapple slices, dried dates, Chinese sweetmeats, melon seeds, peanuts, Mongolian smoked ham, sliced yak tongue, pressed beef, plain beef. Small dishes of sauce (perhaps Soya bean sauce), and a small china ladle were given to each of us for the above, and were retained throughout the meal. A continuous supply of chang was provided, but as there were no chang girls it was poured out with less coercion by the four men-servants who waited on us. All this was by way of hors d'œuvres; now the main courses followed in one or two large and very beautiful Chinese bowls, which were put in the middle of the table so that each person could pick out what he wanted with his chop-sticks or spoon. The smaller preliminary dishes were left on the table for anyone to dip into until the last (and fifteenth) course appeared, when there was no longer any room for them. These courses were as follows:

1. Sharks' fins and minced mutton in gravy.
2. Fine mince rolled in batter with vermicelli, celery and cabbage in gravy.
3. Mince meat in pastry.
4. Slices of a very firm-fleshed fish (probably tunny) with onions, carrots and boiled bacon.
5. Sea slugs in soup with boiled pork.
6. Round meat dumplings.
7. Green peas and mince in gravy.
8. Hard-boiled eggs quartered and attached to a similar quarter of mince in sauce.
9. Damp pastry dumplings.
10. Bamboo roots with boiled pork in soup.
11. Eels in gravy with pork and onion.
12. Rice with raisins, cherries and other fruit in syrup.
13. Small squares of sweet fried bread dipped in syrup.
14. Jam dumplings with sponge-cake.
15. (a) Shark's stomach; (b) boiled pork and carrots; (c) minced yak beef; (d) pieces of mutton; (e) steamed rice with varieties of wet bread-pastry in the form of flowers, peaches, horse-shoes; and also soup.

One is not expected to sample all the preliminary dishes, but each major dish should be tasted. The dumplings (courses 3, 6, 9, 14), two or three on a small dish, were brought round to each person. The food was extraordinarily good, being very rich and highly flavoured. My great criticism is that there was always so much to eat that one could not do justice to the meal without going into training for some time beforehand. At the end of the lunch the cook—a short Tibetan in a very grimy shirt—came in to receive our congratulations as well as a more substantial reward for his skill.

Many of the above dishes are Chinese, and such delicacies

as sea slugs and sharks' fins are imported dried from China (usually, I believe, through agents in Calcutta). Such meals are for formal occasions, and as most Tibetan cooks cannot prepare this food, a few experts are shared among many households.

In the course of these visits we entered most of the residences of Lhasa. Tibetan houses are built very much in a set pattern. Take, for instance, a typical mansion in the city. Between two stalls in a squalid Lhasa street is a large and heavily carved wooden gate, the upper part of which is protected from the sun by a striped and chequered valance rippling in the wind. A whitewashed stone incense-burner stands on one side of the door. Inside there is a large cobbled yard with several fierce mastiffs tied, all too insecurely, to granite posts, there are many mules laden with wool, and riding-ponies standing in covered stalls which run along one side of the courtyard. On the other side are outhouses and storerooms, for the yard is entirely surrounded by buildings. Opposite the entrance gateway is the front of the house with the living-room windows on the first floor, gay with flowers as a rule but now hidden by canvas and yak-hair curtains because the family are using a smaller room while the weather is warm. Brown and white pleated valances protect the paintwork above each window. In the centre of the flat roof is a vase-shaped whitewashed incense-burner, and behind it a cylinder draped with bright silk skirts of the lucky colours—blue, white, red, yellow, green. In addition there are usually " banners of victory " on the corners of the roof. These are small turrets about six feet high draped with black yak-hair, and banded by a white cross of cloth. Often they are surmounted by a trident of brass. On some roofs are wind prayer-wheels, resembling the cup anemometers used by meteorologists. There are also bundles of sticks with fluttering prayer-flags attached. The walls of the first storey are built of courses of square granite blocks bordered by small fragments of stone. Above the first storey the walls are often of sun-dried bricks, though sometimes they are built entirely of stone.

Passing the square granite mounting-blocks one enters the main doorway, which has a protecting stone porch or screen on the inner side. On the plaster of the screen is a large fresco called " Mongolian Leading Tiger ". This is a sign of welcome, and is found in the porchway of almost every house. The man is in Mongolian dress, and there is plenty of action, as his long ear-ring is flying and the tiger strides fiercely at the end of his chain. As a symbol of welcome it becomes less convincing when it is seen that the man crushes small mortals beneath his feet while the tiger treads on representatives of the animal world; but this is intended to be symbolic of the victory of virtue over vice.

Another painting that is usually found on a wooden door-screen or beside a window is known as "the Four Friends". It shows an elephant—usually with engagingly pink ears—and a monkey sitting on his back; the monkey carries a hare, which in its turn supports a magpie. These four creatures are supposed never to quarrel.

The lower rooms are just offices and storerooms, so we climb a steep wooden ladder to the first floor. On the landing is a row of prayer-wheels which are turned by everybody who passes. The chief room is the private chapel of the house, where there are gilt images of Lamaist saints and deities in ornate glass-fronted cases, rows of small brass Buddhas, gold or silver butter-lamps, holy books in pigeon-holes, and vessels of holy water. There are several religious banners hanging on the walls, which are ochre-coloured and surrounded at waist level by bands of blue and scarlet, bordered by thin gold lines. A frieze resembling pleated cloth hangings is painted at the top of the wall. One side of the room consists entirely of windows, two rows of detachable shutters being formed by stretching yellow waxed canvas over a carefully carved trellis-work frame. In the centre of each upper window is a small pane of glass. The square pillars and beams supporting the roof are elaborately carved and painted, and these in turn support innumerable smaller cross-beams used in lieu of plaster and arranged in herring-bone pattern. The ceiling is usually painted a bright matt-blue, except for the main beams, which are red.

The smaller room, in which the family are living at the moment, is built up above the level of the rest so that its windows open out onto the flat roof, on which are rows of flowers in pots. This room has a floor of beaten gravel, stamped and polished to resemble marble. A row of square silk-covered cushions, or rather mattresses, line one wall, and in front of them are low

Tibetan tables lacquered red and gold and deeply carved with dragon or lotus designs. In front of the door is a wooden screen running from floor to ceiling. At the top it is carved in an open-work petal pattern. Lower down is a panel on which there is a painting in low-relief, depicting the eight lucky signs or glorious emblems combined in a design. They are: (1) The Victorious Wheel of an Empire on which the sun never sets. (2) The Lucky Diagram called by the Buddhists "Buddha's entrails", but really a symbol of endless rebirths in worldly misery. (3) The Lotus Flower of heavenly birth. (4) The Vase of divine ambrosia of immortal life. (5) The two Golden Fish of good fortune, the mascots of Yamdrok Lake. (6) The White Umbrella of Sovereignty. (7) The Conch-shell trumpet of Victory. (8) The Victorious Banner.[1] Another favourite screen-panel shows a gold-painted dragon supporting on his head a bowl of the lucky jewels, which are of such size that they resemble fruits. There is also an altar and a few images in this room, and several banners. Two long-spouted chang jars stand in front of the altar together with a pair of Ming cloisonné vases.

Other rooms are locked with the ponderous and complicated Tibetan padlocks, but the steward gets the keys from the lady of the house and opens them. One is full of stored furniture—square Chinese chairs, tents, small folding tables, and carpets rolled up. On the wall are bows and arrows and masks such as are used in the lama dances. Another room is full of bales of wool. Yet another is used for brewing barley beer, and from the roof are suspended large joints of meat which, in the dry Tibetan air, will keep until the following year. In another up-stairs room is the house latrine. At each end of a bare earth floor are two slits about two feet long and four inches wide. These are usually built up in wooden frames about a foot above the ground and are covered by wooden lids. Beneath this room is a cesspit on the ground floor. Ashes from the yak-dung stoves are poured down from time to time so the place does not smell unduly, though it would be intolerable in a warmer climate. The contents of the cesspit are removed at rare intervals —for in winter everything is frozen solid—and heaped in the less frequented streets. The granaries occupy a large part of the house

[1] I am indebted to Waddell's *Lhasa and its Mysteries* for this list.

and contain wheat, barley and peas. Grain is poured in through
an opening at the top and drawn out from a trap-door below.
Grain in the dry Tibetan atmosphere, and in the absence of rats,
will last for as long as a hundred years. Outside one room an
old woman is weaving woollen cloth on a primitive loom, and
near by is the kitchen—a smoke-blackened room with stone grates
and rows of huge copper pans. A heap of mustard-straw is being
used for fuel, but there are piles of dung-cakes too. Servants
are continually passing to and fro; they are extremely dirty and
clothed in filthy grease-stained garments. Only on high ceremonial occasions are they properly clad. From a closed door
comes the monotonous rising and falling of a monk's voice as he
prays for the dead of the household, thus ensuring that they shall
have the best possible rebirth. Now and then he rings a bell,
beats a gong or clashes small cymbals. Half the rooms in the house
seem to have some religious significance, and several monks are
always in residence. This house is typical of many in Tibet,
though as a rule the better houses have three stories.

In return for all this hospitality we used to have equally formidable luncheon parties at the Deyki-Lingka; but whereas each
official had to ask the Mission to lunch, we could invite several
at the same time. In this way we avoided complete inundation.

At the end of September we gave a luncheon party to the
officials of Cabinet rank. These were the three Shap-pes (the
Kalön Lama being away from Lhasa), Trimön Shap-pe (retired),
Tsarong Dzasa, the Lord Chamberlain, and the Duke. Unfortunately the Duke almost forgot the engagement and only
arrived in time for tea. Ringang came as additional interpreter,
and our lay and monk guides attended *ex officio*. For entertainment we hired the town orchestra, the dancing girls and the
chang girls. Great features were the microphone and loud-
speaker, which Nepean had rigged up so that people performing
in his tent behind the house could be heard in our upstairs room
or in the luncheon tent. Our guests insisted on having songs
from the dancers and chang girls several times as loud as normal,
and gramophone music equally blaringly played. Then Tsarong
and Ringang had a long argument before the microphone, much
to the delight of our guests. After tea and liqueurs in our sitting-
room we sat down to lunch under an awning in the garden.
We provided a solid six-course luncheon of " English " food,

starting with hors d'œuvres and working through soup and asparagus to roast mutton with vegetables, and then subsiding to cold tongue and fruit salad. The Shap-pes showed less obvious enjoyment in sampling our food than we had theirs, but they did their best, and the party was an undoubted success.

A more fortuitous entertainment was provided by a chang girl trying to deal for the first time in her life with a soda-water syphon. Having poured some whisky into a glass, she pressed the handle of the syphon with such enthusiasm that the whisky was shot entirely out of the glass, most of it into her face. Luckily she agreed with us in seeing the humorous side of it. It took the girls some time to learn that whisky must neither be poured out nor drunk in the same way as chang. It was their natural inclination to fill the glass with neat spirit and to make the unfortunate guest drink it straight off. Before our guests departed—at five o'clock in the afternoon—all the servants, including the all-important cook, who is usually overlooked on such occasions, were lined up and presented with scarves and a small bag of rupees. Similar largesse was distributed to the orchestra, the dancers and the chang girls.

Two days after we had returned the hospitality of the Shap-pes we invited the Prime Minister to come to lunch. He showed considerable interest in the wireless, and a message was transmitted on his behalf to the Chief of Signals at Jubbulpore. We sometimes wonder if the latter thought somebody was having a practical joke at his expense! A few days later we gave a lunch to eighteen guests who were mainly fourth-rank officials; many of the more important ones could not come, as the Regent was at this time preparing to leave Lhasa in order to visit Samye Monastery. On the following day, making our seventh party in a single week, we gave the last of our big luncheon parties. This time the guests were all below fourth rank. They included the secretaries of the various Government departments, Tendong, the Gyantse Dzongpön who had been our guide from Gyantse to Lhasa, the monk telegraphist, and many younger sons of noble families.

Although there were rumours that the Tashi Lama, together with his controversial Chinese escort, had reached Jyekundo on his way to Tibet, the Regent set off on 6th October to visit Samye Monastery, to the south-east of Lhasa, on the Tsang-po river. This incident is only too typical of the happy-go-lucky Tibetan outlook. The political situation was as bad as it could be, yet he took two of the four Shap-pes with him and—to take photographs—the only depön who had any knowledge of machine-gunnery. So that during his absence—and he was away for six weeks—no important decision could be made; the army was even weaker than usual, and, for all the Tibetans knew, the British Mission might have had to return at short notice to India. But this religious pilgrimage had been planned for some time and could not be delayed any longer. Possibly the Regent, who was at this time in a state of great uncertainty and vacillation, hoped that events would tend to settle themselves in his absence and thus save him the trouble and responsibility of making difficult decisions.

## CHAPTER SEVEN

### HISTORICAL INTERLUDE

THE early history of the Tibetans is obscure. Their own " Book of Genesis " tells how a certain monkey who was an incarnation of the God of Mercy or the Compassionate Spirit (Avalokita in Sanskrit, Chen-re-zi in Tibetan) met a she-demon who had been born in misery owing to the wickedness of her former life. She inveigled him into marrying her, and they produced six children, who are the ancestors of the Tibetan race. Although the early writers are at pains to explain how their saintly ancestor succeeded in getting rid of the tails and long hair of his children by bringing them up on a diet of sacred grain, yet this traditional explanation of the origin of the Tibetan race is not accepted by the anthropologists, who declare prosaically that they are a branch of the ancient Mongolian stock which has inhabited the high plateau of Asia from time immemorial.

The earliest monarchy is supposed by Tibetans to date from the fifth century B.C., but little is known for certain of the rule of the early Kings of Tibet until in the seventh century of our era King Song-tsen Gampo came to the throne. Although Buddhism was first introduced into Tibet in the fifth century it had made little headway against the earlier Pon religion of pure animism, whose chief activity was the propitiation of innumerable malignant devils. The new King, by introducing a reformed system of laws and by other acts of general enlightenment, prepared the way for a more adolescent faith. Moreover, after great military successes in Burma, China and Nepal, he took two queens, one from Nepal and the other from the palace of the Emperor of China, and it was these two Buddhist ladies who inspired the vigorous introduction of the more theistic development of Buddhism which was then prevalent in India, China and Japan.

The original faith of Gautama Buddha (who lived in the sixth century B.C.) was essentially a fatalistic doctrine of negation and despair based on the less nihilistic tenets of Jainism and Brahmanism. It held, as Waddell summarizes it, " that man's sole Salvation was strenuously to try to escape finally and completely outside Life and Existence in any form, with its supposed endless cycles of rebirths after death for the same individual soul, into the haven of Total Extinction of all Existence in Nirvana (literally ' blown out ' like an extinguished candle flame) ".

A faith which demanded that its adherents must abandon wife, home and worldly goods, and live as a mendicant upon the charity of others in order to accumulate sufficient merit to attain Nirvana in a remote future birth, was hardly likely to become a popular religion for the many. Moreover, woman was only capable of salvation if, in a future rebirth, she should be born as a man. However, the great ruler Asoka (whose grandfather had successfully kept Alexander the Great out of India in 327–325 B.C.), by adopting Buddhism, in its more humanized form, as the State religion for his vast Indian Empire in 261 B.C., saved this faith from probable extinction. And it was this Asoka who, for the first time, caused to be recorded the life-story and sayings of Gautama Buddha and, by dispatching missionaries, propagated the faith throughout the Orient.

From these foundations sprang a theistic development which created a less remote Buddha who was called Amitabha, " The Boundless Light " (Öpa-me in Tibetan), but who was still so far removed from mankind that he was provided with an archangel in the form of Avalokita, the Saviour, or the God of Mercy. This more popular form of Buddhism flourished in India during the early centuries of our era and was, as has already been recorded, introduced to Tibet by the wives of Song-tsen Gampo; but it will be seen that present-day Lamaism has in many ways reverted to the earlier form, in which half the population lived parasitically on the working laymen, who had little hope of salvation. An alphabet of Sanskritic characters was brought from Kashmir so that the Scriptures could be translated and written down, and these have survived in Tibet while their originals in India were totally destroyed by the iconoclastic Mohammedan invaders in the twelfth century. Monasteries were erected and the country ceased to be a land merely of nomadic herdsmen, for now the ancient civilizations of China, India and Nepal were introduced by Buddhist missionaries and the returning soldiers of Song-tsen Gampo. This King also built himself a palace on the hill where the Potala now stands.

One of Song-tsen's successors possessed communistic tendencies; he ordained that every Tibetan should have an equal share of the country's wealth. But it was found that the poor, finding themselves suddenly rich, became indolent and soon lost all they had. Three times he ordered the equal distribution of wealth, but at this stage, we are told, the King was poisoned by his mother. The priests astutely ascribed the failure of the scheme to the doctrine of the transmigration of souls, by which men do not start equal in this life but bring with them a heritage of good or bad from previous existences.

The Buddhist faith gradually extended during the eighth and ninth centuries, and Tibetans went down to study in Nepal and India. It was at this time that Ti-song De-tsen and Ral-pa-chan reigned; these two, together with Song-tsen Gampo, are revered by the Tibetans as " The Three Religious Kings, Men of Power ". That they were men of power is attested by the fact that Tibet was then at the zenith of her military power. Having subjugated Turkistan, Nepal and the western part of China, only the hatred of hot climates and the fear of disease can have saved India from the incursions of these conquering hordes from the north of the Himalayas.

When Ral-pa-chan was only forty-eight years old he was slain by his brother Lang-dar-ma, the head of the anti-Buddhist party, and for nearly a hundred years religion suffered a severe set-back, although the fratricide himself ruled for only three years before he was slain by the Black Hat Dancer. After this the famous line of kings ended, and for some three centuries the country was ruled by petty chiefs whose forts can still be seen dominating the villages over which they held sway.

When Buddhism again asserted itself it was in a changed form known as Lamaism, much influenced by the more mystic teaching of India and Nepal, where the purer faith of Gautama had degenerated to mere sorcery and the practice of black arts.

In the twelfth century the grandson of the great conqueror, Jenghiz Khan, invited the chief monk of Sakya monastery, who was then the most important man in Tibet, to visit his Mongolian court. The Mongol armies of Jenghiz Khan, and later of Kublai Khan, in their victorious progress across high Asia did not molest Tibet; due possibly either to the comparative poverty of the country, or to some racial or religious affinity.

In the thirteenth century Kublai Khan had conquered the Chinese Empire and established a Mongol dynasty. In the year 1270, wishing to receive the blessing of the Pontiff of the greatest Church in Asia, he, like his predecessor, invited the then ruler of Sakya, whom alone in all Asia he admitted as an equal, to visit his court; and his history records that the Emperor, adopting Lamaism as the State religion of the Mongols, gave the temporal sovereignty of Tibet to this hierarch, who thus became the first priest-King of Tibet.

This hierarchy lasted for some seventy-five years until it merged into the second monarchy, which, now that the Tibetans had lost something of their martial ardour, was more or less dependent on China. This dynasty lasted for nearly three hundred years, that is, until 1635. During this latter period came a much-needed religious reformation. Tibetan Buddhism had absorbed too much of the later debased form of Indian Buddhism, which had been further adulterated by the devil-worship already prevalent in the country. The reformer was Tsong-kapa, " The Man from the Land of Onions ", who was born in 1358 in Amdo in north-eastern Tibet. His followers, who became known as the Gelugpa, or Yellow Hats, to distinguish them from the Red Hats of the existing priesthood, were not allowed to marry and were expected to lead a life of devotion and simplicity. It was Tsong-kapa who founded the great monasteries of Ganden and Sera on the outskirts of Lhasa, and his successor founded the Tashi-lhünpo monastery of Shigatse, which was destined to become the residence of the Tashi Lamas.

Tsong-kapa's successor died in 1474, and some years later it was claimed that his spirit had passed into the body of a child; and it was this infant who received the title of Dalai Lama from a Mongolian ruler, a title that was held by each subsequent reincarnation of the head of the Yellow Hat sect.   Thus was solved the difficulty in finding a successor to a celibate ruler; and the system of reincarnation has become so popular that there are now about a thousand incarnate lamas in the Tibetan priesthood.

The fifth reincarnation was Lob-sang Gyatso, a man of peasant origin.   He set himself to subdue the decadent Red Hats, and for this purpose called in the help of the Mongols, who, as a reward for his energy and piety, gave the Dalai Lama the temporal sovereignty of Tibet.   Lob-sang then started to build the Potala Palace on the rocky hill-top where lay the ruins of the earlier edifice of King Song-tsen Gampo.   The Dalai Lama's old tutor was made Grand Lama of Tashi-lhünpo and was considered to be an incarnation of Amitabha, "The Boundless Light".   The Dalai Lama himself was from this time regarded as an incarnation of Avalokita (The God of Mercy).   As Amitabha is on a superior spiritual level to Avalokita, it follows, metaphysically speaking, that the Tashi is senior to the Dalai in spiritual affairs; and many Tibetans, especially those from the Shigatse district, consider this to be so.   But as the Dalai Lama lives at Lhasa, the religious and political capital of the country, he has always tended to take the lead in secular affairs.   The Dalai is the active and the Tashi the passive element of the Godhead.

Soon after the Manchus had forcibly replaced the Ming dynasty, Lob-sang visited Peking, and was received by the Emperor with all the honours of an independent sovereign.   But this desire for recognition by the Emperor was destined in the future to disturb the peaceful isolation of Tibet and to draw her into the vortex of world politics.   For both China and Mongolia recognized their responsibility to the Dalai Lama as the spiritual head of their Church, and from time to time found it necessary to interfere with the conduct of his affairs.   After reorganizing the government of Lhasa, Lob-sang died in 1680.   During the latter part of his reign he followed the custom of leaving secular affairs in charge of his Chief Minister while he devoted himself to religion.   The

Potala, much in its present form, was completed a few years after his death. Until the reign of the last Pontiff he was considered the greatest of the Dalai Lamas, and is known in Lhasa as " The Great Fifth ", while others are referred to merely by their numbers.

The next Dalai Lama was not interested in religious matters and spent his time carousing and love-making. He was also a great poet, and some of his songs are still sung in Tibet. Naturally many of the Tibetans, and more especially the Chinese and Mongols, thought that there must have been some mistake in the selection of this incarnation; and during the dissensions that arose the Dzungarian Mongols swept across Tibet, and the Chinese took the opportunity of increasing their influence at Lhasa. They annexed parts of Eastern Tibet, garrisoned the Tachienlu–Lhasa road, and in 1706 put the young Dalai to death and substituted another whom they declared to be the true incarnation. But the Tibetans, backed by the Mongols, refused to recognize the Chinese candidate. Already they considered the incarnation of the God of Mercy to be beyond the machinations of worldly conquerors. Fearing a Mongol–Tibetan combination against China, the Emperor dispatched an army in 1718 which, though defeated at first, eventually entered Lhasa; and from that time until the Chinese revolution in 1910 the Emperors have endeavoured to station representatives, called Ambans, in the capital. In 1750 the Ambans murdered the Regent. In revenge all the Chinese in Lhasa were put to death by the Tibetans, but this merely resulted in the arrival of another Chinese army to strengthen the power of the unpopular Ambans.

Towards the end of the eighteenth century the warlike Gurkhas had gained the ascendancy over the other minor kingdoms of Nepal. Having attacked Sikkim, they occupied parts of southern Tibet and in 1791 sacked Shigatse, the second largest town, which lies just beside the Tashi Lama's monastery at Tashi-lhünpo. At this a large army of Chinese and Tibetans marched across the high passes and desolate wind-swept plateaus of northern Tibet in the middle of winter, and in one of the most remarkable campaigns in history defeated the Gurkhas several times and followed them down to within a few miles of their capital, Katmandu.

After these victories the Chinese increased the power of the two Ambans, who were given equal rank with the Dalai and Tashi Lamas and were even to take a prominent part in selecting the incarnations of the more important Lamas; moreover, the Dalai Lama could now only approach the Emperor through the Ambans. But there has always been a wide divergence between the edicts of the Emperor at Peking and their enforcement at remote Lhasa, where the independent nomad blood of the Tibetans still resents any interference. From the time of the Chinese ascendancy until the birth of the present Dalai Lama in 1876 the Dalais invariably died young; for the Ambans found it easier to control a Regent who was dependent on their favour than one who was the spiritual head of the whole Buddhist Church and a God-King in Tibet.

In the nineteenth century there was further trouble between the Tibetans and the Nepalese. A tribe from Nepal overran northern Sikkim, which was then a Tibetan dependency, and were only expelled with the aid of Tibetan troops. In 1855 the Gurkhas again invaded Tibet and gained the right to establish a Nepalese Agency at Lhasa, and various other concessions.

So far we have only considered the relations of Tibet with other Asiatic powers. It is now time to see how the Tibetans were forced, in spite of their policy of exclusion, to meet the representatives of European civilizations.

In 1626 a Portuguese Jesuit priest entered Tibet, but did not penetrate far. (Marco Polo, by the way, had crossed the Pamirs but never set foot in Tibet.) In 1661 two Jesuits, an Austrian and a Belgian, left Peiping and passing by the Koko Nor Lake travelled south-west over the Chang Tang until Lhasa was reached. They spent a month there and then went on to Katmandu, the present capital of Nepal. It was one of them who described the fifth Dalai Lama as " Devilish God-the-Father who puts to death such as refuse to adore him ".

When Warren Hastings was Governor of Bengal, and the power of Britain was making itself felt in India, he decided that we could no longer tolerate the Bhutanese raids on the borders of Bengal. During the consequent subjection of Bhutan the Tashi Lama wrote to intercede for the vanquished country, which was at that time under Tibetan suzerainty. So it was in 1774, to follow up friendly relations instigated by the Tashi Lama, that Hastings sent George Bogle, a young writer of the East India Company, to visit Bhutan and then to proceed to Tashi-lhünpo to meet the Tashi Lama. Similarly, in 1783 Samuel Turner went up to Shigatse. In 1811 an eccentric Englishman, George Manning, who was a friend of Charles Lamb, went to Gyantse and, owing to his knowledge of medicine, was allowed to go on to Lhasa. Unfortunately he was a very poor observer, to judge by his inadequate account of the journey; though his much-quoted verdict on Phari: " Dirt, dirt, grease, smoke. Misery, but good mutton ", is worth recording.

After the Gurkha campaign of 1792 the Chinese, thinking that we had assisted the Nepalese, encouraged the Tibetan policy of exclusion. In 1850, having annexed Sikkim, we found ourselves neighbours of Tibet and in control of the trade route between Lhasa and India. But it was found impossible to open up any sort of communication with Lhasa. China was at that time the suzerain of Tibet, and the Chinese Ambans at Lhasa found it in their interests to encourage this policy of exclusion, which was almost fanatically maintained by the Tibetans. Suspicion of the intentions of the Government of India was further increased by the remarkable secret explorations of the Bengali, Sarat Das and others. The adventures of these famous surveying " Pandits " make fascinating reading. Recording distance with the beads of their rosaries, and hiding instruments and records in their prayer-wheels, they were able to visit and map Lhasa, even receiving a blessing from the Dalai Lama, whose omniscience fortunately failed to penetrate their disguises. But this was achieved at the daily peril of their lives. The village headmen were held by the Lhasa government as personally responsible, under penalty of death, that no foreigner should pass their village. This responsibility and threat were passed on by the headman to every villager; and fearful were the tortures meted out to the incarnate lama who, after much importunity, assisted Sarat Das to reach the Holy City of Lhasa in disguise. This was only sixty years ago.

In 1885 Macaulay, a secretary to the Government of Bengal, obtained Chinese permission to conduct a Mission to Lhasa; but when the Tibetan authorities refused to allow it, the project was abandoned. Soon after this the Tibetans, instigated by the State Oracle at Nechung, occupied part of British Sikkim. Protests addressed to the Chinese and Tibetans remained unanswered and peaceful messengers were maltreated, so in 1888 General Graham attacked the fort, expelled the Tibetans and advanced up the

Chumbi Valley.  At last, in 1890, the Sikkim Convention was signed by China and Great Britain, recognizing a British Protectorate over Sikkim, delineating the boundary between Tibet and Sikkim, and stipulating that the question of trade facilities across the Sikkim–Tibet frontier should be discussed at a later date. As a result of the last clause a trade mart was established at Yatung in the Chumbi Valley in 1893.  But the Tibetans, who had not signed these treaties, refused to recognize them and obstructed all attempts to develop the trade mart at Yatung and to mark out the frontier between Sikkim and Tibet.  When, in 1900, we tried to treat direct with the Dalai Lama, letters were returned unopened, for the Lhasa Government feared that the British desired not only to increase their territory at the expense of Tibet but to undermine the influence of the monasteries and generally to counteract their cherished policy of seclusion.

The late Dalai Lama, born in 1876, was two or three years old when he was identified.  A few years later he was brought to Lhasa, where he took up his residence at the Potala.  His four immediate predecessors had all died under mysterious circumstances before they were old enough to exercise any power, so that Tibet had been administered by Regents for a hundred years. As the Dalai Lama grew up the power of China seemed to be waning.  True, the Amban remained at Lhasa, but his power was chiefly nominal; this was especially brought home to the Tibetans when the results of the Sino–Japanese war became known in Lhasa.  At this time the young Dalai Lama had a Russian tutor, one Dorjieff, a Buriat monk from Siberia, and this man persuaded the leading Tibetans that Russia, since her recent advances in Mongolia, was embracing the Buddhist religion more and more, and that it was therefore to powerful Russia that Tibet should turn for help against British intrigues.  Consequently in 1900, and again in 1901, Dorjieff escorted an envoy from the Dalai Lama with letters for the Tsar of Russia.  When they returned they brought to Lhasa a supply of Russian arms and ammunition as well— paradoxically enough—as a magnificent set of Russian Episcopal robes as a personal present for the Dalai Lama.  There were rumours—even reports in the Chinese press—of an agreement between Russia and China, by which China had transferred to Russia all her interests in Tibet.  Although these rumours were officially denied, the British Government was very anxious for the safety of the northern frontier of India from Kashmir through Nepal, Sikkim, Bhutan and Assam to Burma. This was before the Russo-Japanese war and the Anglo-Russian agreement: Russia was still looking eastward to fulfil her troubled destiny. The North-West Frontier had been a continual source of trouble and expense, but hitherto, relying on a Tibet governed under the comparatively peaceful suzerainty of friendly China, we had maintained no garrisons on the malarial north-east frontier of India. Now the integrity of this frontier was threatened.

So it was that in 1903 Lord Curzon, the Viceroy of India, proposed to dispatch a Mission accompanied by an armed escort to deal directly with the Dalai Lama at Lhasa, and to discuss the commercial and diplomatic relations of Britain and Tibet. Assurances were at the last moment received from Russia that they had no designs upon Tibet, but that if we increased our influence in Tibet, Russia might find it necessary to advance elsewhere (in, as it proved, Mongolia). However, as our relations with Tibet, especially in regard to trade, were most unsatisfactory, Lord Curzon persuaded the Home Government to send Colonel Younghusband with an armed escort as far as Kampa Dzong, a few miles north of the Sikkim–Tibet frontier. The Mission went up to Kampa Dzong in 1903 and stayed there for five months, but the Tibetans refused to have anything to do with it and vigorously urged its immediate return to India. The Chinese disclaimed any coercive power over the Tibetans, and what had started as a peaceful Mission was forced to become a military expedition.

Younghusband, joined by reinforcements, marched up the Chumbi Valley, occupied Phari Dzong, and advanced towards Gyantse, halting at Tuna, beside Dochen Lake, until March 1904. In spite of considerable opposition from the Tibetan soldiers the expedition captured Gyantse Dzong and, crossing the Karo La, a pass over 16,000 feet high, fought its way to Lhasa. The Tibetan authorities, while continually urging the return of the Mission, for a long time refused to consider coming to terms. Although the Tibetan soldiers had no sort of modern equipment they showed great courage, partly because this was their first experience of modern warfare, nor had they any conception of the strength of their foe. The lamas, who were really behind their stubborn resistance, had given them charms which would, they assured them, afford protection from the British bullets. So the Tibetan

soldiers, armed with antiquated muzzle-loading guns and broad-
swords, advanced with complete nonchalance against our service
rifles and machine-guns. There were of course many casualties;
but the lamas decided they had only given them spells for copper
bullets, and as the British ammunition was of some other metal
the magic had not worked!

The Dalai Lama, advised by Dorjieff, fled to Mongolia and
eventually reached Urga, 1500 miles, as the crow flies, to the
north-east of Lhasa. Later he returned southward to Sining and
at last reached Peiping, where he stayed until the end of 1908.
The Chinese issued a proclamation deposing the Dalai Lama, but
this was completely disregarded by the Tibetans, who have always
ignored any Chinese interference with the power of the Dalai
Lama. They continued to refer all important matters to him.
Meanwhile, on the twenty-seventh day of the seventh month of
the Wood Dragon year (7th September 1904), a treaty was signed
in the Potala Palace at Lhasa between the representatives of Britain
and those of the Dalai Lama's Government, the Chinese Amban
and the Nepalese and Bhutanese representatives. Apart from the
payment of an indemnity by Tibet and the British occupation of
the Chumbi Valley until this was paid, the treaty was concerned
with strengthening trade relations and guaranteeing the maintenance and safety of the trade route between Tibet and Sikkim.
With this object a trade mart was to be established at Gyantse,
half-way between Sikkim and Lhasa, in addition to the existing
mart at Yatung.

From this time onwards the relations between the British and
the Tibetans entirely changed. Before the 1904 expedition they
had regarded us with extreme suspicion: from then on they came
to realize that we had no desire to subvert their religion or to
occupy any part of their territory. We wanted a strong independent Tibet, possibly under the suzerainty of China, but free from
the interference of other countries. The Tibetans were also
favourably surprised that having captured the Holy City—which
they had considered impregnable—we should almost immediately
have retired. The behaviour of our troops and our treatment of
the wounded also created a very good impression. The Tibetan
administration was not interfered with and the monasteries and
other holy places were not desecrated or looted. When grain
and other supplies were bought, a liberal price was paid.

KAMPA DANCERS

A TINY INCARNATION LAMA IN THE REGENT'S PROCESSION

DANCE BY SOLDIERS WEARING ANCIENT ARMOUR

In 1906 the 1904 convention was ratified by the Emperor of China with modifications which gave the Chinese a practically free hand in Tibet while we guaranteed not to annex any territory or to interfere in the internal administration of the country. In the following year an agreement was signed by Great Britain and Russia imposing a policy of non-interference in Tibet and binding both Powers to negotiate through China in Tibetan affairs. The Tibetan Government, however, were not consulted in either of these matters.

Apart from fostering trade between India and Tibet, the object of Great Britain in the 1904 Mission and the subsequent agreements had been to assure the territorial integrity of Tibet and to safe-guard the northern frontier of India by maintaining her existence as a peaceful autonomous State; but the chief result, paradoxically enough, was to put Tibet more and more under Chinese domina-tion, and to give her cause for complaint in that we had once again concluded a treaty with China concerning her without consulting the Lhasa Government. The 1907 agreement between Great Britain and Russia further weakened our position in Tibet by binding both Powers to negotiate in Tibetan affairs through China alone.

China immediately set about reasserting her power in Tibet, wherein she was helped by this treaty and by the apparent lack of interest in Tibetan affairs shown by the British Government of the day. While the Dalai Lama was still absent a Chinese Amban came to Lhasa. The Tibetan indemnity to Britain was paid off by China, and we accordingly evacuated the Chumbi Valley. The Tibetans were persuaded that it was only fear of China that had induced the British to withdraw so soon from Lhasa and to leave no representative there. Trouble broke out once more on the eastern marches of Tibet, in those turbulent semi-independent States inhabited by people of Tibetan blood but under more direct control of the Manchu Emperors than the rest of Tibet.

In 1727, as a result of the Chinese having entered Lhasa, the boundary between China and Tibet was laid down as between the head-waters of the Mekong and Yangtse rivers, and marked by a pillar, a little to the south-west of Batang. Land to the west of this pillar was administered from Lhasa, while the Tibetan chiefs of the tribes to the east came more directly under China. This historical Sino-Tibetan boundary was used until 1910. The

K

States Der-ge, Nyarong, Batang, Litang and the five Hor States—
to name the more important districts—are known collectively in
Lhasa as Kham, an indefinite term suitable to the Tibetan Government, who are disconcertingly vague over such details as treaties
and boundaries.

In 1860 the aggressive Tibetans of Nyarong invaded and conquered several of the neighbouring States who were also under
the nominal protection of China.   But when they appealed for
assistance against the warlike chief of Nyarong the Chinese Government were unable to help them, but the Dalai Lama sent a Tibetan
army into Kham and the power of Nyarong was broken.   This
State, although to the east of the 1727 boundary, was henceforward
administered by the Lhasa Government with the full acquiescence
of China.

After the 1904 expedition to Lhasa the Chinese started to
impose their domination over Tibet, not only diplomatically in
Lhasa but forcibly in Kham.   Chinese troops entered by Tachienlu
on the Szechuan frontier and attempted to interfere with the
powers of reigning chiefs and lamas.   As a result of this the
nomads and lamas of Batang rose and drove out or slew the
isolated Chinese garrison.

In 1905 General Chao Erh-feng was put in charge of punitive
measures.   His policy was to reduce Tibet to the status of a
Chinese province, with the Dalai Lama as a merely spiritual
figure-head.   Great monasteries were besieged and razed to the
ground, monks were killed and local chiefs beheaded.   Chao
Erh-feng's relentless and harsh measures led to a renewed and
fiercer revolt.   But the Tibetans lacked organization and modern
methods, and were, especially in Der-ge, torn by internal dissensions.   Kham was gradually overpowered.   By the end of 1909
Batang, Der-ge and Cham-do were occupied by Chinese troops
and the road to Lhasa lay open.

In spite of Tibetan protests, the Chinese continued to advance.
Resistance to them was sporadic.   The Lhasa Government,
realizing the power of China, wished to avoid direct conflict.
They were also beguiled by the diplomatic persuasiveness of the
Amban at Lhasa, who assured the Tibetans that no more than 1000
Chinese troops would come, and that their real object was to
police the frontiers and roads.   So, in February 1910, for the third
time in history, a Chinese army marched into the Holy City of

Tibet. It is interesting to note that on each of these three occasions China was stimulated by the inroads of other Powers—the Mongols in 1720, the Nepalese in 1790, and the British in 1910.

Let us return now to follow the fortunes of the unfortunate Pontiff of the Buddhist Church. In the summer of 1904, as the British expedition entered Lhasa, the Dalai Lama fled northwards from the Potala Palace. After a long journey he at last reached Urga, the capital of outer Mongolia, nearly 1500 miles north-east of Lhasa, a city regarded by the Buddhists of High Asia as a Holy City second only to Lhasa. After a year at Urga, and two more at a great monastery near Sining, he at last reached Peiping in 1908, having been invited to an audience with the Emperor. But whereas the Great Fifth Dalai Lama had visited the Chinese Emperor as an equal, now great care was taken to stress his position as a vassal of the Manchu throne. In addition to his title of Great Good Self-Existent Buddha of Heaven, an additional title of honour—Loyal and Submissive Vice-Regent—was conferred upon him as well as an annual allowance. Leaving Peiping in December 1908 and travelling by way of Kansu, Sining and Jyekundo, he reached Lhasa in December 1909, after an absence of five years.

Two months later 2000 Chinese troops appeared at Lhasa. The Dalai Lama had once more to flee from the Potala Palace. The efforts of the British Trade Agents at Gyantse and Yatung to promote friendship between Tibet and Britain had not been in vain. During his long exile the Dalai Lama had had much time to think. He did not forget the manner of his reception at Peiping. Now he fled for his personal safety, and this time it was to British India that he fled.

The advance-guard of the Chinese army had had special orders to capture him, but they were just too late. In the middle of the night the Dalai Lama, accompanied by six ministers and a small escort, fled southward across the Tsang-po to the Chumbi Valley. The escort were left at Chaksam to deal with the pursuing Chinese soldiers. In the ensuing fight—according to the Dalai Lama's own letter—two Tibetans and seventy Chinese were killed. At Yatung the Chinese soldiers were only a short distance behind His Holiness.

Nine days after leaving Lhasa the exiles crossed the border into Sikkim, having ridden almost 300 miles and having crossed passes of 15,000 and 16,000 feet—a phenomenal achievement for men of advanced age who normally took little exercise. The party proceeded to Darjeeling, where they were given sanctuary and hospitably entertained for nearly two years. During this time the Dalai Lama and his Ministers went down to Calcutta at the invitation of the Viceroy, Lord Minto. This further augmented the feelings of friendliness between Britain and Tibet.

Sir Charles Bell, with his great knowledge of the Tibetan language and affairs, arranged for the accommodation and entertainment of the Dalai during his exile in British India. His was the unpleasant task of telling the Dalai that the British Government would not intervene between China and Tibet, and that they could only recognize the government set up in Tibet by the Chinese. To such an extent were our hands tied by treaties that we could do nothing to interfere since the Chinese had guaranteed not to alter the administration of Tibet, or to convert it to the status of a Chinese province. It seemed that as long as China kept her hands off Nepal, Bhutan and Sikkim, we were prepared to abandon Tibet to the Chinese. His Holiness, realizing that the recent Chinese aggressions had been brought on—however unwittingly—by the British Mission to Lhasa and its subsequent retreat, was speechless with distress. He and his Ministers even denied any sovereign rights of China over Tibet; and they repudiated the 1906 Convention, which, indeed, they had never even been invited to sign. It seemed that Tibet had no friend to whom she could turn. It was at this juncture, in 1911, that the revolution against the Manchu Dynasty broke out in China.

Once again the tables were turned. General Chao Erh-feng, a great man in spite of his ruthlessness, who had become Viceroy of Szechuan, was treacherously beheaded by the revolutionaries, and the Chinese lost control of most of the frontier districts.

In June 1912 the Dalai Lama and his Ministers returned to the Holy City and Tibet became once more an autonomous State.

In eastern countries which have had spiritual rulers the power has usually been in the hands of a chief minister, while the religious head lived a life of contemplation and seclusion. But the late Dalai Lama, being a man of exceptional character and ability, set himself to follow the example of the " Great Fifth " and to rule the country himself. Not only did he control the organization of the monasteries and the religious life of the people, but he took under his personal supervision more and more of the details of secular government. Perhaps it was these centralizing tendencies of the Dalai that, more than anything else, aroused the alarm of the Tashi, and led to the long and unfortunate quarrel between these two mysterious figures.

In 1904, after the Younghusband Mission had returned from Lhasa, Captain (now Sir Frederick) O'Connor, who had been the chief interpreter to the Mission, was left at Gyantse as the first British Trade Agent in Tibet. One of his first duties was to visit Shigatse, the second town of Tibet, to make the acquaintance of the Tashi Lama, who lives half a mile away in his walled monastery at Tashi-lhünpo which houses 4000 monks. As O'Connor was the first European ever to visit him, he was somewhat surprised when His Serenity said what a pleasure it was for him to renew his previous friendship with British officers. O'Connor suddenly realized that he was referring to the reception afforded more than a hundred and thirty years previously to the two officers sent up by Warren Hastings. The Tashi Lama was identifying himself with one of his previous incarnations.

Captain O'Connor found that the Tashi was then a young man of twenty-two years of age, very friendly, straightforward and intelligent, but at the same time very spiritually minded and strangely aloof from worldly matters, living a cloistered life given up to prayer and meditation. He was much interested in what O'Connor could tell him about the outside world and accepted the invitation of the Government of India to come and meet their Royal Highnesses the Prince and Princess of Wales (later King George V and Queen Mary) on their forthcoming tour of India.

In 1905 His Serenity, with a suite of some 300 monks and laymen, set off with Captain O'Connor for India. As His Serenity was carried in his palanquin the Tibetans came from afar to line the route in the hope of touching his palanquin and receiving a blessing. It is recorded that these villagers, who are not easily moved to tears, were so overcome that they wept with emotion. Although the Tashi Lama had never before spoken to any woman except his mother, he conversed for some time with their Royal Highnesses and impressed everybody by his quiet spiritual voice and charming natural manners; at the same time he met Lord Kitchener, Lord Minto, the Viceroy of India, and other important figures. He also witnessed a review of 60,000 troops at Rawal Pindi. Before returning to Tibet he made a pilgrimage to the holy places of Buddhism, and held a service beneath the famous tree at Boddh Gaya, where his great predecessor, Gautama Buddha, of whom he is believed to be the earthly personification, obtained enlightenment some 2400 years before.

In 1906 Sir Charles Bell was invited to visit His Serenity at Tashi-lhünpo and found him extremely friendly and much interested in the political situation. He feared that the Chinese, who were regaining their hold over Tibet, might have been annoyed by his visit to India. He also feared the Lhasa Government, who suspected that he was trying to secure the aid of Britain to help him to set up independent rule at Tashi-lhünpo. For the Tashi Lama has temporal power over three small districts, though not over Shigatse itself, which is administered by a dzongpön appointed from Lhasa.

It is unfortunate that there is considerable jealousy between Lhasa and Tashi-lhünpo. When the Chinese troops were in control of Lhasa the Tashi Lama's Ministers, several of whom were openly pro-Chinese, had secret relations with them, and refused to take up arms against China until compelled to do so. When the Dalai had been deposed by the Chinese in 1910 the Tashi had been invited to take his place. Though he had wisely refused to do this, he actually went to Lhasa and is said to have sat on the Dalai's throne. In 1912, when the Dalai returned from his exile at Darjeeling, it was arranged that the two Lamas should meet and discuss their differences at Ralung, but nothing came of this.

In 1912 the new republican government dispatched an army from Szechuan to Tibet to restore the Chinese position there; and Yuan Shih Kai issued a Presidential Order that Tibet was to be regarded as on an equal footing with the provinces of China proper.

In 1913 Russia concluded an agreement with China whereby the former recognized China's suzerainty over Mongolia, but Russia was allowed privileges which would give her a large measure of economical and political control over the country. Tibet has always been on very friendly terms with Mongolia, and now that that State was controlled by Russia it became all the more necessary for us to insist upon a strong and autonomous Tibet. Dorjieff had become active again and, using the authority of a letter given to him years before by the Dalai Lama, he engineered a " treaty " between Tibet and Mongolia. The

Kalön Lama was sent to Kham to drive back the Chinese, and from now on the border skirmishes developed into a frontier war between China and Tibet. The power of Lhasa at this time extended east to the Mekong, and north to the southern watershed of the Yangtse.

In order to settle these various differences a conference was arranged in 1913 at Simla between representatives of Great Britain, China and Tibet. The Dalai Lama wanted for Tibet complete control of internal and external affairs; to consult with the British only on more important external relations; to have no Chinese representatives or soldiers in Tibet, and for Nyarong Der-ge, Batang, Litang and the country up to Tachienlu—that is, all the regions inhabited by persons of Tibetan race—to be included in Tibet. The National Assembly, and later the Dalai Lama, also desired a British representative at Lhasa. The Chinese entered the conference with the hope of recovering the position they had held in Tibet at the conclusion of Chao Erh-feng's conquests. The object of Great Britain was to restore Tibet to the position of an autonomous State under Chinese suzerainty; to establish at Lhasa a stable and friendly Tibetan government free from all outside interference, and to restore peace between China and Tibet.

The Simla Convention was initialled in April 1914 by the three parties. Chinese suzerainty over Tibet was recognized, on condition that China did not convert Tibet into a Chinese province. A Chinese Amban with a suitable escort was to be re-established at Lhasa, and the British Agent at Gyantse was authorized to visit the city if necessary. The British Government promised the Tibetans diplomatic support, and reasonable help in securing munitions. But as regards the boundary question the Chinese and Tibetan points of view were so divergent as to make agreement seem impossible. Both sides ignored the 1727 Manchu boundary and, while the Tibetans claimed all the States up to Tachienlu, the Chinese wanted to push the boundary to within a few marches of Lhasa. Eventually Tibet was divided into two zones, " Outer Tibet " (as visualized from China) and " Inner Tibet ". The automony of Outer Tibet, which included Lhasa, Shigatse and Chamdo, was recognized. Inner Tibet, including Batang, Litang, Tachienlu and a large portion of Eastern Tibet, was to remain under the nominal control of Lhasa but the Chinese were to be allowed to send troops and officials there and to plant colonies.

China objected to the frontier which had been established between herself and Tibet, but otherwise agreed to accept the Convention in all respects. At this stage the Great War broke out, and there was an armed truce pending the resumption of mediation by Great Britain. During this truce the Tibetans had time to increase and modernize their army, but the worn out Chinese forces, owing to internal dissensions, were neglected and left to live off the country, so that they deteriorated into brigands and military adventurers.

A Chinese General broke the truce and made a sudden attack while the Tibetans were celebrating one of their many religious festivities. The Tibetans, however, soon rallied and drove the Chinese practically back to Tachienlu and thus recovered the greater part of Eastern Tibet. At this stage the British Consular Agent at Tachienlu was called in to mediate and the truce was re-established in 1918, with a provisional boundary through Batang, and one therefore much more favourable to the Tibetans.

A year later, in 1919, the Chinese proposed to resume the frontier negotiations, but for various reasons nothing was done. The Tibetans were by then running out of munitions, being now prohibited, in spite of our promise to help them in this respect, from importing them through India; and, feeling that we had not given them adequate support, they were forced to agree to receive a Chinese Mission in Lhasa. In 1920 this Mission reached Lhasa and remained for five months treating directly with the Tibetans in the presence of no British intermediary or witness. However, no definite agreement was made. During the same year, 1920, Sir Charles Bell, who had maintained his friendly relations with the Dalai Lama and who had frequently been invited by him to visit Lhasa, was at last allowed to conduct a Mission to Lhasa to endeavour to clarify the political situation.

Although the Tibetans had repeatedly proved to the world that they were competent to maintain order and peace in their own country, Tibet could not stand alone unless she was left alone. It became increasingly clear that, surrounded by Russia, China and India, and carefully watched by Japan, Tibet must rely on a stronger Power. If we could not guarantee her peace she must arm herself, and if we could not supply her with munitions she must turn elsewhere. The Tibetan reception of Sir Charles Bell's Mission was her final effort to secure our assistance.

Sir Charles Bell, accompanied only by Lieutenant-Colonel Kennedy of the I.M.S., spent eleven months at Lhasa. As both had long experience of dealing with the Tibetans, and spoke the language fluently, they were able to establish far more personal and friendly contacts than had been possible hitherto. The Dalai Lama showed his more than friendly intentions by receiving Sir Charles, at the very first interview, informally, sitting with him at a small table in his private apartment, with no witness present. This was regarded by the people of Lhasa as a special honour, as it was the custom for His Holiness to receive even the highest Tibetan officials while seated on his dais. His attitude was always most cordial: often he asked advice about the Tibetan army, some problem of education, finance or even on matters of justice. It was through a personal request from Sir Charles that the Dalai gave permission for the first attempt to climb Mount Everest, though Nepal had already refused to allow the expedition to reach the mountain from the Nepalese side. When it was probable that the Government of India would recall the Mission after it had been in Lhasa only a few months, the Dalai Lama, the Prime Minister and the Shap-pes begged, with the utmost urgency, that Sir Charles should remain longer; and when he eventually took the road to India the Dalai Lama's last words were: " We have known each other for a long time, and I have complete confidence in you, for we two are men of like mind. I pray continually that you may return to Lhasa." A month or two later His Holiness wrote to the Viceroy of India: "All the people of Tibet and myself have become of one mind, and the British and Tibetans have become one family ".

## CHAPTER EIGHT

### LHASA CITY

BEFORE visiting Tibet I had read of the horrors of winter travel, of the unmitigated grimness of the scenery, of the filth and benightedness of the inhabitants, and the squalor of their dwellings. After spending seven months in Tibet I had to amend my preconceived conclusions. True, in winter the high plateaux are swept by relentless dust-storms, and the thermometer falls below zero; but if one starts before dawn, has the good sense to follow the Tibetan way of dressing, and reaches one's destination before midday, when the storms usually start, even winter travel can be enjoyable. The country is bleak and forbidding at first sight; the hills as bare as the rocks of Aden, the valleys frequently sand or stone deserts—but what depth of colouring, what marvellous contrasts! The silver-gold barley rippling in the wind, the tremulous willow-groves, the dun and olive hills swept by deep violet shadows as the heavy cumulus clouds sail across the pale turquoise sky. And, for those who have eyes to see, the hills, bare at a casual glance, are bright with gentians, primulas and delphiniums, and teeming with innumerable species of rare and brightly coloured birds.

It is true that the common people do not wash, that their houses are, by our standards, filthy, and that they live in a state of serfdom—but what delightful folk, nevertheless! What finer men are there in the world than the nomads of the Chang Tang?

So far, I disagree with many of the earlier writers; but when it comes to describing Lhasa itself I am bound to say that they are right. Manning, the first Englishman to visit the Holy City, wrote of it in 1811: "There is nothing striking, nothing pleasing in its appearance. The habitations are begrimed with dirt and smut. The avenues are full of dogs, some growling and gnawing bits of hide which lie about in profusion and emit a charnel-house smell; others limping and looking livid; others ulcerated; others starved and dying, and pecked at by ravens; some dead and preyed upon. In short, everything seems mean and gloomy, and excites the idea of something unreal. Even the mirth and laughter of the inhabitants I thought dreamy and ghostly."

Though I disagree with his impression of the cheerlessness of the people, Manning is right; and Lhasa, the most conservative city in the world, is the same today.

For instance, suppose one were to follow the progress of a religious devotee who, having followed the weary track from India, enters the city and rides to the heart of it to visit the great Jo-kang, the Mecca of Lamaism, the holiest building in all Tibet. As the pilgrim approaches Lhasa along the main trade route from India, the city is completely hidden by the two rocky excrescence on whose summits are the Potala and the Medical College. With what excitement does he first see the sun glittering on the golden roof-pavilions of the Potala wherein are enshrined the mortal remains of former Dalai Lamas. On either side of the road are *lingkas*, park-like enclosures, which are one of the most attractive features of Lhasa. These belong to the Government and are controlled by special officials. Graceful white poplars and willows are grown in these lingkas, the latter being pollarded every three or four years to provide wood for building purposes. The road now enters the western gateway (Pargo Kaling), built in the cleft where the ridge connecting these two rocks drops to the level of the plain. This gate is in the form of a magnificent chorten through which an archway has been pierced. There are subsidiary chortens built on the rocks at some distance on either side; and strings of bells tinkling in the breeze, which connect the three summits.

Beside the gateway are always swarms of beggars sitting against the wall and, with obtruded tongues and upraised thumbs, whining for alms. Many of the beggars are strong and healthy and could easily work for their living, but in Lhasa begging is a privileged profession, and a beggar would consider it far beneath his dignity to accept any kind of work. Others are aged and loathsome, blind, crippled and diseased. They just sit there all day, nodding in the sun, only waking up to start their thin whining as somebody rides by. Lhasa is full of such medicants: any child will come and ask for money; any monk will surreptitiously hold out his hand. Beyond the chorten, on the eastern wall of the Iron Hill, are some attractive little houses precariously built into the vertical wall. They seem to be fairly clean, and all manner of flowers are growing there—nasturtiums, stocks, petunias and phlox predominating.

Just inside the gate is a wooden sentry-box where a " policeman " sits sewing a yak-hair boot-sole or telling his beads. As we splash through the flood-water he takes no notice, then rather shamefacedly remembers that he is on duty and gets up to salute. He wears a tattered and ancient khaki coat, a battered topee and ragged trousers and boots. His face is extremely dirty.

Floods cover the waste ground beside the road, in some places flowing right across it; the water is dark and slimy and stinks to heaven. The Tibetans have no idea of sanitation; you see them, men and women, just squatting down in the street like dogs. Were it not for the cold climate they would surely be afflicted by every variety of epidemic. On the other side of the road, between it and a pleasant-looking park, are great piles of offal eight and ten feet high. The women of Sho, the hamlet across the road, empty every sort of garbage on to this heap. Amongst the filth, some of which is indescribable, are two semi-decomposed dead dogs which are being torn at by others of their species and by three ravens, which are remarkably tame.

These dogs are one of the most disgusting and pathetic sights of the city. They seem to have no owners; nobody cares for them except for a few devout old women, who throw them scraps as an act of piety. In a Buddhist country it is not permitted to take life, so when an unwanted litter of puppies is born they are just turned out to fend for themselves. Domesticity, while providing no food for them, has yet robbed them of the power to hunt. These dogs are of no recognizable breed; in one you see a resemblance to a fox-terrier, in another to an Eskimo husky, but most of them are like nondescript sheep-dogs with prick ears and medium coats. Some of them, usually those that are regularly fed, dislike the smell of foreigners and bark furiously whenever we pass; but the majority have not that much strength, and lie motionless, perhaps in the middle of the road. There was one wretched animal that we saw day after day, with one eye, or rather the place where the eye should have been, swollen up to many times its normal size, completely raw and discharging.

In front of the hamlet of Sho there are several stalls, kept by women whose faces have been daubed with black pigment to protect them from the sun and wind. Most of them have black patches of plaster, the size of a halfpenny, stuck on to their temples to cure headache. They wear dusty homespun robes and greasy striped aprons. Their tousled hair looks as if it has not been washed or combed for months. On the right wrist a bracelet made from a white conch-shell is worn. One or two wear the triangular Lhasa head-dress; but there is no false hair hanging from it, and it merely looks like a distorted halo. These women are selling meat, yak-meat judging by the size of the joints; and there, towering behind them, is the Potala, the palace of the Vice-Regent of Buddha, the very essence of whose teaching is that life should not be taken.

Some children are flying kites; this was a favourite craze during the late autumn. Others, most of them women, are playing another street game which requires considerable skill: a shuttle-cock is made by sticking a few feathers into a piece of wood and this is kept in the air by kicking it with the side or back of the foot. The girl usually removes her boot to play this game; hopping on one foot and holding her skirts out of the way, she kicks the shuttlecock either in front of her or behind her back. Some of them could in this way keep it in the air for five or ten minutes on end.

Just beyond Sho there are two small pagodas on the left of the road; these shelter stone inscriptions recording Chinese victories. On the other side of the road is a four-sided stone edict pillar erected by the Chinese with inscriptions in Tibetan, Chinese and Manchu. Raised on several stone steps, it is about twenty feet high. The inscription refers to the Tibetan conquests in China during the eighth century A.D. It can be seen that in some places words have been obliterated, and the Tibetans state that the Chinese, having obtained permission to make a copy of the inscription, effaced the names of the places in China which Tibet had conquered. Near the monolith is a well where the women stop to gossip as they bring earthenware or wooden vessels for water. There is, at any rate, one point in favour of these towns-women—unwashed though they may be—they are always laughing.

Soon after this the road divides: the left-hand fork, completely under water, leads past park-lands and monasteries to the northern part of the city. In this fork, beyond a small flooded park, is the mansion of the Yuto family, represented at present by the spruce young general who came to call on us. As the original house was burnt down some years ago the present mansion is very fine and up to date. It is a solid-looking square four-storied house with a courtyard and outbuildings on the southern side. The windows are of the casement type, and fitted with small panes of glass—a convenient size this, when glass has to be brought from India on the backs of yaks and mules. On the summit of the roof is a cylindrical banner draped with successive layers of the lucky colours.

The right-hand fork, just before it meets a chorten, turns to the right and crosses a stream by the famous Yuto Sampa, usually known as the Turquoise Bridge, as it is roofed in the Chinese manner with tiles of a greenish (but not turquoise) colour, and has golden dragon-heads at the corners, and conical ornaments along the sides. At each end of the bridge there are always beggars to be found; usually the same ones sit there day after day —a blind man with a thick black beard and a small yellow dog, a wrinkled white-haired old woman, and two youngish men revolving prayer-wheels. After turning to the left the road runs through a plain Chinese gateway leading to a large open space. To the north (left), across some unpleasant-smelling flooded land and heaps of offal, are the ruins of Tengyeling monastery, which was destroyed after it had sided with the Chinese in 1912. In part of the remains of the building is the Post Office, run by an intelligent English-speaking monk who was trained at Kalimpong.

Having passed this gate we are really in the city. To the south is a ruined gateway and part of the old city wall. Along the eastern side of this square in former times was the residence of the Chinese Amban, with its considerable barracks, theatre, restaurant and gardens. The place is completely ruined, but two Chinese lions of granite still stand in front of the ruined wall, eloquent of their vanished power.

The city itself is surprisingly small, a compact square of buildings only two or three miles in circumference. The houses are all flat-roofed and two or three stories high. They are whitewashed for the most part, and have the usual Tibetan window narrowing at the top and shaded by wide carved lintels usually valanced with cloth of striped or diamond pattern. The windows are surrounded by a dull black plaster border. Little glass is seen, usually a piece of canvas is stretched across the frame. The window-sills and balconies are gay with flowers, and often with singing birds in cages. At each corner of the roofs are square towers holding bundles of sticks with prayer-flags attached. The beams along the eaves below the parapets, and over the windows and doors are often carved with an intricate chequered pattern and picked out in bright colours with red predominating.

The centre of the town, both in position and importance, is the Jo-kang, the most holy place of pilgrimage in all Tibet, the real Lhasa, the Place of God. This is usually referred to by Europeans as " The Cathedral ". Unfortunately it is so surrounded by other buildings that it is impossible to obtain a comprehensive view of the outside, which is little higher than its neighbours, though its golden roof-pavilions rise above the drab sea of surrounding roofs, like the snow-capped peaks of a distant mountain-range. The Jo-kang was built in A.D. 652 to enshrine the images brought by the two Buddhist wives of the great King Song-tsen Gampo. Since that time the original shrine has been added to considerably, until some three centuries ago it attained its present dimensions.

Just outside the main gate, at the junction of two squalid streets, are two ancient weeping-willows which, having been struck by lightning in 1924, are now much reduced in size. They are supposed to have sprung miraculously from the hair of the Buddha. The Tibetans considered the breaking of the branches a most inauspicious event, and the Government ordered special prayers to be said in all monasteries to avert the suspected evil.

Beneath the shade of the willows' branches is a somewhat mutilated tablet, put up at the end of the eighteenth century by the Chinese, giving instructions how to combat the dread scourge of smallpox, which in the past has frequently decimated the population. As recently as 1925 some 7000 died from this plague in Lhasa alone. Near by is another stone monolith bearing record of a treaty between Tibet and China. The main gate is set back between two blocks of Government offices. The first thing that strikes one is the crowd of beggars in front of the doors, for nowhere else does the gift of a coin reflect so meritoriously upon the donor. There must have been nearly a hundred of them, some diseased and decrepit, exciting unutterable pity, others able-bodied and clamorous, needing nothing so much as a good whipping. As we approached they set up a piteous wailing, bowing up and down, sticking out their tongues, and stabbing the air with up-turned thumbs.

Several immense fluted pillars of wood support an overhanging roof. In this stone-flagged portico a number of pious beggars and pilgrims are continually prostrating themselves, muttering prayers all the time. They stand facing the Temple, go down on their hands, which are protected by wooden " shoes " studded with nails, lie flat on their faces with their hands stretched out in front of them, draw in their arms, stand up once more and bring their hands together in readiness for another obeisance. Sometimes several thousand prostrations are made in a single day, either to wipe out some personal crime, or, in return for a fee, to earn by proxy good reward in Paradise for some more wealthy worshipper. They were so absorbed in this muscular devotion that they hardly noticed our approach. Above the pillars is a deep maroon-coloured band such as is found along the top of the roof of nearly every Tibetan monastery or important house. It is made by laying willow twigs horizontally and then cutting them vertically to form such a surface as is found in a half-used haystack. These osiers are stamped down with mortar which has been mixed with a reddish dye. The resulting matt surface, in the Cathedral as in other buildings, forms an ideal background for the golden mono-grams and emblems which are usually placed there. The flat roof is higher at the sides, and from the lower central portion hangs a very ragged brown yak-hair curtain. On the walls of the portico are vast paintings of the four Celestial Kings of the Quarters. Their faces are of different colours and one holds a stringed instrument. Two massive wooden doors with engraved bosses and hinges lead to an outer courtyard which is open to the sky and surrounded by a dim cloister. The stone flags are rutted to a depth of six or seven inches in some places, not only by the feet of pilgrims but by the activities of the " prostraters " which are being carried on within as well as without the gates. The whole courtyard is extremely dark and dirty; huge frescoes can just be distinguished on the walls. On one side is a prayer-barrel eight feet in height, which, turned by an impassive-faced old woman, rings a bell at each revolution. This outer court leads to the main temple, which is also open to the sky and of great size. In the central part of the court many flowers, lit by slanting rays of sunshine, grow in pots: hollyhocks, coreopsis, phloxes, antir-rhinums, asters and even two rose bushes.

The chief shrine is at the far or eastern end of this temple; it is protected from thieves by an iron curtain before which several monks are always stationed. On each side are gilt images of the Coming Buddha, who is always depicted seated with his legs hanging down in the European attitude. One of these figures is of colossal size. The central image is a life-sized figure of Gautama Buddha, which Landon considers to be " beyond question the most famous idol in the world ". It is supposed to have been brought from Peiping by the Chinese wife of the builder of the temple. The features of the Buddha are gross and unpleasing,

A LHASA STREET WITH CEREMONIAL FIRE PREPARED

AN OFFICIAL'S LHASA HOUSE

THE REGENT'S BAGGAGE PASSING SHINGDONKA

but the figure is thickly encrusted with precious stones, which represent the accumulated offerings of the faithful for more than a thousand years. On the head is a large golden diadem containing enormous uncut gems. Innumerable butter-lamps, many of them of solid gold, light up the shrine, which with its riot of dimly seen gold and fabulous glinting gems gives the impression of some fantastic treasure-house from King Solomon's Mines.

The main hall is surrounded by a cloister from which many smaller shrines open. We followed our guide into one dark evil-smelling chamber after another, each guarded from thieves by hanging curtains of iron chain-work. One small shrine is devoted to the pacification of the Water-Demon of the lake on which Lhasa is supposed originally to have been built. In another are a thousand small images of Buddha in different attitudes. Before one altar is a loose stone, and prayers uttered while standing on this are certain to be answered. Nearly all the images in the temple have been self-created, miraculously transported, or are credited with supernatural properties.

We were then taken to the shrine of Palden Lhamo, the Buddhist equivalent of the Hindu god Kali, the wife of Shiva. It is this goddess that is supposed by the Tibetans to have been incarnated in the person of Queen Victoria. There are two images, showing her in angry and unpleasant mood. In one she appears as a frightful black monster, clad in the skins of human victims and eating the brains of others from a human skull. Surrounding her are emblems of disease and death, hideous masks, and a strange collection of antiquated weapons of war. Her face is so horrible that it is usually covered, but we were allowed to gaze upon her distorted and hideous features. Near by she is depicted in more amiable mood, wearing clothes of rich brocade and adorned with gold and precious stones, necklaces and innumerable charm-boxes.

It was curious that these two shrines were infested with small pale-brown mice, which ran in and out among the egg-cup shaped butter-lamps and over the monks who were on guard. I was anxious to put one in my pocket, in case they were of some rare species, but as they are supposed to be incarnations of former guardians of the shrine, I decided that it would be unwise.

These shrines were dimly lit by the smoky flames from the butter-lamps; and after the continual stooping, the heavy fetid smell of the damp and greasy floors, and the general rancid airlessness, we were glad to go up on to the roof. There is something repellent and sinister about the place, as if at any moment one might come upon priests performing barbaric rites and offering sacrifices of human blood before their sardonic inscrutable idols.

To the south of the Cathedral is the main square, which is used as a market-place. To the north of this square—and therefore built right against the Cathedral—is the Kashag, the meeting-place of the Tibetan Cabinet, from which its name is taken. Here also is the Government Treasury and other official buildings. For some distance in front of the Kashag the ground is set with cobbles, and there is a large incense-burner. It is here that the Dalai Lama, or Regent, preaches a sermon to the people on the occasion of the Tibetan New Year.

Round the Cathedral buildings are the main shopping streets of Lhasa. Some of the shops are in the form of wooden trestle-tables out in the middle of the square; others are simply collections of wares spread out on the cobbles of the street and protected by an umbrella. The larger shops consist of basement rooms opening on to the street, often with tables just outside, displaying a selection of more attractive wares. The better shops are kept by Nepalese and Ladakis; those in the open air are usually Tibetan and are almost invariably in the charge of women. This is customary; the women look after the retail trade and the shops, while the men carry on the larger commercial ventures and the journeys connected therewith. Almost everything you can imagine is sold on these stalls, and a good deal besides. The cloth-shops sell bales of coarse woollen cloth such as is made in most Tibetan households, squares of silk from China, cheap printed material from India. Often all the permanent shops in a certain district will sell the same commodity, and this is true to a certain extent of the movable stalls. The butchers and tanners, who carry on trades connected with the taking of life, are segregated to special streets, usually on the outskirts of the city. In one place are the food-shops. Here you see trays of different sorts of grain, including maize and rice from Bhutan; fresh vegetables—usually peas, potatoes, cabbages, turnips and radishes all grown near by; spices—trays of red chillies, cloves, nutmegs and all kinds of dried roots and leaves; and always the dried bricks of tea from China in varying grades usually pressed into balls about the size of a grapefruit.

One man sells holy-water vessels to place before the house altars, together with rows of shallow brass cups and a few libation jugs for storing and pouring out the sanctified liquid. In one place is a jeweller's stall. Necklaces of amber, coral and agate are there, as well as cheaper imitations; gold filigree charm-boxes with small brocade-clothed Buddhas inside, such as are worn across the back or chest of those undertaking journeys; gold and turquoise charm-boxes for the women, threaded on necklaces of large beads; turquoise ear-rings and uncut pieces of jade and amber. Here, again, is the street of the bootmakers; one man sits at his work surrounded by pairs of the scarlet-and-black cloth Kham-pa boots; another sells the black or brown leather boots from Mongolia which are often ornamented with an appliqué pattern in green leather; and always there is the bright scarlet-and-green women's boot with a thick sole of leather or woven yak-hair. Other stalls sell small china bowls for tea or rice, polished birch or maple tea-cups such as are carried in the flap of almost every Tibetan's coat, assorted cartridges, electric-torches from Japan, candles, damascene stirrups, sticks of incense, mirrors, toys—one could go on indefinitely. And always beside the stall-keeper is the earthenware teapot, the cup, and tsamba bag.

All Tibetans are born traders. The noble families, such as the Surkang and Ra-ka-sha, employ their own traders, who make long journeys to Mongolia and India. The courtyard of the family mansion is often stacked high with bales of wool, bags of borax or salt, and other articles for export. Similarly the great monasteries, as well as private monk officials, indulge in com-mercial ventures. Wool forms by far the most important export of Tibet. Yak-tails (as used in Hindu temples), hides, salt and borax, are also sent down to India, and musk, horn and various medicinal herbs to China. In return come cotton and woollen goods, hardware, glass, sugar, biscuits, dried fruits, tobacco, hoop-iron and a thousand domestic odds and ends. As the total import both in value and bulk falls far short of the export, bullion and coin in the form of rupees are brought back from India. It is common to meet whole trains of pack animals laden with small heavy boxes of silver or coin.

Perhaps the best-known trader in Lhasa is Pangda-Tsang, who lives in a large mansion in the middle of the city. He trades mainly in wool, silk and furs, but anything else from jewellery to horses can be bought through him. He is also the largest transport contractor in Lhasa. I went to his house one day with a friend who wanted to buy some stone-marten skins. Of these he had an enormous stock, as well as skins of snow-leopard, lynx, fox, otter, marmot and many I could not identify. His courtyard was at that time filled with some fifty mules which were ready to set off to Kalimpong with loads of coarse wool, of which he must have had many tons packed all round the yard right up to the surrounding roof.

The Lhasa streets always seem to be crowded, and wherever we went we were watched by innumerable pairs of eyes—but practically always in a friendly way, for the Lhasa crowd is as amiable as could be wished. Only occasionally does a monk gaze at one with sullen malevolence, perhaps realizing that we represent progress, and that progress spells the end of the unquestioned and unquestioning power of Lamaism.

The first thing that struck me, apart from the filth and the beggars, was the extraordinary number of women in Lhasa: some wearing the hooped Gyantse head-dress, some with the triangular Lhasa type, and others with tousled unadorned hair. This is partly due to the monastic system, which draws so large a proportion of the men to a life of theoretical celibacy; and partly to a system of polyandry which in the country districts leaves a surplus of women who naturally gravitate to the town, where they can find employment and contract promiscuous marriages, for the moral level—at any rate judged by our standards—must be as low at Lhasa as in any city of the world. This practice of polyandry is not confined to the lower classes. I once went to photograph the wife and child of a young lay official. He explained to me that the child was not actually his, as his two brothers shared his wife; and that this child was the son of his younger brother—who happened to be a monk official. Another friend of mine, upon being asked who a certain small boy was, replied that one could never really answer such questions; and that in his case, for instance, he had had three fathers and found the problem of relationship very difficult.

But why polyandry should flourish in Tibet of all countries, when so many thousands of men are debarred from marriage, is a problem I could never solve. Tibet is a poor country, and the system probably originated with the idea of keeping the family patrimony intact and undivided. When the Tibetans were still a pastoral people the men were too poor each to support a wife and home, also they would rarely be at home at the same time : one son would till the fields, while another would look after the herds of animals on the pasture-grounds, and the third would join the local monastery.

Among the cosmopolitan Lhasa crowd were always a great number of nomads; these are the finest people, both in looks and character, that we met in Tibet. They are swarthy independent folk with easy swinging gait and the open faces of mountaineers. Many of them, as the weather grew colder, came down from Golok, Amdo, Hor and the Chang Tang—the high wind-bitten plateau that covers all central Tibet. There are many different types, but the Lhasa people just call them Khampas (people from Kham) or Drok-pa (nomads). The men have short tousled hair and do not wear ear-rings. They wear a single rough sheep-skin garment hitched up to the knees, and boots of a design different from those made in Lhasa. They grow no hair on their faces. The women wear a long full robe of sheep-skin with the fur on the inside. Often one arm and shoulder is slipped out of the garment, and it is then clear that nothing is worn beneath. The most remarkable thing about these nomad women is their head-dresses, which exhibit untold variety. One woman (I think from Nagchuka) had her hair tied into innumerable minute plaits, each no thicker than blindcord. These were divided into two bundles and looped up to her belt. Over the nape of the neck and hanging from her hair was a square foot of cloth ornamented with cowrie shells and, apparently, white bone trouser-buttons. Over her forehead was a rosette the size of a saucer, of small blue, white and red beads. Another head-dress was even more remarkable : the woman's hair was again tied into tiny plaits and these were sewn on to a long strip of cloth woven in green and scarlet squares that reached almost to the ground. These squares were ornamented with Chinese dollars, Indian rupees, pieces of coral and turquoise, rows of cowrie shells and carved ivory; and in the centre was a beautifully embossed disc of silver. I wondered how often she washed her hair ! Some women wear two lumps of amber as big as plums on top of their heads, and usually a few turquoises or corals between. Sometimes strips of black, green or scarlet cloth are sewn on to the border and sleeves of the sheep-skin garment. This is very effective.

The black yak-hair tents of the nomads could often be seen on the Sera plain surrounded by their flocks of yaks and sheep. The former carry wool and the latter small bags of salt or borax, which is collected on the shores of the great brackish lakes to the north of Lhasa. Part of this is paid to the Government as their year's taxation; the rest, together with bales of yak-dung, is exchanged for barley, which they cannot grow in their own country. They do not need much money. A certain amount of brick-tea, a few odds and ends, such as needles, matches, mirrors and jewellery, are bought in the Lhasa bazaar, and they are off home again—perhaps a five months' journey.

While they are in Lhasa, in fact this may be the primary object of their journey, they visit the shrine of the Dalai Lama and the Cathedral. The nomads, in the off season, are notorious brigands, making it unsafe for pilgrims or merchants to cross the Chang Tang except in large caravans, which are formed at regular times each year for mutual protection. They rarely rob their victims of money or valuables that are being taken as an offering to the Jo-king or the Dalai Lama's tomb, for the nomads are notoriously pious, and sometimes they will save up for years and present surprisingly rich gifts to these shrines. Their language is quite different from that of the Lhasa Tibetan; indeed they can hardly understand each other.

In part of the Cathedral buildings there is a religious cloister, the circuit of which must be made at frequent intervals by the devout. In the course of this perambulation several hundred prayer-wheels, set in racks almost touching each other, must be turned. There is also an intermediate circle around the block of buildings of which the Cathedral forms the centre. Enormous prayer-poles surmounted by yaks' tails and chortens mark the course of this circuit. The third and outer circle runs right round the entire city and Potala. It is called the *Ling-kor* or "park circle". All Buddhists are supposed to go round this each day, especially on holy days, the fifteenth and last of each month. And as to walk round it gives one a glimpse of many sides of Lhasa life, I will describe the circuit in some detail.

The Sacred Way runs past the square mud-brick archway leading out of the Deyki Lingka. We have to turn left because the circuit must be made in a clock-wise direction; prayer-wheels are also turned in this way, and when chortens are encountered they must be passed on the right-hand side. To do these things in the reverse direction would stamp one as an adherent of the Pön religion, and would nullify the good work of others.

As we meet the Lhasa-Norbhu Lingka road at right angles there is a pile of stones marking the spot from which the Potala again becomes visible. On the other side of the road are sitting two or three beggars, clad in patchwork garments of filthy rags and wearing necklaces composed of fragments of conch-shell bracelets. Along the main road comes a gang of coolie women carrying a long block of granite to be used in the building of some nobleman's house. As they walk they chant a peculiar and monotonous dirge to keep in step. Sometimes these stones are carried on a wooden two-wheeled cart—the only wheeled vehicle used in Lhasa. The Ling-kor, only ten feet wide here, runs between walls of sun-dried brick striped at regular intervals with splashes of whitewash. Beyond the walls are parks of white poplar and pollard willow trees.

A gateway on the right leads to Gundeling monastery, which can be seen through the trees, with the gable-roofed Chinese temple above. In the latter, behind a wooden balustrade, are two enormous painted figures on mounts like rocking-horses. We overtake a man who is measuring his length round the Sacred Way. As the total distance is between five and six miles, he must make nearly 3000 obeisances per circuit. This man has short hair but does not wear monk's dress. He has a long leather apron strapped over his front and wears on his feet wooden clogs protected with heavy iron nails. He stands with his feet together muttering prayers, brings his hands together in front of him, then lies flat on his face with his arms stretched out beyond his head. He stands up, brings his hands together again, and then walks forward to the point reached by his hands. Sometimes he stops to rest beside the road, marking his progress with a small stone. Unless he is a very notable sinner, I don't think he is doing this on his own account, as I see him at work almost every day. Probably he is wiping out the transgressions of some high official—for a consideration. These exalted people excuse themselves from this

form of devotion on the grounds that their presence would distract
the other worshippers; they must, however, practise it in the
privacy of their own houses.   Nevertheless, I have met the Duke
and Langchungna Shap-pe in the evening on the Sacred Way.
The latter was turning a golden prayer-wheel and wore dark
glasses and a flat-peaked eye-shade projecting a foot in front of his
forehead; he was followed by two or three servants.

Soon the Ling-kor turns sharp right as it meets the sandy bank
of the aqueduct and the main road from India coming in from
the left.   This aqueduct, called the Kaling Chu, was built in 1721
to preserve the city from the encroachments of the flooded plain
to the north and west.   It diverts the streams of the valleys on
either side of Sera monastery and leads them in a semicircle eight
miles in length to join the Kyi Chu below Drepung.   The Kaling
Chu is several feet higher than the surrounding plain and is
enclosed between two immense walls of sand.   The Ling-kor,
here little more than a couple of yards wide, is constricted by an
outcrop of rock.   This is being gradually scraped away as it is a
remedy for rheumatism if taken internally.   It is very sandy here,
and fifty or sixty bright-plumaged sacred cocks attached to the
Chinese temple strut about in the road.   A train of mules laden
with wool comes from the direction of the city on its way to
India, and a mounted woman, with her head so wrapped up in
scarves that only her eyes can be seen, takes the same road, followed
by her two servants.   Above, there is an unusual view of the
Potala; seen end-on from here it looks quite small and is dwarfed
by the rock on which it stands.

The track is confined between the steep sandy wall of the
aqueduct, here fifteen or twenty feet high, and a row of willows,
on the other side of which are Government barley-fields.   Several
dogs, with their noses tucked under their tails, lie curled up with
one eye open for anybody who will give them food.   Now there
is a stream just beside the road; some goosanders and mallard
swim in mid-stream, allowing us to get within ten or fifteen yards.
Looking back I can see as many as fifty people following; practically all are turning prayer-wheels or telling their beads.   There
are very few young people and few men.   Old women pre-
dominate.   It is only when their time in this life becomes short
that they seriously start to prepare themselves for the next.   They
are well muffled up, as it is cold in the early morning.   Many of

them wear a very practical peaked hood which comes down over the shoulders and buttons across the chin, leaving exposed only the eyes and nose. Some of these women lead small dogs which look like crosses between Lhasa terriers and Chinese spaniels. Others lead pet sheep. Some of these are so tame that they follow of their own accord. Both sheep and dogs have many bells tied round their necks. A good number of the followers are nomads with a look of childlike ingenuousness in their eyes. Every morning of their stay in the Holy City they walk round the Lingkor in the early dawn.

A bridge bearing the road from the Lhalu mansion and the Sera plain crosses the aqueduct on our left, but we turn right, over another small bridge towards the Potala, the back of which is now quite close. There is another lingka on the right, and a row of willows on the left, beyond which is a marshy area where white gulls, bar-headed geese and Brahminy duck are feeding. At the foot of the Potala rock there is a tall prayer-pole and a chorten; but we turn left and follow round the high wall of the Snake Temple lake.

Beyond the chorten is the stable of the Dalai Lama's elephant, which was presented some years ago by the Maharajah of Bhutan. It is used in certain ceremonies but otherwise leads a peaceful and apparently healthy life. Some women are carrying in loads of rushes for its breakfast. The northern side of the walls is in ruins and one catches a glimpse of a small temple surrounded by age-old poplars on an island in the middle of a considerable lake. More gnarled and twisted willows, their trunks often lying on the ground, surround the lake; but in the open water are many varieties of duck—mallard, teal, gadwall, tufted, white-eyed and common pochard, as well as goosander, coot and waterhen.

The temple was considered by the Chinese to be one of the five beauties of Lhasa. We visited it soon after we arrived. There is a causeway of ancient poplar logs, but in September it was submerged and a ragged boatman was there to ferry us across to some stone steps that come down to the water's edge. The ferry is similar in shape to the great rectangular barge at Chaksam, but it is only about six feet by four. As it is cut away at the sides to facilitate getting in and out, it is extraordinarily unseaworthy, and we had to sit very still, as there is only an inch or two of freeboard. At the front—there are no bows—is a wooden model of a horse's head raised on a long neck a yard or so above the water. At the back are some twigs with prayer-flags attached. The boat resembles a floating bedstead and seems to be constructed so as to give the maximum possible resistance to the water. Watching the many-hued dragon-flies, and looking across the untroubled surface of the lake to where the iridescent heads of the mallard drakes scintillate among the bowing rushes, and behind them to the luxuriant willows, it is difficult to believe we are nearly 12,000 feet above sea-level.

In the shade of an enormous poplar is the temple, small and square-roofed, with a curious hexagonal tiled dome and a conventional conical ornament on the summit. Hanging from the six corners of the roof are gilt dragons with raised elephantine trunks; from each a golden bell is suspended with a piece of flat metal attached to the clapper so that they tinkle in the wind. Behind the temple rises the northern escarpment of the Potala, somewhat foreshortened from here but as impressive as ever. The temple, like so many Tibetan shrines, is disappointing inside, nor are there any snakes—at any rate not live ones, though some of the idols have diadems or necklaces of writhing serpents. There is, however, a small chamber with a divan where the Dalai Lama used to come and mediate for hours together.

This temple is the abode of a most powerful demon who is the spirit of the lake on which the city of Lhasa is built. On a certain day of each year all the officials and people of Lhasa must visit the temple in order to propitiate him. Having walked in procession round the city, the Prime Minister and the Shap-pes, dressed in their yellow silk robes, and other officials in all their finery, must present scarves to the water-spirit. Yak-hide coracles are brought in and the officials have to remain for some time afloat. Although we did not see this ceremony, as it takes place in the early summer, we saw a small cinema film that Tsarong had made of it, and though the photography was bad—he had waved the camera about like a hosepipe—it was enough to let one realize what a magnificent sight this must be.

The Ling-kor follows the wall of the Snake Temple and of the flooded reed-covered enclosure alongside. On the left are marshes where grow some of the typical Lhasa willows with gnarled spiral-twisted trunks. This is a favourite haunt for birds; in September we would see flocks of literally hundreds of pintail, shoveller, mallard, pochard and teal, together with the ubiquitous bar-heads and Brahminy ducks. The Sacred Way now crosses some open barley-fields where they are gathering in the harvest and treading out the corn with the aid of a dozen or fifteen yaks, which they drive round and round over a floor of beaten clay. On one side is a pile of grain protected from evil spirits by a brightly coloured prayer-flag. Women are sifting the grain and sorting it by tossing it in basket-work trays, and storing it in striped brown and white yak-hair bags. It has been a good harvest. Luckily there were no hail-storms when the grain was ripening, nor any night frosts. An early drop in the temperature can lay waste acres of barley, though these frosts are unusual in the sheltered and comparatively low-lying vale of Lhasa. Now they are starting to plough up the fields with yaks and dzos harnessed in pairs. This must be finished before the ground is held by the winter frosts.

All at once, close at hand, there is a deep booming noise that sets the air a-tremble; it sounds like a hoarse syren or a large animal in dire distress. It is produced by three monks who are sitting on the ground practising on the twelve-foot-long monastery trumpets. The noise is so great that they have to come out into the fields to practise.

The Ling-kor again approaches the city and skirts the high wall surrounding the Regent's summer palace. On the left of the road are the hovels of the lowest class of Lhasa society, the *ra-gyap-pa*, a community of scavenging beggars whose work it is to dispose of the dead bodies. When Buddhists die, their bodies must return to the elements from which they originated—earth, fire, water, air. In the Tibetan winter the ground is frozen too hard for graves to be dug; where yak-dung is the chief fuel not enough can be spared for cremation; many people drink from the river, so that if the corpses are consigned to water the drinking supply would be contaminated. So the body returns to the air. The ra-gyap-pa may be seen in the early morning carrying on their backs the huddled corpses of the poor. These grisly burdens are taken to appointed places where they are laid out on flat stones and cut into small pieces. These are thrown to the vultures and ravens who crowd round waiting for their share of the loathsome meal. These ra-gyap-pa must also remove the carcases of animals that die in the city. Another of their duties is to seek out thieves and

robbers who flee from the city to the surrounding country. At
the time of the 1904 Mission they were put in charge of convicts,
but the practice has been discontinued. Soon after our arrival a
dozen of these ra-gyap-pa came round to the Norbhu Lingka to
ask for money, or rather to demand it as their right. For all
officials visiting Lhasa must pay them on arrival and departure;
similarly when an official is promoted, and on days of festival,
these importunate fellows appear. If they are not paid they break
into such a frenzied yelling and cursing that it is better to settle
up at once and let them go. Some of the ra-gyap-pa are very
wealthy and wear the saucer-shaped hat and ear-ring of respect-
ability.

Their dwellings consist of a wall of sods into which are built
the horns of animals; over the top is raised a roof of ragged yak-
hair tent-cloth. This is often surrounded by an outer wall made
of the horns of yaks, cattle and sheep heaped together. In the
summer their hovels are gay with nasturtiums and marigolds.
Beside the track an aged wizened woman with short white hair
raises herself from her patchwork sheepskin bag, in which she lies
to keep warm, and in a thin whining voice asks for alms. She
lives in a wretched dog-kennel of a hut which is only just big
enough to hold her. Children run naked in the road. There
are innumerable lean and mangy dogs, too emaciated even to
bark at strangers. But these are the lowest of the ra-gyap-pa.
Further on, though they must still live outside the city, they
have proper houses, built of sun-dried bricks, but still with
neat rows of yak horns let into the face of the wall, like a
mosaic.

On the right, close to the Ling-kor, appears the single golden
roof-pavilion of the Ramoche temple, in which is a huge image
of the Chinese wife of King Song-tsen Gampo. Opposite this
temple a road from Sera monastery and the arsenal comes in from
the left. Already a line of bare-headed, bare-footed monks are
entering the city; many of them carry on their backs bundles
wrapped up in a flap of their voluminous robes. The Ling-kor
crosses another stretch of open country with the tents of ra-gyap-pa
on either hand, and away to the left are open fields with occasional
villas surrounded by lingkas. The great walls of Muru monastery
appear above the lower buildings on the right. Soon the north-
east corner of the city is passed and the road swings to the right

over a stone bridge. On the left are marshes and lingkas with a stony road coming in from the north-east. Next the quarter of the butchers is reached, again without the city walls; and the ground is littered with horns, hoofs, bones and scraps of hide. Inappropriately placed among the slaughter-houses and butcheries is the mosque of the Ladakis, rather a mean and neglected-looking building with a wooden lich-gate and enclosing wall. The main road from north Tibet, Ganden and Nagchuka comes in here, and beside it is a small walled pagoda in Chinese style. This is the grave of a member of General Huang-Mu Sung's 1932 Mission to Lhasa who died after being thrown from his horse.

The Ling-kor now turns east and returns between the Kyi Chu and the city. The leather-workers (also outcasts) live here, and there are several coracles stacked against the side of the road. It is a mean quarter of the town, although a few gateways open on the right to the better-class houses which lie behind. Beside the road are piles of dung and all the refuse of the city, with dogs and ravens searching for tasty morsels. There are stacks of kindling wood here, probably the property of the Government, or of Tsarong or the Prime Minister, whose mansions lie to the left amidst groves of trees.

Soon part of the ancient wall of the city is passed on the right, pierced by a ruined gateway where a group of beggars sit turning their prayer-wheels. Beyond this is a large white-washed chorten and a stone bridge which gives access to an open grassy plain stretching to the willow groves wherein are the pleasure-gardens and summer-houses of the monk and lay officials.

It is the picnic season now—Lhasa's favourite pastime—and each official in turn must entertain his colleagues to a picnic, usually followed by a theatrical entertainment. Often canvas tents are put up and pots of flowers brought out for their adornment. The middle and lower classes seem to spend all the day picnicking. Riding through the lingkas we meet party after party sitting round dicing and drinking chang. They bring out a cloth tent, or simply an awning, adorned with blue and red appliqué work. Carved Tibetan tables and padded cushion seats are also brought. The lunch is often cooked in a smaller yak-hair tent. Tea and chang are drunk all day, and in the evening we would meet parties returning, master, mistress and servants all walking together (sometimes arm-in-arm to provide the stability necessary after taking so much chang) and singing songs in harsh Tibetan voices.

The poorer people were usually more abandoned and we would see them returning only just able to walk. Occasionally a man could be seen fast asleep in the gutter beside the road. The doctor found that the number of his patients increased very much during the picnic season, and as soon as he saw what the man's complaint was, he would anticipate his excuses and say: " I suppose you went to a picnic last week? "

" Yes," the man would sheepishly admit.

"And I suppose you fell down? "

" Yes, yes, that's what happened." And the man would receive his injections and go off to another picnic.

In the stream beside the road are shoals of small fish, and it is considered a pious act to feed them with small fragments of barley dough. A little farther on the main river sweeps in to meet the Ling-kor, and quite near in a deep back-water are any number of huge char. Sometimes we saw as many as a hundred in this one pool. The largest would be eight or ten pounds in weight. This pool is the abode of a powerful spirit and the trees near by are festooned with thousands of prayer-flags. Very often there is somebody burning azalea leaves and throwing food to the fishes on the point overlooking the pool. For quite a long while there was a dead baby at the bottom of this pool, for the fish do not seem to appreciate carrion.

Over the tops of the trees of the largest lingka in Lhasa can be seen the long southern face of the Potala and behind it the dun hills on the other side of Sera plain. Just here, where the Sacred Way swings towards the Iron Hill, there is an enormous cairn of stones with the topmost ones whitewashed. This pile is twenty feet high and more than fifty yards in circumference. Each person as he passes picks up a stone from the road and throws it to the top of the heap. The Tibetan has a passion for piling up stones, particularly white ones. A little farther back along the Ling-kor there is a cleft willow which is almost hidden by the stones which have been thrown into the tree.

And now, before completing the circuit, we must cross the precipitous south-western buttresses of the Iron Hill. It is impossible to keep on the level, because a stream washes right against the foot of the rocks. So the path, with steep crags above and below, cuts over the shoulder of the hill. This is perhaps the most remarkable part of the whole Ling-kor. Beside the track are hundreds and hundreds of carved and painted Buddhas. Some are cut out of the rock itself. Others are painted on flat slates and propped up in niches. There are also the horns of animals and innumerable clay castings of the Buddha, which are baked in a primitive kiln beside the track. The Ling-kor here descends so steeply that those measuring their length may cease their uncomfortable progress and walk to the foot of the hill. On the right are three large prayer-barrels built into the wall; these must be turned as you pass. A little farther on is a vertical wall of smooth rock on which are painted several hundred similar Buddhas in red, blue and gold. They are arranged in ranks both vertically and horizontally. Just below the multiple wall painting is a rock which must be touched with the forehead. It is polished to the smoothness of marble. There is also a small hole in the wall forming the summit of a painted chorten; a finger must be placed here. Another devotional exercise is to crawl under a slab of rock which leans against the foot of the main wall. These actions, especially the last two, are often dispensed with. From the top of the wall long strings of prayer-flags are stretched above the Ling-kor to the trees beside the stream. One more chorten is passed and the Sacred Way runs between two willow groves to the Norbhu Lingka gate where we first entered it.

# CHAPTER NINE

## THE POTALA

WRITING of Lhasa City, it has been difficult not to digress occasionally and to describe the many glimpses that one gets of the Potala, which appears from time to time poised above the flat roof-tops or framed at the end of some squalid street. As Salisbury Cathedral towers above the city and plain at its feet, so the Potala completely dominates the vale of Lhasa.

To me the Potala represents the very essence of the Tibetan people. It has a certain untamed dignity in perfect harmony with the surrounding rugged country; a quality of stolid unchangeableness—it seems to say : " Here I have been for hundreds of years, and here I intend to stay for ever ". Yet underneath this beauty, which is reflected not only in the inspired simplicity of its lines but in the exquisite workmanship of many of the smallest details, there is a lurking grimness, personified, perhaps, in the unfortunate political offender Lungsha, who, having fallen foul of the Government, lies with sightless eyes in a dungeon at the foot of the building.

Certainly the Potala is one of the most astonishing buildings in the world, whether it is seen from afar perched on the summit of the eminence which rises from the level plain of Lhasa, with the sun striking flame from the golden pavilions of its roof, or whether, riding out before dawn, you see the moonlight thrown back with unearthly brilliance from the whitewashed wall of the immense southern face. All the supremely great works of art, in literature, painting or architecture, have an indefinable quality of magic which is born from circumstances usually beyond the artist's control; so, in common with the few unquestionably perfect buildings of the world, the Potala has some transcendent quality derived neither from the inspired skill of some master builder or craftsmen, nor from its historical associations, nor from the fact that it is the cynosure of innumerable religious devotees. That it does possess this divine excellence cannot be doubted.

I have sometimes regretted the presence of the Iron Hill and wished that the Potala rock could stand alone as the only eminence in the vale of Lhasa. But it justifies itself by affording what is to my mind the finest view in all the world. It is from here that the Potala, balanced by the flat-roofed village at its foot, is seen to most advantage. It is sufficiently near for detail to be distinguished, and far enough away to be seen as a whole. From the other view-points it leans back unduly; it is stupendous, awe-inspiring, but not in equilibrium. Seen from the top of the Iron Hill it is as near perfection as anything in this world can be. Buildings in other countries may challenge comparison with the Potala; but to my mind no edifice, so perfect in itself, is placed in such incomparable surroundings.

One looks down on to the three chortens of the Western Gate, and on each side of it a sea of tree-tops, with the tenuous green of the willows set off by the darker poplars. Between the trees

THE POTALA FROM THE SOUTH-WEST

THE POTALA FROM THE EAST.  NOMADS PERFORMING HOLY WALK

are pools of water reflecting the blue sky, or level expanses of grass. A mile away to the east, appearing through the greenery as a broken white line, is the city of Lhasa, with the golden Cathedral roofs catching the sun and leading up to the larger mass of gold on the Potala. At this distance Lhasa is indeed a garden city. The fertile plain is bordered by the Kyi Chu, which runs in a great semicircle from extreme east to extreme west. Beyond the river the mountains rise abruptly, spur after spur coming right down to the water's edge. In the valleys between these gaunt ridges are villages surrounded by willow groves and barley-fields, watered by streams that flow from the mountains which tower another 6000 feet above them. The whole plain of Lhasa is surrounded by this ring of great mountains, over whose high passes have flocked for hundreds of years the pilgrims who came from all parts of Asia to tread the Sacred Way around the city and Potala.

Quite unlike anything else in the world, the Potala yet has something of the New York sky-scraper, a faint kinship with Egyptian architecture, and still more of the massive flat-roofed buildings of the Hadhramaut in Arabia. But whereas New York is a city of sky-scrapers, and the Egyptians were prolific builders, the Potala is an isolated example of the perfection which Tibetan architecture can attain. Although some of the monasteries and forts are built in the same style, they cannot be compared with the palace of the Dalai Lamas, standing alone in superb detachment.

Not only does its beauty of form and colour take one's breath away, but it is of such colossal size. This is best appreciated from the Government lingka below the southern face. In front of one is the level turf where a few yaks are grazing. Beyond this is a line of misty green pollard willows through which appear the flat roofs of Sho, the hamlet that nestles at the foot of the Potala. Behind this starts the great rock, strewn with small willows, on which the palace is built. It is difficult to tell where the actual building starts, as the foundation seems to grow out of the rock, and the whitewash on the walls has run down over the lower buttresses. Huge staircases, protected by walls which are themselves cut into enormous steps, zigzag up to the doorways which, as none of them faces south, are not visible from here. As the whole building leans back, and as each " vertical " wall

L

leans inwards, the impression of height is still further enhanced. It is actually 440 feet high and 900 feet in length. Except for the central part, which is of a rich maroon colour, and a small block which is ochreous, the walls are white-washed, and each block of masonry is picked out with a border of deep red along the summit, surmounted in its turn by a narrow white parapet. The form of the whole is reflected in each window, which is broader at the bottom than at the top and is shaded by a wide lintel.

The Potala gives the impression not of having been built by man but of having grown there, so perfectly does it fit in with its surroundings. It has the pleasing lack of symmetry of a great tree or mountain, yet this apparent aimlessness is focused, first by the red central block and then by the golden pavilions on the roof, so that the eye is naturally led from the less important to the essential, both visually and spiritually; for in so much as the gilded roofs over the mortal remains of the Dalai Lamas are the dominant feature of the architecture, so is the incarnate spirit of these rulers the very soul of Tibet.

Over the central line of windows of each block are draped brown yak-hair curtains striped horizontally with white. The roofs of the terra-cotta central portion and of the wing to the east of it, which contains the Dalai Lama's private suite of rooms, are especially beautiful. Here there is a wide strip of dull maroon bordered above and below with white. In the centre of this rich matt surface, which forms an ideal background for them, are four very large embossed monograms of gold, with several smaller ones on either side. These ornaments prepare one for the larger mass of gold on the roof-pavilions. Spaced along the edge of the parapet and at the corners are golden turrets and cylindrical banners of black yak-hair crossed with white. These serve—as well as keeping off devils—to break the severity of the sky-line, which is further relieved by the roof pagodas.

In the seventh century Song-tsen Gampo, the great warrior-King of Tibet, built himself a palace on what was called the Red Hill, where the Potala now stands, but it was demolished in the wars that followed. The word Potala is taken from the name of a rock at Cape Comorin, the southern tip of India, which was supposed by the Indians to be the abode of the God of Mercy, or Chenrezi, who is incarnate in the Dalai Lama. There is another " Potala " on the east coast of China. It was the great

fifth Dalai Lama, Lob-sang Gyatso, who started the construction
of the palace that is now there, and it is uncertain how much of
any previous buildings he incorporated. He died in 1680, and it
was completed by his competent Minister, Sang-gye Gyatso, a
few years later.

As the Jo-kang is the centre of the purely religious life of
Tibet, so is the Potala the focus of the temporal and spiritual
powers of this ruler, who so strangely combines the offices of
Dictator and Pope. Since its completion it has been the official
residence of the Dalai Lamas, though the last Pontiff preferred to
spend his time in the Norbhu Lingka, only visiting the Potala
when ceremonies demanded his presence.

The Regent, who is not permitted to use the Dalai Lama's
suite of rooms, has his own office there, as also has the Prime
Minister. Every Lhasa official, monk and lay, must, theoretically,
meet in the Assembly Hall once each day at a certain time to drink
tea—though the last Dalai Lama usually summoned them to the
Norbhu Lingka. This is to ensure that the officials remain at
their work and do not leave the city. Nearly all the great
ceremonies of the Tibetan year take place within its walls or on
its spacious roof: the inception of the New Year; the Lama
dances which mark the end of the old year; and the changing
of clothes which represents the beginning and end of winter.
When a high official leaves or returns to Lhasa he must go to the
Potala to report and present his scarf of greeting.

Here are the mortal remains of former Dalai Lamas enshrined
in tombs lavishly ornamented with gold and precious stones.
Here also, in the strong rooms of the Potala, is the almost fabulous
private treasury of the Dalai Lamas, which contains the accumulated wealth of centuries, and possibly the world's finest collection
of old Chinese porcelain and cloisonné, ceremonial brocade
robes, golden images, exquisite gems and jewellery, and other
rare or valuable objects. These were presents from pious pilgrims
and others to the head of the Buddhist Church; many of them
came from the Emperors and Princes of China and Mongolia.
No man knows the extent of this treasure-house of the Dalai
Lamas.

The Potala has its own monastery, called the Namgyal Choide,
whose 170 monks are usually recruited from the better families,
and who have the reputation of being the best-dressed monks

in Lhasa. The Dalai Lama takes his place among their number as an ordinary priest. Within the palace there is also a college for monk officials called the Tse-laptra, the School on the Hill. This takes about thirty boys and trains them for three or four years. It is in charge of the three Grand Secretaries, who choose the pupils among boys from the great monasteries near Lhasa. As the choice is made purely by merit, they are frequently of humble birth.

In September they gave the Potala its annual coat of paint. The whitewash was mixed in the well between the stone monument and the small bridge to the south of the Potala. A bag of lime was attached to the middle of a yak-hair rope and dragged from end to end of the well until all the water had been converted into whitewash—a somewhat drastic method of chlorination! This was ladled into wooden or earthenware buckets and carried on the backs of the women to the foot of the Potala walls. Here it was simply thrown up in small buckets or dippers. The areas of wall that could not be reached in this primitive fashion were covered by wash that was thrown down from the windows. Years of this treatment have given the walls a stalagmitic appearance. In September, too, they removed the hanging yak-hair curtains which protected the woodwork from the glare of the sun. The bare lower part of the wall, below the bottom line of windows, is at certain times of the year covered by enormous religious paintings. At the foot of the southern face of the Potala, towards the western end, are the Government prisons and printing establishment. We did not visit the dungeons; report has it that they are unspeakably filthy and that the prisoners are barbarously treated. The printing press, like all others in the country, is in charge of the monks. Tibetan paper is made of the bark of daphne or other shrubs. We would often see it being prepared, usually by a man out of doors. He would pound up the bark with water by spreading it on one flat stone and beating it with another. The resulting mixture was then spread on a wooden frame four feet square, over which was stretched a fine wire gauze. When dry it was removed from the frame and trimmed. This paper is very tough and coarse and resembles cream-coloured cardboard. Troughs are also used in which the pulp is pounded underfoot. Owing to the poisonous nature of one kind of bark used, no insects will attack Tibetan paper; on the other hand, people who have to spend much time with these books complain of severe headaches. Outside the Potala press we saw a line of men sitting in the sun laboriously cutting out wooden blocks in reverse corresponding to each page, for type is not used in Tibet. These blocks were two to three feet long and about six inches wide. Inside, an enormous hall was taken up with racks holding the sets of blocks. There is here a complete set of the Kangyur, or Buddhist Scriptures, in 108 volumes; also of the Tengyur, its commentaries, in 225 volumes.

Although the outside of the Potala is so superb, the inside is disappointing. True, there are certain details—a painting on the wall, a golden butter-lamp, or even a complete room—which are worthy of the palace, but there is no sort of unity; and the various assembly halls, shrines and storerooms are connected by dark and evil-smelling passages slippery with the spillings of innumerable cups of Tibetan tea, while the whole place is anything but clean.

It was 6th September before we could spare a day to go over the interior of the Potala. We rode up the long western causeway and zigzagged to the doorway on the northern side. From here there is a wonderful view to the west and north. We looked down on to the wide road crossing the flooded meadows past Gundeling and thence leading to the Norbhu Lingka. We could just make out our own Deyki Lingka among the trees over the shoulder of the Iron Hill. From above, one can appreciate how very wooded this side is; willow and thorn scrub stretch in a wide green band beside the river as far as eye can see. It was wise of the Tibetans to surround the Potala by a green belt of linghas and fields. Towards Drepung—westward, that is—the greenery is stopped by a wide marshy area on each side of the road; and to the north is the bare Sera plain. The sandy banks of the aqueduct run in a great arc from the front of Sera almost to Drepung. There is also a good view of the Lhalu mansion, where the 1904 Mission were housed. It is surrounded by wooded gardens and water-meadows and has a large private monastery.

We were shown the assembly room where the 1904 treaty was signed. A huge dark room with a flagged floor, and roof supported by square wooden pillars swathed in cloth or hung with strips of silk. In the middle of this a monk was arranging different-coloured powders on a large tray in the form of a geometric design. The walls of many of the audience halls and cloisters were completely covered with frescoes, but it was too dark to see them clearly. Among the many images were life-sized effigies of King Song-tsen Gampo with his two wives from Nepal and China. There were many images from India, including a sandalwood image of Chenrezi, which is supposed to have been miraculously formed as the tree split. Another image of this god was made by the last Dalai Lama. It is of silver, and has eleven heads and a thousand arms and eyes, one eye being engraved in the palm of each hand. We were shown one golden image from the back of which an avaricious monk had stolen a large piece of the precious metal. As a punishment he had had his hands cut off. There is also a special room which was used by the fifth Dalai Lama and which has been preserved exactly as he left it.

The most impressive part of the interior of the Potala is the mausolea of the Dalai Lamas, from the fifth onwards, though the sixth is excluded owing to his dissolute life, or because he died away from Lhasa. Nor are the last four represented, as they were never allowed to grow up. The embalmed bodies are actually there inside chortens which, instead of being made of stone, are reputed to be of silver; certainly they are overlaid with gold plentifully set with turquoise, lapis lazuli, amethyst, coral, onyx, sapphire, and even rubies and diamonds. As the tomb of the fifth is sixty feet high, and that of the thirteenth even higher, they must be worth a vast amount of money. That of the last Dalai Lama had only recently been completed, and in proportion to his greatness it far exceeds all the others in splendour. It is interesting to see that the work done in Lhasa today is apparently indistinguishable from similar work carried out at various times since the seventeenth century, when the palace, in its present form, was built.

Considerable structural alteration has been necessary to fit in this tomb, which rises through three complete stories of the building. It is a great pity that the chorten is not housed in a larger room so that one could stand back and see it in its entirety.

When this saintly ruler died the pious from many parts of the Buddhist world contributed what they could afford to the building of this shrine. The main chorten is encased in gold embossed with different designs and plentifully encrusted with precious stones. In some places valuable charm-boxes, turquoise ear-rings, onyx and coral snuff-boxes, strings of amber and pearls, and innumerable unset gems have been let in to form designs on the gold background. On several shelves in front are displayed more precious presents, gifts from the ancient and noble families of Tibet and from the rich monasteries of China and Mongolia. Here are rare porcelain vases, exquisite examples of cloisonné work, chalice-like vessels of solid gold, meticulously wrought metal-work, alabaster models of temples, and glass cases containing curiously fashioned flowers with leaves and petals of china. On the eastern wall of the room are pigeon-holes containing holy books with carved wooden covers, many small images and filigree charm-boxes such as are carried by travellers.

In front of the shrine burn several enormous butter-lamps of solid silver. They stand four feet high, and the bowls, with a row of burning wicks floating in the fat, are more than two feet in diameter. Each wick has melted a little lake for itself in the congealed butter. White scarves had been thrown up on to the chorten by pilgrims, and there were vases of artificial and real flowers in different parts of the shrine, while the square wooden pillars surrounding the tomb and supporting the roof are covered by long brocade strips of different colours, each hanging over the next like the scales of a fish. Although certain details of the tomb, such as the crystal globes hanging from the ceiling and a coloured biscuit-tin on one of the shelves, struck a false note, the general impression is a fitting tribute to the memory of this revered ruler.

On the upper story of the tomb, which surrounds the chorten like a balcony, some fifteen of the best Tibetan artists were at work on a series of thankas illustrating the life-story of the Dalai Lama. It was interesting to see them at work. They were obviously men of some standing, as each wore the long turquoise and gold ear-ring. They wore white shirts, indigo or purplish broadcloth robes, and black top-boots. They worked on fine canvas, which had been prepared and stiffened with white paint; this was stretched over a wooden frame about four feet high and two and a half feet wide, which they rested on their knees, as they sat cross-legged on the floor. The paints, made of stones and earths (many of them imported from India) ground up with oil, were in separate porcelain saucers. The brushes, of which each painter used several, appeared to be of hog's bristle. The work was extremely fine and they showed great accuracy and skill, though they all painted in the conventional manner, so that it would have been difficult to pick out the work of individual artists. The Potala, considerably conventionalized, appeared in many of the paintings, also processions of monks, street scenes and landscapes, as well as the usual Buddhas, curly clouds and stiff formal flowers. As is usual with Tibetan pictures, every corner of the canvas was filled up. Each artist had his wooden teacup and tsamba bag beside him, and seemed to drink every few minutes.

After tearing ourselves away from the shrine we climbed a crazy ladder to the roof, which is of sand and gravel beaten to the consistency of concrete. It is here that the Dalai Lama, when in residence at the Potala, takes exercise. And what a superb place to take a constitutional! The whole vale of Lhasa lies spread out beneath one, surrounded by its cirque of wild mountain scenery.

Everywhere there are trees—lines of giant poplars, groves of pollard willows, and beside the river acres and acres of thorny scrub.

On the roof of the Potala, surounded by the seven glittering mausolea of departed Dalai Lamas, one cannot help contrasting this superb building with that drab and squalid city with its stinking puddles and rotting heaps of offal; the wealth of the monasteries, and the poverty of the common people. "The Potala", says Percival Landon, "unconsciously symbolizes the vast erection of power and pride which separates the priestly caste of Tibet from the real truths of the religion they have prostituted." Yet in conclusion he almost forgives this Lamaism that has raised up to its gods so great and enduring a wonder.

# CHAPTER TEN

## THE NORBHU LINGKA

As Lhasa is approached from the west a great walled enclosure can be made out between the road and the Kyi Chu. Above the wall, which is ten or twelve feet high, can be seen the golden turrets of an attractive-looking building surrounded by tall trees. This is the Norbhu Lingka, or " Jewel Park ", the summer residence of the Dalai Lama.

It is a fairly recent building, having been put up in the closing years of the last century, while two of the palaces are of even later date. A metalled cambered road, the finest in Lhasa, leads from the western extremity of the Potala rock—a stone's throw from the Western Gate—to the main entrance of the Norbhu Lingka, which is just short of a mile distant. Having crossed some willow-clad water-meadows by a low causeway, which is flooded in the summer months, the road cuts between Gundeling monastery and a spur of the Iron Hill. For the rest of the way it runs between lingkas of willow and poplar. Here it is bordered by walls of sun-dried bricks with stone coping pleasantly overgrown with weeds. These walls, as is usual in Lhasa, are ornamented every few yards with broad splashes of whitewash. Half-way along this straight stretch of road the Sacred Way is crossed, and from this point both the Potala and the Norbhu Lingka gates can be seen.

In 1904 no member of the Mission was ever allowed within the walls of the Norbhu Lingka. To such an extent has the Tibetan attitude changed that in 1920 Sir Charles Bell frequently went there to converse as man to man with the Dalai Lama; he also visited the Forbidden Enclosure, which is a privilege denied even to the highest in the land.

As there was no Dalai Lama during our visit, we were most generously allowed to go there whenever we liked; and when Gould was recovering from his illness he was invited to make use of the gardens for convalescence. He took full advantage of this, and, as I usually accompanied him to take photographs, we spent many hours in this delectable place. On such occasions they let us wander where we liked, and it was only when we went into the inner enclosure that a Tibetan came with us.

L 2

The Norbhu Lingka consists of a walled enclosure nearly half a mile each way and more or less square in shape. The Tibetans are skilled wallers, and this is as good an example as any. More than ten feet high, it is built of huge blocks of granite laid in lines and separated by smaller fragments of stone set horizontally. The lower part is whitewashed and is separated from the reddened upper part by a string course. Along the ground at the foot of the wall lie huge coping-stones of granite; these were brought with much labour, often as a punishment for some minor crime, from the mountains on the other side of the Sera plain; but as the strength of the wall was found insufficient to bear so great a weight their use has been abandoned and many of them have lately been broken up for other purposes. On the southern side a branch of the Kyi Chu, held back by a masonry embankment, comes almost to the foot of the wall. For the rest, the garden is surrounded by overgrown park-land and open meadows. A narrow aqueduct, at present in a state of disrepair, brings water to the small power-station in an angle of the northern wall. This was formerly used to supply electric light, but this scheme seems to have been abandoned.

The main gate is most impressive, with a roof of highly glazed tiles and the usual golden medallions on a background of dark red. On each side and above the gate is a system of branching woodwork painted red and picked out with flower-designs in bright colours. A row of grinning white demons look down from beneath the roof. The heavy wooden doors, with metal knockers formed by a ring held in the jaws of a lion, open into a portico, the ceiling of which is richly painted. It is a pity that the square pillars here are of granite which has been treated in the same way as wood, for the stone looks out of place and its surface is little suited for paintwork. The first place to be visited is the Assembly Room, where, when the Dalai Lama was alive, the Ministers would assemble each day and, sitting on cushions strictly in order of precedence, would drink ceremonial tea and receive a blessing before discussing affairs of State. Hanging from the pillars are curious cylinders covered with tiger and leopard skin; these, we were told, are symbols of power and justice.

The Dalai Lama's reception room is magnificently decorated. The throne, on which he used to sit cross-legged, is about six feet higher than the polished floor. Over the front of it hangs a wonderful piece of embroidery showing the swastika and sacred thunderbolt (dorje) symbols. On each side are pillars swathed in heavy silk hangings. A row of richly coloured thankas framed in brocade hangs along the back wall. The roof-beams and the capitals of the pillars are especially beautifully decorated with gold and bright-coloured flower patterns.

The Norbhu Lingka comprises three separate palaces, houses for the Grand Chamberlain, Chief Secretary, and other officials attached to the Dalai Lama's staff, reception and throne rooms, an inner enclosure including an artificial lake with two summer pavilions, the royal stables, and the barracks where live the 500 troops of the Dalai Lama's private bodyguard. His Holiness was accustomed to move from one palace to another just as he felt inclined, and we were shown several rooms with padded couches on which he used to sit. Before the low cushions was always a carved table on which were set ready his jade teacup with its golden lotus-pattern stand and cover, his prayer-wheel, and often a bowl of fruit. These rooms, unlike other show places in Tibet, were always scrupulously clean and tidy. It was as if they were all prepared for the imminent return of the next incarnation of Chenrezi. The palaces are storehouses of rich presents that the Dalai Lamas have received in the past from different corners of the Buddhist world. Many were locked away and carefully sealed, but others could be seen in glass cases or were in use as ornaments. There were cones of holy-water vessels on tables inlaid with ivory and mother-of-pearl, huge porcelain vases, innumerable golden images set with turquoise and coral and wearing great necklaces of amber, holy books with carved wooden covers, and hangings of priceless brocade. In one room there were several framed photographs of the late Dalai Lama, one of the Potala, and another of a Chinese temple. Most striking of all were several magnificent examples of cloisonné work : Chinese lions four feet in height, and elephants bearing vases on their backs. The lions showed the traditional characteristics of their sex : the male, with his paw pressed playfully on a ball, depicted gentleness in spite of strength, while the female, playing with her cub, showed affection.

In one room, which had a floor of polished wooden blocks, was a life-size image of the Dalai Lama himself, mitred and swathed in rich vestments like a bishop, sitting on a throne with a silken canopy above his head. The walls of these newer palaces were completely covered in paintings, many of them topical, the work of Chinese artists. There were paddle-steamers crossing lakes, a crowd of people traversing an arched stone bridge, as well as birds, animals and flowers.

The gardens had been skilfully laid out, but since the last Prelate's death they have not been properly tended. The flowers are mainly self-sown, and spring up, together with weeds, in the chinks of the paving-stones. But in spite of this lack of proper care the borders in the autumn were a riot of colour, with red and white hollyhocks, purple phloxes, yellow marigolds, petunias, coreopsis, asters, roses and chrysanthemums. All the flowers of an English garden seem to flourish perfectly at 12,000 feet above sea-level. The trees here, instead of being gnarled and twisted, grow slim and straight to a great height. There is one beautiful avenue of white poplars leading to the newer palaces; it is only spoilt by a granite arch whose spindly columns look out of place beside the more robust Tibetan gateways. In one place a pine tree grows as high as the palace roof; there is a clump of bamboo twenty feet high; there are apple trees, apricots and peaches—though these fruits do not ripen in Lhasa. In the gardens two prayer-barrels are set over streams so that they are made to revolve by water-power.

Behind one of the palaces is the Dalai Lama's garage. Here, beneath a dust sheet, we saw a Baby Austin with a number-plate bearing the words *Tibet I*. There was also a venerable Dodge. These cars were presents to the Dalai Lama from former Political Officers. Some years ago he had a road specially built alongside the aqueduct to the Arsenal (*trab-shi*), some three miles distant, and frequently with his favourite, Kumpala, he would drive down to inspect the troops. But now the road has been largely washed away in the summer floods, the wheels of the car, which are missing, have perhaps suffered a similar fate, and *Tibet I* looks neglected and forlorn.

The Forbidden Enclose of the Norbhu Lingka, which is also surrounded by a high wall, is about two hundred yards square. Here there is an artificial lake overhung by tall trees. A granite balustrade borders the lake, which is square in shape, and a bridge, or rather causeway, leads from a small gated portico to

two islands built up with stone walls and surrounded by ornamental granite fencing.   On the walls of the portico are some
very racy frescoes showing golden pheasants and some dogs
like dachshunds.   On the islands are two pavilions surrounded
by innumerable flowers in pots.   These summer-houses, with
golden emblems along the ridges of their orange-brown roofs
of highly glazed Chinese tiles, represent the inner sanctuary of
the Priest King.   No official was allowed within the walls of
this enclosure, and here he could escape the attentions of the
crowd of servants that surround a king, and enjoy the solitude
that is so often denied to one in his position.   Each day (says
Sir Charles Bell, who was privileged to know him intimately)
he would spend several hours in lonely meditation and prayer
among the birds and flowers that he loved.

His Holiness was always devoted to animals and birds, and had
set up what might almost be described as a zoo in the Norbhu
Lingka grounds.   The Bengal tiger which formerly lived in a
corner of the enclosure is no longer there, but a pair of *Shao*,
the almost extinct Sikkim stag, are tethered on one of the lawns.
The hind is quite docile but the stag very much on the defensive.
On the lake are many bar-headed geese and Brahminy duck;
there are doves in cages, Demoiselle cranes and Monal pheasants
in a wire-netting enclosure, and a monkey chained to a tall pole,
up which he climbs.   There were also many dogs, but these
are now looked after by different ministers.   The Abbot of
Gundeling one day showed us a pair of dachshunds which belonged to His Holiness, and there was also an Airedale terrier
and a greyhound.   The granite kennels, built at intervals along
the outside wall and beside the palaces, bear testimony to the
number of Tibetan mastiffs that he used to keep.   These dogs
are kept chained up in the courtyard of most Tibetan mansions;
at night they are allowed to roam round the yard, from which
they successfully keep away thieves.   As they are tied up all
day they become extremely fierce, and as soon as a stranger
approaches they bark furiously and throw themselves to the
ends of their all too flimsy chains.   Very often they wear thick
ruff-like collars of scarlet wool; this is to protect their throats
from the attacks of wolves.   In colour they are black or liver-
and-black; their coats may be either long and shaggy or fairly
short; they have massive heads, pendant ears and bloodshot eyes.

In the palace gardens there were also several of the other typical dog of the country, the Tibetan terrier or " Apso ". These lively little animals were brought by the Chinese, but in Lhasa the breed has practically died out. The usual colour is sable. They resemble Skye terriers, but have curly tails like Pekinese.

The Dalai Lama's herd of two-humped camels are allowed to roam at large over the waste land between the Norbhu Lingka and the main branch of Kyi Chu, where they browse on the thorny bushes that grow there. There are seventeen of them now, one of them having been born since they arrived as a present from Mongolia. Each morning and evening the Tibetan who is in charge of them rounds them up and prevents them from straying too far. While doing this he usually sits on the back of one that is used to being ridden. There is also a herd of some fifty mules and ponies which are taken from the stables to graze in the park in front of the Potala. Though these are in magnificent condition they are never used; practically all of them were presents to His Holiness. Some of the mules— who are as fat as butter—are of a curious fulvous colour with a black line down the centre of the back and tail and similar striped markings on the legs. One, the strangest of all, is white, covered all over with small black spots, like a Dalmatian.

Perhaps the most surprising thing in all the Norbhu Lingka is the Dalai Lama's stables. The stalls are arranged along three sides of a cobbled courtyard and around another block in the centre. On each side of the entrance gateway are two paintings, the Mongolian leading a tiger, and, in a style that recalls an Italian primitive, a man followed by an amiable-looking elephant laden with symbolic jewels. These paintings one has seen elsewhere, but over every stall is the most enchanting fresco painted in bright colours on the plaster of the wall. Many of these are of equestrian subjects, beautiful Pegasus-like horses, pink, blue, spotted or white, flying over far hill-tops or gambolling playfully together. One of the most interesting shows the anatomy of the horse. It is intended for veterinary purposes, and shows two horses, a front and a back view, standing on their hind-legs. This displays the Tibetan conception of the position of the bones and organs of the animal's body: it is naturally somewhat rudimentary. Other paintings illustrate Chinese proverbs and folk-tales: four figures are trying to move something that looks like an enormous peach; a boatload of people cross a lake while an old man sits wrapped in thought, and a wisp of cloud flowing from his brain is developed to form a vision of the Buddha.

All these frescoes, though slightly splashed and discoloured, are marvellously executed and must be the work of first-class artists. The topical paintings on the palace walls are clearly Chinese; the huge richly-coloured figures of the four Kings of the Quarters on the portico opening into the Forbidden Enclosure are as clearly Tibetan, but these equestrian studies exhibit a rare economy of line and colour and are quite unlike other work I saw in Lhasa.

The palaces and grounds are in the charge of the young Prime Minister, who is a nephew of the last Dalai Lama, and nearly every week we used to see him, with his six servants, riding past our house on his way to visit the Norbhu Lingka. Each article is carefully catalogued and entered into books, and he must go and see that none of the seals are broken, and that none of the massive Tibetan locks are undone. However well he may have looked after the treasures, it is a great pity that the garden has so completely gone to seed; it will take many years to restore it to the orderly state in which the last owner kept it. The man directly in charge is a half-brother of Yuto Depön, who is in charge of the bodyguard and has rooms in the barracks.

The nominal strength of this bodyguard is 500, but many of the soldiers were on leave. The barracks face the river and are separated from it by a stony parade-ground where the troops play football. In one corner of this ground was a huge pile of kindling-wood some twenty feet high, and to go and collect loads of this wood from the waste land by the river seemed to be the sole activity of the soldiers, though several of them made remarkable noises with a bugle. There was always a guard in the sentry-box beside the gate. When we gave notice of our intention to visit the palace, there would be a section ready in charge of an N.C.O. They were usually youths, not so tall as the fixed bayonets they carried—it was necessary to have their bayonets fixed, as they carried no ammunition. As we passed they would present-arms and look very ashamed of themselves. The Tibetans are not a military nation.

Going through the quiet rooms and shrines of the palaces,

obviously tended with such loving care, and more especially walking alone in the gardens, with the cooing of turtle-doves and the fragrance of flowers in the air, one could almost feel the presence of the Dalai Lamas, that mysterious spirit of the universe—call it Avalokita, Chenrezi, what you will—which was at that moment being so carefully sought in the person of a young child. But it is the ghost of the Great Thirteenth alone that haunts the Norbhu Lingka.

During our six months in Lhasa we heard so much of this great figure, whose name was mentioned always with respect amounting to adoration, that we were able to form a clear picture of the Precious Protector. Bell describes him as follows:

" The present Dalai Lama has a somewhat dark complexion, which is pitted, but not very deeply, with the marks of small-pox. His form and features reflect his humble parentage, but he moves and speaks with the natural dignity that is inherent in his race and is still further emphasized by the high position to which he has been called. As is natural in one who has perforce to mix much in worldly affairs, his face has not acquired the quiet expression of saintliness that distinguishes his brother Prelate at Tashi-lhünpo. His moustache, high eyebrows, and keen watchful eyes accentuate the impression of worldly cares, so that one who knew him but slightly would be apt to under-rate his spirituality. In actual fact he is in some ways more strict in his devotions than even the Tashi Lama. The quick deprecatory smile that lights up his features when he speaks, and his courtesy, which never failed, even when receiving unwelcome letters from our Government, could not but impress those who conversed with him."

Even the selection of this Pontiff was different and more convincing than that of his predecessors. When a Dalai Lama dies, the method of discovering his successor is most complicated. The child is usually of peasant stock, though during the time of close alliance between the Tibetans and Mongols the child was sometimes the son of a noble or royal Mongol family. The Ambans in Lhasa, when they had sufficient power, used to assist in making the choice. After a certain number of candidates had been chosen, the names and birthdays of the children were written on pieces of wood or paper and put into a golden

NORBHU LINGKA STABLES

CLOISONNE: LIONESS
PLAYING WITH HER CUB,
AT NORBHU LINGKA

FRESCO: MONGOLIAN
LEADING TIGER, IN THE
NORBHU LINGKA STABLES

urn. From this one would be withdrawn by the Amban with a pair of golden chop-sticks.

Often the Dalai Lama before he dies will give some indication to his ministers of the district or even of the house where he will reincarnate. The spirit does not transfer itself to a child born at the exact moment of the decease of the former incarnation; and as it takes several years to find the child, who must in any case pass beyond the age of infancy before he can exert any power, a Regent is chosen to be at the head of affairs. This Regent, or sometimes another incarnation lama, after spending some days in meditation, goes and gazes into the surface of a certain holy lake not far from Lhasa, where he sees a vision which will direct him to where the child is to be found. The Tashi Lama, the Abbots of Sera, Drepung and Garden monasteries, the State Oracle at Nechung, and other important lamas are consulted; and eventually by visions and other mystic means certain information is revealed as to the date of birth of the child and the occupation of his parents; of the type of country, and perhaps an actual description of topographical features in the neighbourhood of the house where the child is to be found.

At this stage expeditions are sent out from Lhasa to the districts of Tibet where it is foretold that the child will be found. They may be away for many years, crossing high passes and searching remote plateau villages for just such a house or hill or family as has been revealed in visions and dreams. In a likely locality any reports of miraculous births or portents and visions bearing on the whereabouts of the child are eagerly looked into by the search-parties. Eventually several possible children may be found, some uncertainty remaining as to which is the genuine incarnation of Chenrezi. The children are then put through various tests. The true incarnation may recognize servants and officials that he had about him in his former life; he should pick out his own teacup, prayer-wheel, bell and sacred thunderbolt from others, and frequently, in spite of his youth, he can indicate occurrences that happened to him in one of his former incarnations. In addition he usually has certain physical peculiarities which Bell gives as follows:

(a) Marks as of a tiger skin on his legs.
(b) Eyes and eyebrows that curve upwards on the outside and are rather long.

(c) Large ears.
(d) Two pieces of flesh near the shoulder-blades indicating the two other hands of Chenrezi.
(e) An imprint like a conch-shell on one of the palms of his hands.

The last Dalai Lama bore the last three signs. On the occasion of his selection the Tibetan Government assured the Amban that the choice was so certain that the ceremony of picking out the name with golden chop-sticks was unnecessary. The State Oracle at Nechung was also quite unwavering in his choice.

Born in 1876, it was not till he was eighteen that he took up the reins of government, the time between being spent in preparation—mainly of a religious character—for his high office. He was taken from his mother at the age of three and brought to the Potala and put in charge of the Master of the Bedchamber and the Court Physician. His four predecessors had all been " removed " by the Chinese before they were old enough to have any power, and this must have caused him considerable concern. It was not long before he discovered a conspiracy to kill him by witchcraft, in which the Regent, Abbot of Tengye-ling monastery, was implicated. It was alleged that he had condoned the preparation of a pair of boots which were presented to the young Dalai Lama. Sewn into the sole of these was a charm. which, as he walked, would speedily kill him. As a result of this conspiracy being discovered the Regent was imprisoned and treated so cruelly that he died. The other vicissitudes suffered by the late Dalai Lama have already been described in the chapter on the History of Tibet.

Even in these days of dictators one cannot but be amazed at his unrivalled power. Former Dalai Lamas—with the exception of the Great Fifth—had been pawns in the hands of ambitious and unscrupulous ministers, and for a hundred years prior to the accession of the last Prelate they had been quietly done away with before they were old enough to wield the Double Sceptre. But the last incarnation of Chenrezi, who would have been an exceptional man in any sphere of life, escaped by his own astuteness the dangers of poisoning and witchcraft; and despite certain violent and headstrong elements in his character, and the mistakes and vicissitudes of his early years, he built up for himself a position unique in the history of the Dalai Lamas.

In the sphere of internal administration his power was supreme, and he could and did enforce his will against the combined opposition of the Cabinet and Assembly. In foreign affairs he was supposed to act in conjunction with these two councils, but in point of fact he rarely consulted them; and, as the people of Tibet consider him literally as a God ruling on earth, his very words are inspired. Actually his power is limited by the difficulty of communications in Tibet and by the natural independence of the nomadic section of the population. In their mountain pastures there is no one to enforce the laws of distant Lhasa.

The two most important officers of the Dalai Lama's staff are the Lord Chamberlain (Chi-kyap Kempo), who is the head of all the monk officials in Tibet, and the Chief Secretary (Dronyer Chempo), who has ten under-secretaries in his office. There is a Court Physician (La-me Kempo) and four orderlies, who are usually of enormous size. It will be noticed that all these officials are monks, and as the Dalai is precluded by his exalted position from travelling about himself, it is through them that information is communicated to him; their power is therefore very great indeed.

When living at the Norbhu Lingka he would rise at dawn and spend two hours before breakfast at his devotions, praying not only for humanity but for all the animal kingdom—all " soul possessors ". The morning would be given up to matters of State for he personally settled all important questions of secular and religious administration. There might be a dispute between two landowners, a question of monastic discipline, an appeal against some decision of the Cabinet, the details of a ceremony to be arranged, a junior official to be appointed. All this was undertaken by the Dalai Lama personally. After an hour spent in prayer he would have lunch, and the afternoon would be spent in the same way as the morning. Any spare time would be devoted to walking round the Norbhu Lingka grounds looking at the flowers and playing with his dogs and other animals.

Again in the evening two more hours were spent in prayer and meditation; the hours until midnight or even later would be devoted to any especially serious problem that confronted him. At certain times of the year he would go into meditation for days, sometimes for months together, at the Norbhu Lingka or elsewhere. I was shown a room in the private monastery of Lhalu mansion and another in the Snake Temple where he used to stay on these occasions. A great deal of his time was taken up in blessing his subjects. When the Dalai travels, the whole countryside flock to be blessed. The monks from Drepung, Sera and Ganden must be blessed every year, each individual monk being then touched by the Dalai's hand. He was an indefatigable worker and his attendants used to complain that they rarely had sufficient sleep.

The Dalai Lama was much criticized in some quarters, especially by the envious supporters of Tashi-lhünpo, for mixing so much in worldly affairs. It was remarked that as an incarnation of Buddha he had no right in 1910 to order the Tibetans to oppose the Chinese and thereby cause considerable loss of life. He should, they said, have followed the example of his predecessors and have devoted his life to religious duties while his chief minister carried on the administration of secular affairs. He was also criticized by many for his harsh treatment of the plotting Regent of Tengye-ling monastery, whose rigorous imprisonment was said to be tantamount to murder. Naturally there will always be some who from jealousy or other motives criticize one who has the strength of character to assume such autocratic powers. But when the Dalai started to rule in 1893 some sort of reform was essential. When he died in 1933 a friend and protector had been found in Great Britain.

# CHAPTER ELEVEN

## MONASTERIES

IN Tibet religion always comes first, and God, says a Tibetan proverb, can only be approached through a lama. The monasteries are therefore the chief influence in the country. Now that there is a comparatively trained army in Lhasa the power of these strongholds of Lamaism is somewhat curtailed, but it is still incalculably great.

In the vicinity of Lhasa the great monasteries of Drepung, Sera and Ganden, known as the Three Pillars of the State, contain some 20,000 monks. It was with some excitement therefore that I heard on August 30th that we were going to visit Drepung, the largest monastery in the world. I hoped to find some answer to the questions that had continually occurred to me since entering Tibet: "How on earth do all these thousands of monks spend their time? how are they supported? and what good, if any, do they do?"

Drepung is supposed to house 7700 monks, but sometimes as many as 10,000 live there. The name Dre-pung literally means "the pile of rice", which is what the monastery resembles, as its tiers of whitewashed buildings lie one behind the other on a sloping site at the head of a wedge-shaped valley. Looked at from a distance, Drepung resembles a large fortified city rather than a single monastery, and it is only when one climbs the steep mountain slopes behind it and looks down on to its innumerable ramifications that one gets a true idea of its immense size. Looked at from below it is foreshortened and many of the buildings are dwarfed or hidden.

The monastery was founded at the beginning of the fifteenth century by the son of a poor herdsman from eastern Tibet, who was a disciple of Tsong-kapa. It was he also who founded the great monastery of Tashi-lhünpo at Shigatse in the middle of the fifteenth century.

Outside the monastery wall a number of very dirty boys dressed in dishevelled monks' robes were playing among the huge boulders; but in anticipation of our visit the majority of the monks had been ordered to keep to their cells so that we would not be inconvenienced by their crowding round and staring at us. As we entered through a ponderous gate in the long southern wall we were met by two *shengoes* or proctors, who are responsible for keeping order in the monastery. They were dressed in robes more scarlet in colour than the usual dull red of the monk's dress. They wore sleeveless undercoats of red and gold brocade and their shoulders were built up and padded to give them an additional air of importance. These proctors were preceded by two lictors who carried curious square iron maces damascened with golden dragons. Perched on the top of these maces were the proctors' yellow crested hats. As we walked along the narrow ways and steep staircases of the monastery these men preceded us, shouting every now and then in stentorian tones, " Pha gyuk " (get out of the way).

We were first taken along a paved roadway, up a steep hill to the main assembly hall. The heavily bossed entrance door lay at the top of a long flight of stone steps twenty yards in width. Outside the door was an anteroom or portico with its roof supported by several enormous fluted pillars of wood. These were each made of several poplar trunks, the components being held together with iron bands. The walls of this anteroom were covered by vast paintings of guardian deities : one red-faced, with grinning fangs, others pale and terrible. These are the four Celestial Kings of the Quarters who guard the universe against the attacks of the outer demons. Other frescoes depict the tortures of poor mortals in the never-ending lives to come.

The Lamaists are great connoisseurs of hells. They recognize some thousands, of which there are sixteen specially select abodes, eight of which are hot and eight cold. These hells, whose varied forms of entertainment bear a close resemblance to the torments of Dante's Inferno, are carefully graded. As well as a wide choice of punishments for commonplace sinners, there are others worthy of note. There is a hell for doctors who kill their patients through incompetence; in this the victims are scarified and clumsily dissected, only to be reunited and revived so that the process can continue indefinitely. Busybodies are nailed down, black lines are drawn on their bodies as a guide to red-hot saws which cut them to pieces; the tongue, enlarged and pegged out, is harrowed by hot spikes. Those who cast refuse or dead bodies on the public roads are pounded in iron mortars and beaten on anvils. Men who grumble against the weather or obstruct watercourses (an obscure connection !) have molten iron poured down their throats. There is a special hell for stupid people, for to the Buddhist unawareness or wilful lack of perception is one of the major sins. In the cold hells, the sinners are immersed in glacier water and the resulting chilblains are aggravated and torn. There are also hells of tantalization wherein the starving victim is surrounded by choice foods which he cannot enjoy, as his mouth is a mere pinprick; and if the poor starveling does succeed in swallowing anything it is turned to lacerating knives and molten metal.

The celebrated Wheel of Life painting, of which there are some fine examples at Drepung, eloquently depicts the endless birth, death and rebirth of man, which is inevitable unless he can escape this eternal circle and attain Buddhahood. The wheel is clutched by a snarling monster. Outside the wheel are two or more figures of Buddhas who have escaped from the circle. In the very centre, as it were the hub of the wheel, are a cock, a serpent and a pig, each grasping in its mouth the tail of the next. These are symbolic of lust, hatred and ignorance : the three sins necessitating rebirth. The six main segments, divided by the " spokes " of the wheel, show the six worlds of rebirth : Heaven, the home of demi-gods or Titans, the animal world, the various hells, the abode of tantalized spirits, and the realm of mankind. In each region is shown a Buddha, who, like the Dalai Lama, has foregone his right to Nirvana in order to help mortals struggling in the inexorable grip of the wheel. The outer rim, divided into twelve partitions, shows the phases of a man's life as symbolizing the causes of rebirth.

Inside the assembly room there were no windows, and the immense room was only dimly lit through the doorway and by a number of spaces left around the central part of the roof-lantern, which was raised higher than the surrounding cloister. The roof was supported by massive square wooden pillars, the lower parts of which were swathed in dark red cloth. On the floor were long strips of cushioned cloth on which the monks could sit; there were raised seats at the end for the officiating monks. On the walls, as far as one could see in the dim light, were gruesome paintings, recesses containing images, and, higher up, lines of richly coloured thankas framed in brocade. At the end of the hall opposite the door was a row of the usual Lamaist images, some of them of immense size. The smaller images of gold were so covered in white scarves that it was difficult to recognize them. Their head-dresses were magnificently bejewelled. On the shelves in front of the images were rows of butter-lamps, holy-water vessels, libation jugs and curiously wrought shapes in butter and tsamba dough. The hall had a heavy, sickly smell, a mixture of incense and rancid butter from the spillings of the monks' tea. The stone flags on the floor, and indeed everything one touched, were thick with sticky grease from the same source.

Drepung is divided into four colleges, each presided over by an Abbot : it was by the careful appointment of these officials that the late Dalai Lama was able to subdue this turbulent monastery. Each college houses monks from a different locality; one being favoured by Khampas, another by Mongolians, and so on.

We drank tea, or hot sweet milk of a curious mauve colour, with each of the Abbots in turn, and were offered heaped-up dishes of rice, sweet cakes and dried fruits. Before eating any rice it is customary to take a few grains between the thumb and middle finger and to scatter it as a libation to the gods. It took some hours to make the tour of the monastery, and even then we must have left out many of the buildings.

We were shown a room used by the great fifth Dalai Lama; it has been kept exactly as he had it in the seventeenth century, when he left the monastery and set about building the new Potala Palace. This custom of retaining undisturbed a room used by some holy lama is common in Lhasa; we were shown several rooms in private houses, usually furnished as chapels, where the last Dalai Lama had stayed.

We must have seen literally hundreds of images at Drepung, some of them being of gigantic size. They were usually dressed in gold brocade and had a silken canopy above their heads. The expressions of some were formal, of others most life-like. Among the latter was a row of effigies of previous incarnation lamas of the monastery; each was depicted in his monk's robe and crested yellow cap like a Roman helmet. We saw five images of the goddess Drölma (or Mary), each one of which was alleged to have uttered words. In another hall there was a striking image of the late Dalai Lama.

We visited some of the monks' cells. The richer brethren or those of noble family have rooms to themselves or share accommodation with a few chosen friends; the poorer monks live in large dormitories. The small cells that we visited had by way of furniture a simple altar, a padded cushion seat which would serve as a bed, and a low carved table. We saw the kitchen too, a dark smoky hall with a number of copper cauldrons six feet across and three or four feet deep. It is in these that the buttered tea is made which, with a few handfuls of barley meal, forms the daily fare of the monks. It must be an exacting task to be in charge of the catering and cleanliness of so many thousands of men. And although the monks themselves looked and smelled as if they had never washed, yet the streets and byways of the monastery were noticeably cleaner than those of Lhasa. There is an underground sewer running the whole length of the monastery and this takes all refuse to some sort of cess-pit, a settling tank a mile away.

The roofs of the buildings are particularly striking. As a rule they are flat and surrounded by a parapet, at the corners of which, and at frequent intervals between, are cylindrical banners held aloft on long poles. These are to frighten away evil spirits. The roofs of the main halls are surmounted by gilt pagodas of Chinese design, similar to those on the summit of the Potala. To relieve the monotony of the white walls pierced by symmetrical rows of windows, many of the roofs are finished by a layer of dull red willow-twig walling six or eight feet high. These form an excellent background for the circular gold emblems with which the upper part of the walls are ornamented. On the parapets above these red layers are cylinders as much as twelve feet high and a yard in diameter, covered with exquisitely chased gold leaf of considerable thickness. In the very centre of the roof is a similarly worked screen about five feet high and three feet wide which is used as a rest for the long monastery trumpets.

After following the custom of giving a very substantial cash present to the monastery, we departed, carrying with us a confused impression of rows of enormous sardonic images in dimly lit halls; steep narrow alleyways with towering walls leaning back on either side; solid gold butter-lamps; slippery, greasy ladders leading from one storey to another; grotesque but wonderfully richly coloured paintings of hideous demons, and everywhere that all-pervading but indescribable smell—a compound of rancid butter, stale incense, musty age-old buildings and unwashed human bodies.

When we emerged from Drepung we saw that many trestle stalls had been put up just outside the main gate. Nearly all the vendors were women; raw meat was the chief article for sale, but there were also vegetables, dried fruits and cigarettes obtainable. The Tibetans are the most tolerant people in the world. Tobacco is strictly forbidden for the monks—though snuff is allowed; and the ban against taking life goes to the very root of the Buddhist religion. Yet they are sensible enough to realize that in a climate such as is found at Lhasa, meat is practically a necessity. The high lamas satisfy their consciences by saying that the spirit of the yak or sheep that is eaten by them will reincarnate in a higher plane in its next life.

In the middle of October we visited Sera monastery, the second largest in the world, with a nominal total of 5500 monks. Drepung, containing a large proportion of Mongolians, Kalmuks and other aliens, has a reputation for being pro-Chinese and against the Lhasa government, while Sera has a more patriotic record. The arrogant Drepung monks, who had always had too much of their own way, viewed with concern the rising power of the army. They realized that this would limit their power; for in the old days with 20,000 monks in the vicinity of the city, and no one to oppose them, their power was unrivalled. This was especially so at the time of the Great Prayer, the chief annual festival, which lasts for the first three weeks of the Tibetan year. During this time the monks have complete control of the city, and some 30,000 of them billet themselves on the inhabitants.

In 1920, when the Dalai Lama was increasing the army, there was considerable friction, and at the time of the New Year it was feared that the monks would get out of control. Some thousands of the Drepung monks marched to the Norbhu Lingka with certain demands. It was only the prompt and decisive action of the Dalai Lama that averted serious trouble. He put Lhasa out of bounds for the military during the time that the monks were installed there. A few months after this there was some internal trouble in Drepung over a question of discipline, and half the monks came out in open rebellion, threatening to attack Lhasa. The Tibetan Government sent Tsarong, who was then commander-in-chief, to besiege the monastery, which gave in after some resistance. The Dalai Lama, having shown that he would stand no nonsense, treated the culprits with characteristic leniency. It is moreover noteworthy that when the Government troops searched the monastery they found an enormous supply of arms and a complete plant for forging Tibetan currency.

Sera, on the other hand, has always been anti-China and has been repeatedly attacked by Chinese troops. The word Sera probably means " hail ", and is said to have been given to it because the hail of Sera scatters the rice of Drepung; a comparison indicating the abiding rivalry of these two institutions. Another school of thought holds that Sera means " wild-rose fence ", a name given to it by the disciples of Tsong-kapa who founded the monastery in 1419 upon the site of a smaller institution which was surrounded by wild-rose bushes. Sera is supposed to keep a large band of fighting monks who spend their time in continuous training on a secret parade-ground at the back of the monastery. I spent some time searching for this with field-glasses from a convenient station on the steep hill-side behind the monastery, but could see no place where it could exist. But in the next valley to Sera is a long-jump pitch where the monks were often to be seen taking exercise; this is one of their favourite sports. A sloping run is built up so that the take-off is three or four feet higher than the landing pit, the latter being full of sand. The performers that I watched had no style at all; they would go through the air with legs and arms flying in all directions. As with Drepung, it is only from above that one can get a true conception of the great size of this monastery, whose buildings run far back into a deep V-shaped valley. As the slope of the site is only slight, it gives the impression from the front of being about a quarter the size of Drepung.

One of the most cherished possessions of Sera is a sacred dagger which is believed to have been found on a hill-side near the monastery after having been miraculously transported from India. It is the model of the *dorje* (" thunderbolt ") daggers that are used in Buddhist ceremonies for stabbing invisible demons of the air. During the New Year festival this dagger, which possesses miraculous powers, is taken in solemn procession to Lhasa City.

Ganden, the third " Pillar of the State ", lies about thirty-five miles to the north-east of Lhasa. We contemplated a visit there, but it was not till after the main body of the Mission had returned that Richardson found time to go. There are some 3300 lamas at Ganden. The monastery is famous for the tomb of the founder, Tsong-kapa, whose body is embalmed there. It is also the chief seat of learning in a country, where wisdom is considered the highest attainment of man, and where the human mind is credited with such powers as controlling the weather and dealing life and death.

Among the laity it is very rare in this feudal land for a man of low birth to attain to high position; but a monk, if he is sufficiently astute and hard-working, can rise to the highest eminence. Many of the Abbots of the great monasteries are drawn from humble families. These Abbots preside over the National Assembly which is summoned on urgent occasions. And during the absence of the Dalai Lama on the occasion of the Younghusband Mission, the Abbot of Ganden acted as Regent and signed the treaty between the Governments of India and Tibet. In fact the " Enthroned of Ganden ", an appointment that is made purely on qualifications of learning, ranks chief among the non-incarnate lamas of Tibet and next in precedence after the Dalai and Tashi Lamas.

There are several great monasteries in the city of Lhasa. The most famous of these are the four " Lings "—Tengye-ling, Gundeling, Tsomo-ling, Tsecho-ling—which, together with Reting and Murn, have the privilege of supplying a Regent during the minority of the Dalai Lama. Of these, Tenge-ling has been destroyed, its considerable estates confiscated by the Government, and its monks dispersed.

Practically half the revenue of the State is devoted to the upkeep of the monasteries, either in the form of grants of land or in gifts of barley, butter and tea. Up till 1912 the Chinese, as well as paying large cash presents to the monasteries, supplied annually thousands of mule-loads of brick tea. Another source of income is forthcoming in the form of gifts from regular worshippers and pilgrims. Fees are also paid on the innumerable occasions when monks have to be called in, or special prayers offered at the monasteries; when a man sets out on a journey, in case of illness, to avert misfortune, or to celebrate a birth, marriage or death. The monks are not slow to exploit the power that is given to them by the superstitious and credulous Tibetan. The Lamaist mythology, adding the deities and devils of Buddhism and Hinduism to the already overcrowded pantheon of Pönism, is overburdened with an unbelievable variety of Buddhas, saints, Titans, celestial guardians, tutelary demons, she-devils, genii, fiends, furies and familiar spirits. All these must be worshipped, propitiated or appeased, and only the lama, possessing the skeleton key to heaven, hell and all intermediate regions, can act as guide through this formidable maze. Rigidly prescribed offerings must be made, horoscopes have to be cast, auspicious days for journeys and all the events of life must be discovered, prayer-flags and charms have to be correctly drawn up and consecrated, and prayers must be offered. In a thousand ways the co-operation of the lama is needed by the layman to avoid perdition and to give him the highest possible chance of a successful rebirth. It is not surprising that the monasteries are the most wealthy and powerful institutions in Tibet.

Many of the smaller monasteries and nunneries are founded and supported by wealthy families, and the monks and nuns therein recruited from their tenantry. Among the noble families of Lhasa, as their estates are lent rent-free by the Government, the eldest, and often the second son, is expected to go into the service of the State, while the younger son becomes a monk official. For the poorer families the priesthood offers prospects of a career, as any boy with the requisite capacity and energy can rise to the highest positions in the monasteries, or can be nominated to the school for monk officials at the Potala; whereas the lay branch of Government service is almost entirely restricted to the ancient families.

Tibet is a poor country, and the land will support only a certain number of people. If the working families have more children than they can afford to keep, the surplus are sent to the neighbouring monastery or nunnery, where they are brought up at the expense of the State. More than one-sixth of the male population of Tibet are monks. Boys destined for the priesthood go to the monastery when they are seven or eight years old. Sometimes we saw even younger ones there, but these were probably orphans who were being brought up by the monastery from childhood. Not all are eligible. Buddhists, being more consistent in this respect than ourselves, insist that a man's means of livelihood shall be above reproach, so those whose families are connected with trades having to do with the taking of life are not permitted to enter the priesthood. Such are the body-cutters, butchers, tanners, leather-workers and gunsmiths. A high physical standard is also demanded; boys with any deformity of limb or speech are not accepted.

A successful applicant is handed over to the charge of a monk instructor who is personally responsible for his education and discipline. The education consists in learning to read and write and in memorizing passages of the scriptures. At this period he is expected to act as a servant to his tutor. If the boy passes his examinations he is then admitted to a college, and after taking certain vows, he becomes a novice or student monk and is allowed to wear the terra-cotta-coloured robes of the priesthood. Some monks never rise above this stage. After this there are various examinations to be passed, each opening the door to successive well-defined positions. The chief qualification is to be able to memorize page after page of the one hundred and eight volumes of the Buddhist scriptures. Not all the young monks follow a career of learning; at an early stage they can choose a life suited to their special aptitudes. If a man shows outstanding skill in painting, wood-carving or in writing the complicated Tibetan script, his talents can be utilized for the benefit of the monastery. If he shows promise as a healer, he goes to the Iron Hill to study medicine. Should he be particularly agile or graceful, he is trained to take part in the lama dances which mark various religious festivals. He may also be a cook, agriculturist, accountant or even an astrologer or sorcerer. Tibetans are born traders, and many of the monasteries augment their incomes by considerable business enterprise. Some of the monks, therefore, presumably those who find too late that they are unsuited to a life of contemplation and learning, devote their energies to trade.

Many of the larger houses of Lhasa have a special altar-room where several monks at all times of the day are to be heard droning prayers for the benefit of departed ancestors, to avert misfortunes, to advance the fortunes of the house, to bring good health, or for some other purpose. These men are looked after and paid; after a time they return to their monastery and others take their places.

When prayers are being held in the main temple of the monastery the Lamaist liturgies follow traditional lines. On the occasion of our visit to Sera monastery a service was in progress, and we were invited to look in for a moment through the open door of the temple. Errant beams of sunlight percolated through the roof-lantern and slanted across the huge square pillars wrapped in red cloth as though with puttees. A row of richly coloured thankas hung from the edge of the colonnade roof. From the doorway an aisle led to the high altar, where a row of butter-lamps threw a ghostly light on to the images, which were hardly distinguishable from the officiating monk, who was raised on a seat above his fellows.

On either side of the aisle lines of monks faced each other, sitting Buddha-fashion on padded cushions. Row after row of shaven-headed, red-robed monks disappeared into the shadows beneath the overhanging colonnade. As the room was in no way heated, each man wore a heavy pleated cape over his shoulders. Some of them were boys of seven or eight years of age, and these seemed to be in the charge of tutors. Several younger monks came round with teapots, and each worshipper produced a wooden cup from the folds of his robes. After drinking the tea the cup was licked clean and replaced. The service continued. There was a burst of music—shrill notes from the cornets, the clashing of cymbals, the insistent beating of gongs, and then a shattering resonant blast from the long trumpets.

The service seemed to be in the form of a litany : the officiating monk would chant a few sentences, punctuated by the occasional ringing of a bell and the clattering of his skull drum, and then the congregation of monks would return the response, the shrill tenor of the acolytes blending with the preternaturally deep bass of the others. Upon enquiry we discovered that their prayers were to avert a hailstorm whose advent had recently been foretold by the Sera oracle.

Sometimes the monks were simply reciting passages of the Scriptures. This they did in deep complaining undulating voices, the first note of a sentence being spoken in a higher tone. Often they were not all reciting the same passage, for if several chapters are run through by different groups concurrently they naturally cover more ground. At times they swayed backwards and forwards in time to the prayer. The object of their devotion is not only to avert disaster but to heal the sick, to hasten the birth of a child, or simply to pray for all creation—man, animal, bird, fish, insect, all " mind possessors ". When the Great War broke out, for instance, the Dalai Lama, as well as offering us two contingents of Tibetan troops, ordained that in all the monasteries of Tibet part of the time reserved for prayers on behalf of the Tibetan Government should be devoted to praying for the success of the Allies.

The ritual and chanting at once recall a Roman Catholic High Mass. Indeed there are so many points of similarity between the two religions that it has been suggested that Lamaism incorporated some of the ritual of the Lazarist and Capuchin fathers who visited Lhasa in the eighteenth century. Enforced celibacy, the use of the rosary and of swinging censers for scattering incense, the continuous repetition of prayers even though the words are not understood, the method of chanting the services—are points of similarity.

But these are only superficial resemblances. In character the two religions are fundamentally different. The Lamaist monk does not spend his time in ministering to the people or educating them, nor do laymen take part in or even attend the monastery services. The beggar beside the road is nothing to the monk. Knowledge is the jealously guarded prerogative of the monastery and is used to increase their influence and wealth. Another essential difference is in dogma. The Catholics are bound by strict rules, and what they must believe is carefully laid down. Not so the Tibetan monk. As long as he attends the service in the monastery temple and is subject to the lay discipline of the proctors, he can pursue any spiritual goal and can endeavour to reach it by whatever means he chooses. He may follow and teach and believe whatever doctrine appeals to him. Moreover, he shares in no community life. If a monk can afford it he keeps his own establishment within the monastery. If his home is near by he will have meals sent in to his apartments. Another way in which Lamaism differs from Catholicism is in its tolerance, which is as admirable as it is remarkable. Father Desideri, one of the Jesuits who was at Lhasa in the early eighteenth century, wrote a book in Tibetan rejecting the tenets of the Lamaist doctrine and defending those of the Catholic faith; he describes how his house became full of monks, especially from Drepung and Sera, who came to read and discuss his book.

Each summer the monks leave their monastery and have a holiday, which varies in length from ten to fifteen days according to the wealth of each monastic college. One day in the middle of September (the last day of the seventh Tibetan month) we met the Drepung monks streaming towards Lhasa to receive the Regent's blessing before starting their holiday. Mounted in the middle of the straggling procession were the proctors in scarlet robes and yellow crested hats, preceded by their stalwart mace-bearers, whose powerful bellowing rapidly cleared the road. The Abbots and other dignitaries, including an incarnation lama of Drepung, followed, each with his retinue of mounted servants in tall cylindrical yellow hats or the red-tasselled head-dress of the ordinary lay servant. Many of the monks carried sheeps' carcasses, cooking utensils, furniture and tents. On this occasion the monks take their annual bath, being forced to go to the river, wash their greasy clothes, and at the same time give their bodies the one immersion of the year.

DREPUNG MONASTERY, THE LARGEST MONASTERY IN THE WORLD

MONASTERY TO THE NORTH OF LHASA

Once when we visited Gundeling, sometime in early December, a strange ceremony was taking place in a corner of the open courtyard. A bearded monk, wearing a strange fan-shaped hat, was sitting on a wooden throne before an open fire of willow logs. On the other side of the fire were about a hundred monks sitting on the courtyard floor. They were all curiously attired. Some played cymbals, others drums or shrill trumpets. At the side were the long monastery trumpets resting on special supports. Beside the officiating priest was a large table covered with some thirty or forty dishes containing different sorts of herbs and magical ingredients, which would be passed to him in turn by an attendant. He would mutter incantations, make mysterious passes with his hands over each bowl, and then throw its contents into the flames. The chorus would sing, cymbals would clash, drums beat and trumpets boom. Upon enquiry we were told that the object of this strange performance was to prevent disease, which is apt to become rife in Tibet as autumn passes to winter.

As well as the large and famous monasteries there are innumerable smaller institutions. Each village or hamlet has its own monastery, which is usually the most imposing building in the place. And often there are remote monasteries far from the haunts of men, perched up on some precipitous rock-face or away at the extremity of some unfrequented valley. From the earliest times Buddhists, following the example of Gautama, have forsaken, for varying periods of time, the distracting haunts of men and have retired into these desolate hermitages to attain enlightenment or supernatural powers by meditation and self-abnegation. Every Tibetan monk is supposed during his lifetime to spend a period of three years, three months and three days in solitary meditation. Naturally it is not by any means all of them who spend even three days in such confinement.

Near Gyantse there is a hermitage where numbers of monks immure themselves for life. It was founded by Mila-Repa, the great hermit saint, more than eight hundred years ago. At first they retire only for a few months; then after a further period of preparation they are walled in for three years, three months and three days. Once more they emerge before undergoing the final period of entombment, which lasts until they die. The cells are perched among the crags of a rocky hill-side. Once the hermit has been locked into his diminutive stone cell he is in absolute

M

darkness. There is a small drain running through the room, and an opening, closed by a sliding door, through which his tea and tsamba are passed daily. But even the hand that appears to take this food is gloved. Many of these deluded devotees lose their reason before the final lifelong immurement, though they may at any time terminate this self-imprisonment. For a real ascetic to retire into the wilderness or solitary place is a different matter; but these Gyantse anchorites are of a debased type who are capable only of the physical and mechanical part of the hermit's life. This is one of the many ways in which Lamaism has exaggerated the letter of Buddha's laws while being incapable of carrying out their spiritual counterpart.

The Tibetan word for a monastery, *gompa*, literally means "secluded place", and the early monks, like those in our own country, had a genius for choosing the most attractive sites. Unless the building is in the open plain it usually faces south and has its back against the mountains, from which its water-supply is drawn. Often up in the hills above the main part of the monastery is some lonely hermitage where the monks can retire for peace and meditation. Certainly the majority of the monks that one saw in the monasteries or met on the road were anything but ascetic in appearance, but in these remote retreats, far from the disturbing haunts of man, they may have developed that store of occult wisdom for which the Tibetan monk has always been famous.

Lamaism, from the early days of the eighth century when Padma Sambhava preached the debased Tantrik doctrine that had replaced the original pure teaching of Buddha, has always delighted in demonology, oracles and other manifestations of black and mystic arts. Lamaism is still farther removed from pure Buddhism by having adopted many of the practices and beliefs of the earlier Pön religion of pure devil-worship and the propitiation of countless malignant devils both in this life and in the endless cycles of life to come.

The Tibetans have a genius for credulity. They believe implicitly in various psychic phenomena such as are described by that remarkable traveller, Madame David Neel. Though I was never fortunate enough to witness these myself, everybody talked of such things as beyond any possibility of doubt, and many had had first-hand experience of them. Among these powers is that of generating internal heat (*tumo*), which enables ill-clad under-nourished hermits to endure the bitter Tibetan winter at 15,000 feet above sea-level. This power is only attained after a long course of probationary exercises. The breathing must be carefully regulated, and the novice must have the power of dissociating his mind from his body. These men, having once learnt the art, can immerse themselves in icy streams so that the clothes afterwards freeze upon their bodies, and then sit motionless throughout the night, and by concentrating their minds and controlling their breathing can sink into a trance which leaves them oblivious of anything so mundane as the temperature. It was this power that sustained the great Tibetan hermit saint, Mila-Repa, when he was cut off by deep snow and had to winter among the glaciers of Mount Everest.

There are other saintly men who can so control their breathing that they can cover immense distances in a very short time. Men who have met these *lung-gom-pa* declare that they progress in a series of rhythmic bounds with their eyes gazing into the far distance. Their bodies sometimes become so light that they have to be weighted down to prevent them floating away. Other of the supernatural accomplishments of the Tibetans are to send messages by telepathy and to read thoughts. The theory of levitation is also understood: maintaining the cross-legged Buddha attitude, certain men can rise into the air as if they were floating, or perch on the summit of a pile of rice without disturbing a single grain.

To what extent these mysterious powers are really possessed by Tibetans I would hesitate to assert. The power of mind over body is being more and more demonstrated by the study of *Yogi*. It is almost certain that if one *has* the necessary faith, one can, literally, remove mountains. It must be borne in mind that to become possessed of these supernatural powers a course of study lasting for many years is necessary, and then it is not all who can succeed, even when taught by eastern ascetics, who maintain an age-long tradition of psychic research and experience. In any case, it is interesting that many of the holiest lamas believe that these psychic exercises are a waste of time and interfere with the search for true enlightenment.

## CHAPTER TWELVE

### FESTIVALS AND PROCESSIONS

THE Tibetans, in common with most Orientals, are very fond of ceremonial processions and the observation of festivals and saints' days; and during our six months at Lhasa we were the fortunate spectators of several such celebrations, for the Tibetan officials and people, in spite of their general policy of seclusion, were anxious that we, as their guests, should be given full opportunity to witness these scenes of gorgeous pageantry and ceremonial. If we were not formally invited by the Government we would usually receive a special message from Tsarong or from some other official telling us what was toward and where we should with most advantage station ourselves. Apart from the New Year festivities, which are of such importance that they demand a separate chapter, the most spectacular procession was on the occasion of the Regent going on tour.

Although Tibetans in general, being a nomadic people, are great travellers, the Lhasa officials are a strangely sedentary class: the Prime Minister had never ventured farther from Lhasa than Trisum Bridge, about eight miles to the south-west. Many of the officials, unless they had held office away from Lhasa, had never been more than a day's journey from the city. This was partly a matter of custom, and partly due to the difficulty of getting any leave from an official job. But the Regent, by these standards, was a great traveller, and this saved him from the narrow-mindedness which must inevitably limit the outlook of one whose whole life has been spent in a single city. The Regent originally came from Reting monastery, sixty miles to the north of Lhasa, and now he was about to visit Samye, fifty miles to the south-east, on the Tsang-po river. Samye is the oldest of the larger Tibetan monasteries, having been founded by Padma Sambhava, who was summoned from India in the eighth century by one of the early kings of Tibet. Some portions of Samye had been rebuilt and the Regent's consecration was necessary, his presence being of special importance, since he had to preside over the ceremony of replacing the golden ornaments on the roof. On such an occasion the officials who are remaining behind have to present scarves of leave-taking to the Regent after accompanying him for a few miles of the way. As the Kya Chu had to be crossed some four miles to the east of Lhasa, this formed a convenient place for leave-taking, and a large tent had been put up on the bank of the river, so that the officials could present scarves and drink tea there. Gould had intended to present a scarf himself, but in the end it was diplomatically decided that Richardson should deputize for him; so he and Norbhu took their places in the procession while Nepean and I accompanied them to take photographs. We took several clerks and half a dozen scarlet-coated retainers to compete with the Chinese who would also be there. In the eyes of the Tibetans these things are of considerable importance: an official has as many servants and wears as sumptuous clothes as his rank and means will allow.

The procession, which was over a mile in length, was the most brilliant and splendid pageant I have ever seen. Although there were heavy clouds over the mountains, the sky above was clear and the sun shone on an endless variety of exquisitely beautiful costumes. The cavalcade—there must have been about five hundred horsemen—started from the Regent's summer palace between the western end of the city and the Potala, and passed through the whole length of Lhasa. Everywhere the streets were crowded with people trying to catch a rare glimpse of the *Po gye-tshap rimpoche*, "the precious one instead of the king". Monks holding silken banners suspended from long staffs lined the route, while servants dressed in homespun robes and saucer hats kept the crowd back with whips, and drove stray cattle and inquisitive dogs from the roadway.

In the front of the procession was a horseman holding aloft a sacred painting hanging from a pole: this was to ward off evil. Behind him rode half a dozen others carrying staffs surmounted by cylindrical silk hangings. These men were dressed in Mongolian robes of gold and silver thread, and wore tall conical witches' hats. They were followed by a hundred or so officials riding two or three abreast. There were monk officials in mulberry-coloured robes edged with silk, gaily embroidered undercoats and wide-brimmed papier-mâché hats lacquered with dark gold, or yellow woollen hats shaped like legionaries' helmets; Shap-pes in scarlet-tasselled wide-brimmed hats and robes of heavy flowered brocade; tiny incarnation lamas or sons of noble family sitting in bucket-saddles from which it is almost impossible to be thrown. Depöns, Dzasas, Tejis, Dzongpöns—all the officials of Lhasa vying with each other to wear the brightest silks, the richest turquoise and coral ornaments, the most gorgeous horse-trappings.

In the middle of the procession came the Regent himself, carried in a highly ornamented palanquin of dark red-gold lacquer. His six bearers wore wide, flat, scarlet hats, vivid green coats, white trousers and black knee-boots. Beside him, in attendance, walked several high officials, one of them with his hand steadying the palanquin, and a servant with an immense valanced umbrella of State held precariously aloft on a long staff.

The procession passed the Muru monastery, skirted the Mohammedan quarter of the town, and then crossed some level marshy land by a very stony track, lined all the way by people. There were many walled lingkas here between the road and the river, with fine poplar and willow trees and green grass beneath. About three miles from the city, just where the track and the river converged, a company of the Tibetan Army had been drawn up as a guard of honour. Beyond these, just short of some rather fine country houses resting solidly among trees, several tents had been put up. The largest of these was sheltered by a deep canopy ornamented with a blue and scarlet dragon pattern in appliqué work. In front of this tent, open to the sky, was a canvas enclosure wherein the officials would take tea. Under the awning was a pile of silken cushions and a wooden lacquered tea-table for the Regent; in front of this were seats of different height according to rank.

In the smaller tent near by, the tea was being brewed in earthenware kettles over yak-dung and juniper-wood fires. Here were four massive silver-gilt teapots used for taking the tea to the officials.

Nepean and I had ridden ahead of the procession so as to photograph its arrival. Although there were several hundred officials and servants on horseback, at least a hundred had been sent ahead to prepare the tent, and they were already waiting, sitting in groups on the grass or standing about gossiping. All the officials were wearing special ceremonial dress; the higher ones, instead of their saffron-coloured silk robes, wore dresses of a heavier brocade embroidered with blue and gold dragons. There was considerable variety of pattern and material and some of the dresses seemed to be very old. The junior officials wore a most attractive dress called *Geluchey*. This consists of a short jacket of very thick brocade with long sleeves made up of several transverse strips of different-coloured material. Here again there was much variety, and some of the jackets were extraordinarily beautiful. Over one shoulder and across the chest lay a voluminous roll of silk made up of small rectangles of every imaginable colour, and wide sashes of varied colour and design were tied so that their frilled ends hung over the long pleated black satin skirt which came down to high claret-coloured boots decorated with a white crossing pattern. On their heads they wore comic little white cockle hats designed to protect the top-knot and charm-box. On each shoulder, set towards the front, were turquoise and gold ornaments, one shaped like a whelk shell and the other a flat rosette. In former times these were suspended from the top of the head and worn as earrings. The monk officials wore special robes with a wide border of red-and-gold brocade to the skirt, and sleeves of the same material as their mulberry-coloured robes. As always, there were innumerable servants and attendant monks; the former in dark broadcloth robes and wide scarlet hats, the latter bare-headed and wearing the flowing monks' robe and heavy clumsy boots with turned-up toes.

The Regent's palanquin was halted near the reception tent and he walked the last hundred yards through ranks of bowing officials. He was bare-headed and dressed in embroidered silk robes of vermilion and gold. He moved with the awkward shuffling gait of one unused to much walking. When the Regent had taken his seat all the officials prostrated themselves three times before him, touching the ground with their foreheads. Then, carefully shepherded by two of the gigantic monk orderlies, they came forward in order of precedence and each offered a white scarf, which was taken by an attendant. According to rank each was blessed either with both hands or one hand, or with a tassel on the end of a stick.

When all the scarves had been offered the company sat down and tea and rice were handed round. Norbhu and Richardson sat apart from the Tibetan officials directly on the right of the Regent; while the Chinese, who had arrived thirty strong with flying banners and an armed escort, sat in a place of less honour on the Regent's left. After half an hour the Regent left the tent and was carried the short distance down to the river-bank, where two yak-hide coracles had been lashed together and completely covered with yellow cloth.

I had taken up a commanding position on a stone breakwater overlooking the embarking place. I shall never forget that scene: the turbulent green and blue of the rushing Kyi Chu, still swollen from the summer rains; the pale blue sky edged with heavy masses of cumulus cloud casting dark shadows on the surrounding mountains; the milky emerald green of the willow trees fringing the river-bank; a large flock of goosanders flying overhead; the chattering crowd of women coyly pretending to avoid my cameras; and the fantastic coracles sitting right on top of the water like empty boxes, swathed even to the paddles in bright yellow cloth. Suddenly the crowd became silent and, through a gap in the flood-bank, the palanquin appeared and was borne down the sandy slope to the water's edge, making a wonderful mass of colour in the clear Tibetan sunlight—the scarlet, green and white of the bearers, the glowing red-gold lacquer of the palanquin, the mulberry-coloured dress of the Lord Chamberlain and Chief Secretary walking in front, the scarlet-tasselled hats and blue and gold robes of the Shap-pes walking alongside.

The Regent, a small, ascetic, almost apologetic figure, stepped from his palanquin and was helped into a seat of embroidered cushions in the stern of one of the coracles. The more senior ministers got in beside him and, sacrificing the dictates of safety to those of propriety, stood up for the whole crossing. The boatmen pulled out into the current and the light coracles were immediately swept away to land on the farther side nearly half a mile lower down. In another boat a young official—presumably a bad sailor—stood with his arms held above his head in prayer. Farther down, where the river was narrower, they were swimming the ponies across. On the far side another tent and, presumably, more tea were awaiting the party.

Those officials who were staying in Lhasa rode slowly homeward, preceded and followed by their servants in the Tibetan manner. Tsarong joined us, and we had a breakfast picnic on the banks of the river.

On 23rd November the Regent returned from Reting. As he came by Chaksam ferry and Chu-shur he approached the city from the other direction, along the main road from the west by which had we originally reached Lhasa. I take the account of his return from my diary:

*November 23rd.*—While Richardson and Norbhu go, officially, to present scarves of welcome to the Regent, Nepean and I ride out to photograph the procession. Rising at 6.30 A.M. (with a temperature of 18° F. in our tents), we set off in the chill morning air, riding as far as Shing-donka, the butchers' village four miles to the west of Lhasa, to a place we carefully chose yesterday.

There is not a cloud in the pale dawn sky; already the sun is reddening the snow on the western mountain-tops away beyond the Trisum river. In the valley the early-morning light is still more attenuated, having to pierce a pall of smoke over Lhasa city where housewives are already lighting their dung fires and burning fragrant incense to Buddha. Looking eastwards we are amazed to see the Potala looming mysteriously above the coppery haze which hides the outline of its massive foundations; unsubstantial it seems, like some fairy castle conjured up by a magician and poised precariously above the earth. All at once the sun's rays light up the golden shrines on the summit, and the outlines of the building emerge, now to assume, by contrast, the solidity of a vast medieval castle.

Even at this hour can be heard the deep droning boom of the ten-foot-long monastery trumpets, and a monotonous beating of drums and cymbals. As we ride along we pass many of the pious at their morning devotions. Although it is scarcely seven o'clock the beggars have already reached their stations—unless they slept there all night. From one patchwork of rags a goitrous face appears with protruding tongue, while an emaciated arm, with fist clenched and thumb raised, importunes us for alms. Here are the usual line of worshippers taking the holy walk around the city. A group of swarthy nomads gaze at us with wide ingenuous eyes—perhaps they have never seen Europeans before; a man with leather apron and wooden protectors for his hands prostrates his way round the city; some Lhasa women, with dark pigment protecting their complexions, wearing robes of dusty black homespun cloth, turn their prayer-wheels and mutter the sacred formula.

Today there seems to be more traffic than usual; much of it is the Regent's baggage sent on ahead. Here is a train of sleek

M 2

mules with his tents and camp furniture; farther on, the road is blocked by a herd of sleepy, slow-moving yaks returning to Lhasa for more barley-meal or wool. Respecting their sharp horns, we leave the track and canter along on the grass where the hoar-frost glitters like amethyst in the thin sunlight. On the marshes bordering the road are immense flocks of bar-headed geese, Brahminy duck and mallard. Skeins of geese, with their lavender and black and white plumage set off by orange beaks and legs, flash in the sun as they circle round with harsh cries. The dark bottle-green of mallards' heads can be picked out among the dun marsh grass.

In honour of the Regent a line of stones has been put down on each side of the road, and every few hundred yards improvised incense-burners have been built of sods and painted white. As he passes azalea and artemisia leaves will be burnt to produce clouds of fragrant white smoke.

Passing below Drepung monastery we reach Shing-donka at eight o'clock. We have been told that the procession will pass the village at about half-past eight; but as time means very little in Tibet we expect to wait an hour or two before anything happens. We set up our cameras on a flat roof overlooking the village. The track rises sharply here to cross a rocky spur of the mountain as it comes down to the loop of the Kyi Chu on which the village lies. On our left, stretching for several miles across to the main channel of the river, lies a level sandy waste covered with thickets of willow and thorny scrub. At this time of the year it affords some scanty grazing and is a source of firewood; in the summer it is under water.

On the ridge above us are many small shrines and bundles of sticks from which prayer-flags flutter; on the rocks Buddhas and prayers are carved. The bare hills, of which the tops are powdered with snow, rise four or five thousand feet. As a rule the outlines of the Lhasa mountains are gently modulated and smooth, but above Shing-donka there is a mountain crested like one of the Dolomites with huge pinnacles of rock. Up above, quick to realize that something unusual is about to happen, are lammergeyers and vultures wheeling in great circles with apparently effortless wings. Shing-donka, at any rate in the summer-time when the river valley is flooded, must be a strategic position, guarding as it does the main approach to Lhasa from the south and west. We could see that the village had once been fortified by the Tibetans; there was still a ruined wall of mud and stone, while below the village was a modern square Chinese fort and barracks unused since 1912, when the Chinese troops evacuated the city.

For two hours there are no signs of the procession, but many evidences of its approach. Lines of mules pass, their loads covered with cloths of the Regent's colours—golden-yellow bordered with scarlet. Then a group of servants in wide red hats appear in a cloud of dust and, dismounting hurriedly, go into what is apparently the headman's house to see that all the necessary arrangements have been made. These servants are mounted on fine ambling ponies or mules. A little later a group of monk officials come by, in mulberry-red robes and gold-lacquered hats. Monks seem to ride mules in preference to ponies. More officials pass, hurrying on to see that the tea will be ready at the required time. The small son of the Kung rides by with a group of his father's servants, some of whom wear silk. The child is only four, but he sits in a high criss-cross saddle of wood from which it is impossible to fall. He wears long boots, a yellow silk robe and a conical hat, with a coral-and-turquoise brooch on the front. After this comes a tiny incarnation lama similarly mounted, but led by a monk servant. The child wears miniature monk's boots with turned-up toes and brocade sides, a claret-coloured robe and yellow hat. Slung across his back is a gold charm-box containing an image of Buddha almost as big as himself. The child looks portentously solemn.

At last a cloud of dust heralds the approach of the procession itself. Women who were flailing barley beside the river drop their wooden flails and hurry to the roadside; a dozen incense-burners on the house-tops and beside the road start belching forth smoke; another party of mounted servants hurries past to clear the road ahead.

It is difficult to see the procession clearly because of the cloud of dust it raises—the standard-bearers, the long line of monk officials, the green-coated palanquin bearers, the fluttering State umbrella, the brocaded senior ministers, more monk officials and always scarlet-hatted servants. The Regent is in a special light palanquin with a movable hood; a less pretentious conveyance than is used away from the city—a touring model, so to speak. I notice that two spare teams of bearers ride at the back of the procession. We pack up our cameras and, giving the procession a respectfully wide berth, overtake it and are ready again when the Regent stops at a gaily coloured tent for tea and rice. The officials leave their mounts with grooms who have suddenly appeared. The monks dispense with their hats—which are only worn on horseback—and form into bowing ranks as the Regent, leaning on the arms of his intimate monk officials, walks from his palanquin to the tent. I notice that the Regent's own horses, gaily caparisoned with strips of brightly coloured silk and gorgeous saddle-cloths, are led by scarlet-robed grooms in case he gets tired of being carried and wants to ride.

Although the route of the procession led only a mile below Drepung monastery, I was surprised to see that none of the monks came down to pay their respects to the Regent. He was educated at Sera, and perhaps this is an unfriendly gesture symbolizing the age-long jealousy between the two institutions. Or possibly the Abbots, realizing that the presence of some thousands of monks would increase the dust-clouds, ordered their charges to keep to their cells.

After one more halt for tea and rice, the procession went on to the official reception, which took place a mile from Lhasa in the Garden of the Mystics, where our Mission was received on its first arrival in Lhasa. Scarves were presented by those officials who had not accompanied the Regent. The Chinese representative, who had also come to present a scarf, joined, indeed for a time actually led, the homeward procession. He was escorted by several mounted standard-bearers, a section of heavily-armed Chinese soldiers, and the local bazaar band disguised as his retainers. The guard of honour, drawn up on the open plain to the west of the city, was the centre of a great crowd of people who had come out from town to watch the procession. Thus does the representative of God on Earth return to his Holy City.

On the fifteenth day of the tenth Tibetan month, November 28th by our calendar, there was a great procession in the city. An enormous image of the goddess Palden Lhamo was taken from the Cathedral and carried through the streets. This all-powerful goddess is the guardian of all Tibet and especially of the Government. She is the deity of whom our good Queen Victoria was supposed by the Tibetans to be an incarnation. The eloquent Landon describes her as follows :

"Palden Lhamo is a dark-blue lady with three eyes who sits upon a chestnut mule drinking blood from a skull and trampling underfoot the torn and mutilated bodies of men and women. Her crown is composed of skulls, her eye-teeth are four inches long, and the bridle, girths, and crupper are living snakes kept in position by the dripping skin of a recently flayed man."

I had been invited to watch the procession from the house of my friend Surkang Se. The goddess was to be taken out of the Cathedral and escorted round the inner road of the city. She would be halted in front of each important house and the owner would have to make some contribution.

It is always difficult to obtain exact information from the Tibetans, whose accounts are so often contradictory. A Tibetan told me that this powerful goddess, when the world was young, was about to destroy all creation, but at the last moment a husband was found for her, and he, apparently, appeased her wrath. On the day that she is taken for her annual tour of the city, her husband, who is kept in a monastery on the other side of the Kyi Chu, is also taken out, and they are allowed to behold each other at a distance of several miles.

The streets were densely crowded; the luckier ones, like myself, watched from the flat roof-tops. Several hundred monks took part in the procession; many of them wore special pleated cloaks and a strip of rainbow-coloured brocade hanging from a diamond-shaped turquoise and gold ornament between their shoulder-blades. They also wore the yellow woollen hat shaped like a fireman's helmet. A group of very youthful monks, hardly yet in their teens, walked past with drums on their shoulders. Others carried golden chargers, swinging incense-burners and silver teapots. Several trumpet-stands, carved in the likeness of dragons' heads, were put up for half a dozen long silver and gold trumpets. A way was cleared for the goddess, who appeared, grotesquely ugly, among a group of monks wearing masks representing different animals. The invisible man who was supporting the goddess took short quick steps so that she appeared to be tripping along with mincing tread, mopping and mowing as she went. This accorded ill with the hideous fixed expression on her face. A few white scarves had been thrown up on her head and shoulders. As the goddess approached the main gateway of the Surkang house there was a deep blast from the long trumpets, a clashing of cymbals and a sustained beating of drums. The goddess was put down in the middle of the road and I saw that a chair was pushed under her skirts, so that the man supporting her could rest. Soon afterwards cups of tea were passed in for his refreshment. The masked monks performed various dances in front of the goddess, and in a side street a large pile of straw surrounding an image of butter and barley-flour was set alight. After more chanting and music the goddess was carried onwards, followed by an immense crowd of people. When she returned to the open space in front of the Cathedral an image of coloured butter and tsamba—which is always prepared by the monks of Muru monastery, who seem to be in charge of the whole ceremony—was broken into small pieces and thrown to the crowd. These fragments are much prized as amulets against the attacks of evil spirits.

Ten days after this ceremony, on December 8th, there was held the Festival of Lights in memory of Tsong-kapa (literally, " the man from the onion country "), the celebrated reformer who established the Yellow Hat sect. He also founded Ganden monastery in the first decade of the fifteenth century, and inaugurated the Great Prayer festival in Lhasa.

The anniversary of the reformer's death, the twenty-fifth day of the tenth Tibetan month, marks the official ending of summer and the beginning of winter. Before this day all officials wear their silks and clothes of summer; only after it, however cold the weather may be before, are they allowed to wear the fur hats and fur-lined robes of winter. (On the eighth day of the third Tibetan month, about April 20th, winter ends and the thin silks are once again worn.) In the morning all the officials of Lhasa collect in the Potala dressed in their thin silks. After prostrating themselves three times before the Regent and presenting scarves, they retire into dressing-rooms and return in a few minutes wearing the wide fur hats and fur-lined robes of winter. After drinking tea, they return to their homes. Norbhu told me that most of the officials wear fur under-robes if they find it cold, but anybody who is caught is heavily fined and may even be degraded.

That night, in memory of Tsong-kapa, all the monasteries, State buildings and private houses were lit up with innumerable tiny lights. There were rows of butter-lamps along every window-sill and along the parapets surrounding the flat roofs. Lhasa itself was completely transformed, and as one had no criterion by which to judge the size of the lights, it resembled some immense distant city with regular lines of lamp-posts marking its long thoroughfare.

Drepung was similarly illuminated. From the Deyki Lingka we looked across to it from a distance of some three miles. An island of a million twinkling lights in the surrounding blackness of the hills, it had an unearthly aspect, like some fairy city floating in the frosty night.

## CHAPTER THIRTEEN

### OUR LIFE IN LHASA

WE soon found that the Deyki Lingka in summer was a very pleasant place, except for innumerable black and ravenous mosquitoes, which appeared each evening from the surrounding marches; there were also many flies and bluebottles. But once we had cut the long grass that grew in our garden their numbers decreased.

This small walled garden, the haunt of turtle-doves, great tits and hoopoes, was a great boon to us. A row of tall double hollyhocks grew in front of the house and there were rose bushes, peach trees, a few ornamental conifers and a fine walnut tree. Beyond the wall grew white poplars, and one looked between their slim grey trunks to the olive-green hills across the river. The house was surrounded by groves of willows and poplars and was therefore free from the infected dust of the city. Just over the other side of the garden wall ran a small branch of the Kyi Chu, with the blue sky and an overhanging clematis mirrored in its still surface.

Leaning over the bridge, one could always see some char swimming idly amongst the undulating water-weed. Parts of this river resembled a Hampshire trout stream, and I continually regretted that we could not fish. But as water is the purest element, so the body of a fish may be the temporary resting-place of some holy lama, whose hope of immortality one would not willingly jeopardize. Beyond the stream a strip of sandy waste-land covered with thorny scrub ran down to the Kyi Chu.

We found the actual house somewhat small for our requirements. Gould and Neame occupied two minute rooms upstairs; the doctor took possession of an even smaller ground-floor room opening off the tiny kitchen courtyard, while Richardson and I put up our tents in the walled garden. There was one rather gloomy downstairs room which we used as a dining-room, and a more cheerful one above with a veranda that we roofed in with canvas and used for receptions. Neame's bedroom afterwards became Gould's office, while the five Sikkimese clerks had a large office a hundred yards from our house. The kitchens and stables were part of the main building. Norbhu found quarters just outside our main doorway between the kitchens and the stables. We were looked after by the staff from the Gangtok Residency, augmented by some of Richardson's servants from Gyantse and a few local recruits. As is usual in the East, they were all men, though a few coolie women were recruited as water-carriers. The chief pivots of this most efficient staff were two Mohammedans, the " Butler ", Mir Khan, and cook, Jakob Khan, both of whom had been with Gould for many years. Although they were elderly they never complained of the height or climate, though they had a great deal to say about the laziness and lack of cleanliness of the Tibetans. There was a Hindoo " sweeper " who always looked unutterably miserable, a " dhobi " or laundry-man, of the same religion, and another dozen or so servants who were all Lepcha orderlies from Sikkim, and therefore Buddhists.

One very serious misfortune that beset us soon after we had settled down in the Deyki Lingka was the illness of the Political Officer. On September 2nd, a little more than a week after our arrival, he went to bed with a chill, which steadily got worse and developed into serious gastric trouble. Day after day he could take no food and was tortured by continuous hiccoughs and vomiting which precluded his getting either sleep or nourishment. Morgan sat up with him at nights and tried every sort of remedy, but he became ever weaker and weaker.

This was especially serious because Mr. Williamson, the last Political Officer, had, under tragic circumstances, actually died in Lhasa, also from internal troubles. Had the same fate befallen Gould it would have been the end of our prestige in the country. For so superstitious are the Tibetans that if two successive representatives of Great Britain had died in the Holy City they would have taken it as a sure sign that the gods desired them to have no more dealings with Britain.

The Tibetans, with the quiet fatalism of the East, were quite certain that he would not recover; and the Doctor looked more and more worried. It seemed that in the rarefied atmosphere of Lhasa he was not going to get better, and then the question was whether he had strength enough to survive the long journey down to India. We even borrowed a small sedan-chair from one of the officials, so that if necessary we could at any moment set off from Lhasa.

Each night from our tents in the garden we could hear him racked by the interminable hiccoughs. He became so weak that he could barely lift a glass of water to his lips. And there was nothing we could do. To fly him down to India was impossible; we knew that there was no machine in India capable of crossing passes of 17,000 feet and carrying enough fuel for the return flight, though the landing conditions in Lhasa are more than adequate. After a week of this distress the Doctor's efforts were rewarded: the hiccoughs gradually stopped. In a few days Gould was able to get up, and on September 13th he was strong enough to receive the Shap-pes, though he still looked terribly ill and haggard.

Apart from this we kept extraordinarily well, except for occasional chills and colds in the head. Living at 12,000 feet, we found, had no ill effects on our health or spirits, though most of us lost weight, becoming somewhat desiccated by the dry Tibetan air. Occasionally we got on each other's nerves, but that would have happened to the same extent at sea-level. We were a well-assorted party—an Irishman, a Welshman, a Scot, and three Englishmen. I can only say that if I ever had the chance of repeating the expedition I should be happy to go with the same companions.

People often say to me: "What on earth did you manage to do with yourselves during those six months? Weren't you awfully bored?" Yet in point of fact we had remarkably little time to ourselves. In the first place, a tremendous amount of time was devoted to receiving visitors and returning their calls, and subsequently in luncheon parties and cinema entertainments.

For me many hours were taken up by such pleasant occupations as sight-seeing, photography and natural history work, and though I do not complain of overwork, I have never known so little spare time for reading or writing as there was on the Lhasa Mission.

Gould was occupied with the major policy, expenditure and organization of the mission, which involved the exchange of long cypher messages with the Government of India, Army Headquarters and other departments. He was therefore engaged in those telegraphic duels which seem to be necessary before the powers that be will take any sort of decision that might possibly place them in a compromising position. The North-West Frontier looms always so large in the minds of Foreign Office and Army officials that they shelved or indefinitely delayed issues that were all-important and urgent to us in Tibet. Gould, too, spent many hours in involved conversations with Norbhu—involved because Norbhu has such an intuitive knowledge of Tibetan affairs and people that his conclusions, however fantastic they may appear, are practically always right; but when he comes to justify them, his arguments are inconsequent and contradictory. Even in a dead calm he knew which way the wind was going to blow. Gould had also to supervise, through Norbhu, the work of the five Sikkimese clerks (though two of them were from the office of the British Trade Agent, Gyantse) and the twenty or so servants from his Gangtok house.

A man of tremendous mental activity and with an unbelievable capacity for work, we found Gould took a great deal of living up to. Struck with a sudden idea, he would, during dinner and afterwards, write out a long telegram to the Government of India; Richardson and I would spend many hours of the night laboriously putting it into the incredibly intricate double cypher that His Majesty's Government seem to consider necessary to outwit the ingenuity of hypothetical foreign agents. At breakfast Gould would appear with an entirely new draft, having been awake since four o'clock reading up all available information on the subject, in a dozen bulging files. I would then spend the morning re-encyphering the message.

Brigadier Neame, alas! could only be spared from his military duties in India long enough to allow him three weeks in Lhasa, and during that time he was naturally very busy finding out all he could about that remarkable organization, the Tibetan Army. One of our earliest acquaintances in Lhasa was the Yuto Depön, who came on the day of our arrival with presents from the Cabinet. He was one of those young officials who had been chosen to be sent down to Quetta to receive training as an artillery officer. We then made the acquaintance of the other moving spirit in the modern Tibetan Army, Jigme Tering, who had been at St. Paul's School, Darjeeling, and who, unlike Yuto, spoke flawless English. Both these young depöns were dressed in extremely smart khaki tunics with well-cut riding breeches and shining field-boots. Tibetan officers can choose their own badges, and so both wore several stars of dark orange-coloured Tibetan gold. These, together with their long turquoise ear-rings and charm-boxes, added greatly to their attractive appearance. We also received calls from Changra Depön, the lay Commander-in-Chief, and Chapay Depön, his assistant, and, as already described, from the monk Commander-in-Chief.

Changra was made depön at the age of forty-eight, having previously held only civil appointments. Two years ago, at the age of fifty-six, he was made Commander-in-Chief, and although he knew that many reforms were needed he did not know where to begin. Chapay, his assistant, had been for many years a depön in Kham. All these officials spoke very freely to Neame and he was able to discover much useful information. It appears that since the death of the late Dalai Lama all military training has lapsed, and only now, with the threat of the Tashi Lama's Chinese escort and further outbreaks in Kham, were the Tibetans becoming anxious. Although they still possess the natural courage and endurance of their Tartar ancestors, a thousand years of Buddhism has undermined their military ardour.

The higher command is often in the hands of officials who have absolutely no knowledge of military affairs, and who have been pitchforked from civil appointments. In Kham the organization is such that each of the four depöns works independently and takes his orders from the Lhasa Cabinet, except when the Kham Commissioner happens to be on the spot. The instruction of the troops is in the hands of a few officers who were trained at Quetta or Gyantse several years ago and who have since forgotten all they ever learnt. Yuto, for instance, was actually given a civil appointment after his training at Quetta. Experienced soldiers cannot rise beyond the rank of *rupön* (theoretically major, but in practice more like a sergeant-major in charge of about 250 men), all higher appointments being made from the ranks of the civil officials.

The army is recruited on a feudal basis, each landowner having to supply so many recruits; there are also several purely military estates. In this way some 3000 regulars were raised, but after the troubles with the Chinese in 1910–12, and the subsequent clashes with Chinese and communists on the Kham frontier, the size of the army has been trebled. The new levies, however, are unreliable and badly officered. The soldiers are ill-fed, and paid practically nothing; they are forced to batten on the civil inhabitants, amongst whom they are consequently unpopular. The regulars, to save the expense of feeding, are frequently allowed home on leave; and during service are often used as navvies for civil undertakings, instead of being allowed to train. As of recent years all available regulars have been sent to Kham, in Lhasa itself there are only a few thousand infantry, including the bodyguard and a battalion of armed police, and many of these are away on semi-permanent leave. They are all equipped with fairly modern service rifles, but live ammunition is so rarely used for practice that their marksmanship is necessarily poor. The ammunition is sealed in strong-rooms and none can be issued without the personal attendance of the Prime Minister, the Cabinet and the two Commanders-in-Chief. Some years ago the Tibetans started manufacturing rifle ammunition in Lhasa. A depön told us that it looked all right, weighed the correct amount, and fitted perfectly, but when fired it frequently burst the barrel of the rifle and seriously injured the soldier. There are also a few mountain machine and Lewis guns, but the men are not fully trained in the use of them and have rarely practised with live ammunition. Naturally, too, they become somewhat weary of cleaning weapons that are never fired, and many of these are said to be badly corroded and even dangerous. The troops, as we noticed when we passed the guard of honour on entering Lhasa, wear battered Wolseley topees, ill-fitting khaki drill uniforms and European boots. Naturally the effect is ludicrous and is further exaggerated by their long pigtails and

enormous ear-rings. The Commanders-in-Chief have just introduced a new uniform which is eminently sensible and most
attractive to look at. A khaki felt hat is worn with ear-flaps
normally tied together on top of the head with blue ribbon.
The tunic, of khaki homespun cloth, buttons on one side in the
Tibetan fashion, and comes down to the knees. Locally made
high boots are worn instead of stiff leather ones.

Having heard so much in disparagement of the Tibetan army,
we were much interested to hear that a review of all available
troops, about five hundred, had been arranged near the Trab-shi
(a building incorporating the barracks, arsenal, and mint) so that
Neame could see them drilling and carrying out range practice.
Yuto and Jigme explained that many of the gunners would be
firing their weapons with live ammunition for the first time,
and they were afraid that the Brigadier would find the whole
display merely ludicrous.

It was a great day. Gould was indisposed at that time, but
the rest of us, including Nepean, who had arrived the day previously from Gyantse, rode out alongside the aqueduct to the
arsenal, some two miles to the north of Lhasa. This roadway,
in the days of " Tibet I," had been carefully built up on a causeway above the surrounding flooded land, but the granite bridges
over the rivulets had broken down and it was nobody's business
to mend them again. It was a blazing hot morning with a
scorching sun and heavy cumulus clouds over the hills. Lammergeyers and kites circled languidly above us, while ravens and
magpies gaped with open beaks on the dry sandy banks of the
aqueduct.

We were received in the barrack square outside the Trab-shi
by a guard of honour, officered by Yuto, by the Commander-in-
Chief, and later, in a reception room, by the Cabinet. Soon
afterwards the Prime Minister arrived—in Tibet, as in other
countries, the higher the official the later he arrives—surrounded
by servants and retainers. As his horse was led through the
barrack square the Shap-pes stood and bowed to the waist. It
took some time for the Prime Minister to drink his tea and to
receive the various military officers, for this was the first time he
had inspected the army or visited the arsenal.

On the dry stony plain outside the Trab-shi stood a row of
white tents ornamented with patterns in red and blue appliqué

work. In the central tent sat the Prime Minister on a high dais with the Shap-pes on one side of him and the Commanders-in-Chief on the other, all of course, on lower seats. There were several tents for other officials, while our tent was on the right of the " royal " one.

Practically all the inhabitants of Lhasa had turned out to see the fun, including several thousand monks. They stood or sat in a wide circle, protected by umbrellas from the scorching sun. The more enterprising women had opened small stalls, where they sat beneath umbrellas selling apricots, greasy-looking cakes, tea and cigarettes. The crowd, which was fairly orderly, was controlled by junior officials and several of the gigantic monks armed with whips.

Soon a column of troops appeared with their colours held high above them. Both the bodyguard and police had bands which made a very creditable noise. One was an ordinary military band with a big drum (the drummer complete with leopard-skin) and the usual bugles and kettle-drums, while the other was a bagpipe band. I am neither military-minded nor musical, but I was greatly impressed by these Tibetan bands, although I must admit that when they played the one tune I *do* know (" God Save the King ") I did not recognize it until I saw the others standing to attention.

The company drill was very ragged, the dressing and marching being bad; while on one occasion a platoon commander got lost and had to sprint vigorously to recover his position. The orders were given in English. After Neame, looking very smart on his white pony, had ridden round watching the drill, he got off to inspect the rifles, some of which were over thirty years old and definitely unfit for firing. The next item was rifle target practice, but as no Lhasa soldier had fired his rifle for the last six years, the sights seemed to have got out of adjustment, and not a man failed to register several misses out of his five shots. The machine-gun fire was more successful, although one gun frequently jammed and only Jigme could persuade it to work, while the others frequently ran across its line of fire in their enthusiasm.

After this we adjourned for a Tibetan lunch in a small room of the barracks, which was decorated in true military fashion with large Chinese drawings of beautiful women.

After lunch there was some Lewis-gun practice, and then two

mountain guns were unloaded from mules, put together and fired at a whitewashed wall over a mile away on the plain. This was the most popular feature of the day. After the report of the gun there was a moment of breathless excitement, and if a direct hit was scored it was greeted with cheers from the crowd, who had converged in their eagerness so as to leave only a narrow channel for the line of fire. At the end of the day the Prime Minister received all the military officers, from the Commanders-in-Chief to the N.C.O.'s, and presented them with white scarves in appreciation of their gallant efforts.

In another section of the Trab-shi is the Government mint, which we visited one day with Tsarong and Langchungna, who are in charge of it. We saw silver and copper coins being stamped out, and paper notes being printed, mostly by up-to-date electrically worked machinery from England. There were two or three venerable home-made hand-power stamping machines with vast wobbly brass fly-wheels. We also saw a new machine made entirely of brass (for they cannot work steel) in process of construction under Ringang's expert direction. In the forge, where women worked marvellous skin-bellows, they were melting bars of silver, mixing in 10 per cent of alloy, and recasting. We were all presented with a set of newly minted coins. It was odd to see Tibetans at work like this, but they seemed to be very skilful. I had heard that owing to the fact that the paint on the paper notes will dry only during the three months of summer, the Tibetans are saved from the dangers of inflation; but this story, attractive though it is, is not true. Owing to the debasing of the coinage and lack of backing for the notes, the *tranka*, which twenty-five years ago was three to the rupee, is now twenty-five. The *tranka*, together with its Chinese and Nepalese variants, was formerly the only Tibetan coin; if smaller amounts were needed the coin was cut into pieces. The Indian rupee, being more stable and harder to cut, is used very largely for more important commercial transactions.

Richardson, as British Trade Agent, Gyantse, maintained a separate office with his own confidential adviser (Sohnam Kazi) and clerks. His job was not only to work with Gould in the straightening out of Tibetan problems and the laying down of a more definite line of policy, but to establish personal contacts with the officials so that when they passed through Gyantse, or if he were again in Lhasa, they would call on him to ask his advice or to supply useful information. The Political Officers of Sikkim have practically always served their apprenticeship to Tibetan affairs by being posted as British Trade Agents, Gyantse; and as they seem to spend the intermediate period in places as far away from Tibet as possible, they must rely on this early training for their subsequent knowledge of the country and people.

Both Richardson and I spent much time learning the language, but it is extremely difficult to acquire. In the first place, in a country where communications are so poor there is a great variety of dialects, though that spoken at Lhasa is the purest and the most widely understood. There is also a great difference between the literary and spoken language. The grammar is very complex and bears little relation to that of European languages; it is said to be most akin to Burmese. Apart from ordinary difficulties of pronunciation there are various tones, so that the same word said in different pitches of voice will assume as many entirely separate meanings. The order of the words in a sentence is exactly the opposite of what it is in English. But the chief difficulty is the use of honorific terms, which necessitates the learning of three vocabularies instead of one. If I talk to a servant or man of muleteer class, or of myself, I use the ordinary language; if I speak to equals or people of higher rank I use the honorific language, but when I speak to members of the nobility or the highest lamas I use a still more exalted form of honorific. These changes are not merely in prefix or suffix, for usually the whole words change. To come, for an equal is *dro-wa*; for a superior, *phep-pa*; for a high official, *chhip-gyu nang-wa*. And as all these verbs mean to go, as well as to come, it will be seen that the language is no easy one.

Some of the words are rather delightfully derived: thus a chair (a non-honorific one) is *kup-kya*, bottom-prop; the word for distance is *tha-ring-thung*, way-long-short; a bribe is *pak-suk*, secret push; an office is *yik-tsang*, nest of letters. The sentence, " Thank you, I have enjoyed looking round the monastery, now I must take my leave ", would be, " *La thu-je-chle, te-ring chho-je yak-po she-tra chung*; *ta gong-pa shu-ki-yin* ".

Gould had had a considerable knowledge of the language

twenty-five years before when he had been British Trade Agent at Gyantse, but having had to learn many Indian dialects since then he had forgotten how to speak it, though he remembered enough of the peculiarities of the language to enable him to teach Richardson and me. Gould had, in fact, spent much time over the problem of the language and had compiled a number of stock honorific conversations to be learnt by heart. (One of these sentences is given above.) In a language with such complicated grammar and vocabulary as the Tibetan this is an excellent way to start and gives much confidence.

It was always a source of gratification to the officials that we had learnt enough to carry on a conversation with them. The Chinese, who always considered the Tibetans as mere barbarians, made a point of never troubling to learn the language, relying on their temporary Tibetan wives as interpreters. We did not trouble to learn the Tibetan letters; there was little enough time to spend on the spoken language. Personally I did not trouble about the honorifics, except to learn by heart a few pages of stock compliments and salutations. If we wanted to talk to officials there was always an interpreter available. My object in learning the language was not only to talk to my servants but to be able to carry on a conversation with any muleteer or nomad that I met in the hills. And this I was able to do. Though I had little grammar, I could chat for half an hour with any fairly intelligent fellow-traveller and discover all his history and anything else I wanted to know.

One morning towards the end of our visit I had to go round to see the Regent and explain to him the workings of a Zeiss camera we were going to present to him as a New Year's gift. Unfortunately, Jigme, who was supposed to be coming as interpreter, mistook the time, and I was left alone to explain the intricacies of range-finders and exposures in the highest honorific terms! The Regent was extraordinarily kind and helpful, and what might have been a most embarrassing interview turned out quite successfully. It so happened that we were all lunching with the Prime Minister that day and I had been asked to go earlier in order to photograph his wife and small child. Here exactly the same thing happened; Sonam, who was going to interpret, was delayed with the rest of the party, and I spent another half-hour struggling with high honorifics.

Captain Morgan, assisted by the genial Rai Sahib Bo and two native orderlies, set up his surgery and hospital in a curious square outbuilding half-way up our drive. This barn—for it was little more—consisted of a square room which relied for lighting on a large uncovered opening in the roof. Once it had been whitewashed all over and furnished with an operating-table and a neat shelf to hold the bottles demanded by the profession, it looked most business-like.

It has always been part of the policy of the British Missions to give free medical attention to the Tibetans, and every morning a motley collection of patients could be seen awaiting treatment. The majority of these came for inoculations for venereal diseases, complaints that are almost universal in Lhasa. These must, together with the systems of polyandry and monasticism, account for the decreasing birthrate. But the Tibetans are a hardy race, and they seem to be establishing a national immunity. Venereal diseases were by no means confined to the lower classes, still less to the lay population. One day Morgan was asked to go and give injections to a certain high official and his wife. Two other brothers, who shared the wife, came in for similar attention, and then, while they were still all in the same room, the official and one brother asked if they might bring in several other of their " wives ". The family seemed to be living in complete promiscuity, and no one seemed the least embarrassed.

There were broken limbs to be set, sores and cuts to be dressed, glasses to be fitted, and teeth to be extracted. For dentistry cases Morgan was assisted by a Nepalese dentist who practises in Lhasa; he used to visit our surgery every day. There was little accommodation at the hospital, and patients who needed continuous treatment or who had come from a distance had to bring their own tents; it was no uncommon sight to see a dozen cloth or yak-hair tents pitched beneath the trees around the hospital. For several weeks there was a tent containing a cheerful small boy who had broken his leg; another child had fearful wounds owing to a thrashing from his monk employer. Most amusing was what we called " the ophthalmic ward ", which consisted of a single piece of yak-hair sacking stretched between two trees, and affording shelter for a grimy old beggar-woman who was being prepared for a cataract operation. This complaint is very prevalent in Tibet, and Morgan must have operated successfully on at least thirty patients whose sight had practically gone. Monks and nuns were conspicuous amongst these cataract cases, and one would see these aged people, supported on the arm of a friend, hobbling around with their eyes swathed in bandages—for the eyes must not be used after the operation until the skin of the iris has healed. This was indeed a miracle for them; and patients, hearing of the Doctor's fame, would come in many days' journey for attention. Luckily for them, Morgan, unlike the majority of men in the Indian Medical Service, had behind him many years' experience gained in a busy practice in England, where he had done his own surgery work and dispensing.

In Tibet a doctor sees many cases which have advanced much further than they would be allowed to do in a country where medical attention is always available. Sometimes patients would come only after the monks had already failed to cure, or even aggravated, the ailment. Occasionally they would interfere with his treatment of a case, forbidding the patient to take his medicine and reversing all his orders. For in Tibet the lay practitioner has little following and the art of healing is a pre-rogative of the monks, who abuse it in no uncertain way. These meddlesome quacks were a continual exasperation to the Doctor's quixotic Welsh temperament.

Just behind our house rises the sharp peak called the Iron Hill (*chak-po ri*). On the summit of this is the Medical College of the monks, which is supplied with students by each of the large monasteries. The course of instruction takes about eight years and consists chiefly in learning by heart long spells and incanta-tions. Except for a certain knowledge of herbs, the Tibetans seem to be completely ignorant of medicine; and of the func-tions, or even the positions, of many of the organs of the body they have the most fantastic notions. A certain holy lama once said that a woman's heart is on the right-hand side of her body, and as far as they are concerned on the right side it is; no amount of argument and practical demonstration will make them change this opinion.

If a patient is suspected of having an infectious disease his pulse is felt at the end of a long string. If the lama cannot lay hands on the required medicine he will write the prescription on a piece of paper, burn it, and make the patient swallow the ashes; probably it is just as efficacious, perhaps it is more so, since the most revolting concoctions are used for medicines, including the excreta of animals, land-crabs, powdered stone, as well as aconite, musk, camphor and other preparations known to Western medicine. In some cases a cure is sought by getting a high lama to spit upon an affected part. Pills made from the excreta or urine of the Dalai and Tashi Lamas are also considered a sovereign remedy for any sort of complaint.

In the afternoons Morgan would ride out to see private patients; either those who were too ill to visit his surgery, or officials who did not want to advertise their ignominious afflictions. In this way he got to know more about the homes and private lives of the people than any of us, and some of his experiences were staggering revelations of the abuse of monastic power and of the complete lack of any moral sense in a large section of upper-class Lhasa.

Morgan, who was once a well-known rugby footballer, is one of those very large but extremely gentle people who are so beloved by children; and his popularity among the Tibetans, who themselves have all the charm and many of the faults of children, was immense. And, as Gould himself recorded, Morgan's unremitting and skilful work as a doctor and his genial personality contributed very largely to the success of the Mission.

Of the activities of the wireless officers I lack the technical knowledge to write with discrimination. It will be remembered that at Gyantse we discovered that the wireless charging motor would not work owing to the great height above sea-level, so Dagg returned to Calcutta in order to procure a hand-power charging-set while Nepean remained at Gyantse to sort out other wireless gear. It was not until 6th September that Nepean reached Lhasa. Dagg arrived three weeks later with a hand-charging motor that he had had constructed in Calcutta. This was to be operated by coolies, who turned its handles and thereby charged the accumulators. The advantage of this was that if we went beyond Lhasa to meet the Tashi Lama we could provide our own power for wireless transmission. In Lhasa itself the accumulators were usually sent along to Ringang to be recharged. There was not enough wire in Lhasa for the town electricity supply to reach the Deyki Lingka, and we had to rely on accumulators for wireless transmission and for working our cinema projectors.

Our transmission station was capable of sending the cypher messages to Jubbulpore or Rawalpindi, so that if necessary we could be independent of the Lhasa land line. The wireless officers worked on a regular programme with stations in India, and in this way we were always in touch. In addition to this official work a large amount of experimental transmission and reception was done. Once they did a twenty-four-hour test to find out at what time of the day conditions were best. They were also in communication with amateurs in China, Hong Kong, the East Indies, Assam, South Africa, Mauritius, Brazil, Australia and many countries of Europe. A great deal of their time was taken up in devising entertainments for our guests. The cinema projection had to be adapted to run off accumulators; and they were always rigging up transformers, loud-speakers, microphones, telephones and other subtle devices. Most of us had sets by our bedsides. At seven in the morning I used to lie in bed and listen to the midnight news from London. It seemed absurdly incongruous to lie there as the sun rose and listen to Big Ben striking midnight, and to hear the announcer's synthetic voice wishing me good night.

We were able to supply much current news to the Tibetans: Gould, listening in at three o'clock one morning, heard that Marshal Chiang Kai Shek had been released, an item of news that the Tibetans would not otherwise have discovered for weeks.

It was by this means that we first heard scattered rumours of the abdication of Edward VIII. At first we were incredulous, but then, long before there was any official declaration from home, we read the whole distressing story in a Chinese-American weekly. We were apprehensive as to how the Tibetans would receive this news; but they considered it the most natural thing in the world that a King, having reached the age of forty without providing an heir, should abdicate in favour of his brother.

I, being Private Secretary to the Mission, had a variety of duties and considered myself much overworked! Telegrams arriving at any hour of the day or night had to be decyphered; a single message might take as long as four hours to disentangle. Cypher work is much quicker if there are two people on the job, so anybody who happened to be free at the moment was called in to assist. I also kept a meteorological log; collected and pressed some six hundred species of flowering plants; dried a number of seeds, some of which we had been asked to collect for His Majesty the King; made notes on the bird-life of Lhasa; and kept a general diary accompanied by photographs, which was sent off each week to the Government of India. But it was photography that took up most of my time. During our seven months in Tibet I took, on behalf of the Mission, some 2500 still-photographs, most of which I developed in Lhasa; 13,000 feet of standard 35-mm. film (all silent), 6000 feet of 16-mm. Kodachrome colour-film and 3000 feet of 16-mm. black-and-white. I used the following cameras: a 35-mm. Bell Howell Eyemo with 2-inch and 6-inch lenses. This was invariably operated from a panotilt tripod, as at Lhasa's altitude it is almost impossible to hold the camera steady, especially if one has been walking just beforehand. I had three 16-mm. cameras: a Model K Kodak with 1·9, 30- and 6-inch lenses, an ancient Model A Kodak that Gould had bought for £10 some years before, and a Siemens' magazine ciné of my own.

Of still-cameras I used five. A quarter-plate Zeiss Nixé film or film pack camera, two 6 × 9-cm. Zeiss Super Ikonta II, one of which was always loaded with colour-film, and two Contax cameras with 2·8 and 3·5 lenses, with a 6-inch 4·5 telephoto lens which would fit either. As I wanted to keep some check upon exposure and general results I used to do all my own developing of still-photographs. The Lhasa water was suitable for this if strained through a handkerchief. I used to do this after dinner; and often it would be long after midnight before the films were fully washed and hanging up to dry.

The cutting and splicing together of cinema film occupied many complete days. Sometimes 1000 feet of film would come back from Calcutta, and it all had to be cut and edited before it was fit to be shown to our discriminating audiences. On one occasion I had two miles of 35-mm. film carefully cut and hanging in lengths from the wires I had rigged up at one end of our dining-room; but in the end we decided not to project any full-sized film as the light from our accumulators was not sufficiently strong to throw a bright enough picture.

Sometimes I would be using all this formidable battery of cameras more or less at the same time.

If we visited a monastery and knew we would not go there again, or on such an occasion as the visit of a high official, we needed a record in big film, colour and still-photography. Take, for instance, the occasion when the Shap-pes came on a ceremonial visit. I would carefully choose my position with due regard to the angle of the sun and the probability of dust, and then, as the Tibetans have no idea of time, I would set up my cameras an hour before they were expected. More usually they were an hour late. As soon as they came into view I would " shoot " them with the 35-mm. telephoto, then take a medium 16-mm. colour " shot ", return to the big camera again and take a near shot, repeat this with the colour-camera, meanwhile firing off any still-cameras that I had been able to fix in the right position. Luckily Nepean became fairly skilful with the 16-mm. cameras, and we used to work together.

When we visited some important place it was a fearful mental strain to use all these cameras, each of which requires a different technique and uses film of different sensitivity or colour value.

Luckily the Tibetans did not object to these activities. At first they were a little suspicious, especially the poorer people, and more particularly of the big cinema camera which made a formidable noise and, with its long telephot lens, resembled some new-fangled automatic gun. Once we had shown them photographs of themselves they were delighted and did all they could to help. The Kodachrome colour-film, as soon as possible after exposure, had to be sent down by post-runner and baggage animal, and finally by train to Calcutta, thence it was sent by air to London, which was the nearest place where it could be processed. It was returned to Lhasa by the same expensive means. But the results were worth it. Except for some of the film that passèd through Calcutta in summer and deteriorated owing to the heat, the results were extraordinarily successful; and when the officials saw themselves and their wives in all the finery of their gay clothes, in natural colour, moving on the screen, they were simply delighted. This was by far our most successful form of entertainment. They were also anxious to receive enlargements of themselves and their families; so, like a court photographer, I used to receive requests to go round and photograph many of the higher officials at their homes.

These cinema parties were a great feature of our life in Lhasa, especially during the last few months.  I shall describe a typical evening.

One day in December, Tsarong with his two wives, Jigme, Mary, the Dele Rabdens (who stay with Tsarong), and eight children aged from four to seventeen years old, are invited to dinner.  They arrive an hour early—at five o'clock—but Norbhu keeps things going and gives them tea until we have finished changing.  The big lower room is needed for projection and Nepean is busy there with transformers and a network of wire, so we assemble upstairs for preliminary drinks.  Tsarong has whisky and the others rather reluctantly take a glass of Cinzano or crème de menthe—Tibetans are not great drinkers.  Then we go downstairs and our older guests sit in chairs while the children crowd on the floor in front.  Then some of Tsarong's senior servants come in, together with a number of monks attached to his private chapel, and a few of his retainers who have heard of the show, and with their children stand round the room or sit on the floor.  Our own servants crowd in at the back.  By this time there are sixty or seventy people in a room that would be licensed by the London County Council to take twenty at the very most.  The smell is indescribable—the clinging musty smell of old silk robes, smothered by the rancid pungence of monk and servants' butter-sodden garments.

We start with a black-and-white film of the Potala and the Lhasa bazaar as a curtain-raiser; some of the audience have never seen films before, and we break them in with something they know.  The bare white walls of the Potala shine with a strange radiance against a dark velvety sky—a simple matter of yellow filters, but the effect transcends the original, and the audience make sharp exclamations of delight, " Ha-le ! ha-le ! "  Anon the scene changes to the city, and they see some familiar shop-wife standing, oblivious of the camera, behind her stall.  Suddenly she wakes up to what is happening and becomes grotesquely self-conscious, hiding her face with her hands, and eventually bolting indoors.  The crowd is delighted, and Tsarong makes some ribald remark which convulses the males of the audience.

Crowd scenes are always popular, as the individuals are known to everybody.  This is followed by a colour-film of the army, by request of Tsarong and Jigme, and the latter sees a close-up of his handsome face and smart uniform, enlivened by his long

A TIBETAN LEWIS-GUN SECTION, SHOWING OLD AND NEW UNIFORMS

LHASA UNITED FOOTBALL TEAM

RUGBEIANS ALL : MONDO, KYIPUP (CITY MAGISTRATE) AND RINGANG

turquoise ear-ring. There are comic incidents too: a soldier with ludicrously battered topee and long pigtails pulls a cord to fire one of the mountain-guns. The cord breaks and he falls over backwards. A group of four Ladakis, wearing red fezes, are revealed sitting on the grass gambling. After a short colour-film of the Political Officer's Residency and garden at Gangtok, it is time for dinner, and our guests, after a stroll in the garden, reluctantly go upstairs.

It is difficult to accommodate some twenty-five people in so small a room, so we sit round with our backs to the wall on padded cushions, and eat from Tibetan tables. Norbhu, Doctor Bo, and Sonham are there as interpreters. The Jigmes can, of course, speak English. The cook deals with the problem by serving a number of hors-d'œuvres-like dishes on the low Tibetan tables. Cups of soup, potato salad, sardines, tinned salmon, sausages and then a substantial dish of rice and curry, is followed by fruit-salad, and anything they like to drink; usually lemon-squash for the children, Cinzano for the ladies, and whisky for the men. But they don't really like our food and drink. Why should they? their own is so much better.

Suddenly Gould, who had slipped out of the room, reappears with an armful of crackers, and the spirit of the party, flagging for a moment under the weight of all this food, suddenly revives. We are amazed by the perfect manners of our guests. They laugh without reserve and yet they avoid becoming boisterous. The children never seem to cry, and without ever being fussed by their parents they behave perfectly. A Tibetan mother never says, "Don't"; yet the child doesn't. A four-year-old girl fearlessly holds a firework, while her brother, aged six, who had previously been told to behave exactly like his father, smokes a cigarette with apparent enjoyment. They are all so obviously delighted that it is a joy to entertain them. The Doctor walks down the room to talk to a child who is sitting, quite happily, alone; but he is so belaboured about the head with balloons that he cannot pass, and pretends to burst into tears; the girls, non-plussed, stop for a moment, and by the time they have discovered his subterfuge, he is at the other side of the room. At eight o'clock, bedecked with paper hats, and Tsarong adorned with a false nose, we go downstairs to continue the film show.

We were going to show a film I had taken in Greenland, but

N

there are shouts of, " Shepada, Shepada," and we weakly give in. " The Shepada " is the Tibetan version of the Shepherd Dog, a name they have given to " The Night Cry ", a five-reeled Rin-Tin-Tin film that has made a tremendous hit in Lhasa; it is simple, moving and of a subject with which they are familiar, nor does it leap inconsequently from scene to scene in the way of more modern films, which are almost incomprehensible to any but the most assiduous picture-goer.

The story is that the hero's dog, Rinty, is accused of slaying the lambs of the rival gang. The latter insist that the hero shoot his dog. He pretends to do this, but actually hides Rinty in a cellar. Lambs continue to disappear, so the villain, in the absence of the hero, enters his house and insists on searching it. In spite of the gallant efforts of the hero's wife Rinty is discovered, but puts up a terrific and realistic fight before. . . . But meanwhile the hero has revealed to the rival gang that the raider is an enormous condor. This bird, tiring of a diet of lamb, approaches the hero's house and carries off (on wires) his small child that has toddled out of doors while its mother was struggling to save Rinty's life. Locked by the villain into a room, she sees this happening, but it is an agonizingly long time before she can work the bolt loose. Meanwhile Rinty, having slain his assailant, also sees the dread bird gradually approaching the baby, but by the time he can break his collar it is too late. Then the three—hero, wife and Rinty—wildly pursue the child, who is carried by the bird to the summit of a crag. At last, after a desperate climb, the child is recovered, and the bird and Rinty, locked in a grip of death, fall to the foot of the crags.

We are continually asked to show this film, and, as it lasts an hour and a half, we are most heartily sick of it. But not so the Tibetans; they gasp and shout encouragement as Rinty vanquishes the villain. As the hero's wife struggles in vain to escape and go to the rescue of her child the women weep on each other's shoulders and themselves shout ineffectual warnings to the child; finally, when the child is saved, and all ends happily, they are quite weak with emotion.

It is then necessary to have a Charlie Chaplin to restore their composure. Of these we have a great stock, mostly of venerable pre-war vintage. And next to the " Shepada " and shots of themselves, these are the favourites. And what wonderful films they are! We have "Easy Street", "The Waiter", "Shanghaied", "One o'Clock in the Morning", "The Crook" —all the old favourites. The irresistible humour of Charlie knocking people over the head with a hammer, of dropping ice-creams down the backs of old ladies' evening-dresses, appeals strongly to the Tibetan mind and never fails to cause a pandemonium of shouts and laughter.

The next item—we have only been going for two hours so far and the night is young—is a film of Tibetan celebrities. The Regent's palanquin leaving Lhasa, the Shap-pes coming to call, the pomp of the Nepalese representative, the Prime Minister and his family at home, and Tsarong himself trying to look stern and then bursting with laughter. Here, again, there are comic interludes; the old Lord Chamberlain, the head of the ecclesiastical party and a total abstainer, rides away from one of our luncheon parties, with his gilt hat at a most rakish angle; Norbhu is blessed by the Regent and the small scarf gets caught up in the charm-box on top of his head, and requires several servants to disentangle it.

A reel of Hendon Air-Pageant, 1929, follows this; another Charlie Chaplin, and then a very popular film of King George V's Jubilee Procession, in which they are amazed at the cleanliness of the streets, and the fact that the horses of the royal coach are not amblers. And so, after four concentrated hours of it, the show stops, and after a final drink our guests mount their ponies and ride home through the clear Tibetan night.

We had a similar cinema party for all the chief officials of Lhasa. Each could bring his women-folk, children and friends. One evening we had an "Old School" party, which was attended by the three Rugbeians, Ringang, Kyipup and Möndö; Jigme, who was at St. Paul's School, Darjeeling; Surkang Se and Derge Se from Ludlow's school at Gyantse. About this time we were shown a letter from Tsarong's sixteen-year-old son, who was at school at Darjeeling, in which he wrote: "Is there any talking picture in Lhasa? I heard there is talking picture in Lhasa and every gentleman doesn't work, but go to see picture every night. I have nothing more to say."

One evening, I think it was when the Duke's family had come to dine, we realized, as we came downstairs, that something unusual was afoot. It transpired that Norbhu had told three or four of the Potala monks that we were having a cinema show that night, and that if they kept the information to themselves they could come. But the walls of the Potala, like other walls, have ears, and about thirty boisterous monks, reinforced by as many soldiers from the neighbouring Norbhu Lingka barracks, had climbed over our wall and " gate-crashed " the room; and while several monks had already taken the chairs reserved for our guests, the rest of the crowd effectively blocked all ways of approach. We made those who were already in the room sit on the floor, while the others were ejected—forcibly where necessary. During the reluctant retreat of a party of monks Morgan was hit on the hand by a stone. After that I have seldom seen monks move faster.

The Regent was very anxious to see our films, but as his sanctity precluded his visiting the Deyki Lingka he asked us to arrange a private view in the throne-room of the monastery in front of his palace. This meant much carrying round of accumulators and other gear, but Nepean and Dagg managed the electrical part with their usual skill; though there was a slight hitch when it was discovered that four of the coolies had stopped at a chang-shop on the way and had got too drunk to complete the journey—luckily this was before the dress rehearsal.

After a Tibetan lunch with the Regent we went across to the monastery roof, where the public-address outfit was blaring forth Scottish military music to an astonished collection of people on surrounding roof-tops. The Regent was delighted and insisted on a three-hours' programme, only letting us go then on condition that we promised to arrange another show later on, which we were able to do in January.

After his return from his visit to Samye in November the Regent became a different man. Whereas before he had been nervous and irresolute and had looked emaciated and ill, now he seemed very much stronger both in mind and body. When he was away from Lhasa he could ride and take a certain amount of exercise, whereas in his Palace this was impossible—though we discovered that he had started playing football with " Simple Simon " and had sent round to Norbhu to ask if we had a spare ball. This alone seemed to justify the Mission! We could never quite fathom the extent of the Regent's influence, or in what direction it was exerted. He always seemed very friendly to us, and declared his intention to visit India some day, and yet there were rumours that he was in communication with China and had even accepted presents and decorations.

The story is told that when he was younger he was due to appear before the Dalai Lama to be examined for a degree corresponding to a Doctorship of Divinity. The Dalai, who knew that the Regent had done no work at all, wrote to him advising him not to sit. But the Regent insisted on coming up, so the Dalai conferred the degree without examination. He became Regent much against his will and continually wanted to be allowed to resign. As some stable figure-head was essential in the critical times which succeeded the death of the Dalai, the Shap-pes persuaded him to stay on, which he would only do on condition that they guaranteed to obey all his orders. Surely this argues a more than ordinary political discernment.

When the Prime Minister heard that we had given a performance in the Regent's house, he demanded one at his home, although we had already given a special cinema party for him at the Deyki Lingka. Another film show was given in the throne-room of Gundeling monastery to the hundred monks who live there, and finally one at the Norbhu Lingka to the bodyguard troops. Had we been able to arrange entertainments at Drepung and Sera I am sure that we should have done a great deal towards establishing even more friendly relations with the monks.

One festivity that must be described was a children's party given at the end of December to celebrate the Political Officer's birthday. Anybody passing the Deyki Lingka that morning might well have imagined either that the Pied Piper had just passed that way or that we were starting a school. By lunchtime about seventy of the sons and daughters of the Lhasa officials had arrived. They came on horseback, either independently, preceded and followed by red-hatted servants, or sharing the saddle with a nurse or groom. The youngest child—Mary Jigme's daughter—was only three, but the majority were in their teens. They wore full-length silk or broadcloth robes, lined with fur, and high-crowned hats with fur-lined ear-flaps. In this becoming dress they resembled gnomes in winter clothing. Mrs. Jigme and Mrs. Ringang came to help with the organization. As soon as the children arrived they were taken upstairs for tea and Christmas cake; it was lucky that a good many were late, as there were more than we had expected and it was difficult to find a seat for everybody in our small room. The Duke's children, true to family tradition, were the last to arrive; they were just in time for tea.

At about one o'clock the cinema show started. The " Shepada " (inevitably), Charlie Chaplin, Aeroplanes, the Grand National, Jubilee Procession, more Charlie Chaplin—it must have been a bewildering experience for children who had never been away from Lhasa, never even read a book (other than the Tibetan Scriptures), much less previously seen a cinema show. After three hours of this they staggered out to the garden for a breath of fresh air in the late evening sunshine.

This was followed by " supper " upstairs. We were much struck to see how charmingly they behaved to each other: if a child was unable to master the difficulties of spoons and forks his neighbour helped him; when one boy spilt his curry into his lap the others laughed with him—not at him—and helped to clear it up. Then came the great event of the day, the Christmas-tree; admittedly a synthetic one made by tying fronds of evergreen on to a carefully pruned poplar. Nevertheless when the children came down to our darkened dining-room, at one end of which the tree glowed like a miracle, lit with electric bulbs of every colour, glistening with tinsel and balls of crystal, and festooned with teddy-bears, humpty-dumpties, scarlet soldiers, and other wonders entirely new to them, they gasped with astonishment and delight.

Then Norbhu, disguised as Father Christmas, but rendered less unfamiliar by the addition of a helmet-shaped monk's hat, made a speech in Tibetan (probably the first time Father Christmas has had to use this tongue) explaining the tree, drew the inevitable comparison between the infant Jesus and the child Dalai Lama, and wished them all a Happy Christmas. After that each child was given a present, and at six o'clock, still looking quite bewildered but clutching in their arms dolls, drums, trumpets, and mechanical toys, they mounted their ponies and rode away for home. We heard afterwards that the chief topic of conversation on the way was whether we would still be in Lhasa next Christmas.

## CHAPTER FOURTEEN

### CHRISTMAS HOLIDAY INTERLUDE

DURING the early part of December the Government of India decided that in view of the troubles on the North-West Frontier they could no longer spare us two wireless officers. This was unfortunate, as there was more than enough work for two. Not only were Nepean and Dagg transmitting cypher messages direct to the Government of India, but they were carrying out most valuable research in exchanging messages with amateurs in different parts of the world, and working such stations as Jubbalpore and Rawalpindi at scheduled times. In addition to their wireless programmes they had a great deal of electrical work to do in connection with our entertainments. When we had luncheon parties they arranged loud-speakers so that gramophone music could beguile our guests into making the best of English food; and in awkward pauses before and after meals they would arrange for two Tibetans with a gift for comic entertainment to carry on an argument or sing a song in front of the loud-speaker so that it could be relayed to our sitting-room. Much of their time was taken up in working the projector for our numerous cinema shows; if these took place away from our house—at the Regent's monastery or at the Prime Minister's home—hours of preparation were necessary, especially as all the accumulators, the screen, and the projector had always to be carried round by coolies, who usually seemed to get lost or to stop for a gossip on the way. The wireless officers also had to do their share of cypher work, lunching out, sightseeing, and attending functions of one sort or another, so they had as little spare time as the rest of us.

Looking back, it has often struck me how extraordinarily busy we were : not that we were overworked, but we seemed to have absolutely no time to ourselves. And if anybody had a moment to spare from his own job he would always be inveigled into helping with cypher work, mending something, using one of my cameras when several different records were needed of the same thing, or working out Gould's latest " scheme ", for I have never known a man so prolific of ideas or so meticulous of detail as the Political Officer !

So it was that, in spite of Gould's remonstrances, Nepean had
to return to India in the middle of December. As I had not
slept away from Lhasa since our arrival there, Gould decided
that I should be allowed a holiday and would go down with
Nepean to the Yamdrok Tso to watch birds, and should wait
either at Pede or Nangartse until Major Finch, the new officer
in command of the escort at Gyantse, should appear on his way
up to Lhasa to spend Christmas with us.

The Tibetans had been tactfully sounded by Norbhu, who
reported that they had got so used to our presence that it seemed
quite natural that Nepean should be needed by his Corps, and
that Finch, the only other European in Tibet (except for the
mysterious Kaulback and Tracey, somewhere down in the south-
east—if they were still alive, which seemed doubtful), should
come up to Lhasa to spend Christmas with us. I will take the
description of this journey from my diary:

*December 14th, Monday.*—How marvellous to be travelling
again! I don't think I have ever in my life spent so long in
one place, and I have longed to be off, though there has been
far too much to do for any hint of boredom. Curious that
when one stops work one so often gets attacked by some germ
or other. I woke up with a vile cold today. Up at 5 A.M.,
14° F., clear, but thin mackerel clouds to the east. These tents,
built for comfort and to impress, are not much good for keeping
out the cold, especially when one has to wash and shave in them.
Packed-up and all ready in time for eggs and bacon at six o'clock.
Usual snags before starting: Nepean found that the pony supplied by a local transport contractor had a fearful sore back.
The Tibetan in charge satisfied his reputation by beating his
muleteer across the shoulders and by giving Nepean a tiny
black pony which jogged along at the most comic slow-motion
canter I have ever seen: it had no pace between this and a funereal
walk, but it always kept its ears forward and never stumbled.
My pony, Marpo, rather sleepy today.

Nepean had seven baggage animals; I had two, one carrying
a pair of boxes and the other the groom's belongings and my
bedding-roll. I have ten days' food with me and a climbing-
tent; half a mule-load is taken up with cameras and photographic
gear.

Sonham Minghu, an orderly lent to us by Richardson, went

ahead to arrange accommodation. Nurgul, Nepean's Pathan servant, is staying to hurry on the transport, which ought to have got away before us. So we have only Iamtso, my groom, with us. He carries two huge horse-hide saddle-bags, which I had made to carry cameras, lunch and spare clothes. Iamtso was only a grass-cutter at Gangtok; he has made a fairly efficient groom, and now he will have to look after me generally while I am alone at the Yamdrok Tso. Till then, Nurgul, who is most efficient not only as a cook, but at the more difficult task of making Tibetans hurry, will look after us till we part. So we have only four servants—including the muleteer—for two men : a very meagre allowance in this country !

Very cold morning, but not a breath of wind : sun on us now, and the thin cloud has vanished. Curious amethyst-tinted frost on the grass, and iron-hard frozen mud away from the road, very bad for the ponies' feet. How grand to have no ciphers to do and no films to develop ! One must earn a holiday to enjoy it fully. Plenty of traffic on the road, which is blocked in places. Met some sheep, each carrying small loads. Probably salt from the great lakes. Big flocks of yaks, goats and sheep below Drepung waited to be slaughtered.

All the people gaze at Nepean's yellow fur-lined Afghan coat. I wear a long purple corduroy robe, lined with fleece, and with fox-skin cuffs and collar. The long Tibetan sleeves, coming right down over the hands, allow one to hold the reins without gloves. Although Marpo is pulling like the devil, my hands are perfectly warm. We both wear Gilgit boots (made of thick felt coming above the knee), though we have had to get special wide stirrups for them. We also have Tibetan hats with fur-lined flaps coming over the ears and back of the neck. We would be better off still in Tibetan felt boots, for these Gilgit boots are not good when it comes to walking over rough or wet roads. Many bar-headed geese and Brahminy ducks standing on the ice and beside the few pools kept open by the current. Lammergeyers and vultures circle silently above. Many desert-chats about and a few robin-accentors and white-winged redstarts.

Passed Shing-donka, glad of the excuse to walk down the hill to get warm. The sweet smell from the incense-burners atones for the slaughter-house atmosphere here. Yaks and oxen laden with the carcasses of sheep are already leaving for the city, and

there are piles of entrails, hides, hooves and other offal down by
the river.  At Trisum bridge, where I stopped to take some
colour-films, great chunks of ice were being swept down by the
current—made me feel quite home-sick for the Arctic.  All the
way today met coolies and animals bringing up iron plates and
girders for the next span of the bridge.

Soon after this saw immense flocks of twittering snow-finches
coming up from the south, flying quite aimlessly; probably
just local movements.  Several ravens seen to-day, and many
choughs with bright crimson beaks, one party of fifteen.  Innumerable sparrows, and parties of thirty or forty twites.  Occasional rose-finches—what gorgeous birds they are !

At Nethang we missed the main road and found ourselves
among a maze of irrigation channels.  Iamtso tried to cross
one, but his pony never thought of jumping and went in up to its
belly.  Luckily the camera-bags kept out of the water.

Stopped for lunch by the track where it crosses sand slopes
that have been blown up against the bare hills.  Watched some
Tibetans, laden with great bundles of thorny weeds they had
collected in the hills for firewood, sliding down a four-hundred
foot sand-chute to the track.  Good lunch : half a chicken each
and baked potatoes, tea from a thermos.  Boiling hot sun now,
and we have to take our heavy clothes off.  I climbed a hill
and made an ascent of a curious pillar of hard-baked mud with
lumps of granite embedded in it.  I am not sure if it is the
remains of an old fort or an outcrop of natural conglomerate.

The track is very difficult here; though the floods have sub-
sided, it is only a narrow path cutting up and down across
precarious rock faces.  Met many donkeys with loads of glass,
sheet-copper and lengths of strip-iron; also yaks carrying skins
of butter and bags of tsamba.  One has to be very careful
meeting these animals suddenly at a corner of the track with
a drop of a hundred feet often straight down into the river.
There is usually only one driver to every seven or eight animals,
and many of them are half out of control.  Stampeding past
with their bulging loads, they might quite easily push one over
the edge.  I usually lead Marpo past such hazards, as he is very
jumpy and always puts up his ears at yaks.  There is usually
strong competition for the inner side of the track and the mule's
persistent nature usually wins.  Except for these places where

the track is forced up into the hills by the river, the country is much the same: wide fan-shaped valleys sloping gently up to their apexes with tributary valleys on either side. The lower stretches are stony and barren, but at the top, before the stream has dried up, there is usually a monastery surrounded by stunted trees and terraces of cultivation more than half of which are no longer kept up. The hills are gaunt and rocky low down, but rounded and smooth above, where yaks can occasionally be seen grazing. Down by the main river there is often considerable cultivation where the irrigation has been maintained. In some places part of the river has been dammed up with a wall of stakes and stones to divert the water into well-constructed canals which are dry at this time of the year.

Met several old monks walking along with bundles of holy books tied on to their backs. They look at us with hard arrogant unfriendly faces; other wayfarers regard us with amazement, but they usually smile, especially when I salute them. The monks sometimes don't even reply.

Reached Jangme at three o'clock. Seven and a half hours including lunch, about twenty miles. I like Jangme. A trim village of about a dozen houses built where a high rocky spur comes down to the river. Each house has its own yard, surrounded by outhouses and stables, the flat roofs of which form a balcony accessible from the living-room windows. Here was Sonham Minghu, who showed us to the guest-room in one of the houses. A clean bare room with mud walls and floor, and shuttered windows. Some good frescoes on the walls, the Mongolian Leading Tiger, the Four Friends and a six-armed eleven-headed Chenrezi. The only furniture is some mattress-like cushions on the floor and a couple of Tibetan tables. We didn't expect the baggage for a couple of hours, so we clambered up the spur for a thousand feet or so and came down by a sand-chute.

At the back of the village there are several huge wizened willow trees with sprawling spiral-twisted trunks. Near these are some mud-flats and unfrozen pools. Saw four greenshank here: pale grey heads and necks, and long dark upturned bills; dark wings show in flight. Their liquid fluting note, three or four times repeated, recalls instantly the first time I heard it one night on the Solway marshes. Three or four wood-sandpiper

too, much darker and with barred tails, give shrill " pluie " note.
Thirty mallard, with the sun lighting up their bottle-green heads.
As many teal, and two pairs of goosanders, the males with long
drooping black scapulars and pink-flushed breasts.  Put up a tiny
wren, dark and scolding.  At least a couple of hundred bar-
headed geese in the fields, and odd Brahminy ducks.  Four
bottle-shaped swallows' nests between the rafters outside our
window.

Nepean put up his camp-bed; I spread my sleeping-bag over
the square cushions on the floor.  Supper after a day's hard
travelling is more a sacrament than a meal.  Nurgul produced
mulligatawny soup, boiled mutton and vegetables, tinned
peas, caramel pudding and welsh rarebit, washed down with a
bottle of stout.  Spent an hour or two learning Tibetan, though
the yak-dung stove smokes so pungently that it is difficult to
read.

*December* 15*th, Tuesday.*—Hell of a day!  A day that will be
remembered among many grim days—unless it be obliterated
by innumerable future memories of winter-travel in this bleak
land.

Nurgul brought tea at five o'clock, but I had taken some
aspirin for my cold and awoke in a clammy sweat at midnight,
and was kept awake by a cock *in* the house which had a rasping
clarion note.  Went out, to see a dawn full of stars—The Great
Bear, Capella and many friends—more than friends.  Incredible
to think I used to steer my sledge on those very stars, and that I
used to gaze at them after staggering out of my tent in Lapland
or on the Greenland Ice Cap with exactly the same feeling of
reverence and delight.  A second in their lifetime has elapsed
since then: whole ages in mine.  Soon the Brahminies and bar-
heads started calling sleepily on the pond beside the house, the stars
began to pale, and the tinkling bells of pack animals could be
heard already leaving the village.

Packed up.  Porridge, fried eggs, potato and sausages.  All
sorts of snags this morning.  We hung about while Nurgul
packed up the gear, and it wasn't till 7.30 that we got away,
just as the sun lit up the hill-tops.  A sudden violent burst of
song from a wren just as we started; bar-heads, mallard, goosander, Brahminies, and teal on the move.  Lammergeyers
always soaring above.  A big crowd of peasants sitting round

drinking tea at the end of the village; I think they are clearing out one of the irrigation canals. I wish I could understand what they said as we passed! The track is exciting here. Many wandering corners under huge overhanging basalt cliffs, and the river rushing past just on our left. Saw many dark-coloured fish here. Buddhas painted on the rocks, and always prayers carved, strings of flags, and piles of holy stones to which each wayfarer adds his contribution to ensure his safety round every sudden corner.

Came out onto the long open plain before Chu-shur. Stony, sandy and barren most of it is, with only the thorny vetch growing. We are still meeting girders going up for the bridge; yaks, mules and donkeys with miscellaneous loads. We kept on the right, on a special track prepared for the recent tour of the Regent. The stones have been removed from the way and have been arranged in lines on each side, leaving an even, sandy surface, fifteen or twenty feet wide. We cantered along most of this. At ten o'clock we saw an important-looking party of horsemen approaching on a parallel track to the left, so we cut across and found, as we expected, that it was Tsarong and his younger wife, also his son and two daughters, and Norbhu's son, who are all returning from school at Darjeeling. Tsarong and his wife have been down to Chu-shur to meet them. The boys wore horn-rimmed glasses and short hair and long silk robes lined with fur. Tsarong, as befits a man of his independence, wore an aged khaki coat and a leather flying-helmet. Anyone else who tried that in Lhasa would be degraded. His wife wore a tall peaked hat, and had her face swathed in scarves with only her eyes showing They had about a dozen servants with them. It was a very embarrassing interview, as the children did not know what to say. The younger Tibetans could speak English, but they were completely tongue-tied, and all my conversation was with Tsarong in Tibetan, luckily he doesn't expect many honorifics! Reached Chu-shur at eleven o'clock.

Many black-necked cranes on the plain and odd flocks of snow-finches, Elwes' horned-larks, rose-finches, etc. Many Tibetan great-tits at Chu-shur. How different it looks now that the floods are down. Found Sonham Minghu here (he said he left Jangme at 3 A.M.) and changed Nepean's stalwart little pony for a too independent-looking mule. Noticed clouds of sand blowing high into the air, along the valley of Tsang-po.

Followed a winding built-up track beside the river and then turned left across shingle banks to the ferry at Chaksam. There is a very attractive smallish monastery on the far side of the river, and a long iron chain running out to an island in mid-stream. This is the remains of a remarkable suspension bridge which is reputed to have been built five hundred years ago by an ancient king of Tibet, whose image is worshipped in the near-by Chaksam monastery. By the time we reached the river we were enveloped in the sand-storm which was roaring down the course of the Tsang-po from west to east. It was absolute hell. We breathed sand and gritted it between our teeth; it filled our eyes so that we could not see, it got into our noses and ears, stung our faces and made life quite intolerable. My camera-bags were filled with sand. The ponies would hardly face it, indeed they were often stopped dead by the sheer force of the wind.

There were two ferry-boats, both on the far side—crude rectangular wooden boxes about twenty feet by eight. The boatmen refused to come over for half an hour or so, as it was too rough. We waited miserably, breathing sand and impatience. The boats are propelled with crude wooden paddles; but the men do not have to row very much: they creep up the steep bank under cover from the wind, making use of a back-water, then they row furiously in the middle until they come into another eddy, which brings them across. It was rather a hazardous business, and most of the time water was being shipped, as the sides of the boats are cut away in the middle so that the animals can get on and off more easily. When we came up against the force of the current and the wind it looked as if we were going to be washed down towards the island. The ferry has one huge steering oar used against an upright beam in the stern. A similar beam at the other end—one can hardly say bows—has a carved horse's head at the summit and a bamboo pole with prayer-flags attached.

No sign of our baggage animals yet. A fine young Tibetan crossed with us; he wore a hat of a complete fox-skin with the tail hanging down behind, and carried slung across his back a Mauser rifle and a beautifully worked silver charm-box with an image inside. I had a long talk with him and discovered he was returning to Chung-ye, having been up to Lhasa to conduct some business concerning a Government estate which had gradually absorbed his own family property. He told me that before anyone would take any sort of action it was necessary to visit Lhasa many times. Letters, apparently, remained unanswered. He invited us to go and stay with him.

A tricky job getting our ponies off the ferry, as it is half full of ice. The track then led along at the foot of a rocky hill, with little hermitages 1000 feet above the river. It seems to be an exceptionally holy place. There are many chortens here and painted Buddhas recessed in the rocks and protected by wire-netting. Whitewash has also been splashed over the rocks. The storm is dead against us now, and we can make little pro-gress, as the ponies try to turn back. The way leads over miles of sand-dunes, so that the track is obliterated and the drift so bad that we almost decided to turn and try again early tomorrow. At two o'clock, having eaten nothing for eight hours, we stopped to have some lunch inside a ruined barn; but we ate more sand than anything else. The wind was most exhausting and our eyes were very inflamed.

Gradually the path diverged from the river and rose along the foot of a range of rounded grassy hills on our left. Below was a level plain of very fertile cultivated land, running down to the sandy waste which marked the summer flood-limit of the river. There are some fine-looking isolated farms with swastikas and other lucky signs whitewashed on the walls. After an hour we turned up to the left, following a wide fan of flood débris brought down by a monsoon watercourse. The floods must be terrific in summer, as the walls of this river-bed are about thirty feet high and quite vertical. The sides are often a hundred yards apart. But the bed of the watercourse makes a tolerable track for us. Passed a village where we ought, if we'd had any sense, to have stayed the night, but it is ignominious to cut down one's allotted stage unless absolutely necessary.

The Kamba La is a formidable pass. We had to rise nearly 5000 feet from the Tsang-po. The track zigzagged steeply upward for miles and miles, and it was rapidly getting dark. I walked all the way up, as Marpo was tired. Nepean was abso-lutely dead-beat and only just kept going. Luckily his mule is very strong and could carry him. We reached the summit of the pass at 5.30, by which time it was dark and very cold. On the way up Sonham Minghu passed us. He had waited behind at Chu-shur to change the baggage animals, and when he reached the ferry they said at first it was unsafe to cross. Sonham, on his own sturdy little Tibetan pony, trotted practically all the way up the hill. I shouldn't have thought it possible, but I suppose the ponies get used to it, as no Tibetan ever walks if it is safe to ride. They have a proverb that if he can't carry you up any hill he's nò pony; if you can't walk down you're no man. Heard a snow-cock up in the hills and saw mountain-finches again. There are mouse-hares up here too; I should have thought they would have had the sense to be hibernating.

The descent in the dark was terrifying, as we lost the track and got on to a very precipitous watercourse; we also lost the village of Tremlung until some thoughtful person shone a light for our benefit. At last, at seven o'clock, we found the rest-house. It was terribly cold waiting for our baggage. Our accommodation is a low stable-like room, about twelve feet by thirty, with two pillars supporting an open rafter roof covered with sods. The walls and floor are of rough stones and mud. A door and windows with boarded shutters open on to a balcony which is the roof of the stables. A piece of cloth is hung against the roof to keep the dust from falling on to the cushions and tables. It was bitterly cold, as the wind roared through the room. We borrowed a butter-lamp and a couple of sheep-dung stoves and then drank cup after cup of Tibetan tea. It is the very thing for an occasion like this. Nurgul arrived at ten o'clock quite unperturbed, though the muleteers had wanted to turn back and he had had to use a torch to pick a way over the pass. One pony, with a load of wireless gear, had fallen from the track and turned several somersaults, but seemed none the worse. Supper of Maconochie rations, sardines, cake, Scotch woodcock and tea. Nurgul is a great man! I wish these dung stoves wouldn't smoke so much. They produce pungent fumes which are like moss saturated with chlorine.

It is curious what vicarious pleasure one derives from physical exhaustion and discomfort. It is a strange paradox that the more intolerable a journey is at the time, the more satisfactory does it become in retrospect. Our sensibilities and characters were made to be sharpened against the hard forces of Nature. But how few people nowadays get any chance to test their physical endurance to breaking-point, to feel cold fear gnawing at their hearts, or to have to make decisions that hold life and death in the balance? That is why men flock so easily to war; to test a manhood that is perverted by the present state of civilization.

*December 16th, Wednesday.* Blew hard all night and still blowing, but no sand drifting. A lovely clear morning; warm reddish tints on the hill-tops opposite; a deep-blue lake with white horses chasing each other across it and on the far side rounded grassy mountain-tops. No trees up here except for some wind-bitten thorn bushes. My pony has gone lame so I rode Iamtso's, while he hired another. Marpo is running loose; he will have time to recover at Pede.

A short stony descent to the shores of the Yamdrok Tso, then alternate rough-going round spurs, and easy fast-travelling in between. Bitterly cold with a violent wind from the Nangartse end. Down there on the mud-flats sand-devils were being swirled for 1500 feet into the air, but as a rule we are free from them at the Tremlung end. Plenty of fellow-travellers: a party of brigand-like men with dark sunburnt faces and long sheepskin robes; they were all armed with rifles and were followed by even wilder-looking retainers similarly armed. A monk came striding along the road with part of his red robe tied round the top of his head for warmth; he carried a big pack, and on top of it were two tiny dogs fast asleep. A hundred or so yaks laden with planks of wood. Many flocks of sheep and goats in charge of ragged-looking shepherd boys. A couple of post-runners carrying spears on which bells are tied, which jingle as they jog along.

Birds very interesting, quite different from those of the Lhasa valley. Altogether I saw ten male white-winged redstarts and no females, six desert-chats, eight robin-accentors, about five hundred horned-larks, any number of three varieties of snow- and mountain-finches, two kinds of gulls on the lake, many goosanders—a hundred drakes together in one place, odd parties of tufted duck, pochard, mallard and a few teal, several single grebes diving out on the lake. At Pede I saw about thirty red-headed pochard quite close in, near the ruined fort. There are bar-heads feeding along the shallows, and occasional lammer-geyers, buzzards, peregrines, kestrels and harriers. I have seen no choughs, cranes or rose-finches this side of the pass.

At Pede, Sonham had everything ready. This is a place for changing baggage animals, so Nepean got rid of his mule, which has been getting more and more refractory. I shall go on to Nangartse with Nepean and leave Iamtso here with Marpo, who is still very lame.

An extraordinary number of mouse-hares here; I saw a yellow weasel too. Several parties of gazelle up in the hills. This end of the lake is frozen over, but the birds remain beside open pools and at the edge of the ice. Blowing so much now that we could hardly carry on; no wonder the Tibetans finish travelling by midday. We reached Nangartse at 3.30, having had to stop several times to put on more clothes.

As we reached the village nestling at the foot of the fort, some women seized our bridles and led our ponies up the steep cobbled hill to the guest-house just at the back of the fort. It is almost the highest building in Nangartse. We were taken up a steep staircase, through a long dark passage, across a little courtyard open to the sky, and then to a tiny room with a glass window looking right across to the Karo La, and to the plain five hundred feet below. It is a very superior room: there are some religious wall-paintings protected by glass, and embroidered cloths hung against the ceiling to stop things falling on to the silken cushions and carved tables below. Two earthenware jars of smouldering sheep-dung were brought in, and, in spite of the acrid smoke, they made the room quite warm and snug. The baggage arrived at seven o'clock. The wind is whistling and roaring outside our exposed room. The whole building quivers. Had a grand farewell dinner—tomato soup, chicken with fried potatoes and carrots, cherries and custard, prawns, and the odd tot of whisky. Tomorrow Nepean goes on. I shall spend the morning wandering round the lake and then return to Iamtso at Pede to await Finch.

*December 17th, Thursday.*—Am on my own now. But in this country one cannot get to know the people. In Greenland one could wander off and be perfectly happy with the Eskimos as long as one could speak the language. There one passed as an equal and lived, ate, hunted, and travelled just as they did. We did very well without servants. Here it is fundamentally different. In this feudal country one is a Sahib, and is judged not by one's prowess as a hunter or as a man, but by the number of servants one keeps and the amount one throws one's weight about. Perhaps it would be different with the nomads of the Chang Tang. I think if a man knew the language perfectly, especially if he were a doctor and could really help the people, he might get to know them.

An awe-inspiring view from our window: we look straight down on to the rocks several hundred feet below us, then over some frozen ponds and ploughed fields on either side of the track, along which parties of yaks are already moving, and behind that to the line of the Karo La mountains. Nepean went off at seven, with Sonham and Nurgul. He will take two days to Gyantse. I walked over towards Samding monastery, feeling rather forlorn. There is something peculiarly poignant about partings like this. For several months you see a man all day and every day—your ways divide, and you may never meet again.

There are about three hundred yaks picketed at the foot of the village. Sand is starting to drift already. Many snow- and mountain-finches out on the mud-flats and calandra-larks with their melodious whistle. Literally hundreds of mouse-hares here; they sit up beside their burrows and squeak as you pass. Spent an hour stalking them with a camera. By the lake a skylark was singing a thin song, and a tiny sandpipery bird ran like a ball along the edge of the ice which runs out for about three hundred yards to the open water. Returned to the village and was almost mobbed by the local dogs; luckily the fiercest ones were tied up. I took some photographs of the fort and of the snow-capped mountains beyond the Karo La, then I packed my saddle-bags and set off for Pede.

Although there could be no question of losing the way, a very aged man on an equally aged pony insisted on accompanying me, and we took four hours to reach Pede at an uncomfortable jog-trot which made me very cross and sore. At first the wind was behind us, so it was sunny and quite warm. Saw about twenty pintail today as well as the usual birds, then later I saw a blackbird fly out of some rocks beside the track. Later it got very cold. The wind was so strong that in some places the water was being blown from the lake up on to the track. I suppose that is why the lake isn't frozen over here, as it is certainly cold enough. The water froze stiff on our clothes.

Iamtso says Marpo is still lame, but Finch won't be here for a day or two. It seems to be a sand crack at the back of the hoof—the same trouble that several of our ponies have already had. Pede consists of half a dozen houses on a low spur between the hills and the lake. The ruined fort looks like a Scottish castle and also recalls Chillon. I walked along beside the lake. Some distance out in the water are close packs of several hundred ducks. Some of these must contain almost a thousand birds. The majority are red-headed pochards, there are also many tufted duck and common pochard; they are not all diving ducks; I can make out mallard, teal and a few gadwall, and, I think, a widgeon. I saw several parties of about a hundred yaks laden with wool coming down an exceptionally steep hill just behind Pede. There is a perfectly good track, but the yaks prefer the bare hill-side. There seems to be one driver to thirty or forty animals. Last year the price for wool at Kalimpong was five-pence per pound; this year it is elevenpence. Normally 12 million pounds go down to India each year, two-thirds going to Kalimpong. This year many fortunes are being made in the wool trade.

I have a draughty upstairs room overlooking a courtyard where noisy mules are picketed. What a remarkable noise they make when they see their food approaching. Only yak-hair curtains keep out the wind. While I was shaving off a three days' beard, some sparrows, who are apparently in the habit of roosting in some holes in the ceiling, tried to pluck up their courage to come in and sat chirping on the curtain. The people here are very interested in me and seem amused that I can talk to them. I have arranged to go up Yasik Ri and Pede Ri tomorrow; these are the names the local people have for the two mountains, about 17,800 feet high, which stand out from the long range at the back of the lake, whose surface is 14,000 feet above sea-level. I shall take Iamtso and a local man to see if I can get any film of gazelle.

*December 18th, Friday.*—Somewhat disturbed by the muleteers who started feeding their charges soon after midnight and were on the road by 1.30 A.M. That's the way to travel at this time of the year. Iamtso, the local man, and I, set off at seven o'clock, just as the sun rose. We went straight up the steep fell behind the house and almost immediately saw a gazelle. Paler than burrhal and with a more goat-like action. Very white face with little upright black horns, most conspicuous white backside and a black scut. Saw fifteen more higher up. They are exquisitely graceful but very wild. I went on ahead while the other two tried to drive them past me. But there wasn't enough cover and they saw me. We had several more drives but it was very difficult. I got some shots with the six-inch lens. I must have seen about fifty gazelle today. The wind is terrific up here and intolerably cold. One can hardly stand. I sent the other two back after taking some colour film, and went on to the summit alone. From here there is a very good view across to Ningdzingzongka, the 23,000-foot peak to the north of the Karo La. Its north ridge is icy and fluted, but the southern ridge is a fairly easy-looking snow slope, with only the last few hundred feet very steep. I might be allowed to try it on the way back to India.

There is a huge block of snowy mountains down to the southwest. Below me the many-bayed blue lake curls round the feet of brown hills. All the last part of the climb was over loose shale coated in snow and ice. The summit of Pede Ri was built up like a huge fort, with a number of rooms, but all roofless. I wonder who can have done all this : it must have taken months of work. There is snow on the north faces of all the hills. Passes run up nearly every valley over to the Tsang-po, but many of them seem not to be used in winter. I went along the summit ridge for two miles to the top of the other mountain, which is higher and further north. Suddenly I felt very ill, so curled up under a rock and went to sleep. I shouldn't have thought I would have got mountain sickness at about 18,000 after living for several months at 12,000. Perhaps I came up too fast, or hadn't had enough to eat. In the distance to the north and north-east I can see a range of snow-capped mountains—far, far away. The Tsang-po valley can be followed for many miles to the east. Came down a track very slowly, feeling weak and ill. All the streams have overflowed and frozen into great slabs of ice. Saw a dipper on the way down, and several wrens. Got back at four o'clock and drank pints of tea, then practised Tibetan on the family who live here.

I am suffering not only from cracked lips and a sore face owing to the dry cold wind, but have most painful open cracks on the ends and sides of my thumbs and fingers, just as if they had been cut with a razor-blade. I have never experienced this before.

*December* 19*th, Saturday*.—Another day alone. Finch might have come today, but will probably arrive tomorrow. Spent the morning trying again to film gazelle. The trouble is that even if you get to exactly the right place they see you the moment they come into the view of the finder and are away in a flash. The best plan is to stalk them from below and " shoot " them leaping away uphill. I got so near to some that I could hear their shrill sneeze-like screams of alarm. I got some quite good " shots " today, but the Tibetans are too impatient and won't give me time to carry out a really good stalk. In the afternoon walked for miles beside the lake. Saw a rough-legged buzzard sitting hunched up on a stone. I also got within twenty yards of a fine drake widgeon who was sheltering in a little bay. A note from Finch, who has already reached Nangartse. He will be along at nine tomorrow. Started *Fire over England*, by A. E. W. Mason, and went on till I had finished it. A thrilling and romantic melodrama in the best Elizabethan style. Practically the first book I've read since leaving India.

*December* 20*th, Sunday*.—Packed up by 8 o'clock. Pony still lame. Went round taking a few more photographs, but something is wrong with the ¼-plate camera. Went along the track to meet Finch. Hundreds of yaks laden with wool going down towards Nangartse. I saw one remarkable yak driver wearing a garment of coarse sheepskin slipped off one shoulder, cold though it was. He had a sparse black beard, an expression like John the Baptist, and an untidy pigtail ornamented with an ivory ring, a charm-box and some odd pieces of coral and turquoise. He was turning a prayer-wheel as he rode along on a huge black yak, and slung across his back was an antiquated prong-gun with half a dozen prayer-flags fluttering from the prongs.

I next saw a party of five horsemen approaching, one of whom soon dismounted. I advanced with a very " Doctor Livingstone, I presume? " feeling! Finch wore a topee and Wellington boots; very English, but he doesn't seem to feel cold. He seems to be just the man for the job—tremendously interested in everything, already a great admirer of the Tibetans and keen to learn the language. He is very excited to be going to Lhasa.

We decided to go as far as Tremlung at this side of the pass today, and to cross the Kamba La to Chu-shur tomorrow, get to Nethang the day after, and reach Lhasa early on the following day. As Marpo is still lame, I rode a hireling which had to be beaten all the time. Finch's Gyantse ponies are very strong and fit. As we rode we discussed everything under the sun, from polo to politics, from Lhasa to the North Pole. We reached Tremlung at two o'clock and after a meal we explored the village. There are many ghost traps over the doors. These, a relic of the old Pön religion, are to avert devils from the inmates of the house. The lower part is the skull of a ram with the horns attached; over this are several flat pieces of wood on which there are paintings rather resembling the court cards in a pack; these are effigies of the people in the house and are meant to divert evil from their originals; above and around these a web of coloured wool is arranged in geometric patterns. The village is extremely dirty: there are piles of dung and offal in most of the courtyards. We watched a woman weaving a narrow strip of coarse woollen cloth on a very primitive but efficient loom. After that we walked up the lake for a mile or two in the opposite direction to Nangartse. Watched twelve gazelle up in the hills. Saw a wall-creeper. Returned by a short-cut over a low pass. Finch has a Tilley heater with him, so we made the room very snug and warm and talked till late. After half a day's acquaintance we know each other far better than one ever gets to know people in ordinary circumstances at home.[1]

*December 21st, Monday.*—Got away by 6.30 A.M. and walked to the top of the pass before the sun rose. Looking down to the lake I was surprised to see a wooden rowing-boat pulling across from the other side: I didn't know the Tibetans used them. This must be the highest navigable lake in the world: 2000 feet higher than Lake Titicaca.

We sent our ponies on ahead and, leaving the track, followed a long ridge right down to the Tsang-po valley. Stalked three snow-cock and got quite near. They are big grey birds with striped flanks, buff cheeks, orange-red beaks and tails like

[1] Major Finch, I deeply regret to say, died in England as a result of some glandular trouble from which he was suffering at this time.

black-cock. They run away clucking when one gets nearer than twenty yards. The usual vicious gale and dust-storm at Chaksam, and we had to wait for some time before it was safe enough to cross. Reached Chu-shur at midday and stayed in a very beautiful old house belonging to Tsarong. He had told us to come here on our return and to use his wood-stove.

We used the very dark and ancient altar-room which had a big fresco on the wall showing seven generations of one family all living at the same time. It is a Mongolian painting: Bhon-dong Shap-pe has the same fresco in his living-room at Lhasa, so has Tsarong. Along one wall, over some lockers where the family's best clothes are kept, is a rack full of sacred books. There is a photograph of the Tashi Lama cut out of a news-paper, several gilt images hung with scarves, a row of thankas, and a collection of prayer-wheels, travelling charm-boxes, chang pots and tsamba bowls. The people were very friendly and we showed them the photographs in some books about Tibet that Finch had with him. One of the girls is extremely beautiful. But her skin is absolutely filthy and her cheeks are coated with black pigment as a protection against the weather. Her hair is full of dust and pieces of straw, while her coarse homespun is engrained with grease and filth. But she has perfect features and eyes like a gazelle.

I went for a walk up the very fertile valley to the north-west. There is a very complicated irrigation system up here and several watermills for grinding corn. Some fine trees too, and groves of willows, poplars and walnuts. Watched a family of laughing-thrushes and a hoopoe, who seems to be wintering here. Tsarong says hoopoes hibernate and swears he has found them in disused rooms of his house. I shall believe it when I see it.

*December 22nd, Tuesday.*—A long and fairly uneventful ride past Jangme to Nethang, which we reached in the early after-noon, without much wind. Finch's four servants, some of whom have never been to Lhasa, are very excited at the prospect. At Nethang I went for a walk down by the river and saw flocks of several hundred pintail, nearly all drakes.

At the house where we stayed they were very busy preparing pea- and barley-flour. In a roofed corner of the courtyard there was a large sun-brick stove which was being stoked with dried mustard plants and kept at a roaring heat with the aid of a pair of bellows made from the skin of a goat. A flat pan full of sand was heated up and then handfuls of peas or barley were put in. These became suddenly hot and expanded—just as maize does when it is made into popcorn—the pan being shaken all the time so that nothing was burnt. After that the sand was run off through a sieve and the grain was ready to be ground. The parched peas tasted excellent. This most arduous work was done by the women, who were at it continuously, in spite of the heat, for several hours.

Next day we reached Lhasa without further adventure. The wind seemed to decrease as we went further away from the Tsang-po valley. The sun was shining brightly and we all felt a growing excitement as we approached the scintillating golden shrines on the roof of the Potala.

## CHAPTER FIFTEEN

### TIBETAN NEW YEAR

THE Tibetan calendar, which has been in use since A.D. 1027, is a peculiar mixture of Chinese and Western (imported through India) origins. Five elements—wood, fire, earth, iron and water —are joined to the twelve beasts of the Chinese zodiac: mouse, ox, tiger, hare, dragon, serpent, horse, sheep, monkey, bird, dog and pig. Each element comes twice, first as male, then as female. The elements are thus " used up " by the tenth year; so the first element, in male then female form, is combined with the eleventh and twelfth animals which are left over. This system gives a cycle of sixty years. Last year (1936) was the Fire-Mouse Year. The New Year (1937, or the eleventh year of the sixteenth Tibetan cycle) is the Fire-Ox Year. Next will be the Earth-Tiger Year.

The Tibetan New Year's Day in 1937 coincided with 12th February of our Calendar. As this is the greatest festival of the Tibetan Year we were extremely lucky to be in Lhasa at this time, for no other living Europeans, except Sir Charles Bell and his doctor, Colonel Kennedy, have witnessed these remarkable celebrations. It was unfortunate that the Mission left Lhasa on

17th February, before the second half of the festivities had taken place; but we were in time to see the great Lama Dance at the Potala, to attend the official New Year reception there, to witness the annual trance of the State Oracle, and to see how the New Year is kept in the Lhasa home.   Only Richardson remained in Lhasa to see the latter half of the celebrations during the Monlam, or Great Prayer, when twenty thousand monks are in civil command of the city.

With sound reasoning the Tibetans hold that before they can hope to celebrate an auspicious New Year, all the evil influences that have accumulated in the Old Year must be exorcised and driven from the Holy City.   Accordingly, on the twenty-ninth day of the last month of the Old Year a Devil Dance takes place in the great eastern courtyard of the Potala.   All Lhasa officials from the Regent downwards must be there.

We had been invited to attend this dance by the Cabinet.   From the point of view of photography it was difficult to find out the exact order and times of the various ceremonies; reports were as usual contradictory.   At last Jigme, after consulting Tsarong, gave me a beautifully typed programme of events, but was careful to explain that the times given were merely approximate. In some cases they might start as much as four hours late.   On this occasion I went especially early to photograph the officials riding up to the northern gateway of the Potala.   Jigme and I had examined the track and found a place suitable for photography where the morning sun would shine on the gay dresses of the officials.   Jigme said I ought to be there by seven o'clock, but Ringang assured me that no one would appear until eight-thirty or nine.   However, I preferred to be on the safe side; so the Doctor and I rode out just as the sun was reddening the top of the holy mountain behind Drepung.   The Doctor had volunteered to help, as I wanted records of the procession and dance in every photographic medium.   We fixed up the cameras and waited for an hour as the sun slowly transformed the valley beneath us. It was an admirable setting.   We could " shoot " the officials just as they turned a corner of the steep zigzag road.   In the background was the turquoise pool of the Snake Temple framed by leafless branches.

At first a few old monks and servants straggled up, mounted on mules; then came a group of monk officials, followed by scattered parties of lay officials in geluchay dress. The colours looked unspeakably lovely in the early morning sun: the high monk officials swathed in mulberry-coloured wrappings and with yellow silk showing at the neck and on the crown of their fur-edged hats; a magistrate with basin hat and bright scarlet gown over his silk; and, most resplendent of all, the geluchays, a kaleidoscopic medley of variegated colours. They were all in their best clothes on this day, and I had the impression of watching some gay medieval pageant, some fantastic Hollywood production, or a throng of people in fancy dress. Yuto was wearing a long saffron and green silk robe and wide red-topped fur hat. Tsarong wore a glistening brocade dress with a multi-coloured pattern of scaly dragons. The Shap-pes, who, as befitted their rank, came late, wore brightly patterned robes instead of their yellow silk. They seemed to have even more than the usual crowd of scarlet-hatted outriders, servants and grooms—perhaps because they arrived separately instead of together.

At last there was a great stir down below and we knew that the Regent was coming. For once he was on horseback, and not carried in his palanquin. In front of him rode his usual monk officials, including Simple Simon, grinning from ear to ear and looking colossal on a minute and unfortunate mule. The Regent was dressed in yellow and vermilion silk, and his pony was hung with gay trappings. He wore a large yellow hood, exposing only his face, and dark glasses. I was photographing furiously with one camera after another, but he did not seem to mind. In fact he smiled to us as he passed, as did all the officials except old Lungchungna, who doesn't approve of such new-fangled things as cameras, and one rather apathetic Tegi who had never called on us because he said he could not afford a present. The Ringangs were the last to arrive just as we were moving off at about nine o'clock. Morgan told big Ringang that he ought to carry his pony instead of riding the wretched thing up the hill. This seemed to amuse him vastly. After that we went inside the Potala and down the steps into the eastern court, where the Devil Dance was to be performed.

Here everybody was bustling about getting things ready. They had hung a lovely scarlet, green and gold silk curtain with a huge dragon pattern at the top of the steps. Above some of the windows are large scarlet and yellow pelmets, and over the triple staircase a fringe of many-pointed strips of different-coloured silks gives the impression of a patchwork quilt, except that there is a regular pattern zigzagging through the separate pieces. Right along the northern side of the courtyard an awning with a brightly coloured valance was supported by a series of cords running across to the southern side. The top-centre of this is ornamented in blue appliqué work with a huge scarlet and yellow dragon's head. Beneath it the monk band were collecting their drums and trumpets. There was a very striking stand for the long trumpets, carved in the semblance of two gilded skeletons.

As we did not want to make ourselves too conspicuous, the Doctor and I went up to our balcony immediately above the eastern entrance to the court. We had been offered the one above as being more honourable, but as the lower one is better for photography, Gould decided to leave the upper one to the Chinese, who will think they are one up on us and be duly pleased. I rigged up my cameras (seven of them) while a young monk in a very decorative gold and scarlet braid undercoat brought us Tibetan tea in a great silver-gilt teapot. This was most welcome, as there was a bitter north wind blowing and we were in the shade. It was clouding up by now and threatening snow. We wondered if this would be auspicious.

Down below us the courtyard is gradually filling with a motley crowd of men-at-arms in all kinds of antiquated and dilapidated armour. A few minor officials with ragged pigtails and wearing faded scarlet cloaks over their silk robes are drilling the soldiers— of whom there are several hundred—into some semblance of order. They are in two lines now; some of them are blowing small brass trumpets, while others sing a dirge and stamp to and fro as if the two ranks were enacting a mock battle. Those who are not actually taking part form a great circle round the edge of the court. There seems to be a series of scenes acted by different units. One group wears enormous plumed head-dresses ornamented with bunches of white fluff, and dances a stately minuet; another has the black tail-feathers of a cock streaming from his hat like an Italian soldier. One scene is acted by solemn spearmen with daggers in their belts. The two ranks close and some argument seems to be carried on, chiefly by the leaders, while they make dignified passes at each other. Their places are soon taken by bowmen who have enormous conical basket-work shields; they

wear khaki-coloured uniforms and a halo of rolled cloth round
their leather or iron helmets. Their armour consists of metal
plates, about two inches long and half an inch in width, threaded
loosely together.

The most interesting of these war dances is done by men with
incredibly ancient flint-lock guns with rusty barrels encased in
wood. The soldiers are drawn up in two lines; after the usual
chanting, disputing and goose-stepping, the ranks turn their
backs on each other and, holding their weapons at waist level,
point them backwards at their opponents. At a word from the
scarlet-robed conductor of ceremonies they apply fuses to the
breeches of the guns and, after a tremendous explosion, the
courtyard is completely filled with smoke. Much to my surprise
there were no casualties.

Although they cannot get much practice, these men seem to
know the drill extraordinarily well. After their exertions, all
the warriors sit down on the courtyard floor and are given tea and
tsamba.

Gould and Richardson arrived about this time (ten o'clock),
the former wisely wearing his fur-lined Tibetan coat. Meanwhile other spectators were arriving. The gallery on the south,
and the flat roof above it, soon filled up with ladies of rank and
citizens of Lhasa. We waved to the Tsarong women-folk who
were dressed up in all their finery.

Across the top of the banisters above the triple flight of steps
there was a silver and gilt trumpet-rest. Down the outer staircase
(the central one is normally reserved for the exclusive use of the
Dalai Lama) crowds of officials and monks poured; the former
sat beneath an awning on the flat roof to our left, while the monks
formed a crowd on either side of the foot of the steps. The Regent
and the Prime Minister appeared at a sixth-storey window on the
left of the great eastern façade of the Potala, while the Shap-pes,
Dzasas, Tegis, and other high officials could be seen in one of the
long windows directly above the triple staircase. The more
senior the official, the worse the view: such is the burden of office.

Suddenly there are three resounding blasts from the great
trumpets at the top of the steps, and the fifty or sixty members
of the monk band troop down and take their places under the
awning. As well as the long bass trumpets there are drums—or
rather gongs, shaped like old-fashioned warming-pans supported

on their one leg, beaten with curiously curved drumsticks—two sorts of cymbals, and small trumpets with piercing cornet-like notes. Once more the trumpets boom, and a portentous figure with a vermilion gown hung over his long golden robe and wearing a monstrous grinning mask, strides ponderously down the steps and into the court. Hanging from his neck is an enormous rosary. His progress is slow because after every few steps he pauses with one foot raised. This is Hashang, known the world over as " The Laughing Buddha ", the Chinese priest-god of happiness. With him, hand in hand, walk three pairs of attendants. The inner pair, whose tiny stature emphasizes Hashang's colossal bulk, are two small Alice-in-Wonderland-like figures with smiling masks, long hair and wide blue-black skirts held tightly in at the waist. The outer couple have pale skeleton masks and red and white costumes. The remaining pair have Brahman-like dresses, recalling the early connection of Lamaism and Hinduism. After turning about and bowing deeply to the Regent, they march to a chair, where Hashang is destined to sit, absolutely motionless, throughout the whole performance, his vast bald head making a foreground for most of my photographs.

The trumpets blow again and two dancers in demon masks run down the steps scattering rice from bowls held by monk attendants. They dance their way down the steps, and, to the insistent music of the band, they start to pirouette round the court. After a few minutes they return up the steps and two more dancers differently attired take their place. The dancing is much the same all the time. With arms outstretched to make the most of their long and highly ornamented sleeves, the dancers balance on one foot, turn slowly, hop once or twice, and turn again. The measure is simple but effective, combining stylized posturing with acrobatic pirouetting. Considerable control of balance is required, as they often turn round several times on one leg before putting down the other foot. Some of the masks are horned to represent bulls or stags; others have exaggeratedly hideous faces, scarlet, gold or green, with staring eyes and grinning fangs. Yet they look grotesquely realistic, being skilfully made of wood or papier mâché, while the back of the mask is hidden by a piece of cloth which hangs down behind. The dresses themselves are very long and full enough to flow as the dancer swings and turns. In the front hangs an apron of gorgeous embroidery, and the wide pointed sleeves are cut so as almost to reach the ground. Every imaginable colour is there, with black, red, and yellow predominating.

After nine pairs of these dancers have come and gone, the crowd, which has been comparatively silent until now, suddenly starts to whistle. This is the traditional reception for the skeleton dancers, four of whom now appear scattering white ashes as they hop down the steps. These are ghoulish figures with grinning skeleton heads, large ears, and long bony fingers and claws. Instead of flowing robes they wear close-fitting red garments on which the bones stand out in white, and they dance with considerable agility to a rapid pulsating measure. In the middle of the courtyard there is now a square carpet with the crude effigy of a head at one end, and arms and legs at the corners. Round this " corpse " the figures dance, mopping and mowing and clattering their thin bony fingers.

Meanwhile another actor has made his entry. This is the Ancient Man. Wearing an astonishingly life-like mask, with a tonsured head and long grey beard, he leans on his stick and totters round the court. The crowd shouts with joy as he sinks pathetically to the ground and feebly raises himself, only to fall again and again. Now he is given a large bowl of dried fruits and sweets. At a given signal the crowd rushes him and scrambles for the dainties, in spite of attendants who belabour them with whips. At last a tiger-skin rug is put on the carpet where the Ancient Man carries on his antics. He walks slowly towards it, then gives it a tremendous blow with his stick; after that he rolls over and over with it in mortal struggle until at last he prevails. Now he is suddenly rejuvenated, and, casting aside the slain tiger, he leaps to his feet and dances round the court like a young man. This scene is an innovation (surely a very rare thing in Tibet) of the late Dalai Tama. While he was in China he dreamed this scene, and on his return to Lhasa he included it in the performance.

While the Ancient Man is playing the fool, the skeleton dancers scamper away and the trumpets proclaim the chief actor of the day. This is the Black Hat magician who is to lead the remainder of the ceremony. Although, as a rule, when we asked for any interpretation of the dances the answers we received were vague and contradictory, in the case of the Black Hat dance there is a well-known historical interpretation.

At the end of the ninth century Lang-dar-ma, an adherent of

the Pön religion, having murdered his brother, became king of Tibet, and within a few years had almost exterminated Tibetan Buddhism. Then a certain lama whose monastery had been destroyed determined to put an end to this reign of tyranny. Wearing black robes and a tall black hat, both of which were lined with white, and riding a white horse which he had carefully covered with soot, he attracted the attention of the king by his peculiar dance. Lang-dar-ma sent for this man and made him dance before him. The black-hatted lama, in the course of his fascinating dance, circled nearer and nearer to the king, and eventually shot him with a bow and arrow which he had concealed in his robes. In the ensuing confusion the lama reversed his hat and robe, and splashed through a river on his horse, which, as the soot was washed off, rapidly became white. The search for a black-robed assassin was therefore futile, and the lama escaped in safety.

A most impressive figure is the Black Hat dancer as, with slow dignity, he descends the steps. He wears an immense hat with a wide black-edged brim; a pyramid of gilded woodwork, carved like flames, surmounts some miniature skulls and leads up to a rosette of peacock feathers. From the back of this hat, hanging over the brim and stretching half-way to the ground, is a wide strip of gold cloth. His flowing brocade robes are ornamented with the dorje thunderbolt and with skulls set in a scarlet and yellow border. Over this he wears an apron of beads carved from human bones. His movements are fluent and graceful beyond those of former dancers as he pirouettes slowly round the court with outstretched arms, holding in one hand a dorje dagger with a blue cloth that flaps as he dances, and in the other a small imitation of a human skull, complete with flowing hair. He is weaving spells as he goes, and the crowd are silent once more.

The sun has gone in, and a violent north wind is threatening to tear away the pelmets above the windows. One corner of the great awning has broken from its noorings and flaps furiously as some men try to secure it. There are snow-squalls in the hills and it is bitterly cold.

Soon a procession of monks appears with yellow hats and long pleated cloaks. Between their shoulders a strip of scarlet-fringed brocade hangs from a diamond-shaped gold and turquoise orna-

NEW YEAR LAMA DANCE AT THE POTALA

TSARONG'S HOUSEHOLD DURING NEW YEAR CELEBRATIONS
TSARONG AND HIS WIFE

DELE RABDEN'S WIFE, MARY TERING, DAISY TERING

ment. They bear golden censers and sticks of incense. Many of them blow shrill trumpets. They lead into the courtyard about twenty more Black Hat dancers, dressed like their leader, but less resplendently. Slowly they dance round until they are arranged in a circle about the chief magician, who continues to weave his spells in the centre. Then all the masked dancers who had appeared earlier return and form an inner circle.

The court is now almost full of figures dancing slowly round. The band has become more animated and the continued pounding rhythm has an almost hypnotic effect. Every now and then there is a burst of music much resembling that of bagpipes, and always the clanging of cymbals drowned at intervals by the ponderous booming of the long trumpets.

Just beyond the mock corpse—which has had to be weighted down to prevent it blowing away—a table has been put, covered with a silk cloth, and beside the " corpse " a square tiger-skin rug edged with blue. On the table are various religious insignia, a bell, a dorje, axes, swords, daggers, a chain, and bowls and drums made from human skulls. Behind the table stand several lamas with gold libation jugs and a large golden dish. The chief magician now goes through a complicated ceremony, taking each of these insignia in turn and, after dancing round, brandishes them over the corpse. Finally water and blood are poured from skulls over the corpse, which has now been chained; and the Black Hats, who have been dancing for several hours continuously, are at last allowed to rest.

The wind is now howling round the court, and many of the spectators have gone home. Clouds are sweeping overhead. It seems that the very elements have been invoked in this potent ceremony of driving away the devils.

All at once the rhythm of the band increases to an insistent " Tum, tum, te-tum. Tum, tum, te-tum ", and a tiny figure, dressed in silver and with a huge stag's-head mask, jigs down the steps. This goblin-like creature dances at great speed with his arms held straight out in front of him. He rushes round with flying robes, kicking first one leg then the other high in the air. At last he squats over the corpse, still with his arms stretched out in front. He twitches up and down in time with the music and every now and then jumps right round, landing on his haunches again : he is certainly something of an acrobat.

O

All this time, in one corner of the court, a fire of thorns has been heating a huge cauldron of rancid mustard-oil. The chief magician, with dignified and portentous movements, approaches this and pours a skullful of spirit into it. There is a tremendous flash and the oil blazes up. The stand is pulled from beneath the cauldron, and the burning oil pours over the floor. A paper with effigies of all the devils is consumed in the flames.

This is the end of the dance. All at once, as if the devils that have accumulated in the Old Year are indeed destroyed, the sky is miraculously cleared, the wind drops, and the evening sun shines through once more. The dancers—how weary they must be!— slowly ascend the steps. The band straggles away. The officials are no longer seen at the upper windows. Hashang, with his line of supporters, walks slowly back across the court, his scarlet robe blazing in the evening sunlight. Once more the stage is filled with the motley army—a medley of plumed hats, venerable muskets and shields. Copper trumpets, blown by small warriors, sound from either end of the court, and a procession of monks headed by acolytes with censers streams down the steps. Once they are in the court two enormous thankas are hung in front of the silk curtain.

This is the final act of the ceremony, when a *torma*, or image made of dough and invested with devils, is carried down the Potala steps and burnt beside the obelisk at the foot.

The procession, several hundred strong, is most impressive. It is headed by monks carrying tall cylindrical banners surmounted by tridents; then follow a great number of monks with crested yellow hats and pleated cloaks. About thirty of them carry on their shoulders golden drums, which they beat with the long curving drumsticks. Others have cymbals, bells or trumpets. After these come men in silk robes of a chequered pattern we have not hitherto seen, and with scarlet fur-edged hats. As the procession leaves the court the soldiers give wild war-cries, trumpets are blown, and guns fired into the air. Right down the long zigzag staircase and through the southern gate they stream, then, crossing the road, they stop just beside the stone column on which past history is recorded. Here, after more music and a wild fusillade of shots, the torma is solemnly burnt in a great fire of thorns and mustard-straw.

The people disperse silently to their homes. The sun sets

incarnadine behind the mountains. The devils are finally and effectually driven away from the Holy City.

On 12th February the New Year was officially celebrated in the Potala by a religious ceremony which had to be attended by all officials, wearing robes reserved for this special occasion.

The Tibetan Government paid us a great compliment by inviting us on this day; for the Chinese, Nepalese and Bhutanese representatives came for the second and less intimate ceremony of the following day.

On the first day of the New Year everyone is awakened before it is light and begins the year with a bowl of chang, which must be drained even by small children. Then all officials go at dawn to the Cathedral, where they visit the more important shrines, and then on to the Potala.

The chief of the New Year ceremonies is celebrated in the Dalai Lama's throne-room, a large pillared hall lit only by skylights in the roof. At the northern end of the hall is the high throne of the Dalai Lama, covered in silken cloth and cushions. On the right are much lower thrones for the Regent and the Prime Minister. Next to them, separated by a few yards, are the abbots of Ganden, Drepung and Sera, " The Three Pillars of the State ", muffled against the cold in yellow cloaks with broad edgings of red brocade. Opposite the Dalai Lama's throne are the Duke, Shap-pes, Dzasas and Tegis (the fourth-rank officials). Some of them wear robes with an edging of silver-fox fur on the skirt and cuffs, and with a short cape, similarly bordered, falling over their shoulders; others wear dresses of heavy flowered brocade. All wear wide flat fur hats with scarlet tops. We sit on low cushions on the fourth side of this square while the fifth-rank and junior officials sit behind in their many-hued geluchay dresses. Suddenly the shrill note of cornets is heard and lights flicker in the dark passage. An attendant unrolls a strip of white silk carpet from the door to the foot of the throne. Robes and other possessions of the late Dalai Lama are arranged on the throne to represent his presence. (Tucked into the robes is an object which looks suspiciously like an aluminium hot-water bottle.) When all has been arranged with loving care by the Lord Chamberlain and other monk officials, the lights and trumpeting come nearer, and the Regent enters the hall clad in yellow robes and wearing a mitre-shaped yellow hat. He takes off this cap, prostrates himself three times before the throne, then offers a scarf. The Prime Minister and other officials follow in order of precedence and present scarves to the throne and then to the Regent and the Prime Minister. We also present our scarves, and then the Lord Chamberlain goes round the assembly with an enquiry from the Regent as to the health of all the officers. Tea is then served in a heavy gold dragon-patterned teapot for the Dalai Lama's presence, and in silver for the rest of the company. Each of the officials produces his own wooden teacup from his robe.

The Dalai Lama's tea is first tasted by a monk official, as a precaution against poison. The monk officials go round filling up the teacups, swirling the pot round and round to make sure that it is well mixed.

Two abbots, one from Drepung and the other from Sera, stand on one side of the throne and begin a religious debate, making their points with much pounding of the palm and occasional shrill cries. The smaller one, who is more frail, seems to be completely browbeaten by the other, who speaks and shouts with overbearing vehemence. There are two monks sitting on cushions in the middle of the hall. Upon asking what their function is, we are told they are recording history; but the history of this ceremony must long since have become a matter of mere repetition, and they are not even provided with pens and paper.

A band strikes up, and thirteen curious figures in blue and red flowered robes and flat tam-o'-shanter hats file into the hall. These are the Dalai Lama's dancing boys, a lay troupe whose services are a form of taxation. Each carries a small battle-axe in his hands. The troupe have suffered neglect since the Dalai died (or perhaps it is inauspicious to repair their clothes), for their boots are out at heel and their robes torn and faded. Keeping in line, they perform a number of formal dances, sometimes posturing with hips protruded sideways and striking stylized attitudes, at other times displaying considerable acrobatic skill. The dance is quite short, and is succeeded by a further instalment of the debate and more tea. Each official is then presented with a large bone covered with meat, but this is more in the nature of a symbol and —to our great relief—is not meant to be eaten.

The dancers return, and then messengers come in with letters and presents for the Dalai Lama, and tables loaded with food of all kinds are set out in the middle of the hall. There are great piles of bread and maize-cakes, plates of dried fruits and sweets, joints of beef and mutton, and whole dried carcasses of sheep and yaks, complete with head and horns. There seems to be enough food for an army.

Soon some of the offerings are laid before the Dalai Lama's throne and others are handed round to the officials; after this the Potala servants are allowed to scramble for the rest. There is a rush and the vast pile is covered with struggling figures, who drag away the carcasses and fill their robes with what they can lay hands on. Tall monk attendants belabour the fighting mass with whips and sticks, a precaution against any but the poor taking part, and to prevent anyone getting more than his share; but the victims wear plenty of thick clothes and do not seem to mind the beating.

When the floor is again clear the debate goes on and is followed by a third and final dance. Then one of the abbots recites a long prayer before the throne, ending with a high-pitched cry.

The ceremony is at an end. The Regent and the Prime Minister withdraw in procession as they came, and after them all the officials leave the hall and go up on to the Potala roof for the final part of the ceremony.

This is the real Tibetan New Year's Day, and is celebrated by the Lhasa people in no uncertain way. For days past they have been baking cakes and biscuits and brewing enormous quantities of chang. In front of the family altar is arranged a wooden box containing barley-flour, butter ornaments painted and picked out with gold leaf, bowls of chang, pots of green barley-shoots and other traditional offerings.

Many calls are paid on this day, and as soon as the visitor arrives he is offered the box of barley-flour in which stands a piece of wood ornamented with coloured butter designs and a few shoots of a red-stalked spiraea that grows in the hills. The guest takes a pinch of the flour between the thumb and third finger of the right hand and throws it skywards as a libation to the gods.

The streets of Lhasa are crowded with people in their best clothes, skipping, kicking up the shuttlecock, letting off cheap Chinese fireworks and gambling. A vast quantity of chang is drunk, and the people stagger about arm-in-arm singing songs or dancing.

As soon as we got home from the Potala, Tsarong came to

present a scarf of greeting and a small gift to each of us. He was wearing a remarkable brocade dress of such heavy silk that it would practically stand up even if he were not in it. The general colour was pale saffron, and it had a large pattern of dragons and flowers. We discovered it had cost him two thousand rupees (£150).

During the course of the day several other officials came to pay their respects to the Political Officer, but no one stayed long for there were many other visits to be made.

The traditional greeting is, " *Tashi dela phun-sum tso, tendu dewa thop-pa sho* " ! which means " May you enjoy the three blessings (health, wealth, and good repute), and may your days be filled with peace and happiness."

Several officials told me of a very special ceremonial dress that is stored in the Potala and is worn for this one ceremony of the New Year by thirteen young officials chosen by the Dalai Lama or Regent. They said it would not upset anybody if I went up at about eight o'clock while the officials were dressing-up, to photograph them. I was rather reluctant to " butt in " where I had not officially been invited, but Norbhu seemed to think it was all right, so up I went. Yuto and Kyipup were among the thirteen, and they promised to look after me.

The dress, which is supposed to be part of the actual wardrobe of the ancient kings of Tibet, was even beyond my expectations. Over somewhat tattered silk robes, each wore two long necklaces, one of amber with beads as big as tangerines, and the other of coral. In the centre was a golden breast-plate six inches in diameter set with concentric rings of turquoises. From each side of the head two ornaments were suspended; one, a bar of gold eighteen inches long studded with a row of ancient Tibetan turquoises, was so heavy that it had to be supported in the hand; the other, also of gold and turquoises, was in the shape of a flattened pear, and possibly represented a conch-shell. Two of the thirteen were selected for special ceremonial duties; they wore high-crowned scarlet hats adorned with peacock feathers, while the others wore a smaller silken head-dress. Having photographed these dresses in colour, I slipped away before any of the others arrived.

The ceremony on this day was much the same as the one we

witnessed on the day before; but whereas the other had been the priestly celebration of the New Year, this was particularly for the laymen. The abbots were not present; the debate was conducted by Doctors of Divinity; the dancers carried swords instead of battle-axes, and there was a short Devil Dance. After the ceremony all the officials went up on to the roof of the Potala, where there was much blowing of cornets and of the long deep-toned trumpets.

Then followed a ceremony that all Lhasa turned out to see. In the old days a yak-hair rope was stretched from the roof of the Potala to a stone edict pillar at the foot of the southern staircase, hundreds of feet below. Then several men, protected by leather saddles, slid down the rope at terrific speed. To provide these men was a form of taxation levied on certain villages. The men usually arrived at the bottom in a half-dead condition, and on one occasion a performer slipped beneath the rope in his descent and was nearly killed. So the Dalai Lama stopped this performance on the grounds of cruelty, and substituted another acrobatic feat, which I was lucky enough to witness and photograph from the flat roof of the " War Office " building overlooking the edict pillar.

Here a tall pole, say fifty feet high, swathed in yak-hair cloth to prevent it splitting, was put up on the flat paved platform at the foot of the wide Potala staircase, and was held in position by yak-hair shrouds. Meanwhile crowds of people were settling themselves down to wait on the steps—which are here about eight yards wide—and on the flat-topped balustrade alongside. On the roofs of the neighbouring houses there were many chang parties in progress, and everybody seemed to be laughing and happy. Many ladies of fashion appeared in all their finery of seed-pearl and coral head-dresses, purple silk robes, and turquoise charm-boxes.

The majority wore the triangular Lhasa head-dress, but there were several of the tall-hooped Gyantse fashion. On this day I saw one—the only one I ever saw in Lhasa—of a design which was fashionable (judging by old photographs) some years ago. It consisted of the usual framework studded with turquoise and coral, but it was coiled close to the head like a tiara. It seemed to me to be much more practicable than either of the head-dresses which are at present fashionable.

On the roof next to mine several tents had been put up. I could see a group of buxom nuns in small yellow conical hats exchanging pleasantries with some blue-uniformed Nepalese soldiers who, like most people on this day, had been drinking plenty of chang.

Sitting on the ample steps of the Potala were the poorer people : a party of tousle-headed Khampa shepherds wearing coarse sheep-skin robes; some monks with close-cropped hair and voluminous claret-coloured dresses; some beggar-women spinning prayer-wheels, and in front of the crowd a small boy with a mask over his shoulder shrilly asking for alms.

At last, after most of us have been there for several hours, the orchestra on the Potala roof works itself up to a furious crescendo, and the officials are seen to be descending. There is a sudden stir up above, and a couple of men come rushing down the steps dragging by its legs the carcass of a yak with its sharp-horned head swinging from side to side and effectively clearing a way through the crowd for the officials, who came down the steps in small groups. On this day alone of the year even the highest officials must wear geluchay dress, and I can pick out Tsarong with his white cockle-hat, and the Shap-pes similarly dressed. To-day many of the servants, and quite junior officials, wear silk dresses and scarlet-topped hats. From above, a ribbon of gay colours appears to descend through the middle of the sombrely clad crowd like a rainbow in a stormy sky. Some of the officials, having seen this performance many times before, ride away through the crowd that has by now filled the roadways below.

All at once there is a hush, and a man looking—and probably feeling—singularly like a sacrifice, is swung astride a rope pre-paratory to being hauled to the top of the pole. While he is only just above the heads of the crowd he starts to chant, and drinks a cup of tea which is handed up to him. His head is bound with a white cloth. On the summit of the pole is a small platform on which there is just room to stand. Above this projects a short rod of iron. To begin with, the man, chanting all the time, stands for a moment on the platform; but a strong wind makes this too precarious, and he is obviously not too confident. After all, the pole was only put up a few hours ago, and he cannot have had much opportunity for rehearsals. He takes his boots off and throws them down into the crowd. Several times he stands up with his arms outstretched, but only for a brief moment. Then, tying a bobbin-shaped piece of wood on to his stomach, he fits this over the top of the metal rod and, with arms and legs outstretched, starts to spin round and round. After he has repeated this several times he is allowed to return to terra firma, where he bows down three times towards the Potala, offering thanks that his ordeal is safely over. Many of the crowd throw coins into his hat as they disperse to their homes.

On the following day, 14th February, all the officials, including the Regent and Prime Minister, had to go to the monastery of the State Oracle. We had not been invited to attend this, but Tsarong thought it would be a good chance for me to get some photographs, and offered to take me with him and to look after me.

That morning it snowed for the first time since the early autumn, and the procession was two hours late in starting. But by then, ten o'clock, blue sky appeared through the snow-clouds. There was an inch of snow everywhere and the sun was just breaking through. The Regent's palanquin was well ahead by now, so we had to hurry. The mountains, already glistening white in the sunshine, glowed through the lifting snow-clouds with the remarkable luminosity of icebergs in moonlight which has not yet touched the surrounding waves.

Hundreds and hundreds of monks from Drepung were streaming along the track on their way to the city, where twenty thousand would be assembled that night to take over control of Lhasa during the Great Prayer. Never have I seen a more evil-looking crowd. They refused to get out of the way of Tsarong's pony, and one who was squatting down right in the middle of the track just stayed there while Tsarong had to turn aside. Hardly a single friendly face or smile of salutation did I see. Many of the monks had blackened their faces; Jigme said that this denotes special bravery. When I asked how a monk proved his bravery, he answered, " By fighting with his fellows ".

Not till we reached the turning leading to Drepung and Nechung did we catch up with the procession. Nearly every official in Lhasa seemed to be there. About twenty of them were actually waiting on the Regent, while the others went on in front. Including servants, there must have been about four hundred riders. I rode with Surkang-Se and Yuto—nobody seemed at all surprised to see me. Leaving our ponies under the big trees which surrounded Nechung, we followed the narrow passage to the main entrance of the court. Tsarong found a place for me just beside the entrance but beneath the cloister roof, so I was fairly inconspicuous and the light was excellent. I collected a small table to stand on so that I could take photographs above the heads of the crowd who half filled the court. Eight drummers of the band were sitting on the floor in front of the steps which led to an ante-room in front of the main hall of the monastery. Here seats for the officials had been prepared. On each side of the steps was a white porcelain Chinese lion picked out in green and blue. A rather crude frieze consisting of different-coloured rectangles of cloth was hung right round the court. All the pillars were swathed in red cloth and were decorated with a ring of warlike emblems. There were suits of armour, old muzzle-loading guns, helmets, swords and copper trumpets.

Almost immediately the Regent, Prime Minister, Shap-pes and a crowd of monk and lay officials walked across the courtyard and took up their positions on the raised balcony in strict order of precedence. Tea was brought round, and the dance started.

This Nechung Devil Dance was quite different from that at the Potala. The whole dance was finished in less than an hour, and though the Black Hats were there, most of the dresses were new to me. One party of eight or so monk-like figures, two of whom were tall, but the rest children, wore checkered red and yellow cloaks over their lamas' robes, and wide-brimmed lacquered hats. Another group wore skeleton masks and white costumes ornamented only with two big squares of green, red, yellow, and blue. One act was performed by men dressed entirely in black, and in another, costumes similar to those worn by the Lhasa mummers appeared. There was also a procession of the multi-coloured cylindrical banners held high on poles. After the dance more tea was served, and the Oracle, dressed splendidly in cloth of gold and wearing an enormous jewelled and feathered head-dress, appeared from the door just behind me and walked, unobserved by the crowd, to a side door leading to the main shrine of the monastery, which lay just beyond where the officials were drinking tea.

Now that the droning of the long trumpets had stopped there was comparative silence, except for the crowing of two gorgeously coloured cocks that had wandered on to the dance-floor. Looking round, I was struck by the extraordinarily macabre tone of the decoration. Grinning skulls leered malignantly from the tops of the pillars, and all the back wall and roof of the cloister were covered with paintings of the many Buddhist hells. Here a demoniacal figure with grinning fangs crushed a poor diminutive mortal beneath his tongue, in his hand he held a skull from which the eyes, but recently gouged out, were still suspended. All the varied tortures of the tantalized spirits were graphically depicted. Never have I seen paintings executed with so gruesome a fantasy.

There seemed to be a pause in the proceedings, but from the inside of the main monastery hall could be heard the incessant and monotonous beating of drums and the rhythmic clanging of cymbals where the Oracle was being possessed by the Spirit of Nechung.

All at once there was a stir at the top of the steps: the officials near the inner doorway stood up; somebody upset a table and the cups tinkled on to the stone floor. The Oracle, shaking all over and very red in the face, emerged from the inner room. His outstretched arms were supported by two monks; others were in close attendance.

It was difficult to see exactly what happened, as the Oracle was surrounded by officials in the confined and shadowy space at the top of the steps. I was disappointed that he did not descend into the courtyard. At one moment he became violent: I saw the officials press back out of his way—for on several occasions the Oracles have injured people when possessed—and I could see the attendant monks clinging with difficulty to his outstretched arms. But the spasm passed, and all was still again except for the tremulous agitation of the plumes in his tall head-dress and the movement of a monk who was straightening out the Oracle's robes. For some time he seemed to be whispering to the Regent, who could be seen leaning forward on his throne. Then he swayed gently to and fro until he suddenly disappeared as he collapsed into the arms of his attendants.

The Regent did not disclose what was said to him, and the message to the general public was unintelligible; but in any case it is only understood by his attendant monks, who interpret it as they think fit. But I gather his utterances resemble those of

the Delphic Oracle in being conveniently equivocal. After the
Oracle had been assisted back to the inner hall the officials dispersed,
and I hurried ahead to photograph the returning procession. I
had hoped to take it in the beautiful and unusual setting of snow,
but by now it had all melted. I noted that the monk officials
surrounding the Regent were wearing tall fur hats of a type I had
not seen before. It was like a busby in shape, wider at the top
than at the bottom, and surmounted by a jewelled emblem. I
rode back with Möndö, who seemed much amused by the whole
proceeding. It must be difficult for an old Rugbeian to live up
to the standard of credulity demanded by the Lamaist faith.
Tsarong had said that the snow was most auspicious, and as Yuto
had stated that it was extremely inauspicious, I asked Möndö what
he thought, "Well," he replied, "I don't think it makes any
difference ".

In the afternoon there was an archery competition on the plain
beside the mansion of Lhalu. Tsarong had asked us to lunch with
him in the Lhalu house and then to watch the sport.

Young Lhalu was in attendance on the Regent, who was con-
ducting some ceremony at the Potala, but his wife (if she is his
wife; someone told me she was his adopted mother) acted as
hostess. Lhalu is the son of the ill-fated Lungsha who lies in the
Potala dungeons; but in Tibet they do not visit the sins of the
fathers upon the children, and, having changed his name, he was
taken into the family of Lhalu, which at that time had suffered a
succession of misfortunes and was left without an heir. The lady
of Lhalu was of middle age and extremely stout. She wore the
most wonderful jewellery, and was more made-up than any
Tibetan woman I had seen. Being the daughter of one Kung and
the widow of another, she is one of the first ladies of Lhasa.

We had lunch in a completely bare room with whitewashed
walls, the only articles of furniture being a large table and chairs.
It was little consolation to discover that this was " the English
room ".

Our hostess was wonderfully good company. She and
Tsarong, who were old friends, exchanged lively repartee throughout the meal. The lunch was excellent, but our indefatigable
hostess made us eat far more than we wanted, and absolutely
forced us to drink quantities of excellent but most potent chang.
Tsarong, who had not been let off quite so lightly as ourselves,

remarked as, somewhat unsteadily, we left the house, " That fat Mrs.; very difficult ! " and roared with laughter.

The archery contests were rather spoilt by the fact that the sun had gone in and a bitterly cold wind was blowing. The " grand-stand " consisted of a flat-roofed building shaped like a square with one side missing. The Shap-pes, who were judging the competition, sat under cover at the back; we were given a place on the roof, unfortunately in the direct line of smoke from a thorn fire below us where an immense urn of tea was being boiled.

At the open side of the building the competitors, most of them servants representing various officials, were stringing their bows preparatory to shooting in the long-distance competition. In front of the archers swastikas and other lucky signs had been drawn in white on the ground.

The mark was a flag some two hundred yards distant, but many of the competitors shot almost another hundred yards beyond it. It was noticeable that at nearly every shot the bow-string broke. In Bhutan the strings are made of cord woven from the skin of stinging-nettles; these do not break. In Tibet they use grass or reeds. The bows were made of wild yak-horn or simply of bamboo.

Yuto Depön, in an interval, measured the lengths of the shots (this was appropriate, seeing that depön literally means " lord of the arrow ").

Later on, whistling-arrows were shot at a small ring suspended in front of a curtain. Some of the officers themselves competed, among them an old City Magistrate who is a famous archer; he, in fact, won the competition. The whistling noise is made by a flat-ended square of wood which takes the place of the point of the arrow. It is so pierced that a deep vibrant hum is caused as the arrow cleaves the air.

In the evening we all went to Tsarong's house to see how the New Year is celebrated in the home. Tsarong was very anxious that we should see this, and had made special arrangements so that I could take photographs by artificial light.

In front of his private altar were the traditional boxes of tsamba and grain, jugs of chang, bowls of dried and fresh fruit, plates of sugar and other sweetmeats, and rams' skulls filled with barley-dough and adorned with patterns of coloured butter and gold leaf. There were also intricate ornaments—made by the monks —of barley-dough and picked out in the same way, and the bowls of sprouting barley which were to be seen in every house.

On one side of the room was a high throne for Tsarong, and next to it on the left, another, slightly lower, for his wife, and others, lower still, for the three children. Seats for the guests of the house were arranged on another side of the room. In front of each seat were carved Tibetan tables, also graded in height, on each of which was placed a chang-bowl, a circular wooden bowl with its lid held up on a square column of barley-dough, and a fluted silver basin for scraps. Tsarong wore his heavy brocade robe and fur hat, while the women, as well as their accustomed finery, wore round their shoulders sashes of many-coloured silk similar to the scarf worn in geluchay dress.

A servant then brought round the box of tsamba and grain, and silver bowls of chang; of these a little had to be taken between the thumb and third finger and thrown into the air. Tea, and bowls of a root not unlike truffles cooked in butter, and rice were put in front of each person. These are auspicious food, of which each person has to eat a little. After this a woman-servant held up a bowl of chang in front of Tsarong; and the other servants, of whom there were about twenty, lined up behind her and danced and sang a song of good wishes. The steward then poured out chang from the silver bowl for Tsarong. Three separate draughts had to be drunk; the cup being filled again after each draught. When Tsarong had done this, the steward respectfully hung a white silk scarf round his neck. He then gave chang to each member of the family in the same way and hung scarves round their necks. Then the servants came up with their bowls, and Tsarong now gave chang to them. The servants then brought trays of food as an offering and laid them before each member of the family; finally they took off their hats, bowed, and put out their tongues. The presents were removed and the ceremony was over. It was all very simple, and the atmosphere, although dignified, was friendly, and emphasized the patriarchal nature of the family. It would be hard to find a people who can keep up their tradition with greater dignity and less self-consciousness than the Tibetans.

By now, the fourth day of the New Year, the *Monlam*, or "Great Prayer", had started, some thirty thousand monks having come into the city on 14th February. The object of this festival is to shorten the time which must elapse before the reign of the Coming Buddha of " Conquering Love ".

The Great Prayer was instituted by Tsong-kapa at the beginning of the fifteenth century, and was added to by the fifth Dalai Lama a hundred and fifty years later.

The monks are quartered on the people, and for three weeks two Provosts of Drepung rule the city, assisted by a number of monk " police " armed with whips. Before the provosts are carried the square metal maces which we had seen at Drepung and Sera. In former times the monks used to abuse their power by paying off old grudges against the lay officials and by extorting large sums of money in fines. But the late Dalai Lama very much lessened this abuse.

When we were riding out one evening to pay a farewell call, we met one of these provosts riding in state through the streets, preceded by his mace-bearers and a group of monks who were inspecting the houses. During the Great Prayer the monks insist on a high standard of cleanliness in the streets, and we found that clean valances had been hung over windows and doors, and that the street in front of each house had been swept clean and orna-mented with auspicious designs traced in white ash.

Every day services are held in the great assembly-room of the Cathedral, which is capable of holding 20,000 monks. When we went to bid farewell to the Cabinet in a small room leading off the Cathedral roof, we looked down and saw there thousands of red-robed monks swaying backwards and forwards in prayer, and producing a noise like the murmur of a distant storm.

On the fifteenth day of the first month there is a festival of lights similar to that described to commemorate the death of Tsong-kapa.

After the reign of the monks, several days are devoted to the New Year games, over which two young officials are chosen to preside.

First there is a procession of cavalry dressed and armed like the mounted soldier of the ancient Tibetan kings. Then there are horse-races; the ponies are always riderless, but they are directed by relays of mounted grooms. Each official is bound to send in a certain number of entries, according to his rank. These are followed by foot-races and wrestling contests, and by shooting at targets with guns and bows from the back of a galloping horse.

And in addition to all this, there are religious ceremonies. One day huge images of butter and tsamba are fashioned by the lamas. An image of the Coming Buddha is carried round the city in solemn procession. The Nechung Oracle visits Lhasa and foretells the prosperity of the coming year.

And so, the declining reign of Gautama Buddha is hurried towards its close, and that of " Conquering Love " is brought nearer.

## CONCLUSION

ALTHOUGH, during our stay in Lhasa, there were frequent rumours that the Tashi Lama had actually set out for his monastery at Tashi-lhünpo, it became clear by the end of January that the return of His Serenity was as remote as ever. Except for the matter of the Chinese escort, the Tibetan Government had conceded almost everything that the Tashi Lama had requested; but still he found excuses to remain the precarious guest of China.

It was heard in Lhasa that among the hundreds of camel-loads of his advance baggage was found a consignment of bombs; this did little to convince the Government of the Tashi Lama's friendly intentions.

We were forced to realize either that he was so much indebted to China that he was no longer a free agent, or that the officials of his entourage, wedded to Chinese wives, and in the generous pay of the Nanking Government, were so reluctant to hazard an uncertain welcome in Tibet that they had convinced the Tashi Lama of the futility and dangers of his homecoming without the protection of an escort.

Except that we had been unable to settle this matter, we seemed to have achieved our objects. The maintenance of the Mission was expensive, and Gould had other work to do in Sikkim and Bhutan. A Lhasa official likened the presence of the Mission to the shade of a great tree in the plains of India. Though we had been passive rather than active in our contacts with the people, yet we were on extraordinarily friendly terms with all classes of Tibetan society. Their great need for advice on political questions, the multifarious efforts of the Doctor, the entertainment provided by the cinema projector and the wireless loud-speaker had all done their share in breaking down what few barriers there are between the Tibetans and ourselves—for here there is nothing of the rigid caste system of the Hindus, the purdah of Mohammedan women, or any taboos on food or drink. Many of the officials had formed the habit of " dropping in " to the Deyki Lingka for tea or supper; and we had formed lasting friendships with many of the younger Tibetans.

They had grown used to the presence of the Mission. It had seemed quite natural to them that Major Finch, left alone at Gyantse, should have come up to Lhasa to spend Christmas with us. And when the main body of the Mission left for India, Richardson was left behind to suggest an element of permanency, a reminder that we had not forgotten their problems and difficulties.

Shortly before we left Lhasa the Shap-pes came to have lunch with us. When they arrived they handed to Norbhu a small scroll, together with a scarf of greeting. This was the permission for the 1938 Everest Expedition, which Gould had asked them for a few weeks previously. As Mount Everest is extremely holy to the Tibetans, they are always very reluctant to grant this permission. They were now careful to point out that they were getting rather tired of the matter, and hoped that we would make a great effort to avoid the necessity of asking for it again.

As the time of our departure drew near the officials came to say good-bye and to bring us presents. As the Government of India had paid for those we had given to them on our first visits, these presents were not our property, though in most cases we were allowed to buy them back from the Government of India. Several ponies were presented, various skins—stone-marten, fox, snow-leopard and lynx—Tibetan carpets and quantities of locally woven cloth, ceremonial robes, ornate saddlery, inlaid swords, cloisonné work, china bowls, a few thankas and innumerable silver or copper teapots, pen-cases, chang-bowls and prayer-wheels.

On 14th February we went to pay our official farewell call on the Regent and Prime Minister at the Potala. They received us in the small upper room in which we had first paid our respects to them. As it was a formal visit it was brief; and they both thanked the Political Officer for being able to stay for so long, and for all the help he had given them.

On 17th February, accompanied for a short distance by a guard of honour and a small group of officials, we bade farewell to the Holy City and set off for India.

At the beginning of December, 1937, the news reached Europe that His Serenity the Tashi Lama—that saintly and tragic figure—had died at Jyekundo.

FINIS

# INDEX

ABRAHAM, GEORGE, 30
Acaster, —, 86
Aiguille d'Argentière, the, 31
Alexander the Great, 279, 309
Allwein, Dr., 65
Alpine flowers, 18
Alps, the, 16, 17, 18, 33
Amdo, 281
Amitabha ("Boundless Light"), 279, 282
Amo Chu, 132, 134
Amo Chu River, 196
Ancient man, 414
Ang Babu, 58, 77, 79, 96, 99, 102, 108
Anglo-Russian agreement, 287
Angmagssalik, 27
Ang Nima, 52, 58, 65, 69, 77, 80, 96, 99, 102–109 passim, 112, 114, 127
Antarctic, the, 28, 30
Arctic, the, 27, 28, 164
Arlberg Kandahar, the, 24
Asatulla Mahommad, 255
Asoka, 279
Assam, 226, 287, 381; tea-gardens, 255
Atishu, 230
Atlas Mountains, 34
Australia, 381
Avallon, 23
Avalokita, 279, 282, 336
Aysgarth, 31, 32

Baffin Land, 27
Bailey, Lt.-Col., 87, 210, 226
Baird, Gen. Sir Douglas, 88, 179

Batang, 289, 290, 295, 296
Bauer, Dr. Paul, 43, 52, 64
Bell, Sir Charles, 210, 248, 266, 292, 294, 296, 297, 329, 333, 336, 409
Bengal, 39, 178, 183, 284
Ben Nevis, 12, 16, 18
Ben Rhydding, 8
Bhamo, 81
Bhondong Shap-pe, 237, 408
Bhutan, 39, 41, 44, 90, 123–125 passim, 133, 137, 139, 140, 142, 145, 148, 157, 179, 195, 199, 201, 213, 255, 284, 287, 292, 306, 429, 432
Bhutan, agent of, 255
Bhutan, Maharajah of, 87, 124, 133, 313
Black Force, 9
Black Hat dancer, 280, 415, 416
Black Hats, 417, 426
Black Sail Pass, 29
Borrowdale, 29
Botnia, the, 23
Bo Tsering, Rai Sahib, 202, 217, 227, 256, 378, 385
Boddh Gaya, 294
Bogle, George, 284
"Book of Genesis," 278
Boustead, Major, 64
Bow Fell, 29, 30
Brahmanism, 279
Brandreth, 31
Brazil, 381
Brèche de la Meije, the, 19
Brèche Zsigmondy, the, 21
Britain, 284–294 passim, 340, 369

British Arctic Air-Route Expedition, 26
British Government, 195, 212, 242, 255, 267, 285–287, 295
British Graham Land Expedition, 30
Broad Stand, 29
Broderick's Crack, 16
Bruce, General, 169
Buddha, 209, 303, 304, 335, 340, 353–354, 361
Buddhism, 192, 254, 278, 279, 281, 294, 348, 354, 371, 416
Burma, 279, 287

Cader Idris, 10
Calcutta, 37, 38, 125, 126, 127, 175, 176, 244, 247, 248, 272, 292, 380, 382, 383
Cambridge, 10, 11, 15, 23, 26
Cambridge Mountaineering Club, 11
Campbell, Dr., 62
Cape Comorin, 322
Capel Curig, 11
Capuchin fathers, 351
Carré, Glacier, 20
Catholicism, 352
Cautley Spout, 9
Central Buttress, 14
Ceylon, 35
Chaksam, 227, 228, 291, 313, 398, 408; ferry, 360; monastery, 398
Chalu village, 207
Chamdo, 290, 295
Chamonix, 31
Champithang, 132
Champithang bungalow, 191
Chang Tang, 95, 234, 284, 298, 309, 310, 403
Changlo, 213
Changra Depön, 371
Changu, 129, 131

Changu bungalow, 189
Changu Lake, 130
Chanson Glacier, 105
Chao, Erh-feng, Gen., 290, 292, 295
Chao, F. R. G., 18, 20, 21, 22
Chapay Depön, 371
Chenrezi, 322, 326, 331, 336, 337, 338, 395
Cheval Rouge, the, 20
Chiang Kai-Shek, Marshal, 381
China, 205, 230, 249, 255, 260, 267, 272, 278–279, 282, 284–286, 287–290, 292, 294–295, 296, 301–302, 306–307, 323–328 passim, 340, 381, 389, 415, 432
Chinese Ambans, 224, 283, 284, 285, 286, 288, 289, 290, 295, 302, 336
Chinese Government, 290
Chomiomo, 105
Chomolhari, 105, 123, 124, 131–137 passim, 169, 170, 190 198, 201, 203, 204, 208, 215; ascent of, 138–158; descent of, 158–167; monastery, 138
Chorten Nyima La, 96, 109, 110, 113
Chu-gya hamlet, 202
Chumbi valley, 132, 192, 195, 199, 208, 242, 286, 287, 288, 289, 291
Chungtang, 86, 90
Chung-ye, 399
Chuni, Ranee, 87
Chu-shur, 227, 228, 229, 360, 397, 400, 407; valley, 229
Clough Head, 30
Col de Galibier, 22
Coming Buddha, 304, 431, 432
Cooch Behar, 255
Cooke, J. K., 33, 55, 57, 61, 68–71 passim, 75–84 passim, 88, 90, 92, 94, 95, 98, 99, 103, 104, 105, 110, 111, 112

Coombe Scaur, 8, 9
Cow and Calf Rocks, 8
Crawford, Charles, 125-131 passim, 134, 135, 136, 138, 139, 143, 145, 147, 153, 154, 159, 168
Crib Goch ridge, the, 138, 143
Cuillins, the, 17
Curzon, Lord, 287

Dagg, Lieut. S. G., 180, 181, 204, 206, 219, 270, 380, 388, 391
Dalai Lamas, 81-82, 88, 122, 180, 195, 209-210, 215-223 passim, 232, 237-255 passim, 261-262, 266, 271-298 passim, 306, 310, 313, 321-347 passim, 351, 371, 380, 388-390 passim, 413-422 passim, 431
Dale Head, 29
Darjeeling, 39, 40, 42, 43, 45, 62, 63, 125, 126, 130, 175, 177, 178, 195, 210, 211, 242, 247, 263, 266, 292, 294, 371, 387, 397
David-Neel, Madame, 52
Davos, 24, 25, 26
Dehra Dun, 126, 187
Dele Rabdens, 263, 384
Delhi, 82
Der-ge, 290, 295
Derge Se, 387
Derwentwater, 29
Desideri, Father, 352
Devil Dance, 411, 423, 426
Deyki Lingka, 234, 255, 267, 276, 311, 325, 366-368, 380, 387-390, 433
Dikchu, 46, 47, 48, 87, 121
Dinka Depön, 219
Dochen, 203; bungalow, 205; lake, 203, 204, 287
Dogra force, 256
Doigt de Dieu, the, 21
Dollywaggon Pike, 7, 30

Dolmetsch, Dr., 32
Dongkya La, 62, 63, 86
Dorjè, the, 148, 167
Dorje Phagmo, 224
Dorjieff, 286, 288, 294
Douglas Boulder, the, 16
Dow Crag, 16
Drepung monastery, 122, 231, 232, 233, 241, 312, 325, 340-346 passim, 352, 362, 364, 367, 389, 425; abbot of, 251, 337, 411, 419, 420, 431
Drok-pa, 309
Drölma, 344
Dunmail Raise, 7, 30
Dzara, 222, 223
Dzungarian Mongols, 283

East India Company, 284
East Indies, 381
Easter Gully, 16
"Easy Street", 387
Edward VIII, 381
Emperor of China, 279, 289, 291
Enari, Lake, 32
"Enthroned of Ganden", 348
Eskdale, 29
Esk Hause, 29
Eskimos, 28
Everest, Mt., 15, 28, 33, 43, 63, 88, 89, 105, 123, 157, 297, 355,
Everest expeditions, 42, 52, 117, 123, 124, 126, 134, 433

Fairfield, 30
Faroe Islands, 23, 27
Fell Record, the, 28-30
Fell and Rock-Climbing Club, 169
Finch, —, 54, 55
Finch, Major, 392, 403-408 passim, 433
Fire Over England, 406

Fjord, Lake, 28
Fluted Peak, the, 96, 112, 113; ascent of, 108–112
Forbidden Enclosure, 329, 332, 335
Fort William, 16
"Four Friends", 274, 395
Freshfield, Sir Douglas, 62, 63

Ganden, 122
Ganden monastery, 281, 317, 340, 341, 347, 348, 366; abbot of, 251, 337, 347, 419
Gangorti, 32, 92
Gangtok, 41, 44, 51, 52, 58, 62, 83–90 passim, 113, 117–130 passim, 168, 175–189 passim, 209–210, 248, 256, 385, 393; Residency, 368
Garden of the Mystics, 233, 364
Gartok, 237; Governor of, 250
Gashed Crag, the, 17
Gautama Buddha, 279, 281, 294, 304, 353, 432
Gautsa, 134, 135, 169; bungalow, 196
Geille Tea Gardens, 43
Gelugpa, 281
German Kangchenjunga Expedition, 64
German Nanga Parbat Expedition, 126
Ghonkar, 246
Giant's Fang, the, 144, 146, 147, 151, 166, 167
Gnatong, 126, 129, 131, 133
Gobshi village, 219, 220
God of Mercy, 278
Golok, 309
Göteborg, 34
Gould, B. J., 41, 81, 82, 83, 87, 107, 113, 118, 124, 129, 180, 191, 195, 196, 201, 202, 206, 210, 213, 215, 219, 232, 233–234, 236–
237, 256–258, 267, 270, 329, 346, 357, 368, 369, 373, 376, 377, 380–382, 385, 391, 392, 412, 413, 432–433
Graham, Bob, 30
Graham, Dr., 39
Graham, Gen., 285
Grand Pic, 20
Great Calva, 30
Great Divide, 146, 147, 166
Great Dod, 30
Great End, 29
"Great Fifth", 283, 284, 291, 292, 323, 338
Great Gable, 12, 29
Great Langdale, 12
Great Prayer, 366, 410, 425
Great Rangit River, 62
Great Thirteenth, 336
Great War, 296, 351
Green Gable, 29
Green Lake, 52, 55, 57, 58, 60, 61, 63, 65, 68, 69, 70, 71, 80
Greenland, 26–28, 29, 30, 90, 109, 164, 385, 402; Ice Cap, 396
Grenoble, 18, 21, 22
Grepon, 31
Grialetch Hut, 25
Grisedale, 7, 30
Grisedale Tarn, 30
Guicha La, 63
Gulam Maidin Mahommad, 255
Gundeling monastery, 234, 240, 311, 325, 329, 352–353, 389; abbot of, 333, 347–348
Guru, 210; hot springs, 204
Guthrie, 213, 216
Gyaltsen, 199
Gyantse, 40, 44, 82, 83, 92, 123, 124, 179, 180, 185–193, 202–218 passim, 228, 248, 266, 277, 287–294 passim, 308, 353, 368–380 passim, 387, 392, 403, 423,

433; fort, 210, 287; monastery, abbot of, 213, 266

Hamal, Major, 255
Hamblin, —, 54, 55
Harris, Miss Audrey, 87
Harrison, Jock, 81, 83, 84, 87, 88, 90, 92, 94, 96–102 passim, 105, 106, 116, 119
Hashang, 414
Haslemere, 32
Hastings, Warren, 284, 293
Heather Traverse, the, 17
Helvellyn, 7, 9, 28, 30
Hendon Air Pageant, 387
Hicks, T. E., 12, 15, 33
Hidden Glacier, 67
High White Stones, 30
Himalaya, the, 16, 17, 32, 33, 39, 65, 73, 109, 123, 128, 147, 157, 179, 183, 195, 232, 280
Himalayan Club, 42, 126, 128
Hindscarth, 29
Hinduism, 348, 414
H.M. the King, 381
Holdsworth, R. H. L., 24, 25, 125
Hong Kong, 381
Honister Pass, 29
Hooghli, the, 37
Hooker, Sir Joseph, 62, 186
Hor States, 252, 290, 309
Hor-kang family, 243
Hram Tso, 204
Huang Mu Sung, Gen., 180, 211, 317
Hudson Bay, 27

Iamtso, 394, 401–404
Iceland, 23, 24, 26, 27
Idwal slabs, 11
Ilkley, 8
Inaccessible Pinnacle, 16

India, 213, 229–231, 244, 246, 248, 261, 266, 279–281, 285, 286–287, 289, 292–293, 297, 298, 301, 306–307, 312, 322, 356, 369, 370, 432–434
India, British, 256, 291, 292
India, Government of, 82, 180, 258, 285, 293, 348, 370, 382, 392, 433
Ingram, M. J., 24, 25
Iron Hill, 231, 299, 318, 320, 325, 329, 350, 379
"Isaac", 31–32
Ishwar Singh, 41, 52, 57, 58, 69, 70, 80
Islamia College, 125

Jainism, 279
Jakob Khan, 230
Jangme, 395, 397, 408
Japan, 242, 267, 279, 296, 307
Jelep La, 129, 131, 133, 169, 183, 190, 194, 195, 248
Jenghiz Khan, 281
Jigme Tering, 247, 370–387 passim, 410, 425
Jigmes, 263, 385
Jo-kang, 298, 302, 303, 310, 323
Jonsong Glacier, 104; Peak, 104
Jubbulpore, 277, 391
Jun Singh, 41, 57, 58

Kabru, 157
Kailas, Mt., 193
Kakapu, 123
Kala, 206, 207; valley, 207
Kali, 305
Kalimpong, 37, 39–41, 44, 45, 56, 63, 87, 124, 125, 127, 136, 168, 169, 177–180, 183, 195, 211, 219, 248, 302, 308, 404
Kaling Chu, 162
Kalön Lama, 239, 251, 276, 295

Kamba La, 228, 399
Kamet, 126
Kampa Dzong, 63, 203, 242
Kangchenjau, 60
Kangchenjunga, 32, 40, 41, 43, 63–71 passim, 84, 98, 126, 157, 176, 181; glacier, 66
Kangma, 209
Kangyur, 325
Kansu, 291
Kapshupa, 253
Karasjok, 31, 32
Karesuando, 31
Kargyü monastery, 132, 191, 192; sect, 192, 255
Karo La, 123, 208, 215, 221–222, 287, 401–404
Karponang, 129, 185
Kashag, 122, 306
Kashak, 250
Kashmir, 256, 280, 287
Katmandu, 87, 283, 284
Kaulback, Ronald, 67, 392
Kazis, 89
Kellas, Dr., 62, 63, 109
Kendal, 8; Otter Hounds, 10
Kennedy, Col., 297, 409
Kern Knotts Crack, 12
Kesch Hut, 25
Keswick, 28, 30
Kham, 237, 245, 247, 252, 271, 289–290, 295, 309, 371
Khap-ri, 143, 147, 154, 156
"Kharita", 258
Kidd, —, 126
Kikuli, 126, 134, 135, 138, 148–154 passim, 168
Kilo, 81, 95, 96, 97, 98, 100, 108
King George V's Jubilee Procession, 387, 390
King of Siam's Palace, 262
Kings of the Quarters, 304, 335, 342

Kipak, 58, 65, 71, 80, 81, 92
Kirk Fell, 29
Kitchener, Lord, 293
Koko Nor Lake, 284
Kopup, 131, 190
Korayedu, 109, 113, 114, 115
Kublai Khan, 281
Kumpa-la, 251, 252, 271, 332
Kung, 240, 428
Kyi Chu, 229–231, 259, 262, 312, 317, 321, 329, 334, 357, 360, 362, 365, 367
Kyipup, 233, 246, 247, 387, 422

Labrador, 26
Laccadive Islands, 35
Lachen, 45, 49, 51, 54, 56, 57, 59, 63, 69, 84, 85, 88, 90, 92, 93, 100, 114, 117, 119, 120, 129, 132, 133
Lachung, 49, 62
Ladakh, 213, 256
La Grave, 18, 21
Lagyap La, 130, 188, 189
Lahore, 125
Lake District, 7, 9, 10, 12, 28, 54
Lama Anden, 54, 55, 56, 62, 63
Lama Cabinet, 240, 250
Lama Dance, 410
Lamaism, 281, 298, 308, 328, 340, 351–354 passim, 414
Lamb, Charles, 285
Landon, Percival, 304, 328
Lang-chungna, 237, 238, 242, 251, 270, 271, 312, 375
Lang-dar-ma, 280, 415
Langpo Chu, 94, 95, 96, 109, 112; La, 98, 99, 102; Peak, 96, 98, 103, 104, 105, 109; Glacier, 105
Lapland, 29–30, 396
Lattimer, —, 109
Layden La, 239, 302
Lazarist fathers, 351
Les Trois Pucelles, 18

Passenram Glacier, the, 65, 73, 77
Pauhunri, 62, 105, 140, 157, 202
Pavey Ark, 12, 20
Pede, 224, 401–403; Dzong, 225
Pede Ri, 404, 405
Peiping, 284, 288, 291, 304
Peking, 242, 282, 284
Penlong La, 46, 84, 86, 87, 121
Perim, 35
Peshawar, 125
Phari, 123, 127–135 passim, 136,
    137, 138, 140, 142, 157, 159, 168,
    170, 197–204, 210; bungalow,
    199; Commander, 199; Dzong,
    197–200, 287; plain, 199
Phintzu, 99, 100
Phodang monastery, 47
Pillar Rock, 12, 15, 29
Pipitang village, 132, 194, 210
Pircher, Herr, 65
Pitz Grialetch, 25
Pitz Kesch, 24
Podong Chu, 95; La, 106
Pön religion, 279, 348, 354, 407,
    416
Porchobello Hut, 25; Glacier, 24
Portinscale, 29
Potala, 231–233, 239–240, 244,
    256–257, 260, 265–266, 280–
    291 passim, 298–300, 310–345
    passim, 349, 357, 361, 366, 384–
    390 passim, 409–413, 418–428,
    433; rock, 329
Primula denticulata, 132
Primula Royalei, 85, 119, 139, 144
Primula scottica, 18
Primula sikkimensis, 119, 132
Promontoire Hut, 19
Punakha, 124
Punjab, 210
Purang, 244
Pyramid Peak, the, 73, 74, 77, 96,
    98, 99, 104, 105, 107, 108, 111

Pyrenees, 125, 371, 372

Quetta, 44

Raeburn, Harold, 63
Ra-ka-sha, 249, 307
Ral-pa-chan, 280
Ralung, 221, 222; valley, 222
Ramba, 246, 250
Ramoche temple, 316
Rangpo, 44, 178
Rawalpindi, 293, 381, 391
Recorder, the, 33, 37
Red Hats, 282
Red Hill, 322
Red Idol Gorge, 210, 211
Red Pike, 29
Red Sea, 34–35
Requin, the, 31
Reting monastery, 239, 258, 356,
    360; Dzasa, 257, 258
Reykjavik, 23
Richardson, H. E., 124, 125, 126,
    179, 213, 216, 222–224, 234,
    243, 256, 347, 357, 359, 361, 368,
    370, 375–376, 410, 413, 433
Rinchen Bhutia, 52, 58, 65, 77, 78,
    80
Rinchen Sherpa, 52, 58, 67, 77, 78,
    80, 92, 95–97 passim
Ringang, 244–245, 263, 268, 276,
    375, 380, 387, 410, 411; Mrs.,
    389, 411
Ringbi Chu, 63
Roaf, R. C., 33, 37, 41, 52, 54, 61,
    69, 71, 73, 74–78 passim, 80, 83,
    90
Robinson, 29
Rongni Chu, 129, 183
Russia, 267, 286, 287, 289, 294,
    296; Tsar, of, 286
Russo–Japanese war, 287
Rymill, 30

Sacred Way, 311, 312, 315, 318, 319, 321, 329
Saddleback, 30
St. Joseph's School, 263
St. Paul's School, 371, 387
Sakya monastery, 281
Salomons, Capt., 194, 212, 216
Salur, 37
Salween River, 180
Samada, 207, 208
Samding monastery, 4, 224, 403
Sams, Capt., 81, 87, 100
Samye monastery, 277, 356, 388
Sarat Das, 285
Sarsura, the, 25
Saugang, 211, 212
Sayok Chu, 114, 115; La, 114, 115
Scafell, 14, 20, 28, 29
Schaller, 66
Scott, Capt., 31
Scott, J. M., 26
Seat Sandal, 30
Sedbergh, 8, 16, 28
Sera monastery, 122, 240, 281, 312, 316, 325, 340, 346, 350–351, 352–353, 364, 389; abbot of, 251, 337, 419, 420; plain, 310, 313, 318, 325, 330
Sergeant Man, 30
Sgurr nan Gillean, 16
Shackleton, Sir Ernest, 31
Shanghai, 81
" Shanghaied ", 387
Shap-pes, 235–238, 241–433 passim
Shiday monastery, 257
Shigatse, 208, 213, 219, 225, 242, 248–249, 264, 282, 283–284, 293–294, 295, 341
Shing-donkar village, 232, 361, 362, 393
Shipton, E., 128
Shiva, 305

Sho village, 246, 299–300, 321
Siberia, 286
Sierra Nevada, the, 34
Sikkim, 32, 33, 39, 41, 62, 63, 73, 75, 77, 81, 83, 87, 114, 131, 133, 178, 179, 186, 190, 192, 195, 209–210, 221, 283–284, 285–286, 288, 291–292, 368, 376, 432
Sikkim, Convention of 1890, 286
Sikkim, Maharajah of, 41, 87, 88, 89, 216
Sikkim Residency, 182
Sikkim State gaol, 183
Siliguri, 39, 44, 175, 177
Simla, 295
Simvu, 32, 41, 48, 56, 61, 62–79 passim, 83; glacier, 67, 71, 73, 80; Saddle, 63–73 passim, 106; Upper Saddle, 71, 72, 73, 80
Singhik, 49, 63, 86, 90
Singma Kang-chung, 226
Sining, 290–291
Siniolchu, 32, 41, 48, 56, 57, 61, 63, 66, 73, 74, 75, 77, 84, 105, 157
Siniolchu, Little, 57, 74
Sino-Tibetan boundary, 290
Skiddaw, 28, 30
Skye, 12, 16, 125
Smythe, Frank, 126
Snake temple, 314, 340, 410; lake, 313, 314
Snow Leopard Gully, 110
Snowdon, 12, 21, 31
Sola Khombu, 42
Song-tsen Gampo, King, 278–281, 303, 316, 322, 326
Sonham Kazi, 375, 377, 385
Sonham Minghu, 392–402 passim
South Africa, 381
Sphinx, the, 98, 99, 104; ascent of, 105–107, 108
Spitsbergen, 26

State Oracle, 241, 252, 285, 337–338, 346, 410, 424–431; monastery of, 231

Steel Fell, 30

Steeple, 29

Stefansson, —, 31, 158

Stobart, —, 109

Stybarrow Dod, 30

Sugarloaf, the, 66, 74

Surkang house, 253, 365

Surkang-Se, 247, 365, 387, 425

Sur-La, the, 140, 143, 144

Sutherland, 18

Szechuan, 294; frontier, 290; Viceroy of, 292


Tachienlu, 283, 290, 295, 296

Takapu, 123, 143, 146

Ta Lama, 241, 248–249

Talung, 65, 67, 73, 76, 77, 80, 85; Chu, 63; Glacier, 63, 64; Monastery, 55, 63; Peak, 76, 98

Taly-llyn Lake, 10

Tang La, 52, 54, 123, 198, 199, 203

Tangu, 94, 115, 117, 119

Tantrik, doctrine, 354

Tashi Lama, the, 88, 122, 180, 205, 218–223, 237, 248, 261, 264, 277, 281–284, 292–294, 336–337, 348, 371, 379–380, 432–434

Tashi-lhünpo, 180, 219, 281–284, 293–294, 336–340, 432; Grand Lama of, 282

Teesta bridge, 39, 44, 175, 183; gorge, 39, 40, 62; river, 39, 48, 49, 62–63, 64, 176, 177; valley, 62, 67, 127, 130

Tendong, 215–218, 277; Shap-pe, 237, 252

Tengye-ling monastery, 253, 302, 338–340; abbot of, 348

Tengyur, 325

Tent Peak, 65, 71, 74, 84, 96, 98, 99, 102, 104, 106, 109; La, 106

Terai, the, 39, 176

Tering, 220; Rajah, 212, 216, 219, 247, 249; Rimpoche, 215

" The Crook ", 387

" The Lama ", 62–63

" The Shepada ", 386–387, 390

" The Waiter ", 387

Thomas, Eustace, 29

Threlkeld, 30

Tibet, 33, 39–40 passim, 52, 58, 73, 77, 81, 82, 83, 88, 95, 105, 114, 121–133 passim, 140, 159, 195–196, 213, 235–434 passim; admits Chinese Mission to Lhasa, 179; highlands, 190

Tibetan Cabinet, 306

Tibetan Government, 267–268, 288–289, 338, 346, 364, 419

Tilman, H.W., 88

Ti-song De-tsen, 124

Tobgay Dorje, Rajah, 87, 124

Tobin, Col., 63

Tombazi, N. G., 64

Tong, 49

Tongshyong Glacier, 63

Tour Noir, the, 31

Tower Ridge, 16

Trab-shi, 373, 375

Tracey, 392

Trap-je, 242

Tremlung, 400, 401, 407

Tremo, La, 137, 168, 199

Trimon, 248, 251, 253, 270, 276

Trisum bridge, 231, 247, 356, 394; river, 361

Tryvfan, 11, 17

Tsa Serkang, 205

Tsang-po (Brahmaputra), 176, 208, 226–229, 242, 277, 291, 356, 398, 399, 405; valley, 226, 398, 405–409

Tsarong, Mrs., 263
Tsarong Shap-pe, 242
Tsarong (Tsensar Namgyal), 240–243, 261–270, 276, 317, 346, 360, 375, 383–384, 385–387, 397, 407–410, 421, 423–425, 428–429
Tse-chen, 218
Tsecho-ling, 348
Tse-laptra, 324
Tsetang, 54, 84, 85, 92, 93, 117
Tsomo-ling, 348
Tsong-kapa, 281, 341, 346–347, 365–366, 430–431
Tsungtang, 49
Tumlong, 62
Tuna village, 123, 201–203, 287; hills, 203–204
Tungkar monastery, 196
Turkestan, 280
Turner, Samuel, 284
Turquoise bridge, 302
Twins, the, 64, 65, 71, 72, 84

Urga, 422, 288, 291

Vadsö, 32
Vallorgia Cass, 25
Viceroys of India, 208, 257, 258, 287–297
Victoria, Queen, 305, 364–365
Vizagapatam, 35

Waddell, Col., 210, 275 n., 279
Wager, Lawrence, 15, 18, 21
Wakefield, Dr. A., 28, 30
Wales, North, 10, 11, 17
Wales, Prince and Princess of, 293
Walker's Gully, 15

Waller, —, 86
Ward, Kingdon, 45
Warren, Charles, 15, 33
Wastdale Head, 29
Watkins, Gino, 15, 26, 28
Weir, Lt.-Col., 210
Western Gate, 320, 329
Westman Islands, 23
White, Claud, 63
Williamson, Mr., 44, 211, 368
Winnipeg, 27
Wood Johnson, G., 43, 126
Woodhouse, Bobby, 16, 28

Yamdrok Tso, 224, 391–392, 401
Yangtse, 81, 289, 295
Yapshi Kung, 260
Yasik Ri, 404
Yatung, 119, 131, 132, 133, 137, 169, 193–195, 202, 204, 242, 286, 288, 291
Yellow Hats, 281
Yeumtso La, 63
Yewbarrow, 27
Yorkshire Moors, 8
Young, Geoffrey Winthrop, 10–11
Younghusband, 185, 287, 293, 348
Yuan Shih Kai, 294
Yunnan-Fu, 81
Yuto family, 301; Depön, 234, 235, 247, 335, 371–373, 422, 425, 429

Zemu Chu, 54, 55, 56, 62, 63, 64, 85, 92; Gap, 63, 64, 65, 67, 88; Glacier, 32, 33, 41, 52, 60–70 passim, 76, 95, 106; Ram, 52, 54, 85; Valley, 63, 93

FOR DEPRIVED CHILDREN
N DEVON HOLIDAY HOME
BROTHER JOHNATHAN,
P/O      ALSWEAR

S MOLTON.
N DEVON   EX36 4LH

BISHOPS NYMPTON 294